The New Dog Owner's Manual

To all my dogs
who have given me so much pleasure
and enriched my life
with their antics.

ON SELECTING, RAISING AND BREEDING DOG

The Watermark Press

The New Dog Owner's Manual

Karen Hedberg BVSc

Illustrations by Denise Dufferin

First published 1989 by
THE WATERMARK PRESS
Sydney, Australia.

2nd edition 1996

National Library of Australia
cataloguing-in-publication data:

Hedberg, Karen.
    The new dog owner's manual on selecting, raising
    and breeding dogs.

    Includes index.
    ISBN 0 949284 26 2.

    1. Dogs   I. Title

    636.708

Design by Harry Williamson
Typeset by Leanne Hogbin
Printed by Australian Print Group

Every effort has been made by the author and
publishers to ensure that dosages are accurate.
Readers are urged to check the recommendations
for all medications most carefully and to consult
their veterinarian prior to use.

Contents

Introduction

When selecting the right breed of dog for yourself and your family, time should be spent on determining what breed you like and your reson for buying the dog. New owners often do not consider the long-term suitability of the breed of dog for their family and lifestyle. This includes the eventual size and temperament of the dog in relation to the age of members of the famiily, size of the backyard, and the amount of exercise and care which will be needed with the adult animal. Young puppies grow extremely rapidly, particularly if they are members of a large breed. They can change within six to eight months from being very cute and cuddly, to being heavier than most small children.

The first few chapters assist your choice with a short summary of the different breeds and their general characteristics and, hopefully, will help you in the selection of a sound, healthy puppy. When buying a puppy, remember that you are not buying a toy, but rather, a faithful friend that will give you much joy and companionship for up to 14 years. For the person more interested in buying a dog for the show ring, there are helpful hints on buying good quality dogs from reputable breeders.

Chapters are devoted to the raising and feeding of your puppy, the stages through which it develops, its socialisation and so on. It is vital that your puppy, particularly if it is a member of a heavier breed, is properly fed and that close attention is paid to its bone and ligament development.

The second section of the book is devoted to breeding, including the care of the bitch throughout pregnancy and whelping, and how to steady your nerves thoughout the long haul. Puppy care from birth until leaving home at six to eight weeks is covered, with discussion on health, diet, worming, vaccinations and socialisation.

Genetics, care of geriatric dogs and a chapter on kennel construction and management make up the third part of the book. A section on general health care and emergency treatment round out the book.

I have tried to present the chapters in chronological order from the selection of the new puppy, breeding (if you are mad enough), to care in old age. This book is not intended to be used in lieu of a visit to your veterinarian. Rather it is designed to give practical assistance to the dog owner, from the complete novice to the more experienced breeder, to cope with everyday situations in the life of your dog.

Karen Hedberg B.V.Sc.

1

What Do You Want from a Dog?

New puppy owners often do not consider whether the breed of dog that they have selected will be suitable for their family or lifestyle. They have a breed in mind that they may have seen in someone else's backyard or on a dog food advertisement on television. The breed may be a very nice one, but will it fit in with *your* family, particularly if you have very small children? A Saint Bernard, although a lovely small puppy, reaches 60–80 kg by nine months of age, while your child has gained 6–8 kg (if it is growing rapidly) in an entire year! The Saint Bernard puppy can be a bit too heavy and exuberant to associate with lightweight children. However, an older bitch, one that has got over the puppy stage, can be excellent with young children.

When selecting a dog, care should be taken to choose a breed with a **nature** that the family likes and can live with in and around the house. A quiet gentle breed, e.g. the Italian Greyhound, is totally unsuited to rough handling by young excitable children, yet it is particularly good with older children and adults. A rough and ready terrier, for example, the Australian Terrier, is ideal for 'middle-sized' energetic humans.

Consideration should be given to the following:

(a) **Size** of the dog in relation to the age of any children.

(b) **Area** of the backyard.

(c) **Amount of exercise needed and care necessary** in grooming the adult coat. An Old English Sheepdog, for instance, looks superb when in full coat, but may require 6–8 hours work a week to keep it that way. The vast majority of these dogs are eventually clipped very close to the skin every summer because the grooming cannot be managed properly.

If some thought is given *before* buying a puppy, there would be far fewer unwanted dogs finishing up in the pound. The more thought that is put into determining the type and temperament of your puppy, the greater the eventual enjoyment there is between suitably matched dogs and owners.

To assist your choice of breed, here is a summary of the different breed groups, their general characteristics and temperaments. The second half of the chapter deals with considerations that are necessary before you purchase a puppy. Chapter 2 goes into the selection of a sound, healthy puppy. If however, you have already bought a puppy, all this wonderful advice arrives a bit late, but the following chapter may assist you to understand your puppy's individual traits.

Remember that a dog is a wonderful friend, who accepts you with no reservations. It will not be able to criticise you if *your* temperament and habits do not mix well with its temperament and habits.

The Development of the Various Breeds

To understand the breeds, here is a very short history of the development of the different types and uses of the dogs.

The dog is the first animal to have been domesticated by man. To a certain extent the dog was domesticated because of mutual need and assistance, the dog being a natural hunter and scavenger. Evidence of association of dogs with human settlements extends back at least 12,000 to 14,000 years.

Through the centuries, dogs have aided man in nearly all of his varied pursuits. Not only has man's best friend been the dog, but, generally speaking, the reverse also holds true. As man spread out over the various regions of the earth, so did his environments change and the sources of food supplies become more varied. Adapting to both natural and man-made selection, dogs have evolved diversely, learning to cope with man's changing needs and environments. The dog has a large number of chromosomes for a mammal, which allows for an enormous possible range of combinations of genetic material. Because of this the dog has the ability to adapt rapidly to different climates throughout the world.

SELECTION FOR SPECIFIC OBJECTIVES

The need for dogs such as Wolfhounds (wolf hunting) and Setters (field and bird hunting) resulted in the development of strains that excelled in particular areas. The strains gradually evolved into separate breeds of dog, with most of the clarification and demarcation between the breeds going on in the past 100 to 150 years.

A breed is, by definition, a group of dogs related by descent, and reproducing certain characteristics that the breeders agree to recognise as the ones distinguishing the breed.

Breeds of dogs have been further categorised into **groups of similar function**. The actual breeds that make up a group can vary slightly around the world. The Rottweiler was in the 'non-sporting' group in Australia and in the 'working dog' group in most other countries. Nowadays, the Rottweiler is mostly found in the 'utility' group.

The groups are as follows:
- **hounds** — dogs developed for pack hunting, including sight and scent hounds.
- **gun dogs** — used for hunting and retrieving.
- **working** — developed for animal herding, pulling loads and guarding.
- **utility** — dogs bred for varied pursuits including guarding.
- **toy** — smaller breeds developed mostly as house dogs and lap dogs.
- **terriers** — bred to hunt and kill vermin.
- **non-sporting** — a group with generalised abilities rather than specific duties.

Just as the various breeds that make up a group tend to have a similar function, so do the **temperaments** within a group. This generalisation applies best to the more uniform groups, e.g. hounds, gun dogs, terriers and working dogs. The utility, toy and non-sporting groups are not as uniform in type or temperament, so the comments apply far more loosely to these dogs.

General Function and Temperament by Group

HOUNDS

This group of dogs was developed primarily as pack hunting animals, capable of being 'run' (kennelled) in groups without too much trouble. As hounds are pack animals, they prefer not to live alone — humans are good substitutes for other dogs in this respect! The hounds can be loosely divided into two types, sight hounds and scent hounds, referring to their original use.

Sight hounds love lots of space to run around in, but if their run areas are very open, they can get rather noisy if they can see too far, e.g. a cat strolling by. Greyhounds and Whippets are two members of this subgroup, and love to go hunting for hours — unfortunately they often forget to look out for obstacles when they are chasing and may occasionally leave bits and pieces of their skin behind on the fences. They are affectionate pets, making good house dogs and will get on well with cats and other pets if they have not been taught to 'chase'.

Scent hounds, while not quite as noisy, have a habit of putting their nose to the ground and disappearing — if not recalled, they can go for kilometres before they lift their heads! Popular members of this select group include the Basset and the Beagle. They are very independent dogs particularly in relation to 'rules and regulations', and may gently but firmly, resist attempts to control them. Be braver and firmer in your resolve than they are, and you may eventually have an obedient dog.

Another hound seen frequently is the Dachshund — in all its sizes and coat types. These little dogs were developed as badger hunters and love to go investigating, preferably down rabbit holes. Unfortunately once they are down there they may wish to stay there for a while or, if they are lucky enough to get a rabbit, they often cannot fit through the tunnels on the way out. My family owned one and we regularly had to dig our dog out of deep tunnels in the most inaccessible countryside. We always travelled with a shovel!

Hounds are, as a rule, very exuberant individuals and love to be taken out (on a lead for safety) for walks and social trips. This group does not, on the whole, make good obedience dogs, as their minds (or noses and eyes) are far away and they will often refuse to concentrate for any great length of time.

The hound breeds make good pets with children as long as they (the children) are old enough to be 'pounced' on, as hounds love to play and out of sheer exuberance they may throw their whole weight on top of you!

GUN DOGS

The gun dog group is a very active one. This collection of dogs contains some of the most boisterous breeds in existence. As a group, they require a long time to 'grow up' mentally — they do not like to leave puppyhood behind! Because they are so energetic, they are not good pets for small backyards or apartments, unless yours is a placid individual. If too confined they can be a rather destructive with plants and gardens.

Gun dogs as a rule are affectionate, almost too much so. For people who have an active lifestyle, plenty of room in the backyard and lots of patience while the dog becomes more mature, this could be the dog. They also love to swim — you do not even need to have a river as a pool or even a puddle will do! Several of the breeds, e.g. Golden Retrievers and Labradors, make good obedience dogs, provided you can make them 'sit' in one spot for long enough.

Most of the group make excellent pets particularly for older children. One of the more popular of these is the Golden Retriever, which is reasonably quiet and not over active, yet is very good with children and is obedient. The Labrador Retriever is another such breed, but it can be very boisterous and may take several years to sober up and behave like an adult (usually around four years). Labradors are often attracted by washing hanging on the clothes line as a source of games.

The Setters — Irish, English and Gordon, Springers and Cocker Spaniels, are all very good family pets, but they adore getting out to go hunting, particularly the Springers as they 'spring' over many fences. Good fencing is a must with all dogs, but particularly so with this group as, if they do get out, they are apt to be feather-brained when on the roads.

WORKING DOGS

This group is another active one, although not as boisterous generally as the gun dogs. The various breeds within this grouping have been developed mainly as herding and protective animals. Many of the breeds are of dual function 'working' the herd and guarding against predators. They need a reasonable amount of room, but will tolerate small areas provided they get out regularly. Some, e.g. Cattle Dogs, are prone to boredom if they have nothing to do and they may round up the washing off the line, or guard the chickens, preventing them from grazing. I have seen one bored Cattle Dog round up a pile of stones and then scatter them for the sheer activity of it!

Working dogs (especially the bitches) cope well with children and are good at guarding them from harm. This can even extend to pulling a child out of the water (much to the child's disgust!) when all the child wants to do is go swimming. Several of the breeds excel at obedience, e.g. German Shepherds, Belgian Shepherds, Briards and Border Collies. Those that cannot concentrate for long periods, e.g. Bearded Collies, although they make excellent children's pets, are not the greatest at remembering where they are and what they are doing, particularly in the middle of an obedience trial. Collies and Shelties make wonderful children's pets as they are very gentle and easily handled — rarely if ever will one bite, even under more than reasonable provocation.

The Border Collie is a born agility dog. They are so quick, both on their feet and mentally. They excel in this area, while occasionally overkeen, they move like greased lightning through an agility course, and they *love* it! The Corgis are the smallest members of this group and are probably the least likely to be seen in the agility stakes. Despite this, they are very active little dogs and, like the other breeds in this group, were developed as a working dog to work, believe it or not, with cattle! Rarely seen with the said cows nowadays, the Corgi is one of the more popular pet dogs in homes all around the world.

Some working dogs are 'all rounders', e.g. German Shepherds, who are good at numerous tasks including obedience, guarding and tracking, while being good pets with children of all ages. Cattle Dogs in addition to working animals, if required, make very good guard dogs and would almost be the most popular household guard dog in Australia, after the German Shepherd.

Kelpies, on the other hand, make excellent sheep dogs, but are too 'soft' in temperament to make good guard dogs (on the whole), as they love to turn upside down to say 'hello' to everyone they meet!

Any animal that is used for guarding purposes (this also applies to other 'guarding' breeds in other groups), should be well socialised, as 'vicious' guard dogs are predominantly man-made to suit their owners' needs. People who are wary of dogs should not go for breeds (particularly male dogs) that may become overprotective. More is said further on in this chapter in the section on Temperament. When buying a puppy for a family pet and a guard dog — e.g. German Shepherd, Cattle Dog, Rottweiler — good temperament is *essential* in both the dog's parents and the offspring.

TERRIERS

This group of dogs is very 'feisty' — they love to 'have a go' at anything that invades their territory, and their territory also includes anywhere they happen to be! Terriers were bred and selected to be aggressive hunters and killers of vermin, e.g. mice, rats and other terriers. These days, in the minds of the terriers at least, the 'vermin' come in all sizes, including the Great Dane down the road. As terriers generally come in a smaller size range they do not always win!

The terrier temperament is, for the most part very affectionate, particularly towards humans. Their friendliness does not, however, extend to other dogs (especially of the same sex), and cats! Equal fervour is put into the fighting as into the affection given to their human(s). To these little dogs, fighting is as natural as breathing; some, I am sure, live for it.

Most of the breeds make very good pets for children and adults, however, they do not like to be crossed. They are very stubborn when it comes to having something 'nasty' that needs to be done to them, e.g. injections at the veterinary surgery or nail cuts; their reaction can be a nightmare (especially to the vet's delicate ears) and many a docile terrier temporarily turns into a fiend. For this reason, I feel that terriers are *not* the best breed to have near very young children, particularly the child that likes to pull and prod at eyes and ears, or clasp the dog around the neck in a death grip! It is often necessary to be very firm with your terrier for under that loving exterior lies a great deal of stubbornness.

Probably the most popular breed of this group today is the Bull Terrier. It is said by many to have the ugliest head of any dog, a fact that devoted owners hotly refute. 'Bullies' are very affectionate, amusing dogs with the quaint habit of staring at things that only they can see, e.g. 'fairies under bushes' for 5–10 minutes at a time! They are sudden death to any strange animal intruder. They rarely attack humans as they are fond of them and many will tolerate the cats they have grown up with, and defend them through thick and thin. They seem to have heads made out of concrete — it takes time for the bright ideas to emerge! They are not the best pet for a young child, as they are too boisterous and may consider the child to be below them in the 'pecking' order.

For slightly older children (medium sized and upwards), a terrier can be an excellent pet — I have never seen a better dog for exhausting overactive children than an Australian Terrier! The 'Aussie' is a very good pet for smaller backyards as they do not take up much room and are invaluable mousers — much better than cats! Another excellent mouser in the field is the Jack Russell which, while not officially registered, is a very popular 'activity' dog; they are in on any activity going and would even go mountaineering if someone could keep them from wanting to lead the way.

Terriers come in many shapes and sizes. Among the rarer ones is the Dandie Dinmont and it is often hard to find a local breeder. This is one of the gentlest terriers, devoted to becoming your lap dog and permanent bedfellow. They have enormous eyes and prefer to spend their life looking soulfully up at you — from a distance of 20 cm, that is, from your lap!

Utility Dogs

The dogs that make up this group are not as similar in origin and purpose as the preceding groups. They are primarily working dogs, which in many countries are probably still listed within that group. They include Rottweilers, Dobermans and Boxers; dogs that have been bred for working purposes with the emphasis on guarding and/or defence work. While all are naturally protective, they do differ in temperament to a certain extent.

Some within the group, e.g. Bernese Mountain Dogs and St Bernards, were developed primarily as working dogs and secondarily for defence. Many, such as the Samoyed and the Husky, are from colder climates and mountainous terrain and have thick coats. Some of the mountainous breeds, particularly the Samoyed, are used to roaming over the hills and dales and are so fond of wandering that good fences are needed.

Boxers are a very active breed and never appear to get tired, while Saint Bernards have varying energy levels. Dobermans and Rottweilers can be very protective, occasionally too much so. Dobermans and Rottweilers also have a temperament that is very easy to train for guard work — but they can be very hard to train out of a bad habit.

Generally breeds within the group can be very stubborn, and may 'resist' training — at least this is how it can appear to the novice owner! Stubborn dogs should not be spoilt or left untrained, especially the male dogs and members of the larger breeds, as control is often lost with increasing size — particularly from the veterinarian's point of view!

Many utility dogs make excellent companions for all sorts of activities and circumstances, especially the bitches. I would stress, however, that if you are about to become a first dog owner, choose a female puppy with which to get used to the breed. Females are still naturally defensive, but lack the dominating type of aggression occasionally seen in the males. Most of the breeds within this group have lovely temperaments and, if handled properly, make very good dual purpose pets.

NON-SPORTING DOGS

This is a rather mixed group. This group contains some terriers, but also some working breeds, e.g. the Dutch Barge Dog (Keeshond). Sizes vary from large breeds, such as the Great Dane, to the small breeds, such as the Shih Tzu. The breeds within this group are not particularly specialised as far as guarding or purpose of use.

Origins vary greatly across the group for example, Dalmatians were developed as carriage dogs and Shih Tzus were originally temple guard dogs. Dalmatians as a breed love lots of exercise and can be a little boisterous — they are not particularly known as intellectual heavyweights, more as 'featherweights'.

Dalmatians love to get out and about and go for long excursions. They are also the 'smiliest' breed in dogdom, and you very quickly get used to wrinkled, crinkled lips.

Shih Tzus, on the other hand, prefer a sedentary lifestyle (going outside is occasionally a chore), but are good barkers when there are visitors or when the telephone rings (you obviously couldn't hear it, so they have to get your attention somehow!). The Shih Tzu breed is among the smaller end of the group and these little dogs make delightful house pets. They are affectionate, rarely if ever dream of being nasty, and are ideal dogs to have around children and older people.

Apart from the Poodles, few breeds of this group are regularly used for obedience. Poodles (all three sizes) are very intelligent and are quick to learn. While not necessarily the most courageous breed, Poodles have worldwide popularity as intelligent and happy dogs. As this breed was originally developed as a water retriever, not only are they natural retrievers but they also have a very dense waterproof coat. As they do not drop or shed coat (it is actually more like wool than hair), there is a lot of coat care associated with this breed. On the plus side, they are suitable for most people who are allergic to normal dog hair.

The Great Dane is a breed that was developed mainly for guarding, but not all are particularly brave (occasionally you can get extremes of aggression and shyness). Good temperament is most important in all breeds, more so in the giant breeds. As these are very big dogs, they do need a fair amount of living space, but they are rather lazy, and will cope with smallish backyards as long as they get out occasionally. If you wish to own a Great Dane, be prepared to buy a bigger car and a separate lounge (for the dog, of course). They love to 'lean' on objects, particularly legs — human, table, chair ... Buy sturdy furniture!

TOY DOGS

This term covers a hotch potch of breeds that includes some of the smaller terriers and a mixture (in origin at least) of little breeds. Today the breeds within this group are bred and kept as affectionate house pets, and make ideal lap dogs.

Most of the group have very good temperaments and are terrific children's pets, especially the Cavaliers. Those breeds in this group with terrier in them do not mix well with very small children.

The other major consideration with this group is that they are, on the whole, *very small* and consequently *very fragile* (e.g. Chihuahuas and Italian Greyhounds) and fractures can occur easily. These fragile dogs are more suited to people with slightly older children. The Cavaliers, on the other hand, are more robust, have been bred for centuries as lap dogs and are still excellent at their work. Cavaliers are particularly good dogs for the older person as they are big enough to see easily, require very little coat care and love to be nursed (and don't weigh too much), so they get my vote of ten out of ten for the top sedentary lifestyle dog.

For people with apartments or limited backyards, toy dogs are ideal sized pets. All dogs in the group love to be held and cuddled — not by the vet, however! They are loyal to their owners and most prefer not to be held by strangers. Several breeds are rather highly strung (mildly neurotic, the uncharitable vet may mutter), in particular the Miniature Pinschers and the occasional Silky Terrier and Chihuahua. Mostly this is as a result of insufficient socialisation with other humans, apart from the owners, and unfortunately a lack of discipline given by the owners. Well-socialised and disciplined toy dogs, even if nervous of strange surroundings, make for a far nicer dog which is easily handled by strangers if the need arises.

Many toy breeds end up rather fat due to overindulgent owners, and often develop weight and heart problems in later life, so care should be taken not to overfeed. Often they have bad breath from excessive soft food diets and need to be given hard biscuits to keep the teeth clean.

Points To Remember

Natural instincts, e.g. herding, guarding and protection, are present in all breeds independent of origin, and are exhibited to a greater or lesser degree. These instincts have been selectively bred for within many breeds, and will show up regardless of the intelligence level of the dog. Some individuals can exhibit these characteristics poorly even in supposedly 'aggressive' breeds, while others may over-exhibit these characteristics.

Dogs that are too sharp (too quick to react to a situation) and/or too aggressive do not make good children's pets, nor are they the ideal dog for a novice to handle. A large, powerful aggressive dog (of any breed, of any group) can, in the hands of a total novice, be a disaster — it invariably leads to someone being hurt or bitten. Such a dog then becomes a danger to its owner and spoils the reputation of the breed. The same sort of animal, in the hands of an experienced trainer or owner used to the breed, can have that determination/aggression controlled and turned into a keenness for work.

My advice is to *read up* on the breed that you are interested in. There are plenty of breed speciality books that trace the origins and development of the breed. This will help you to understand the basis for much of your dog's behaviour patterns, and hopefully guide you in the selection of the breed of dog in the first place. There are also books that cover all the breeds in a general fashion and these can be useful in selecting which breed to choose. Unfortunately, many specialist books are very out of date about diets which are changing constantly as technology advances; some of the older diets produce horrendous bone problems in many of the heavier breeds. Much of the information about whelping, vaccinations and worming given in these books is similarly out of date.

Selecting the Type and Temperament of Dog

Every person's idea of the ideal dog varies. This is why we have so many different and diverse breeds including the mixed breeds, which many people admire and love. The advantage of buying a pure bred dog is that to a large extent, you know what the dog's final appearance, size and temperament is going to be. Unfortunately, with a cross-bred puppy you can get a 'pig in a poke', i.e. no idea of final appearance (including coat type), size or temperament. The fact that many turn out to be nice individuals is, I think, a reflection on the good overall qualities of the dog in general.

Your Temperament in Relation to the Dog's Temperament

If you wish to lead a quiet and sedentary life, do not pick a boisterous, noisy dog; if, however, you have a large backyard full of half-grown children, nothing is better at keeping the children company, and for tiring them out! There are usually several breeds that you would like, and of various sizes that are suitable for you, your family and situation. These days there is even a computer service to help you to select the right dog.

Selection should be made according to the size of dog you prefer, the temperament that you like, the amount of care (grooming, exercise etc.) needed, the size of your backyard, whether you have children and their age group, and finally what you want to do with the dog and the dog to do for you.

Unfortunately, most people do not really think enough about the type of dog that is *suitable* for their situation and conditions, let alone whether the temperament suits in the first place. A feather-brained dog may suit many people and is quite often a very affectionate pet that is very good with children, but many people are driven dotty by a dog that refuses to learn what they consider fairly elementary rules of conduct. In the long run, it is better for the dog, the owner and all concerned that the nature of the dog is fairly compatible with the nature of the owner.

Consideration must be given, if there are children, to whether the dog's temperament is suitable to cope with 'midget adults'. Some dogs (more commonly males), will not tolerate very small children or toddlers. It seems to me that the *smaller* the child in relation to the dog's size, the *lower* the dog's regard in relation to dominance; i.e. dogs quite often consider that small children are below them in order of dominance and they feel that if the child annoys them, then they are within their rights to retaliate. These dogs need to be *very firmly* taught that it is *they*, and not the child, that is suffering from delusions — I do not believe that *any* dog should be allowed to get away with such behaviour. Generally a good stint of obedience training will bring such dogs back into line.

If you are not a firm type of person, *do not* get a dog that requires firm handling; get an amenable dog that will not be overpowering to your personality. As women often feed and care for dogs, this should also be taken into account, since it is they, (not the 'man' of the house) who have to deal with the dogs and their idiosyncrasies, and if they are not capable of being sufficiently firm, problems can often develop.

Many of the more popular 'macho' breeds are purchased by the husband, but the wife is the one that has to live with it, feed it and cope with disciplining it. The husband comes home, the dog recognises firmness when it is applied and behaves, which in turn can create quite a lot of marital difficulties as the husband may never quite believe that his 'Rambo' would do anything like bailing up the person who feeds it!

The **size of the area** that you live in can be very important. An active dog that needs plenty of room to run around, e.g. a German Shorthaired Pointer, will obviously get very bored and often destructive when kept in small backyards. The same dog, kept in an adequately large area, can be happier and non-destructive. Little breeds are obviously in their element when they have (to them) a positively enormous backyard that a German Shorthaired Pointer would sneer at! This is not to say that the smaller dogs would not enjoy living in the great outdoors. Some larger breeds, e.g. Great Danes or St Bernards, are very sedentary, and can rarely bestir themselves to go for a walk. Many German Shepherds would secretly prefer to be lounge lizards on a permanent basis, yet love to go exploring with their own personal 'god' on the lead behind them. Small areas such as apartments are, to my way of thinking, not particularly suited to any but the smallest breeds, unless the dogs are very regularly allowed access to parks and other open areas. Even then, many may become bored and can become rather 'crabby' in nature.

Amount of Care Needed

A dog will live 12 to 14 years on the average. With today's technology, dogs, like people, are living longer and the average veterinarian has a number of 'geriatric' patients around 16 years. This means that the dog, its coat and energy will be around for a long time!

The lifespan of a dog should be taken into account before you buy it — especially when you are buying a coated breed. By 'coated', I mean that the coat is long and usually has a heavy undercoat. The breeds that come to mind in particular are Afghans, Old English Sheepdogs, Shih Tzus, Bearded Collies and Poodles. These dogs will need constant attention to their coats throughout their lifetime, not just for six months or so. Quite often, especially if the dog is being bought for a child, the child will 'promise' faithfully to groom the dog and this tends to go quite well for the first few months and then becomes 'somebody else's' job (inevitably mothers get this one).

When buying a heavily coated breed, you should accept the fact that the dog, if being kept as a pet, should be regularly trimmed every couple of months at least. This way everyone, particularly the dog, is a lot happier.

Also, the **environment** in which the dog is going to spend its time should be considered. Owning long-haired dogs in areas with long grass and burrs is asking for trouble from grass seed abscesses in the feet, under the front legs and in the ears. In tick areas, having a long-haired dog is tempting fate, as trying to find *all* the horrid little pests can be nearly impossible. Often the dog has to be clipped off to the skin. If you want to keep a dog like this in a tick area, have the dog regularly clipped off just before the tick season — this usually coincides with the grass seed season, which makes the haircut quite useful. By the end of the tick season (ticks like warm humid weather), the coat is growing back nicely in time for winter.

Another point to remember is that excessively dense coated dogs have great trouble coping with the heat, e.g. Siberian Huskies and Chow Chows, and they will get easily distressed unless ample shade, water and, preferably, a cool room are available.

Exercise

Most dogs will, on the whole, exercise themselves, particularly if there are children around. When there is a small backyard and you have a big breed of dog, it makes exercising the dog a necessity if you do not want the dog to become batty and destructive through boredom and frustration. Generally speaking, all dogs should be taken out a couple of times a week, even if it is just to give them a breath of fresh air. Contrary to popular opinion of the bigger breeds, some individuals enjoy lying about and strenuously resist *too much* exercise.

Several of the larger hound and gun dog breeds are extremely boisterous and will take all the exercising that you hand out and look disappointed when you collapse. These are ideal dogs for joggers! If you want a sedate life do *not* inflict one of these on yourself — you will only get very frustrated and so will the dog.

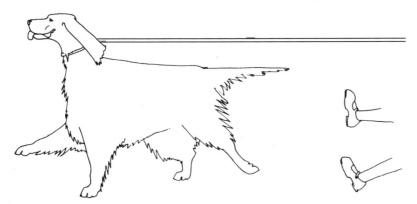

WHAT IS THE INTENDED PURPOSE OF THE DOG?

The reason for actually buying a dog varies considerably. The duties of a dog, as we have mentioned previously, cover many and varied situations. This can be depending on whether they are considered as pets and show dogs, guard and protection, working (i.e. in the 'field'), obedience and agility. Many breeds cross over and cover several fields.

It is important to get your priorities right when selecting a dog. Do you want the dog as a child's pet, a friend for the children to grow up with and not be eaten by, or an all-round pet/guard dog? If you want to do serious obedience training, do not pick a dog that loves to wander or one that cannot concentrate for more than five minutes.

Show dogs are chosen for looks and type first but, unfortunately, temperament and soundness are often overlooked. Working dogs including obedience, agility, armed forces, herding, guard etc. — are selected primarily for temperament, next for soundness and lastly, looks.

Ideally, good temperament, soundness and type for the purpose for which the dogs were bred should be present in the puppy which you buy. The average person would be happy with the first two. All of this has been discussed in greater depth in the section on Selection in chapter 2.

KNOW THE BREED

This can take years to do properly. At least read up a little on the breed and find out its good and bad points. The second may be hard to find as the specialist books very rarely criticise their breed. If you can't locate a reasonable book, ask your vet — the problems usually end up on their doorsteps.

If you are buying a **show** puppy, it is especially important to try to find out as much as you can *before* you buy; even so, the first puppy you buy is the one you usually learn the 'ropes' on and make all the mistakes with. Always go to several people before you make up your mind. If you find after doing your homework that a particular breeder has exactly what you want, be prepared to put an order in and wait. If the delay expected is too long, look outside your local area — this, too, can have its problems. If what you want is not available at the time, you may have to take 'second' or 'third' best (which may eventually prove to be the pick of the litter), for the **value** in the bloodlines that may be unobtainable otherwise. It can mean keeping the animal even if it does not shape up to top quality. This applies mainly to bitches, rarely to male dogs, unless it is of a numerically small breed. Always try to go for soundness of mind and body as well as type.

Occasionally you may hear the expression '**Pick of the litter**' being used and wonder precisely what this means. Pick of the litter means that you get first pick of the puppies within that litter — often it may be pick of a particular sex. Your pick of the litter may differ considerably to that of the breeder.

When you have pick of a litter and you are not completely confident that you will choose the best puppy, ask the breeder which one would be their choice. If the breeder is giving you pick, he/she usually wants you to have at least a respectable puppy as it will invariably be shown and they want a good one to be exhibited. If you do not particularly like that puppy, take another person who is experienced in the breed and (hopefully) is good at choosing puppies and they will give you another viewpoint of the puppies. If you take another person, out of courtesy, always ask the breeder beforehand if he or she would mind.

GROUP 1 TOYS

Affenpinscher
Australian Silky Terrier
Bichon Frise
Cavalier King Charles Spaniel
Chihuahua (Long)
Chihuahua (Smooth)
Chinese Crested Dog
English Toy Terrier (Black & tan)
Griffon Bruxellois
Italian Greyhound
Japanese Chin

King Charles Spaniel
Lowchen
Maltese
Miniature Pinscher
Papillon
Pekingese
Pomeranian
Pug
Tibetan Spaniel
Yorkshire Terrier

List of breeds by groups: international grouping

GROUP 2 TERRIERS

Airedale Terrier
Australian Terrier
Bedlington Terrier
Border Terrier
Bull Terrier
Cairn Terrier
Dandie Dinmont Terrier
Fox Terrier (Smooth)
Fox Terrier (Wire)
Glen of Imaal Terrier
Irish Terrier
Kerry Blue Terrier

Lakeland Terrier
Manchester Terrier
Norfolk Terrier
Norwich Terrier
Scottish Terrier
Sealyham Terrier
Skye Terrier
Soft-coated Wheaten Terrier
Staffordshire Bull Terrier
Welsh Terrier
West Highland White Terrier

GROUP 3 GUN DOGS

Brittany Spaniel
Bay Retriever
Clumber Spaniel
Cocker Spaniel (English)
Cocker Spaniel (American)
Curly-coated Retriever
English Setter
English Springer Spaniel
Flat Coated Retriever
German Shorthaired Pointer
German Wirehaired Pointer

Golden Retriever
Gordon Setter
Hungarian Visla
Irish Setter
Irish Water Spaniel
Labrador Retriever
Large Munsterlander
Pointer (English)
Sussex Spaniel
Weimaraner
Welsh Springer Spaniel

GROUP 4 HOUNDS

Afghan Hound	Finnish Spitz
Basenji	Foxhound
Basset Hound	Greyhound
Beagle	Hamiltonstovare
Bloodhound	Harrier
Borzoi	Ibizan Hound
Dachshund (Long-haired)	Irish Wolfhound
Dachshund (Min. long-haired)	Otterhound
Dachshund (Smooth-haired)	Petite Basset Griffon Vendeen
Dachshund (Min. smooth-haired)	Pharaoh Hound
Dachshund (Wire-haired)	Rhodesian Ridgeback
Dachshund (Min. wire-haired)	Saluki
Deerhound	Sloughi
Elkhound	Whippet

GROUP 5 WORKING DOGS

Anatolian Shepherd	Collie (Smooth)
Australian Cattle Dog	German Shepherd
Australian Kelpie	Hungarian Puli
Bearded Collie	Maremma Sheepdog
Belgian Shepherd (Groenendael)	Norwegian Buhund
Belgian Shepherd (Laekenois)	Old English Sheepdog
Belgian Shepherd (Malinois)	Shetland Sheepdog
Belgian Shepherd (Tervueren)	Stumpy-tailed Cattle Dog
Border Collie	Swedish Valhund
Bouvier Des Flandres	Welsh Corgi (Cardigan)
Briar	Welsh Corgi (Pembroke)
Collie (Rough)	

GROUP 6 UTILITY

Akita	Pyrenean Mountain Dog
Alaskan Malamute	Rottweiler
Bernese Mountain Dog	Samoyed
Boxer	Schnauzer (Miniature)
Bull Mastiff	Schnauzer (Standard)
Doberman	Schnauzer (Giant)
Komondor	Siberian Husky
Mastiff	St Bernard
Newfoundland	Tibetan Mastiff

GROUP 7 NON-SPORTING

Boston Terrier

British Bulldog

Chow Chow

Dalmatian

French Bulldog

Great Dane

Japanese Spitz

Keeshond

Lhasa Apso

Pinscher (German)

Poodle (Standard)

Poodle (Miniature)

Poodle (Toy)

Schipperke

Shar Pei

Shih Tzu

Tibetan Terrier

2

Selecting a Puppy

I t is important to buy a sound healthy puppy — especially if you are paying a large amount of money for the dog. While it is reasonably easy to select a *healthy* puppy, it is far more difficult to select a *sound* one. Buying a puppy that is very typical of its breed, i.e. for showing, is, for the novice, harder still.

What to Look for When Purchasing a Healthy Puppy

1. The puppies should be bright and active, playing with each other, and happy to investigate new humans. If, however, the puppies have just been fed, then they may be reluctant to run around; all they usually want to do after a feed is to curl up and have a sleep. Puppies should never run away and hide; this usually indicates a timid temperament or insufficient handling and socialising with humans. These problems can occasionally be irreversible, particularly in puppies over 10-12 weeks of age. If there has been insufficient early handling and association with humans, the puppies concerned may never develop a normal relationship with man. Bad or poor temperament can, on the other hand, be associated with genetics, and despite good handling and socialisation, the dog may still show these characteristics, especially under stress. These hereditary temperament problems can be minimised by good socialisation, but the problem tends (at best) to remain in the background.

2. The puppy should be of a good size and weight. To gauge the weight of the puppy, lightly run your fingers over the ribs — there should be (at least) a light layer of fat covering the ribs. Some breeds do not carry much fat but, even so, they still should have that light layer. Coated breeds can be deceptive and look fat but under the coat they may be light on for weight. It is important for the puppy to carry a little spare weight at this age as they should be growing rapidly and they usually will not eat well for a few days when they go to their new homes.

Weight is also a reasonably good indication that the puppies have been wormed regularly. If puppies have not been wormed regularly, they tend to be thin over the ribs, 'pot-bellied' and are in poor condition generally. The stress of changing homes on a puppy like this can quite often precipitate gastric problems such as diarrhoea and vomiting up of worms. This can also predispose the puppy to viral gastric infections due to a lowered state of health.

Size is really only of importance if the puppy is going to be shown. The average size of a puppy, relative to its breed, can be difficult to determine if you are unfamiliar with that breed. All you have to go on is the litter in front of you. If you are buying a show puppy and are very keen to make sure that this is the right puppy for you, go and see several litters. You can very quickly see the difference between well-raised puppies and those that have had insufficient worming and generally indifferent care. If there is only one litter available, try to avoid very small, runty puppies unless you really know the breed.

With breeds which have a size limit:

(a) A top limit of size, e.g. Toy and Miniature Poodles, avoid the very large puppies as they may go over the maximum size allowable.

(b) A minimum height limit and no maximum, e.g. Great Danes, avoid the very small, fine-boned puppies as they may not make size.

3. The puppy should have no nasal or eye discharges. The eyes should be clear, the whites of the eyes should be white and not red and inflamed. A light, clear tearing can be normal, especially if the weather has been windy or dusty. Any heavy inflammation of the eyes producing a heavy, yellow-greenish coloured discharge can be an indication of infection, viral or bacterial. At worst it can be a sign of distemper, so be careful.

Heavy but *clear* watery discharge can indicate that there may be eyelid problems, e.g. entropion (inturned eye lids) or extra hairs on the lids which can irritate the eye surface. These conditions are generally easy to correct surgically, but they are also genetic, i.e. inheritable conditions. Several breeds are more prone to this problem, notably breeds with excessively loose eye and head skin folds, e.g. Chow Chows, Bloodhounds and Bassets. While not condoning these genetic problems, they are easy problems to correct, and are not life threatening. Breeders should either fix the problem before the puppies leave or, if it shows up in the first few months, the breeder should help to cover the costs of surgery.

Selecting for tighter eyes without excessive skin folds on the head will gradually reduce the incidence; avoiding affected individuals for breeding is the fastest way of removing the problem from a line.

4. Look for hernias and other obvious defects. Hernias are not a life threatening problem. Umbilical hernias are the most commonly seen and these can range from very small to very large. Small hernias (about the size of the tip of your little finger) are usually self correcting; they normally close over by 10–12 weeks. If you gently wriggle any tissue back in once a week, this assists the hernia to close over.

Large hernias — e.g. if you can fit two to three fingers into the hole — these definitely need correcting and are usually done by the breeder at around 7–10 weeks of age. Hernias of the groin (inguinal) are quite common in some of the smaller breeds, notably the Miniature Poodle, Shih Tzu and the Cavaliers. Again, most are self correcting by 3–4 months, but if very big and the puppy is kept in an overweight condition, these may need correcting in later life.

Scrotal hernias can also occur; again, most will correct, if left alone, by 3–4 months, as long as the puppy is not kept too fat.

To a certain extent, hernias are considered a genetic defect. Within certain lines of particular breeds, there is obviously a genetic problem when 50% or more of the puppies turn up with hernias. However, there are occasionally small minor hernias (mostly umbilical) where only one or two puppies are affected. These cannot all be attributed to genetics; most of these 'random' hernias are probably developmental problems of the muscles not quite knitting firmly prior to birth, and to rough handling by the bitch biting and pulling the umbilical cord at birth. These affected puppies usually go on to have normal puppies with no hernias. Personally, I would, as a breeder, rather have minor hernias than many other life-threatening defects that shorten a dog's lifetime or active working life, e.g. hip dysplasia.

Puppies with obvious defects such as abnormal limbs are usually put down at birth. However, there are occasionally minor deformities, e.g. of tails, which, while not tolerated in the breeding ring, are perfectly acceptable in pets and working animals.

Breeds which commonly suffer from genetic eye defects include Collies, Poodles and Irish Setters. Most breeds that contain the gene for merle colouring also tend to have accompanying eye faults. The safest way to buy stock from breeds that are commonly affected is to ask whether the parents have been tested for those defects.

Some eye defects can be detected as early as at 7–8 weeks of age by an eye specialist, particularly for retinal and lens abnormalities. Other eye defects are often not visible early and may not show up for several years.

5. Vaccinations, worming and diets. Most reputable breeders will have had the puppies vaccinated before they are allowed to leave. This safeguards the puppy, the breeder and the new owner, to a certain extent. If the puppy has been vaccinated, there should be a vaccination certificate, stating what and when the vaccinations were given.

Puppies are usually vaccinated at around 6–8 weeks of age. I prefer that the puppies do not leave the breeder for at least 3–4 days following vaccination as the puppies will not take stress such as long trips, change of environment or change of diet at all well directly after the vaccination. If there is too much stress this can precipitate gastric upsets, which in turn can cause gastric viral infections such as parvovirus.

If a puppy is not vaccinated, I prefer, providing the puppy is healthy and eating well, to leave the puppy alone and let it settle into its new environment for 5–7 days before subjecting it to any further stress. Once the puppy has settled in and is eating well and there are no signs of gastric problems, then vaccinate the puppy.

POINTS TO REMEMBER

Keep your puppy at home until the second vaccinations. Do not take the puppy visiting all and sundry, especially in public places. The first vaccinations are temporary, i.e. they will withstand moderate challenge only. Remember also that vaccinations take 5–7 days to build up a reasonable immune response.

As stated above, if the puppies are not wormed regularly by the breeder they are often thin, ribby and pot bellied. Breeders that look after their puppies properly will have been regularly worming the puppies from 2–3 weeks of age.

When you buy a puppy ask when it was last wormed, when it is next due to be wormed and what they use for worming. Do not worm the puppy as soon as you get it home. Give the puppy several days to settle down before worming as this can upset the puppy's gut and can start off gastric problems.

DIET

Most reputable and caring breeders will give you a diet sheet of what the puppy has been fed on. Do not vary from that diet for several days as again the puppy needs time to settle down before you start upsetting its gut.

The common fault, however, of most diet sheets is that they suggest that you feed the puppy too many times a day. By six weeks of age, three times daily is quite sufficient and usually by eight weeks, the meals are down to twice daily. If you feed your puppy any more frequently, the puppy will either not eat or get very fussy about what it wants to eat. This can be a short road to big problems (see chapter 3 on New owner's syndrome). If you wish to change the diet to a better balanced diet, or one that is easier for you, do wait until the puppy settles in and then gradually change the diet over the space of 1–2 weeks, so as not to upset the gut.

What to Look for When Buying a Sound Puppy

Soundness relates to function and use. A working dog should be able to move well and tirelessly for hours at a time. A lap dog does not need to have the stamina of its working brothers, but to me at least, the dog should be able to run around and play and not be a cripple due to leg faults.

Soundness of movement is particularly important when selecting a show puppy, or a working dog that is expected to work for long hours without collapsing due to hip dysplasia or chronic knee or elbow problems. It also relates to vision, health and heart, so the dog can lead a normal life suitable to its breed ideals. Health soundness is usually checked by your veterinarian. Anything major should have been recognised by the breeder's veterinarian; but it is safer to have your puppy checked, rather than find out there is a problem months later.

CONSTRUCTION

This section is an attempt to give a shortened version about the *ideal* construction of the dog and the whys and wherefores so that the main points are understood. There are several very good books that explain construction and movement in greater detail.

Before we analyse the points of the dog, an overall view of the animal must first be obtained. How does the animal appear to *you*? Does it look like a representative of its breed? Is it balanced front to rear? When moving is your impression one of all parts flowing harmoniously, or three dogs trying to move at the one time?

To assess soundness of construction and movement, it is important to understand the 'bits' that make up the dog. Every dog has the same type and number of bones, but the relative lengths of the bones give the great variation of appearance to the breeds. There are ideal proportions written down for each breed (the 'standard'), but the basic bone structure is similar.

It can take years to develop a good 'eye' for a dog. New breeders may take several litters before they can reasonably assess their own puppies, as they change so rapidly from week to week. Some people unfortunately never develop a good 'eye' for a dog and cannot see where a dog is constructed incorrectly, or why it has gait abnormalities and restrictions.

With puppies, I find the ideal age to assess them is between six and eight weeks of age, when for a short period they 'even' out, i.e. before they start growing up in different sections and looking gangly.

1. Overall view

Think of the dog as a system of levers and pulleys. The back acts as a bridge connecting the front and rear assemblies. *If the ratio of the lengths of the bones of the front and rear are even, then the dog is balanced for that breed.* The ideal lengths vary between breeds, but the principle always holds.

When trying to justify *why* relative lengths of different bones give better movement than others, one can go quite insane if you try to fit all breeds of dog to the one ideal. Having bred German Shepherds, my idea of an ideal construction is very different to someone with a toy dog or a Greyhound. The only way one can look at dog construction is through function. What is the function of the breed, what is the characteristic movement for that breed and so on.

To try to group different construction 'styles', I would divide dogs into three categories:

1. The walking or strutting dog, e.g. Fox Terrier.
2. The trotting dog, e.g. the German Shepherd.
3. The galloping dog, e.g. the Greyhound.

All the breeds range between these three types depending on size, function and individual characteristics.

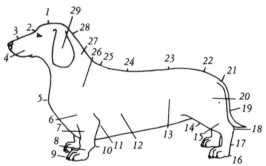

1. skull	11. elbow	21. set of tail
2. stop	12. rib cage	22. croup
3. foreface	13. flank	23. loin
4. muzzle	14. stifle	24. back
5. prosternum	15. lower thigh	25. withers
6. upper arm	16. hind foot	26. shoulder
7. forearm	17. rear pastern	27. neck
8. pastern	18. hock	28. crest
9. forefoot	19. tail	29. ear
10. stopper pad	20. upper thigh	

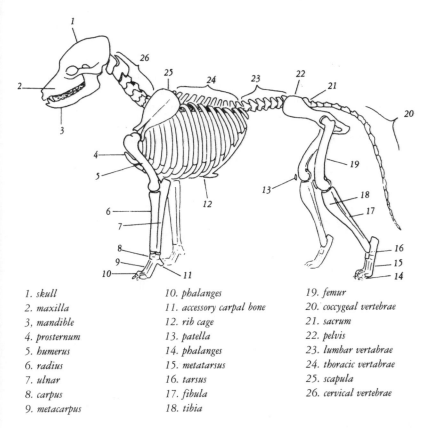

1. skull
2. maxilla
3, mandible
4. prosternum
5. humerus
6. radius
7. ulnar
8. carpus
9. metacarpus
10. phalanges
11. accessory carpal bone
12. rib cage
13. patella
14. phalanges
15. metatarsus
16. tarsus
17. fibula
18. tibia
19. femur
20. coccygeal vertebrae
21. sacrum
22. pelvis
23. lumbar vertabrae
24. thoracic vertabrae
25. scapula
26. cervical vertebrae

Type 1 — the walking or strutting breeds. These breeds have a short bouncy action, where quite often the forequarter assembly is steep, they often have short backs with a reasonable turn of hindquarter for agility. The pasterns are often short and upright. An example of this is the Fox Terrier.

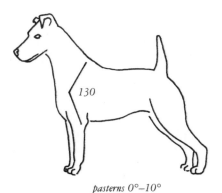

pasterns 0°–10°

31

Type 2 — the trotting breeds. These breeds are used where a tireless, and preferably economical action is called for. Many of the working breeds fit into this category, with differences mostly in the forequarter where added nimbleness is asked for, e.g. the Collie breeds, which are lighter boned and more open in angulation than the German Shepherd. The Shepherd is not being asked to be especially nimble, rather a tireless worker at its natural gait, the trot. The ideal German Shepherd dog is one that covers the maximum amount of ground with the minimum amount of effort, i.e. fewer steps, translating to good reach and drive. Pasterns are longer and more sloping, giving better spring or flexibility.

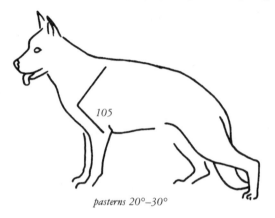

pasterns 20°–30°

Type 3 — the galloping breeds. These breeds are used where great turns of speed are needed. This type is mostly found in the hunting dogs, e.g. Greyhounds. Here the maximum amount of thrust comes from longer, very powerful and well muscled hindquarters which push the dog up and stretch well forwards with very mobile, muscular shoulders. The Pointer breeds show similar structural type, but are not nearly as exaggerated as the Greyhound. Good length of pastern, particularly in the Greyhound types.

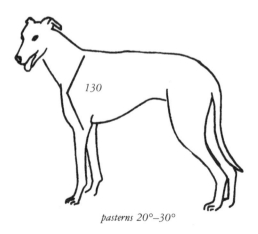

pasterns 20°–30°

Length of reach of the foreleg is determined by the lay of the shoulder *2. Forequarter*
blade, the relative lengths of the scapula (shoulder blade) and the humerus
(upper arm), and the 'arc of movement' that the foreleg moves through.

PLACEMENT OF THE SHOULDER BLADES

The definitions or terms used in this area are:

Well laid back — with the prosternum prominent, which allows for
maximum arc of movement from the top of the shoulder blade.

Upright (steep) — lacking prosternum — disappearing in between the
forelegs when viewed from the side. The effect on movement at the trot
is one of loose elbows when seen coming towards one.

The withers is the area along the top of the shoulder blades, which
obviously in turn relates to the placement of the shoulder. Most breeds
call for a prominent or well developed wither — which often has a
different meaning between breeds. An easy way to obtain an estimate is
to view the dog/puppy from the side; the withers should be higher than
the middle of the back.

The height of wither is determined by how high the top of the
shoulder blades are relative to the top of the dorsal spines of the vertebrae
of the back.

High withers — the tops of the shoulder blades are higher than the top
of the dorsal spines — this obviously gives the tightest muscling over
the top of the shoulder blades (as there are shorter muscles), in turn
giving firmer movement throughout the forequarter. Seen from the side
the wither is higher than the back.

Level withers — where the top of the dorsal vertebrae are level with the
top of the dorsal spines. This gives more room for movement over the
withers, allowing the shoulder to drop slightly in movement. Viewed
from the side the wither is level than the back.

Low withers (flat) — the top of the shoulder blades are lower than the
top of the dorsal spines. This allows a large degree of laxity during
movement, generally causing falling on the forequarter. Viewed from the
side the wither is lower than the middle of the back.

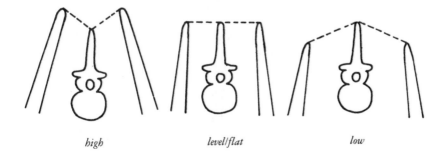

high   level/flat   low

FOREQUARTER ANGULATIONS
Diagrams of the good and the ugly.

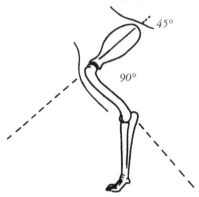

1. Very good forequarter angulation, with a maximum shoulder angle of 90°. This gives very good length and reach.

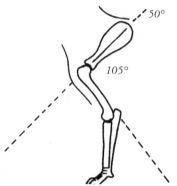

2. Most commonly seen shoulder angulation of 105°, with good length of upper arm — typical of a trotting breed.

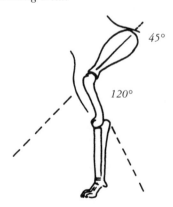

3. Good layback of shoulder blade, but short steep upper arm, giving a restricted reach. Angle 120°.

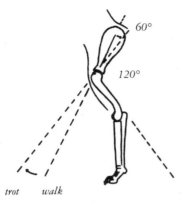

trot   *walk*

4. Steeper placement of shoulder, but good length of upper arm. 120° angle is typical of galloping breeds, slightly restricted in reach during the walk, but at the trot or gallop, the shoulder blade top moves backwards allowing greater reach.

In summary, the longer the upper arm (humerus), the better the reach, regardless of the length and lay of the shoulder blade.

Pasterns. The pasterns act as the cushioning device for the front legs. Short, upright pasterns have a reduced flexibility, and are commonly seen in the terrier breeds, where a short bouncy action is called for. Good length and angle of pastern (15°–20°) will allow great spring and flexibility of the pastern, reflected in a smoother gait as seen in the German Shepherd and the sight hounds. Too long in pastern or too great an angle in relation to the foreleg, will result in loss of spring, over extension of the ligaments and a looseness (paddling effect) when viewed from front-on during movement.

The main points to consider in this area are the chest and the coupling. *3. **Body***

The chest. This is the area bounded by the rib cage and it encloses the heart and lungs. Most breeds ask for a good spring of rib, so as to allow for maximum lung expansion when needed, but other breeds may deem it attractive to be barrel ribbed, e.g. the British Bulldog, and some go for the deep narrow chest, e.g. the Borzoi.

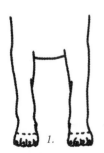  

1. *Correct — the legs drop straight to the ground.*
2. *Barrel ribbed — too wide — wide front movement — elbows out, feet in, paddling effect, 'loose at elbows'.*
3. *Slab sided — too narrow, elbows in, feet out, looseness of pastern.*

The coupling. The length of loin. There is considerable variation between breeds as to what is considered ideal. The length of coupling is what creates the impression of length of body when considering the height to length proportions. Forward placed or steep shoulders can give an impression of length of body.

Dogs which are too short in the coupling cannot extend properly while gaiting. Tall dogs that are short coupled cannot get their hindquarters under themselves sufficiently to drive effectively from their hocks. Most of the thrust of movement goes upwards, not forwards. Dogs which are too long in the coupling dissipate much of the forward drive along the back, particularly if the ligaments of the back are soft. The result is a back which bounces during movement.

1. Good length of coupling - the drive is transmitted without loss along the back.

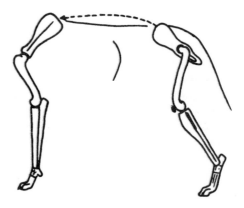

2. Too short in coupling, resulting in a restricted reach and drive, as much of the drive is transmitted up and over the back.

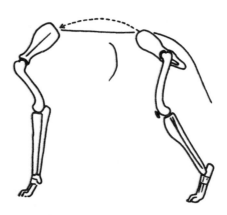

3. Too long in the coupling, where the drive is lost in the centre of the back due to the length, causing a bouncing movement.

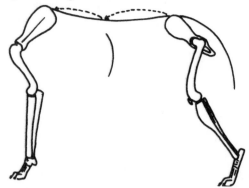

Correct angulation. This must be seen relative to what is desired in the breed and it can be assessed from where the hind leg is positioned when the hock is perpendicular to the ground. The ideal angulation is one where the length of the femur is equal to the length of tibia/fibula (lower thigh). The longer both the femur and tibia/fibula are, the greater the turn of stifle for that breed. A quick way to check for equal lengths of femur and tibia is to raise the hock (perpendicularly, of course) up to the back of the pelvis. If the point of the hock extends beyond the rear edge of the pelvis, then the tibia is too long in relation to the femur. Rarely is the femur too long.

4. Hind-quarters

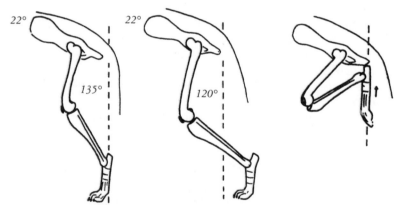

Equal lengths of upper and lower thigh. The longer the bones, the greater the turn of stifle. The hock, when lifted straight upright will be level with the end of the pelvis.

Overangulation. This occurs when the bones of the lower thigh (tibia/fibula) are too long in the relation to the length of femur. This results in the hock (when perpendicular) being placed considerably further behind a line dropped behind the pelvis than when the lengths are equal. (The term overangulation also occasionally applies to those breeds with well-turned stifles, e.g. the German Shepherd.)

The longer the lower thigh is in relation to the length of femur, the greater the amount of turn of stifle. The longer the hock in combination with a longer lower thigh, the more unstable the hock during movement. Shorter hocks will give greater stability, particularly where there is a longer lower thigh.

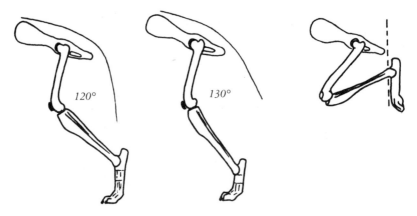

1. *Short femur, long lower thigh, long hock.*
2. *Short femur, long lower thigh, short hock.*
3. *Short femur, longer lower thigh, where the point of the hock is behind the end of the pelvis when raised perpendicular from the ground.*

Insufficient angulation (straight stifled). This is desired in some breeds, excessively so in the Chow Chow. It is, however, *not* a good direction to follow due to the increasing instability of the knee as the leg becomes straighter, placing more and more stress on the knee during exercise. The knee is the major pivotal joint of the hindquarters and it takes all the strain of braking and twisting. Hock problems can be present as they become very upright, and will occasionally even bend forwards ('double jointed').

In a hindquarter lacking angulation, the hock when perpendicular does not extend behind the end of the pelvis.

Hindquarter too steep, e.g. the Chow Chow

The knee (or stifle joint). This is (from side to side) not as stable as is the human knee which is a lot wider. Due to this narrowness and in conjunction with a straight stifle (lack of good turn at the knee), the knee cap (the patella) can become unstable, and **patella luxation** may occur. Patella luxation is when the knee cap 'jumps' out of its groove and the dog cannot bear proper weight on the leg. This condition is considered genetic in origin, particularly so in toy breeds, but can also develop after accidents involving the ligaments of the knee. If the patella groove is deep, then patella luxation is less likely to occur.

The relative instability of a straighter stifle can cause the larger breeds to be more prone to damaging the anterior cruciate ligament — like a human football injury. This type of injury is not however, totally confined to those dogs with straighter stifles. It can occur in any hyperactive dog.

Due to the abnormal stance from a straight stifle, problems associated from excessive wear of the cartilages of both the hocks and knees can occur in the heavier breeds, particularly Rottweilers. This condition is often associated with overweight young dogs.

Hocks. Tightness and firmness of the hocks during movement is desirable. The stability of the hocks is related to the relative lengths of all three sections — the upper thigh (femur), lower thigh (tibia/fibula), and the hock. Too long a hock, particularly when accompanied by a long lower thigh, allows for considerable instability of the hindquarter drive. Some breeds may stand cow hocked due to more angulation of the hindquarter e.g. German Shepherds, but during their natural gait (the trot), the hocks should be firm and remain upright.

Length of hock relative to end size in puppies. Long hocks tend to go with increased size of the adult dog and a straighter hindquarter. Shorter hocks are more desirable in most breeds as they often go with better hindquarter angulation and firmness of hocks (therefore better transmission of drive). This is well worth noticing when purchasing a puppy, particularly in breeds with a top size limit of adults.

The back is an area which many people overlook as it seems to be so obvious that it connects the back end to the front. The back is, in effect, a bridge between the two halves of the dog, and the strongest bridge has a slight rise over its apex. The ideal back is firm in movement. Movement of the back will cause loss of forward drive.

5. Backs and croups

The length of back can also affect movement. If it is too short, the movement is restricted, and the dog is unable to drive properly; if it is too long, there will be bounce and loss of drive (see section on coupling).

The **croup** affects the angle at which the hindquarter functions. Some believe that the croup has little effect, but most agree that too short and steep a croup, results in loss of hindquarter drive through an upwards rather than forwards motion. Ideally, a croup should be of good length and laid at a gentle angle to the back so that the drive up through the hindquarter **flows forwards** along the back without a break. A croup that is too short and steep will reduce the arc of movement possible from the hindquarter, causing restrictions in drive.

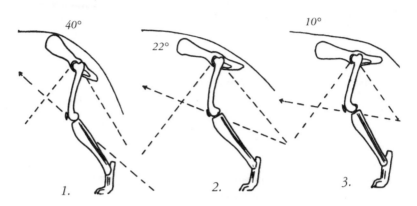

1. At 40° — *too steep, where the angle of drive is too high, causing the back to rise during movement. Restricted in rear swing of the hindquarter due to the steep croup.*
2. At 22° — *croup good, the angle of drive is not too steep, where the thrust is forwards along the back. Good swing of the hindquarter (both forwards and backwards) is allowed by the croup.*
3. At 10° — *croup too flat, angle of drive is lower than the back, and considerable thrust is lost as it is not transmitted forwards. The forward reach of the hindquarter is slightly restricted.*

The ideal angle of the croup would be between 20°–30° (from the line of the back). This variation is needed to allow for differences in lengths of backs and croups. The stronger back would probably tend to the 30°, whereas the longer back would tend to the 20°. The angle of the croup should ideally flow in smooth line from the backline, allowing for maximum transmission of drive along the back. The steeper the angle of the croup, the more it will affect the forward motion of the drive or hindquarter thrust.

6. Transmission

Transmission is the force generated from the hindquarter thrust (or drive), which transmits along the back pushing the forequarter forward. The forequarter movement is more of a reaching, grabbing movement; and the hindquarter thrust allows maximum use of the forequarter construction.

If there is good hindquarter construction and poor forequarter construction, the hindquarter drive tends to overrun the forequarter and so create the impression of 'running down hill' or falling on the forehand.

The transmission is up through the back, then down, i.e. a pounding effect, as the drive is excessive in relation to what the front can achieve.

If there is good forequarter construction and poor hindquarter construction, the hindquarter drive is insufficient to move the forequarter properly and consequently movement is restricted both front and rear and the hocks do not reach under the dog to achieve a good drive.

If the back is good, then the transmission of the drive from the hindquarter through the back into the forequarter, will be transmitted smoothly and without loss of power. If the back is too soft or too long then the transmission forward is somewhat dissipated and the overall picture is one of a reduced 'flow', i.e. the back will bounce around losing much of its power. Dogs with backs that are too short or too roached are similarly affected.

With balanced construction both front and rear, and moving with a firm back; a dog of moderately good construction can out move a dog with just a good front, or a good rear end.

HEADS AND COATS

These vary greatly from breed to breed. Read up as much as you can, go to several shows and at least find out a little about the breed before buying a puppy of a breed in which the head and coat are of major importance. Heads can change greatly from an early age — what may look promising at six weeks can occasionally look horrid at 12 weeks. Also check the mouth and the bite. (See chapter 4 on Teeth.)

TYPE

This can be an extremely ambiguous area for the novice. This is also of major importance to people buying show puppies, but may be of no importance to the pet, working dog, obedience or tracking animal. To other people soundness is of prime significance.

Type means that a dog looks like a good representative of the breed — unfortunately this does not go hand in hand with soundness which, speaking as a veterinarian, is a great pity. However, people are becoming more aware of breed constructional problems and are trying to gradually change the breed standards to produce not only good looking but healthier and sounder animals.

Type can mean the difference between a good show dog and a pet, which if pointed out to a novice, can usually be easily seen. For example, take a Basset; if the dog has a poor head, short ears and longish legs, it may still be a Basset, but it is not of the correct type. A Basset is characterised by a slightly wrinkled skin over the eyes when the head is down, the head should be well chiselled and in proportion to the body; the body should be low to the ground and of reasonable length one third height to two thirds length); the ears should be long and extend at least to the tip of the nose.

If there is too much wrinkling of skin over the eyes, then eyelid problems and excessive drooping of lids occur; creating possible surgical problems. This issue is really over type, i.e. the standard taken to the extreme by some breeders and judges (who are often breeders as well).

Type, just to confuse the issue further, can mean many things to different people. 'Type' can range from one breeders line to another to the extent that you can pick them at a dog show without even looking at a catalogue. 'Type' can also mean a range of extremes of the breed standard, from too big, too little, excessively coated (most go for that one) to very lightly coated (better for the 'working' members of the breed), and so on.

Most extremes do not worry me, but if it affects the dogs overall soundness when walking and breathing (with the excessively short forefaced breeds, e.g. British Bulldogs, Pekingese and Pugs), I do object most strongly. As stated earlier, they are finally starting to change some of the breed standards but I only hope that the judges and breeders are told!

If you are choosing a puppy, the above section should be of assistance to you. If you are buying a puppy, try to learn as much as possible before going to buy, and see several breeders (if possible) before making your choice. The first breeder may be the one you buy from but you can at least compare differences in litters, care given and temperaments.

Selecting a Puppy from Reputable Breeders

In the background are the reputable breeders. These people are usually trying to do the best for the breed by trying to improve the breed's overall soundness. They are usually members of breed clubs which have schemes to try and reduce and eliminate the incidence of major genetic problems. Participation in these schemes is usually voluntary. Some members may, unfortunately, prefer to keep their heads in the sand and pretend things like hip dysplasia and other genetic problems do not exist. Gradually, the general public is becoming more aware of things like hip dysplasia schemes and the fact that people can advertise that their dogs have been x-rayed or tested and the result published. By doing so, they gain more credibility in the eyes of the public.

Getting in touch with breed clubs is usually not very hard. An area body or a national kennel control will usually give you the phone number of the secretary of a particular breed club, and clubs often advertise in dog magazines.

The secretary of a breed club will give you the names and phone numbers of members who currently have litters. If the club has any schemes going, the list of litters available should be of those of the members who participate in the schemes.

Breeders that really have the breed at heart will usually be very helpful especially to novices. Remember, they are besotted with their dogs and generally once you start them talking they will not stop. If you are buying a show puppy, they will quite often help you learn the ins and outs, the do's and don'ts. These people are usually interested in following the progress of the puppy, especially if the puppy turns out to be the best thing they have ever bred.

Not all puppies sold as show puppies succeed as show dogs. Occasionally the puppy's mouth may go wrong or the dog may go over size. If the fault is very bad, a reputable breeder *may* either replace the dog, offer another at half price, or come to some other arrangement. These arrangements are always between the breeder and the owner and can differ widely. Usually the possibility of the dog not coming up to scratch is touched on at the time of purchase, and/or conditions of 'guarantee' are outlined.

A puppy may develop a genetic problem despite the breeder's attempts to avoid it, e.g. hip dysplasia. The possibility of this is usually mentioned in a guarantee. Again, what the breeder will offer to do will vary considerably according to the case at hand e.g. What do you want to do with the dog? Do you want to keep it despite the problem and other considerations? The breeder quite often will ask that their own veterinarian examine the animal as well.

Problems like bone and/or mouth abnormalities may arise because *you*, the owner, have not fed the dog correctly, either by giving it too much food or the wrong type, for example too much meat. In these cases I do not believe that the breeder (unless they gave you an incorrect diet) is always entirely liable for all of the end result. The best way to avoid creating these problems is to follow the diet chart provided by the breeder (as long as it is good) or the general one in this book. Also, read New owner's syndrome in chapter 3 — this may apply to you. Regularly check in with the breeder, especially in the first few months and this way you may not have any major problems.

DEALERS

Avoid buying from dog 'dealers' on the whole. These are people who buy in puppies and occasionally adults from all over the place. The trouble is, that you are often buying the puppy or dog second hand and there are few if any guarantees offered. You are usually buying the dog at a vastly inflated price, then at the first sign of trouble — no sign of the 'dealer' or they will refer you to the dog's original breeder who will usually say that the animal concerned was sold strictly as a pet. This inevitably means the dog comes as is, flaws and all.

You will normally get much fairer and professional treatment from breeders direct (although it is still possible to meet some strange breeders). The best advice is to try looking around at several kennels before buying as you will have a much better idea of what you want plus who you want to buy it from. Do not go out on the spur of the moment wanting a 'Bloggs terrier' or that fluffy thing you saw on a television advertisement. Go to several dog shows if you are not sure of the breed that you want, decide what suits your temperament and environment and then start looking in earnest when you know definitely what it is that you do want.

PRICE

To obtain a reasonable idea of the price range to expect to pay for a puppy, ask the club secretary. The secretary will give you the range currently being asked for that breed by different breeders. There is a range of prices obviously between pet and show. Just because a puppy cost you a fortune it does not necessarily relate to its quality.

Always try to find out if there are schemes available in the breed that you are getting which will possibly help you to obtain a sounder puppy. The puppy will grow and hopefully live 12–14 years on average, so try to get a healthy one. People who say they don't need to do any of these things as their stock couldn't possibly have anything wrong, are either hiding from the problem or are too scared to try and find out if they do have problems.

In the long run, buying a puppy from a breeder who is trying to do the right thing by both the breed and the buyer is the safest way. It may cost you a little more to start with, but in the long term, you *should* obtain a sounder animal which is going to cost you a lot less in vet fees and anguish.

Summary

The breeder builds the foundations but you, the owner, build the house. The soundness of the 'house' depends on both the 'foundations' and the 'building'. A healthy dog internally, externally, and mentally, is a lovely animal and a pleasure to own. Both breeders *and* owners should try to do their best to keep it that way!

Remember — *caveat emptor* — let the buyer beware!

3

New Owners

A Puppy's First Day at its New Home

Well, the big day has finally arrived, you have just picked up your precious little bundle of joy and are taking him or her home! Hopefully the puppy was not fed in the past 2–3 hours or you will have a very soggy puppy (and lap). Many puppies will dribble and drool as they are unused to car travel; some will be car sick even if they have not been fed. The safe way to travel home is to have a small box or an old towel, so that if mishaps occur (as they inevitably do), everyone stays a lot cleaner including the puppy. If you have a long way to travel and it is a hot day, take some water for small drinks for the puppy, and a towel to wet if necessary and put under the puppy if it is distressed by the heat. The puppy will be panting very rapidly and heavily and its tongue will be hanging out halfway to China!

When you get home the fun begins. There is an initial settling in period that can last up to 10–14 days, where adjustments are made on both sides. A lot of your preconceived ideas may fly out the window; the puppy, while having no preconceived ideas at all, is more than willing to make *its* own rules but only if *you* let it.

SLEEPING AREA

You may think that the puppy is going to sleep outside. If you have another dog and preferably good kennelling, this will keep the puppy company and it may not howl the place down. However, if you don't have another dog, you are in for a few noisy nights and days. The puppy will naturally prefer to sleep with you, preferably the closer the better. This is a fairly noiseless way to sleep, but the puppy will usually expect to sleep with you for the rest of its life.

Generally speaking, the best way to get over this period is to put the puppy in the laundry or garage at night, shut it in and leave it with a few old blankets and plenty of water. Some people leave a ticking clock wrapped in a fluffy old blanket — it may or may not work (you may end up with a shredded clock). Leaving the radio on is also very helpful.

It will take 4–5 nights before the puppy will settle down; some are good and after 1–2 nights will not make a sound. Give the puppy a few nights' grace, as you cannot expect a puppy to go from a litter situation to being by itself and in a strange environment, in the space of one night.

However, if the puppy is a real screamer and the neighbours complain, explain that you have only just got the puppy, and could they please be tolerant for a few nights until it settles down.

If the puppy is still shrieking after three nights, then here are several hints (not necessarily nice), on how to control the puppy:

(a) Do not go out and cuddle the puppy if it is crying — it will only cry harder and sooner.

(b) If yelling at the puppy has no effect, go in, pick the puppy up and shake it hard, give it a 'NO', and leave the room — you may have to do this several times before the message sinks in.

(c) If despite all attempts the puppy still barks or howls, get a small bowl of water and open the door, yell at the puppy and throw half the water on the puppy. Close the door and wait, then if it starts again, whip open the door, yell and throw the other half. (Do not throw much — half a cup is ample and preferably don't do it on a cold night.).

FEEDING

See the diet sheet on page 183–4 and New owner's syndrome on page 49 — and don't forget that it applies to *you*, too!

It is suggested that you re-read New owner's syndrome at the end of one week, just to refresh your memory of what not to do. It is very easy to fall into bad habits without realising as it occurs gradually.

Always leave water for the puppy; it should be in a low, shallow dish if the puppy is very short to the ground. Then as the puppy grows you can change it for larger and/or higher dishes. If the puppy likes to spill the water and, naturally, play in it, put a heavy object such as a brick, in the middle of the dish or use a concrete trough.

Do not leave deep, high dishes where the puppy has to struggle and jump to get water as the puppy may:

(a) not get any water at all.

(b) get caught in the bucket/dish and possibly drown.

Always think of the availability of water from the puppy's point of view, so place it close to the ground.

HOUSE TRAINING

If your puppy is going to be a house pet, then the household and the dog must get on and a few rules have to be laid down and learnt.

House training is usually relatively easy to accomplish if you remember two things:

(a) Always take the puppy outside immediately after it has been fed and wait until it 'goes'.

(b) Always take the puppy outside as soon as it wakes up. Wait until it goes to the toilet, preferably both sorts; praise the puppy and let it in again. The hard part of house training is being there in the first place.

A dog will prefer not to dirty an area that it sleeps in, if given the room to do so. A puppy cannot discriminate between what is and what isn't a suitable area in which it can urinate and defecate. Most dogs are very clean and once they have been house trained may hold on and last nearly 24 hours before messing anywhere.

If a puppy has been raised on newspaper, put some newspaper down by the door, and gradually move the paper out and away from the house. If the puppy does make a mess, pick it up, shake it, say 'NO' loudly, and whiz it outside or onto the newspaper. Do not wait to find something to hit the puppy with — you will only make the puppy afraid of 'stick' type things, and lose the instant effect of chastisement of a 'foul' deed done right in front of you. **House training is not instantaneous!**

Some puppies learn very quickly, especially if someone is at home with them during the first few days, and makes a point of being very vigilant about 'catching' the puppy *before* it makes a mistake. Other puppies can be very slow at becoming house trained, especially if their owners are slack about trying to train them. It is easier and far quicker to make an all-out effort in the first two weeks and have a well house-trained dog for life, than make a half-hearted attempt and have a sloppily trained dog who will occasionally revert to its 'sloppy' habits. Remember, you have been warned.

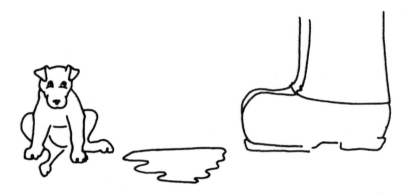

SOCIALISATION

As mentioned elsewhere, young puppies, even if they have been vaccinated, are not particularly well covered against a strong challenge to that vaccination. The puppy's immune system is immature at this age, and it cannot develop a high level of protection against parvovirus, distemper and other problems. If the puppy is dragged all over the countryside, and to public places like parks, shopping centres and dog shows, then the risk of the puppy coming into contact with these diseases is greatly increased.

A puppy should basically stay at home, in its own backyard, at least until it has had its second set of vaccinations. It may seem boring to you, but it is safer for the puppy. People can come and visit — provided they do not have any sick puppies. The puppy can play with or be near your other dogs, if they are healthy, reasonably up to date on vaccinations, and have not been sick lately but definitely *not* if they have had gastric or any problems recently.

Plenty of handling, playing with the puppy and elementary leading lessons are a good thing at this stage.

Adult dogs should only be allowed to play with young puppies for short periods that are preferably supervised! Too many puppies end up sore, bruised and battered by older dogs who, while they may mean no harm, will cause damage and occasionally fractures by their sheer weight. Puppies should be kept in separate runs to adult dogs; next to adults but not running with adults.

Children can play with puppies at this stage quite happily, in fact you won't be able to stop them! Very young children should, however, be supervised, as puppy teeth are very sharp and kids don't appreciate it when puppies are being too rough. Young puppies, likewise, do not appreciate it when children are being too rough and, occasionally, cruel. Both the children and the puppies need a little time to appreciate the good and bad aspects of each other, and generally after a short time there is an understanding between them that is amicable for all concerned. This does not mean that one should tolerate a puppy that bites non-stop. It is best to pick the puppy up, shake it hard and smack it saying 'NO' very firmly.

Generally speaking, *never* hit the puppy on the head as it tends to make it hand-shy, usually a tap on the bottom or the side of the body is sufficient — *it is more the indignity of the slap than the force of the slap that counts!* If the puppy tries to growl and bite you, shake it harder and smack it, close the mouth, hold it shut and shake the head saying 'NO' till it calms down. When it has calmed down, hold it for a few minutes, pat it and only then let it go.

A puppy should never be 'vicious'. This is mostly the result of bad, incorrect handling and/or poor discipline; *you*, the owner have let the puppy get away with bad habits, which if left to develop, will cause an unmanageable dog.

POINTS TO REMEMBER

What not to do with your new puppy, especially in the first 7–10 days:

- Do not change the diet drastically — minor changes can be made gradually — preferably do not use pasteurised milk as it can upset puppies' stomachs — use low-lactose milk, which is very good and non-allergenic, as is natural yoghurt.
- Do not travel long distances with the puppy, especially in the heat.
- Do not take the puppy visiting — leave it at home.
- Do not worm the puppy in the first few days or you will upset its stomach. Wait a few days and then use something mild.
- Do not vaccinate the puppy (if it has not been vaccinated) immediately after the purchase — wait for several days, preferably at least 4–5 days to make sure the puppy has got over the stress of change of environment. If, however, the puppy is off-colour, vomiting and/or has foul-smelling diarrhoea, take the puppy immediately to your vet.

Stress in any form is to be minimised at all costs.

'New Owner's Syndrome'

Upon selling a puppy, the breeder usually furnishes you the buyer, with a diet sheet and instructions on how to care for your puppy. The problem is that you are usually too excited to take much notice of what the breeder is saying and fail to pick up the important points. The other major problem is that the puppy is going from a litter situation, to where it is quite often the only dog or pet.

When a new puppy goes to its new home, it explores, settles down and sticks to you like glue. All seems wonderful. Then you try to feed it. This is a major difficulty — you give it what the breeder suggested and quite often the puppy will not eat it or eat very little. Personally, as a dog breeder and a veterinarian, I suggest three-quarters dry dog food to one-quarter fatty meat, table scraps, chicken, cheese etc. The new puppy going home will usually gulp down the meat or cheese and leave the dry food because there is no competition for the food.

This is often when new owners may start making mistakes:

- They tend to leave uneaten food and/or dry food lying around, which encourages the puppy to nibble at, but not really eat the dry food.
- They think because the puppy likes the meat or chicken, everything is fine. At least it's eating something, so they tend to give more and more meat in the diet. The end result is a picky eater, in the first case, and possible bone problems in the second.

New owners should be told as they usually are but they forget, that a puppy will be finicky with its food for about one week after going to its new home. Not having all the other litter mates around trying to grab the next piece of food, in strange surroundings, with new people; all these circumstances tend to make the puppy less keen to eat.

The problems then compound themselves as the puppy loves the meat and table scraps but will not eat the dry food — or very little of it. The breeder usually does not see the puppy until it is 3–4 months old, by which stage you may have a complete dietary problem on your hands.

Common problems include stunted front legs, down in pasterns, mouth problems, over- and underweight puppies and legs that would do a Basset proud! This is called the 'all meat syndrome'. *It will usually never occur if the puppy is fed at least two-thirds and preferably three-quarters good quality dry dog food.* Meat is very high in phosphorus, especially kidney, liver and heart. The higher the phosphorus in the diet, the lower the calcium absorption. You may be adding calcium and have no signs of absorption, because the high phosphorus level in the diet will actively push down the calcium absorption.

The larger the breed and the heavier boned the puppy, the more important it is to keep the meat in reasonable proportions.

POINTS TO REMEMBER

- The puppy will often be finicky with food for the first 7–10 days.
- Do not leave dry dog food lying around (or any food for that matter). Leave the food down for 20–30 minutes — no longer — if not eaten, remove it!
- New puppies tend to go off sloppy food. By 7–8 weeks the dry dog food should not need to be soaked at all. Put it out as is and pour on some milk, watery vegemite or something to flavour the dry food,

e.g. a canned puppy food, meat or cheese. Always mix the food thoroughly so they don't just eat the 'strawberries' on the top.

- Cut down to two feeds daily by eight weeks or the puppy will start to leave food and wait for the next feed to eat the goodies and leave the rest. Cut out breakfast gradually between 3–4 months.

- If your puppy is not eating well (and properly) after 1–2 weeks with you, phone the breeder. Do *not* wait until 6–8 weeks have passed, when you may have caused problems. If you don't think that your puppy is eating well, but the weight of the puppy is good, the problem may be that *you* are fussing. To check the puppy's weight, just run your fingers lightly along the ribs. There should be a light layer of fat between the ribs and the skin. Not too little, but not centimetres!

- The stress of a change of environment, new home and people, can cause the puppy to be a bit loose in its motions, especially for a few days. Avoid milk (especially pasteurised), canned food or anything that is too rich for a few days until the puppy's gut has had a chance to settle down. If the puppy has had to travel a long distance to reach its new home, this is an added stress factor. Worming the puppy immediately is again a stress factor. I like to settle a puppy in for a few days before worming, vaccinating (if it has not been done) or changing the diet too drastically. A good bland diet, especially if the puppy's motions are loose, is a combination of cooked chicken, natural yoghurt, dry dog food and/or cooked rice. None of these things should upset the gut. This diet is good for dogs at any age that may have an upset gut or are invalids. The natural yoghurt is very good at settling the gut lining and helping to restore the normal gut bacteria.

WORMING

Do not worm the puppy in the first few days. Worm every two weeks until 14–16 weeks of age. This is done mainly for round and hookworms. Tapeworming is usually only needed every 6–8 weeks.

After 16 weeks of age, worm every 6–8 weeks. By 10–12 months, i.e. adulthood, a 3–4 month interval between wormings is usually quite sufficient. Start heartworm treatment as soon as you get the puppy home.

The final piece of advice to the new owner is to phone the breeder after about two weeks and let them know how the puppy is developing.

My advice to the breeder is that if they have not heard from the new puppy owners after two weeks, attempt to contact them and find out how the puppy is coming along. It is always easier and quicker to correct possible mistakes at this early stage than in 6–8 weeks time, when irreversible damage may have occurred.

Responsible Pet Ownership

Responsible ownership involves a duty to care for the animal, consider the rest of the community and comply with appropriate legislation.

With any new pet and particularly for the first time pet owner, it is important that owners realise their responsibilities both to the pet for its own well being and welfare, and to the community in general. While the benefits of pet ownership can clearly be seen, pet owners as a whole must learn to control and manage their pets taking into account the interests of the community at large and the protection of the environment.

In our increasingly urbanised society, pet owners need to be aware of all factors of dog care. Dogs should be under effective control at all times. This means that your dog must be kept within your boundaries unless on a lead in a public area. The only exception to this is in council designated leash-free areas where the dog is still expected to behave in an obedient manner even if off its lead. Whilst walking your dog, try to ensure that it defecates in an area that is away from public walkways or preferably, use a pooper-scooper. Secure fences are a must for the keeping of any dog, especially for those guard breeds that will quite readily attempt to patrol the whole street if not kept confined to their owners' property. Unfortunately, not all people love pets and many are scared of large dogs, particularly if they are roaming in the street accosting people (even if it is a gesture of friendliness), or chasing other dogs, cats or cars.

Dogs should be well socialised from puppyhood onwards by attending puppy preschool and obedience training. This makes for a far more sociably acceptable pet when in public. Another area where owners must make an effort is in the control of excessive barking, which can often occur when the owner is absent and invariably late at night. Environment enrichment by adding chew or play objects, or the introduction of a friend to play with, will help reduce a dog's boredom. Regular outings also keep dogs much happier.

In the event that your dog accidentally escapes from your yard, it should have a positive means of identification, i.e. a legible dog tag with a contact telephone number. Other identification techniques such as micro-chips or tattoos are extremely helpful as your dog's details can be registered with a central body and its rapid return is usually ensured. As an owner, you are legally liable for any damages that your dog causes when off your property, e.g. biting another dog, damage to cars etc. Your dog is far safer inside your fences than out on the roads. Allowing your dog out at night shows a lack of consideration to other members of your neighbourhood as well as placing your dog at risk of care accidents and confrontation with other similarly uncontrolled dogs.

Your dog must have access to shade, shelter and an adequate supply of clean water at all times.

4

Raising a Puppy to Puberty

This chapter is in several sections, and the amount of material that needs to be covered could fill several books let alone one chapter. It is most important to raise a puppy properly so as to have a healthy, well-developed adult that has a minimum of problems and which should stay that way for the majority of its life.

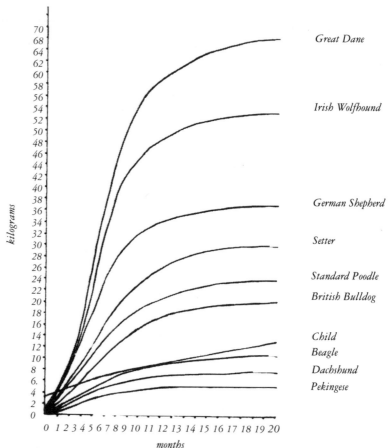

Growth Rates

Growth is a complex process whereby the body grows and develops. The body has a very finely tuned mechanism which is delicately balanced by hormones. The hormones involved in growth are many and varied — the average person thinks only of sex hormones, but there are many other hormones in the body besides these. Hormones are the *regulating mechanisms* which tell the body, among other things, what it needs to eat, absorb, when to grow and when to stop. If you upset one hormone by too much, or too little of something in the diet, then it can affect the other regulating hormones.

Feeding your dog a diet that gives a *balanced* intake of energy, protein, carbohydrates and minerals is extremely important. *What you feed your dog from puppyhood to adolescence, can determine the dog's eventual soundness for life.* It greatly influences the final height and boning (as well as minimising leg fractures in the 'delicate breeds'); tightness and firmness of ligamentation for breeding later on; teeth and bites and coats.

What you feed your dog and what it needs at the various stages, will depend on its weight and rate of growth. Always remember that a young dog is eating not only for daily maintenance, but for growth as well, i.e. up to twice that of a normal adult. This gradually reduces to a maintenance level by 8–10 months of age. *The amount of food fed reduces as the rate of growth decreases.* Proportionally, a puppy eats far more per unit of body weight than does an adult.

A puppy grows extremely rapidly, growing from around ½ kg at birth to 20–30 kg by 8–9 months in the average medium-sized breed. A child grows at nowhere near the same rate — the equivalent growth may take 2–5 years. This rapid growth is even more exaggerated in the giant breeds where a 60–70 kg dog by 10 months is not uncommon. Due to this tremendous expansion in both size and weight, the diet must be capable of delivering available minerals and a balanced supply of energy, proteins, fats and carbohydrates.

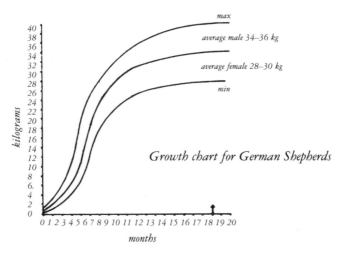

Growth chart for German Shepherds

This is an example to show you the variation in weight gain that is possible between a male and female puppy, and between a small and heavy puppy within the same breed. The males are obviously in the top half of the range and the bitches should be in the bottom half of the line.

Feeding

Sound common sense is the most important thing to remember with any diet. Stick to good quality foods. A growing dog requires more food than an adult dog as it is eating for growth as well as maintenance of body weight. A pregnant bitch requires more food for growth of puppies and her own body maintenance. A lactating bitch needs up to three times the normal diet to produce sufficient milk output to feed the growing puppies and to be able to maintain her own body weight. Puppies grow very rapidly to about two thirds adult weight, i.e. 6–7 months of age, then the growth rate slows down, and they gradually mature at around 18 months of age. Smaller breeds are often fully mature by 9–10 months of age.

WEIGHT

It is important to keep an eye on your dog's weight. As mentioned earlier, a simple test is to run your fingers over the ribs and there should be a thin layer of fat between the ribs and the skin. A growing dog, especially between three and six months of age, should not get too thin or too fat as it is growing very fast and either excess is not helpful to the firmness and soundness of the eventual adult dog. Elderly dogs can carry a bit more weight, but this should never be excessive.

POINTS TO REMEMBER

- Avoid excessive protein intake in young puppies. Feed a good quality highly digestible diet. Avoid overfeeding as this will *force* the growth rate beyond the ideal and can result in the development of metabolic bone disorders such as cartilage defects and bone soreness.
- The bigger the breed the lower the meat intake. Meat is very high in phosphorus and protein. Excessive meat intake can cause flat feet, poor under jaw growth, swollen growth plates and causes the average calcium additive to be very poorly absorbed.
- Watch the feet and pasterns to assess how the dog is coping with its diet and the absorption of calcium in the diet. If the feet are not improving despite changing the diet, consult your veterinarian.
- Watch the weight of your puppy — do not let the puppy become too overweight. If you can keep your puppy trim (not fat, not thin — and definitely not sloppy) until 8–9 months for the average to large breeds (12–15 months for the giant breeds), then you will have a fairly sound boned and ligamented dog for life. Fat, sloppy youngsters tend to make fat, sloppy adults!

FEEDING VERY YOUNG PUPPIES

You can start to feed puppies at 2–3 weeks of age — as soon as their eyes open. With small litters, the start of weaning can be left until 3–4 weeks, but take care with the smaller breeds to avoid calcium deficiencies that can turn into milk fever. The earlier you start, the sooner the drain is eased on the bitch. Use a good-quality dry puppy food, one that soaks down readily, such as Supercoat Puppy®. Dry dog foods are better 'starter' cereals than human baby food preparations as they are formulated specifically for canine rather than human requirements.

A small amount of low lactose milk (e.g. Di-Vetelact®, Biolac®), natural yoghurt or junket, can be added. These are good as they do not upset the gut; one quarter of the total amount fed should be finely minced meat or a canned puppy food. Make this into a sloppy porridge and feed three times daily. The entire day's feed can be made in one batch providing it is refrigerated until needed and then diluted/mixed with hot water before being fed to the puppy. This certainly saves time in meal preparation. Another advantage of preparing a day's feed is that additives can be spread evenly over three feeds.

Try to avoid a separate feed of meat, as most puppies prefer to eat meat and having filled up on meat, refuse to eat the soaked dry dog food. If it is all slopped together, then they will eat well, and not become fussy eaters. Also, avoid feeding meat by itself when just starting to wean puppies as they overeat it and can become constipated as a result. If the meat is mixed with the milk soaked food, constipation rarely occurs.

Encourage the puppies to eat by taking the bitch away for about an hour before feeding. Feed three times daily until eight weeks, then twice daily; at around four months reduce feeds to one per day. Also ease the soaking of the dry food so that by eight weeks the food is given mainly dry to bigger breeds. Small breeds may require soaked or semi-soaked food till 3–4 months of age, as their teeth come through later.

Do not leave food that is soaked lying around especially in hot weather, as it will go off in the heat, attract flies and cause gut upsets.

If you stick to three-quarters dry dog food to one-quarter fatty meat (or other substitutes), you can rear just about any breed without too many problems or additives — just remember to stick to good quality complete dry foods. Many of the new speciality dry foods are excellent, particularly with puppies, as they have a higher digestibility, available protein and fat levels than those previously available. When selecting a puppy dry food, I would aim for at least 20–24% protein with around 10–14% fat levels. The greater the amount of meat based protein present, generally the higher digestibility. Giant breeds which are growing extremely rapidly have very high requirements for energy to sustain optimal growth and may require in excess of 26% protein levels in the diet during these early weeks. Very small breeds often have marginal liver function as puppies, so they require frequent feeds of good quality and high digestibility (see section on Sugar drop in chapter 10).

This diet applies to all breeds of all ages. Demands for higher protein and digestibility exist in stress situations such as growth, heavy work and lactation. Diets high in digestible proteins are good, but should not be overfed, particularly in puppies where the growth rate is increased beyond the limit which the bones can cope with. This can result in the development of cartilaginous defects, and generalised soreness in the bones. Carried to an extreme, this can cause premature closure of the growth plates in the distal radius, giving a typical 'French front', with reduced length of foreleg.

For the extra quarter of the diet — Pal Puppy Food®; fatty meat which is better than lean, as a certain amount of fat is necessary in the diet. Other things that can be substituted for this quarter are chicken (not all the time as this is not a good weight producing protein and is low in iron), cheese, sardines (twice per week is sufficient), eggs (2–3 times weekly, highly poached) or table scraps but no burnt bones and, with very young puppies, no bones at all.

Adult dogs can quite happily have larger amounts of meat if you wish, as the demand for calcium for bone growth has decreased and they no longer need as balanced a diet, but this should generally not exceed 50%. Mutton flaps are good, as are brisket bones for adding weight and cleaning teeth and gums.

ADDITIVES

Meat is very high in phosphorus and the higher the level of phosphorus in the diet, the lower the level of calcium absorption. Therefore, the demand for an increased level of calcium occurs when a percentage of meat is introduced in the total diet. This is extremely important to remember when organising a diet, and the amount of calcium added obviously relates to this. Ideally there should be a ratio of 1.2:1 of calcium to phosphorus in the diet.

Certain types of meat, such as liver, kidney and heart, are excessively high in phosphorus , so use these meats only once or twice per week at most, and preferably in small quantities. Kidney, liver and heart are also very high in vitamin A, and excessive vitamin A can cause irritation to the bones, particularly around the joints.

Most good-quality dry foods are already supplemented with sufficient calcium, so little if any supplementation is needed when feeding the correct proportions of dry food to meat. If feeding in excess of one-third meat, then small amount of calcium supplementation may be required. Only use low doses of supplements if and as needed.

CALCIUM

The absorption of the calcium added to the diet is the important factor. As stated above, calcium problems are usually related to excessive meat and phosphates in the diet, which in turn can greatly reduce the absorption of the available calcium in the additive.

Types of calcium additives:

Calcium carbonate — 40% Ca^{++}ion — availability 6–20%.

Calcium lactate & calcium gluconate 28% Ca^{++} ion availability — 6–20%.

DCP 340 (di calcium triple phosphate) 26% Ca, 24%P, available Ca 6–10%.

Calcium Sandoz — a liquid Ca-sugar combination 22 mg Ca/mL, available 6–20%.

Keylomin calcium — tablets 200 mg Ca each, powder 96 mg/g, available 90–95% (chelated calcium).

Calcium is mostly fed in the form of a salt — a combination of calcium with another molecule. To absorb the calcium, the body must break down the bond with the other molecule, attach a protein and then absorb the calcium attached to the protein. This process can with some compounds take some time, so only a proportion of that which is added has time to break down and be absorbed.

The *chelated* calcium is a form that has the calcium ion already bound by a protein coating, so very high absorption rates can be achieved. Because the possible absorption rates are high, care should be taken not to use over the recommended amounts.

When giving calcium it is important to notice several things:

- The dog's feet: toes should be nice and tight and the pasterns upright or gently sloping The feet should not turn out too far, i.e. 'east-west'. If the feet are flat and the toes are splayed out, and the pasterns are very loose and sloping, the dog is probably getting insufficient calcium.

- Not all dogs will absorb calcium efficiently. If there is a balanced diet and sufficient calcium is 'available' in the diet, yet despite this, the dog's feet and pasterns are down; you may have to change the type or amount of calcium that is being given to the dog.

- Around 3–4 months of age the puppy is teething and may require extra amounts of calcium. Watch the feet and if they are okay, you do not need to increase the calcium. In some breeds, the effect can also be seen on the ear carriage, particularly of erect-eared breeds.

Very heavy boned puppies and/or breeds may occasionally need small amounts of calcium added to the diet if the feet and pasterns suddenly change. Use only low doses to effect, when you get the response, reduce the dose and if okay, stop. The odd tablet given around 4–5 months is often all that is required.

When puppies are showing signs of calcium deficiency, add small amounts of calcium. If there is no improvement within one week, the diet should be assessed. The problem may not be calcium related, rather any one or combination of the following: zinc, iron, B group vitamins or trace element deficiencies. Often a small addition of zinc (Keylomin Performance® tablets are excellent) will result in dramatic improvement.

Too much calcium is as bad as too little.

VITAMIN D

This is manufactured by the dog by exposure to sunlight; it is useful in helping to absorb calcium. Too much vitamin D can cause the body to start reabsorbing calcium from the bones. Vitamin D lasts for quite some time in the dog so it is important not to give too much. If the weather is bright and sunny, it is unnecessary to add any extra vitamin D.

Cod liver oil is a very rich source of vitamin D. If you wish to add cod liver oil, twice a week would be the maximum. One teaspoon twice a week for a large sized breed at 6–8 weeks is quite sufficient. This can be increased to two teaspoons at three months and one tablespoon at four months (maximum); small breeds should keep to the teaspoon amount. Sardines in oil will do the same — it is not as concentrated, so one can twice a week is sufficient.

During prolonged periods of overcast or wet weather, young growing dogs may go down on their pasterns. This can be from a lack of exposure to sunlight; during these periods, a vitamin D supplement can be given up to three times weekly if necessary.

VITAMIN C
Some believe this is very beneficial and may help bone development. I think moderation is best, 500 mg daily is quite enough for a growing puppy of a larger breed. It can be of considerable benefit in fast growing puppies that are sore in the bones and joints.

MULTIVITAMIN SUPPLEMENTS
Most are fairly good providing they are not given in vast quantities. Many of the vitamins and minerals are quite readily available in a well balanced diet with a small amount of supplement. Multimineral supplements will supply trace elements that may be lacking in some dry dog foods. Adverse conditions, such as drought, can create a deficiency of certain trace elements in cereals.

PUPPY GROWTH
- Watch your puppies, remember they are individuals and within the litter can vary considerably in their bone, size and rate of development.
- Never 'push' the puppies' nutrition too fast, i.e. making them too heavy, too soon for the bones to cope with the forced growth rate.
- Keep your puppies trim, not fat and not thin. This way you will end up with sound adults for life.
- Over 9–10 months you can start to fatten your dogs up if you wish. The dog should remain fairly sound, despite your efforts.

PREGNANCY AND LACTATION
A pregnant bitch needs extra vitamins and calcium during and after pregnancy. Usually I suggest giving a *small* amount of calcium from 4–6 weeks pregnancy. Larger breeds may not need additional calcium until the last trimester of pregnancy. After whelping, the demand for calcium doubles. Again, keep an eye on the feet of the bitch while she is feeding the puppies.

Larger breeds usually do not get calcium deficiencies during lactation unless they have very large litters and/or are rather neurotic.

Smaller breeds have a proportionately far greater drain of calcium than the big breeds and it is most important to remember this during lactation (see the section on Milk fever in chapter 8).

POINTS TO REMEMBER
- Only give additives if really necessary. Use small amounts to effect. Check the diet if no response.
- Any calcium or multivitamin supplements can be reduced by half by 6–8 months of age as the growth rate has slowed considerably by this age. By 10–12 months they can be stopped altogether.

Dietary Problems

Diets, particularly in the last 4–6 years, have been changing very rapidly. Gone are the days of 'don't feed your dogs high-protein diets'. Research over the past 10 years has largely debunked the high-protein myth. The aim today is to feed a balanced diet of good digestibility with high quality protein and fats.

The better dry foods should be able to provide the dog with a broad base of necessary amino acids to ensure good health and to cover stress situations such as rapid growth, lactation and hard work. This type of dry food can be combined with a quarter to a third fatty meat. Protein in dry dog food diets comes from two sources, animal and cereal-based protein. Meat-based protein has a high digestibility (90–95%), while cereal-based protein is not as digestible (60–65% varying slightly according to the grain type).

Many of the dry foods which have a high cereal component have in excess of the recommended levels of calcium as the digestibility and absorption is lowered by the cereal component. Adding meat to this diet will increase the calcium availability, as meat protein increases the digestibility. This is why one can feed up to a quarter to a third (maximum) meat in the diet without adding any additional calcium.

The exception to this would be 'Eukanuba' which has a very high digestibility and a high component of meat-based protein. Eukanuba has been made to feed without meat being added, so giving meat in excess of 10% of the diet will alter dietary parameters.

Some breeds of dogs can have tremendous rates of growth, going from less than ½ kg at birth to in excess of 30 kg (in the average medium-sized breed) in the space of 8–10 months. A sound diet is most important to the eventual soundness of the adult dog.

The other commonly heard argument is that dogs in the wild eat no additives and live on an all-meat diet, therefore this is the correct thing to feed — wrong! Three important facts are overlooked in this area:

1. In the wild, a dog eats all of its kill — stomach contents, bones etc. — not just the meat.

2. Modern medium to large breeds of dog are on the average one-quarter to one-third heavier than they were 100 years ago. The selection has been for increased bone and substance so that the German shepherd during this period has gone from 20–22 kg (bitch) up to 28–32 kg, and dogs 24–28 kg up to 34–40 kg. Toy breeds are the exceptions in this area. The height standard has not changed, but the weight gain has been predominantly one of increased bone and substance. Quite a few old breeders of different breeds bewail the fact that formerly they never had to 'add things' to the diets but now their dogs are showing signs of deficiencies. In fact the breed has changed around them. The weight of an adult wolf is lucky to exceed 25 kg, yet some big breeds exceed this weight by 4–5 months of age.

3. The last point to consider is that most of the grains and meat used in the diets are from heavily used agricultural land, where trace elements are missing or severely depleted. The chance of trace element deficiencies developing may increase over time. Elements such as zinc, iodine and selenium are commonly low and lack of these elements can affect growth rates as well as the functioning of various glands, in particular the thyroid gland.

All three points are well worth taking into consideration when feeding your growing puppy — particularly the larger breeds and especially the heavier boned individuals.

POINTS TO REMEMBER

- Always go by the individual — due to the differing metabolic rates between individuals and breeds; one cannot ever state the exact amount of either food and/or additives to give any one individual. Generally additives are given per unit of weight, but give according to need rather than an exact amount. Some dogs, regardless (almost), of diet, will do well on a rough and ready diet with little or no supplementation. Others, however, may end up as a dietary mess at a veterinarian's, where hopefully it can be recognised, treated and rectified fairly quickly. The heavily boned individuals may require careful attention to diets and growth rates and may require some supplementation of trace elements. Small breeds rarely need extra additives during their growth stages, but require proportionally higher amounts of minerals during pregnancy.
- Always check the feet and toes — these should be tight together and the pasterns upright. If the toes are flat, spread out or even rolling over to one side, there is a problem. If the feet are east-west from the pasterns, when as puppies they were correct, again there is a problem.

Some breeds will, admittedly, have east-west facing feet, but usually this is not excessive.

i) Correct — good when viewed from the front and side-on.

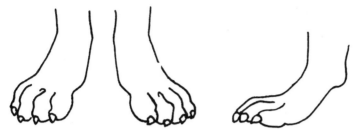

ii) Poor — east-west front on; down in pastern side-on.

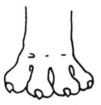

iii) Splayed toes.

- Always check the growth plates — these are the thickened areas just above the wrists of the front legs. If these seem enlarged or swollen beyond normal, they can be an indication of a dietary or malabsorption problem. This is particularly important around 4–6 months, when the puppies are growing very fast and teething.

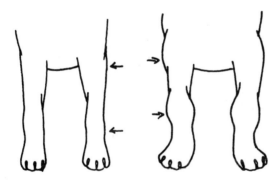

This can be a very demanding time, for growth. The diet must be able to deliver sufficient digestible energy and minerals.

- Not all dogs absorb different types of additives well, and not all breeds will do well on the one sort of dry dog food. By trial and error, you will eventually find which sort of basic diet best suits your breed of dog.

The same applies to additives as well — the main thing to remember about additives is always use a *registered product*, i.e. it must have written on it the amount of mineral, vitamin or whatever per unit of measure, so that if you wish, you can work out the exact amount that you are adding. If the product states the absorption rate per unit; this is extremely useful, as not all (or very rarely), is the absorption rate above 20–30% of the total (often only 10%). Recently, however, there have been minerals and vitamins attached to proteins in their raw state, which means that up to 90–95% absorption rates are now possible; these are usually called mineral or vitamin proteinates. Use these products with care. While they are extremely good, they are also very strong and can be over absorbed. The appearance of over absorption can be similar to malabsorption.

If you have your dogs on a well balanced diet already, and feel that you must add extra minerals, use only low doses. With the proteinates or chelated minerals, use only half to a quarter of the recommended rate, even on growing puppies. The only time I use a higher dose is on lactating bitches, or on a severely deficient animal until it returns to normal.

Go by the individual — look at and assess your dog constantly while it is growing.

OVERNUTRITION

Overnutrition is produced by feeding your dog *too much*, usually of a high-energy diet. The end result is that the body is pushed into growing too fast, i.e. the hormones that regulate growth and the absorption of minerals, especially calcium, go out of kilter. This in turn sets off other regulating hormones and starts a vicious circle, which, once started, is quite often exacerbated by excessive amounts of calcium, vitamin C and vitamin D, particularly if the diet remains *unchanged*.

This can, at the critical times in a puppy's growing life, i.e. from 5–8 weeks until 8–9 months, cause immense damage to the bones. Overnutrition can cause thickening and failure of growth of the long bones; remodelling and bowing of the distal radius; osteochondritis dessicans (cartilage defects) of the shoulders, elbows and hocks; increased angulation of the heads of the femur, which in turn causes increased wear (i.e. accelerates changes) due to hip dysplasia.

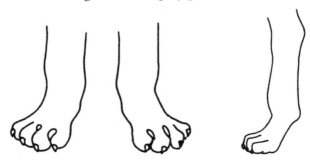

Overnutrition initially produces increased growth and weight gain, then the growth plates start to look too prominent, the pasterns start to sag, the feet and toes flatten out and spread, and the bones between the wrist and the elbow start to look thickened and too short in proportion.

If the problem is not corrected fairly soon after these changes are first observed, then irreparable damage may occur. Unfortunately, many of these dogs are not seen until around 6–8 months by which stage major damage may have taken place.

The typical story is of a dog that is reluctant to stand, moves very stiffly, is very sore (the areas of soreness vary and can appear to change) and is reluctant to play and run around. The dog will usually present in an overweight condition, the pasterns are down compared to normal and the feet east-west, the distal growth plates of the radius and ulnar are prominent and thickened. Extreme cases are usually seen at around 3–5 months of age with 'foreshortened' front legs, flattened or spread-out toes, together with any or all of the above mentioned problems. Often the young dogs will arch their backs, both at stance and during movement.

The other typical features of the stories accompanying these animals is their diet and the fact that most of their owners will tell you that the dog is a very 'fussy' eater — despite its overweight condition! These dogs are usually being fed 80–90% meat and the owners state that they will not eat dry dog food (kibble).

Unfortunately, occasionally these dogs have been to other veterinarians who have never asked what the dog is being fed and attributed the problems to hip dysplasia; the shortened forelegs to 'genetic' problems.

Most of the bone remodelling and loose ligamentation is reversible to a large extent if seen early enough. Basically 'soreness' and/or minor front leg problems will improve within three weeks of correcting the diet, regulating the additives and resting the animal. The owners usually report that the dog, after a week, is much more active and is moving more freely. The occasional owner will state that 'their little darling will not eat anything but fillet steak' — I usually have to get very firm and state that if the dog is hungry enough, it *will* eat. It may take 7–10 days, but they must be firm! The owners occasionally come back saying their dogs didn't eat for 3–4 days (which, as most of them are overweight and part of the objective is to lose the weight, does not do any of the 'little darlings' any harm), but after the first few days they ate with a will!

One of the common mistakes that creates this type of dog is to leave food lying around — this *must* stop. Food is only left out for 15–20 minutes and then it disappears completely! Feed only once a day after 4 months of age — if the dog is not hungry the first day it will learn very quickly to eat what is put down or it gets nothing. Most dogs learn this lesson in 3–4 days, to the surprise of the overanxious owners. (See New owner's syndrome in chapter 3; this is where the problem invariably starts. Overnutrition is often an extension of this bad beginning!)

Severe overnutrition or the 'all meat syndrome' can be very hard or almost impossible to reverse completely. It may take a lot of hard work by both yourself and the veterinarian to change the diet, carefully vary the mineral intake according to the dog in front of you, and possibly rest and confine the dog for several weeks. If the dog is very sore, it may need aspirins (usually for 3–7 days at most), rest and possibly the use of different drugs to help reduce the soreness (preferably not cortisone). If the distal growth plates of the radius have closed, causing bowing and twisting of the front legs, surgery may be necessary — but try to correct all the elements that caused the condition in the first place before considering surgery. This way, if surgery has to be performed, the dog can at least heal well after the operation!

Wheat and Wheat Gluten Free Diet

Before we leave the diet section, a short section on a homemade diet for those dogs that do not tolerate commercial dry dog food. The affected dogs have trouble maintaining a formed stool and retaining weight on commercial diets. The majority of these dogs will gain weight quickly when placed on a wheat free diet, so the underlying problem may be a wheat gluten or wheat sensitivity causing an allergic type reaction. Without going into great detail, an example of a home made cereal mix is as follows:

Cereal Mix

Rolled oats, linseed meal, flaked barley, flaked rye, cornmeal.

Use 50% rolled oats to 50% of the other cereals mixed in equal quantities. Add water, mix and cook as you would porridge. The same mix can be made into a biscuit by adding 1–2 eggs to 4–6 cups of cereal mix, warm water and one tablespoon of cornflour. Mix to a biscuit consistency and cook as you would biscuits (five minutes in the microwave). You can add to the biscuit mix malt, molasses, kelp and/or Vegemite for flavouring.

For breakfast — give the porridge with goat's milk and honey (or molasses).

For dinner — meat (one-quarter) with cereal biscuits.

The variety of such diets is endless, some use brown rice rather than rolled oats as the base grain. Regardless, if you have a dog that appears not to tolerate commercial dry dog foods, it is worth giving this type of diet a try. Books on human diets around similar allergies are available.

Worming

For convenience, I have tried to put the majority of the relevant material in the one large section, rather than offer small pieces here and there. This section is applicable to all age groups.

POINTS TO REMEMBER

There are two important facts to remember in any worming program:

- Worm eggs hatch in warm, humid weather. There are two periods of the year — spring and autumn — when there is a high pick-up of worm larvae and worming should be more regular (every 6–8 weeks) during these periods. During the colder and drier periods worming can be less regular — every 3–4 months.

- Immature round and hookworms undergo migration through the body and during this stage they are not susceptible to worming preparations, i.e. the first 10–12 days of their life cycle. Therefore, if you wish to have an effective worming program, it is often advisable to worm dogs *twice* for round and hookworm at a 10–14 day interval.

THE WAYS IN WHICH WORM EGGS ARE PICKED UP BY DOGS

The majority of worms are picked up by the ingestion of contaminated material. Worm eggs hatch from the faeces that were passed by infected animals. Eggs that pass out into the big wide world do not always hatch immediately; they have a thickened shell which protects them from adverse conditions, and worm eggs can lie dormant in the ground for long periods of time. When conditions are ideal; with warmth, moisture and/or humidity — the eggs will hatch. The hatched eggs are ingested by the dog when the dog eats a bone, for example (there is usually some dirt on it that gets eaten as well), or digs holes. Hookworm larvae (i.e. the hatched form of the egg), can also penetrate the skin, giving another method of worm pick-up.

Tapeworms are transmitted to dogs by the ingestion of the 'intermediate host' which is the flea. Heavy flea infestation obviously means a fairly continuous tapeworm pick-up, so more frequent tapeworming may be necessary.

Another aspect to consider is how infected is the ground where the dogs are kept. Areas where dogs have been running and kennelled for long periods of time (years) or where there are large numbers of dogs usually have a high contamination level of worm eggs.

Ways to try to reduce this level include regular heavy liming of the dog yards/areas. Use ordinary building lime — leave it on for a day then water it in well. Do not let dogs run on it immediately as it can cause a 'burning' irritation of the feet. This at least keeps the problem of increasing worm pick-up to a minimum. Do this every 3–4 months. Do one area, wait until it is well watered in, then move to the next area.

Fleas are much harder to control and it is important to concentrate on sandy and dusty areas. Flea control can be very tedious as fleas can develop resistances to the different chemicals that are used. Further control methods are discussed in greater detail in chapter 18.

THE PREGNANT BITCH

Bitches can pass immature round and hookworm larvae via the uterus to the puppies during pregnancy. This means that puppies can be born with immature roundworm and hookworm, which then develop. There can be adult roundworms and hookworms in puppies by 2–3 weeks of age. Puppies can die from heavy infestations as early as 3–4 weeks of age!

It is an idea to worm the bitch prior to mating — this is usually done during the first week of her season. Once the bitch is pregnant there is a lowered immunity to worms in general and the bitch can pick up heavy infestations more readily. I suggest the bitch is rewormed at five weeks and again at seven weeks of the pregnancy — for round and hookworm. This will not affect any immature larvae already in the uterus, but it will reduce the burden on the bitch. Worm bitches for tapeworm once only during pregnancy — usually around six weeks.

It is not a good practice to worm or use heavy chemical rinses on bitches especially during the first few (three) weeks of pregnancy. During the first trimester of pregnancy, the foetuses (developing puppies) are especially sensitive to any sudden changes and temperature rises going on in the bitch. Very high temperatures or excessive stresses on the bitch can cause developmental abnormalities in the puppies. The chances of this happening (due to worming) are remote, but I feel that it is wise during this sensitive period to avoid any unnecessary risks.

Be very careful with the type of wormer that is used in pregnant bitches — some can be harmful — check with your veterinarian!

PUPPIES — FREQUENCY OF WORMING

- Start worming puppies at 10–14 days of age.
- Repeat once per week until 6–8 weeks of age.
- After this worm every two weeks until 14–16 weeks of age.
- From 4 months of age, worm every 6–8 weeks, until 12 months of age.
- Adults — worm every 3–4 months.
- Puppies can have life-threatening burdens of round and hookworm as early as three weeks of age.

LIFE CYCLES OF WORMS

Hookworm The hookworm's life cycle can be as short as three weeks.

The signs of infestation of hookworm in puppies (regardless of age) are poor condition, dull dry coat and pale mucous membranes of the mouth due to anaemia. These changes occur because the hookworms are blood parasites. They latch onto the inside walls of the intestines and use the blood they absorb to live on. The puppies are reluctant to move around and tire easily. Motions often tend to be dark and 'tarry' — which is actually broken down, digested blood. Hookworms are found in the small intestine, high up the intestinal tract. Hookworms are rarely seen as they are small and resemble short pieces (2–4 cm) of cotton thread.

Hookworm

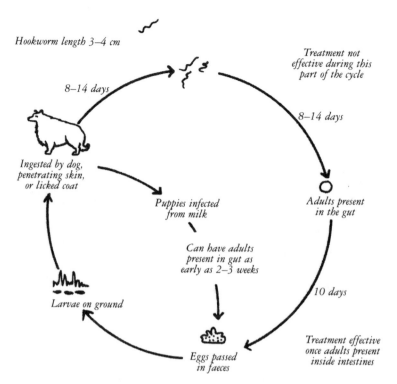

Hookworm length 3–4 cm

8–14 days

Treatment not effective during this part of the cycle

8–14 days

Ingested by dog, penetrating skin, or licked coat

Puppies infected from milk

Adults present in the gut

Can have adults present in gut as early as 2–3 weeks

10 days

Larvae on ground

Treatment effective once adults present inside intestines

Eggs passed in faeces

Puppies need to be treated immediately and usually several times (once a week), before the problem is properly controlled. Severe cases may need to be re-treated after five days. It is a good idea to keep the puppies restricted in a small area until their anaemia starts to show signs of recovery (usually within 7–10 days).

The roundworm's life cycle is 4–6 weeks.

Infestations of roundworm are not as commonly seen these days where the mother of the puppies is on heartworm tablets. The heartworm tablets have a useful side effect of treating for roundworm. Roundworms live in the small intestine and the upper areas of the large intestine. Roundworms are quite large and can reach 15–20 cm long — they look like pieces of 'spaghetti'. Heavy roundworm burdens can cause deaths due to bowel obstruction and malnutrition if there are sufficient present.

The signs of roundworm infestation are pot-bellied puppies, failure to thrive and/or 'weedy' looking puppies, dry coats, poor appetites and a 'whingey' attitude. Puppies will, under conditions of stress and heavy worm burden, pass roundworms and occasionally vomit them up (it does look as bad as it sounds).

Once treated, puppies usually pick up very quickly and can have 'overnight' miraculous recoveries. Keep treating once a week until you have a 'clear' week, then worm every two weeks.

Roundworm

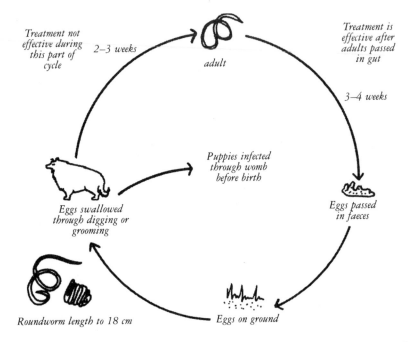

Treatment not
effective during
this part of
cycle

2–3 weeks

adult

Treatment is
effective after
adults passed
in gut

3–4 weeks

Puppies infected
through womb
before birth

Eggs passed
in faeces

Eggs swallowed
through digging or
grooming

Roundworm length to 18 cm

Eggs on ground

Adult dogs should be wormed every 3–4 months. In spring and autumn in particular, there is a heavier pick-up of worm eggs due to the humidity and warmth, so re-worm 10–14 days later for round and hookworm. The re-worming 10–14 days later catches any worms (mainly round and/or hook), that were undergoing migration at the first worming. By waiting the 10–14 days, the immature worms that were unaffected by the chemicals used (as they were migrating here, there and everywhere), will have developed into adults in the intestines and be susceptible to chemicals.

Puppies can die by 3–4 weeks of age if they have heavy worm infestations.

Whipworms have a life cycle of 3–4 months and are not transmitted via the uterus. Therefore it is not necessary to worm for whipworm before 3–4 months of age as this is the earliest age that there can be adults in the intestine; after this worm for whipworm at 3–4 monthly intervals. Whipworm can unfortunately be rather difficult to shift and is tedious to clear up, i.e. it may need several treatments before removing it completely.

Signs of whipworm infestation are a dry coat, failure to gain weight and motions with small amounts of fresh-looking blood in the faeces. Whipworm is to be found in the large intestine and rectum, hence the fresh-looking blood. Once treated successfully the dog picks up fairly rapidly.

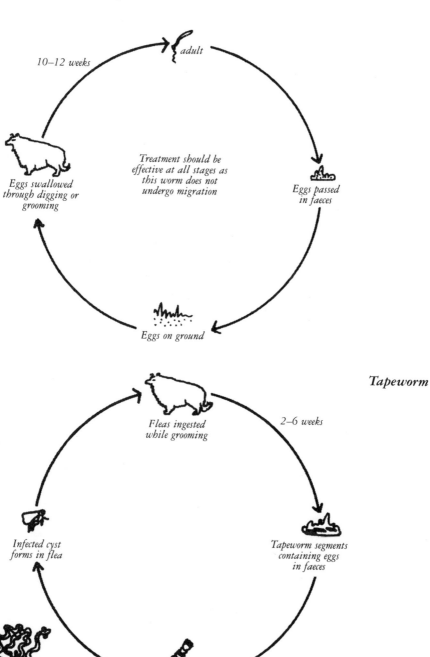

Whipworm

Whipworm length 4–7 cm

adult

10–12 weeks

Eggs swallowed through digging or grooming

Treatment should be effective at all stages as this worm does not undergo migration

Eggs passed in faeces

Eggs on ground

Tapeworm

Fleas ingested while grooming

2–6 weeks

Infected cyst forms in flea

Tapeworm segments containing eggs in faeces

Flea tapeworm length to 50 cm

Eggs eaten by flea larvae

The tapeworm's life cycle is 6–8 weeks.

The flea is the intermediate host of the tapeworm. In the flea season tapeworming every 4–6 weeks is necessary if you have a flea/tapeworm problem. If, however, there is good flea control, every 6–8 weeks is quite sufficient. During the rest of the year, once every 3–4 months is adequate. Tapeworms can be difficult to shift, and occasionally it may be necessary to use a higher or repeated dose to clear the parasite.

Tapeworms are found throughout the small and large intestine. Segments of tapeworm are passed with the faeces and have an appearance of cucumber seeds, that can be white to pinkish. Tape segments are flat, they wriggle and wave at you, and have a characteristic stretching forward and then contracting motion — so moving along. Segments are often found around the anal area and on the droppings. A tapeworm can be as long as the intestines, i.e. over a metre long.

Tapeworms do not on the whole cause much trouble — unless accompanied by heavy burdens of other internal parasites and/or if the dog is living in stressful conditions.

Signs of tapeworm include scraping or 'scooting' around on the bottom, chewing and licking around the anal area, failure to gain weight despite ordinary worming, dry coat and an ill-thrifty appearance.

Tapeworms come from a different family of worms to other internal parasites as they are flat and segmented. As such, they will not respond to drugs that affect round, hook or whipworms. It is usually necessary to worm separately for tapeworm to get effective removal.

Hydatid tapeworm This is another type of tapeworm, one that is far more dangerous to humans. This tapeworm is short in length and the eggs are shed in the dog's droppings where they are ingested by various animals, mainly grass eaters. The eggs then form hydatid cysts in many organs, principally the lungs, liver and kidneys. The cycle is completed when the dog ingests contaminated offal (lungs, liver, etc.,) from an animal carrying hydatid cysts.

The major human health risk is that the accidental ingestion of hydatid eggs on the coat of the dog (generally through poor hygiene) can cause hydatid cysts to form in the human organs. These cysts are rather like large abscesses, except far more dangerous as the contents, if spilled, can form many more cysts. It can be a fatal disease in humans. This problem is far less common these days when the cycle can be effectively stopped by not feeding dogs offal unless it has been passed fit for human consumption, i.e. has been through an abattoir where the carcasses are all inspected prior to use.

Country dogs should never be fed offal from home-killed carcasses of sheep or cattle. Children should always wash their hands before eating, particularly if they have just been playing with the dog. If you are concerned about the hydatid tapeworm, you should regularly worm your dog, particularly if you have young children, every 6–8 weeks if need be.

Hydatid tapeworm

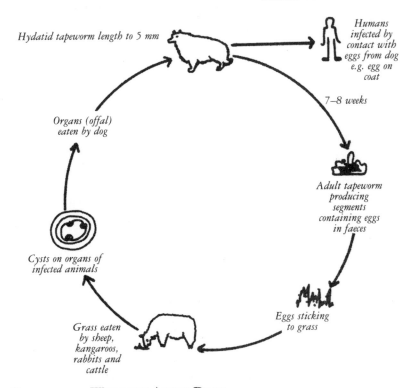

Hydatid tapeworm length to 5 mm

Humans infected by contact with eggs from dog e.g. egg on coat

7–8 weeks

Organs (offal) eaten by dog

Adult tapeworm producing segments containing eggs in faeces

Cysts on organs of infected animals

Grass eaten by sheep, kangaroos, rabbits and cattle

Eggs sticking to grass

ROUTINE FOR WORMING ADULT DOGS
This should be done every 3–4 months.

1. Use a broad spectrum wormer for roundworm, hookworm and whipworm (e.g. Canex Plus®).

2. Skip one day, then use a tapewormer (e.g. Droncit®). There are new wormers that can do both together (e.g. Drontal All Wormer®).

3. Follow up 10–14 days later with a wormer for roundworm and hookworm to kill any immature worms that may have been missed in the first worming. This is like a double worming and is very effective.

EFFICIENCY OF DRUGS USED FOR WORMING
The efficiency of a drug refers to its ability to affect what it is used for. Most drugs/chemicals used for worming do not have 100% efficiency at killing all the worms that they are supposed to affect — the average is more likely in the 80–90% range.

The other problem with wormers is that the worms themselves will over a period of time, e.g. 5–10 years, gradually develop a resistance to various drugs, especially if the same drug is used all the time. This effect is very slow, but is worth remembering for the long term.

The range of drugs and chemicals used for worming is quite wide and varied. Some of the common wormers are listed below, by chemical, not commercial brand name:

- **Piperazines** — These are very good at removing roundworm (about 85%), but have no effect against hookworm. Many so-called 'puppy and kitten' wormers have only piperazine in them and will therefore only clear the roundworms and not touch the hookworms. So, if you are just using a piperazine wormer, the puppies may be clear of roundworm, yet could be dying of anaemia caused by hookworm.

- **Pyrantel Pamoates** — (Canex®, Pyrate®, etc.) These are good at removing both hookworms and roundworms (90–95%). However, it appears that there may be some resistance developing to these drugs; at present it is still fairly effective. The pyrantels vary in the solubility of the tablet (as do all wormers in tablet form). A tablet should dissolve when placed in a glass of warm water and left for no longer than 15 minutes. If it does not dissolve, it may not dissolve properly inside the dog.

- **Pyrantel plus Oxantal Pamoate** — (Canex Plus®, Pyrate Plus®, etc.) This is the same as the above with the addition of an extra pamoate which is effective against whipworm. It is a one dose treatment and is fairly effective (90–95%).

- **Bendazoles** — (mebendazole [Telmintic®]), (fenbendazole [Panacur-liquid®]) This family of wormers is fairly good (90–95%) on roundworm, hookworm and whipworm. It is also effective against the Taenia species of tapeworm, but has very little effect against the ordinary dog tapeworm. This group of wormers is very safe to use and is generally used as a three day course. Whipworm especially is particularly hard to shift, and the three day treatment is very effective. This family of wormers is useful as a change from the above group. I do, however, avoid using them on pregnant bitches, as the three day treatment may upset the pregnancy.

- **Piraziquantel** — (Droncit®) This is a tapewormer and is effective against all types of tapeworm including hydatid tapeworm. The drug is very safe and does not cause vomiting like several other tapewormers. Tape segments are not commonly seen after treatment as they are often digested before being passed. Occasionally tapeworm is difficult to shift and double dosing of Droncit® is quite safe. Efficiency is 90–95%.

- **Bunamidine** — (Scolaban®) This is another tapewormer. Unfortunately, you need to 'starve' the dog, i.e. give on an empty stomach with a small meal, and vomiting after treatment is not uncommon. The efficiency is 70–80%. I prefer to use a drug that has very little side effects of any kind.

There are many other sorts of wormers, but quite a few have harsh and occasionally severe side effects i.e. they may be fairly good wormers if the dog survives the treatment!

Do not use the old-fashioned 'bombers' under any circumstances, as they often have very dangerous side effects.

Quite a few of the newer wormers are combinations of existing drugs — but they can double up on their side effects. Ambex®, for example, (niclosamide plus levamisole) is a combination of a tapewormer (niclosamide), which has very few side effects, and a broad-spectrum wormer levamisole, which is a drug also used to treat heartworm, with side effects include vomiting, wobbliness and depression. Elderly dogs and young puppies can get 'knocked around' by this drug combination. Dogs that have heartworm and/or are just getting over heartworm can be also adversely affected. Use these types of wormers with care. If in doubt ask your vet.

Drontal® is another combination drug which aims to cover the four major worm groups seen in dogs. This is a combination of piraziquantel, pryantel embonate and febantel. This is really Droncit® (for tapeworm), Canex Plus® (roundworm, hookworm and whipworm) with the addition of fenbantel. This is quite effective, but again I would not use it on pregnant bitches as the febantel component may, on rare occasions, cause abnormalities and abortions.

Read the instructions carefully before worming a dog, to determine the correct dosage. Find out whether there is any recommendation against worming a pregnant bitch with the worming compound. If there is such a recommendation, do not use the product at all during pregnancy, and preferably do not worm bitches in the first three weeks, or the last two weeks of pregnancy.

Ask your vet before using any 'new' drug.

HEARTWORM

Distribution

Heartworm is far more widespread than most people would care to believe. It occurs in the tropical and temperate zones throughout the world. With the widespread transportation of dogs, in particular racing Greyhounds, few if any are required to be tested for heartworm prior to transport, and so the spread of heartworm is greatly facilitated.

Once heartworm has been established in an area by infected animals, the local mosquitoes assist in the spread of the parasite. The mosquitoes that carry the infective larvae prefer warm humid conditions and the incidence of heartworm is far higher around river and coastal areas.

Life cycle

The life cycle of the heartworm takes 6–9 months, i.e. from the time the dog is infected to the time that there are adult heartworms in the heart producing offspring (microfilariae). The minimum time it can take from the dog being bitten to the microfilariae showing up in a blood filter test is six months. There has been the odd case of a dog showing up positive after five months, but this is uncommon.

Heartworms are blood parasites that usually live in the greater vessels of the heart — the right side; but they can develop and live in the lungs and liver upon occasion. The heartworm can grown up to 15–18 cm causing considerable obstruction to blood flow and tissue damage.

Heartworm

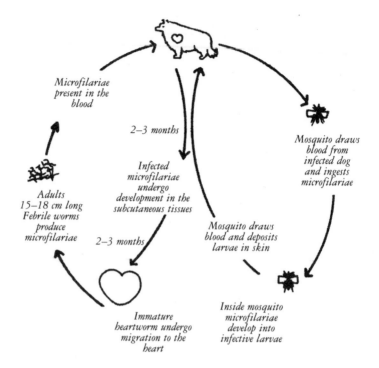

Microfilariae present in the blood

2–3 months

Infected microfilariae undergo development in the subcutaneous tissues

Mosquito draws blood from infected dog and ingests microfilariae

Adults 15–18 cm long Febrile worms produce microfilariae

2–3 months

Mosquito draws blood and deposits larvae in skin

Immature heartworm undergo migration to the heart

Inside mosquito microfilariae develop into infective larvae

Signs of infestation are a slight cough that starts at night and/or after strenuous exercise, weight loss and poor coat condition. The ends of the coat are dry and starey. The dog tends to tire easily and get unusually distressed in hot weather. Changes are usually gradual and are often attributed to the dog 'getting older'.

Infection occurs when an infected mosquito bites a dog, injecting infective larvae into the layers of the skin. These larvae then gradually develop in the tissues under the skin; this usually takes 3–4 months. The immature heartworms then begin to migrate through the body, occasionally causing liver and lung damage. They finally arrive at the heart 4–7 months after initial infection. The heartworms now mature (1–2 months), start producing microfilariae 6–9 months after the initial infection.

Microfilariae can live up to two years within the blood stream. They cannot develop into adults, unless they get ingested by the mosquito to complete the cycle. The actual number of microfilaria present in a blood filter test does not relate to the number of adult heartworms. Recent infections with young healthy worms will produce high numbers of offspring; over a period of time the production of microfilariae will decline. So, an older dog with a long-standing infection of heartworm may have very few microfilaria showing up on a slide, whereas a young recently infected dog may have large numbers. The cases and situations are endless.

Mosquitoes ingesting blood from infected dogs also ingest microfilariae which undergo changes within the mosquito to become infective larvae in 2–3 weeks. Mosquitoes (if they were uninfected to start with) cannot go from one infected dog, hop on the next and so on down the line. If however, the mosquito is infected anything is possible

It is impossible to have microfilariae developing into adult heartworm, without first going through the mosquito stage of the life cycle.

Heartworm can only be transmitted via the mosquito, never by dog to dog contact.

It is also important to realise that a pregnant bitch with heartworm can only pass microfilariae to her puppies through the uterus and that these can then live up to two years (usually 12 months or less), and may show up in a blood test as a 'false positive'. If this situation occurs it is quite easy to treat the puppies with a dose of the once-a-month heartworm tablets, given at any stage from four weeks onwards and this will kill any circulating microfilariae.

A blood sample must be taken from the dog. Usually 1–2 mL is sufficient. A filter test was originally used when testing for heartworm. However, where the heartworms are immature or old, there are few if any circulating microfilariae. The number of infections that can be missed by this method can be as high as 20–25%.

Testing for heartworm

A heartworm antigen test has been developed which is highly specific for the antibodies that develop in the presence of adult heartworm. This test has a high degree of accuracy and will correctly diagnose over 95% of heartworm infections. This enables the veterinarian to pick up the majority of the false negatives or 'occult' cases of heartworm that may be missed with the filter test and this is now the blood test of choice for heartworm detection.

Any dog that has been filter tested *negative*, but reacts badly to the heartworm tablets, i.e. vomiting, staggering or depression, should be immediately taken off the tablets and re-tested with the antigen test. This is one of the situations where the antigen test can be invaluable in diagnosis, with a very high degree of accuracy.

The levels of infection differ from area to area, but a general rule of thumb would be that the higher the number of mosquitoes, the greater the risk of the dog being infected with heartworm.

There are several different treatments available and providing the dog is reasonably fit and healthy, and the owners are careful especially in the first two weeks after treatment, the vast majority (over 95%) will recover with very little trouble.

Treatment

The treatment regime is variable according to current methods of treatment and the preferences of the individual veterinarian. Severely affected dogs are generally stabilised on medication for 10–14 days prior to treatment.

1. Arsenic intravenous injections (Caparsolate/Arsenolate) — morning and night injections are given for a total of four injections according to the dog's weight. Confine for 10 days, then re-check by your veterinarian. Mild exercise for 20 days, then one injection of ivermectin and place the dog on once-a-month heartworm tablets. Retest with an antigen test six months later. Collies go straight on to the once-a-month tablet after 30 days as they cannot be given high doses of ivermectin.

2. Immiticide (intramuscular arsenical) — the newest current method of choice. Dogs are given two injections, one day apart into the deep lumbar muscles. This form of treatment has fewer side effects particularly on the liver and has a higher rate of clearance of the adult heartworm, i.e. lower rate of re-treatment needed. Severely affected dogs are stabilised first, may be given one injection, wait one month to re-assess, by this time the dog's health has generally improved. The dog will usually take the two injections quite well.

3. Homoeopathic — approximately 60% effective — good for elderly dogs and those at severe risk. This can take 10–12 weeks to complete. When finished have the vet reassess the health of the dog and see if the dog can tolerate the Immiticide treatment.

Possible problems associated with each treatment

Treatment 1 Arsenic intravenous injections (Caparsolate/Arsenolate) were the standard treatment prior to the development of Immiticide treatment as the majority of the dogs treated respond very well. However, not all dogs tolerate the arsenic dose, and some may become jaundiced after one or two injections; usually less than 10–15% of dogs are so affected. *Aftercare is most important* — complete rest for 10 days and any signs of being off-colour, not eating, should be reported immediately to your vet. What is happening is that the heartworms are dying by 3–5 days after treatment, and then the dead heartworms have to be broken down and removed from the blood stream by the body's 'garbage' system (the macrophages). Excessive exercise or jumping, can cause a dead heartworm to be dislodged and cause blockages in the lungs, liver or kidneys. The body's reaction to this blockage can be very severe, and this is what can cause deaths from the heartworm treatment.

Normally it is not the arsenic injections that cause the problem, so much as the disintegration of the body of the dead heartworm afterwards. Aspirin is very beneficial in helping the lung tissue to settle adverse reactions to the dead heartworms after treatment. Aspirin is often started prior to treatment in severe cases to help stabilise the lungs.

Cortisone may be necessary in addition to the aspirin, where there are signs of heavy lung involvement. Antibiotics are often given routinely for the first 5–6 days. The majority of the dogs treated have little or no signs of any trouble and, after the first few days, are very hard to keep quiet.

After 10 days, the dog is usually returned to the vet for a check-up and the lungs and heart are listened to and carefully checked. Any congestion and/or valvular difficulties may require further rest and tablets. If the dog is healthy, allow the dog gradually increasing exercise over the next few days and, if there are no signs of coughing, free exercise for 20 days.

At the end of 30 days the dog comes back, gets re-weighed and is treated with an injection or an oral dose of ivermectin to kill the immature microfilariae. The dogs are then placed on the once-a-month heartworm tablets and retested with the antigen blood test six months after initial treatment. This covers the dogs from possible re-infection while waiting for the circulating antibody level to drop. Retesting sooner than 3–4 months post treatment can occasionally show up a false positive as the test is so sensitive. By waiting 5–6 months, any remaining antibody levels will have dropped and the test will accurately reflect the heartworm status of the dog.

Ivermectin (and its related compounds) is the active drug present in the once a month heartworm tablets. Ivermectin is also a powerful wormer and at higher doses will kill most internal parasites as well as external parasites such as sarcoptic and demodectic mange mites. However, Collies and Shetland Sheepdogs have been known to have adverse drug reactions to ivermectin at higher dose rates and it can kill these breeds (and some susceptible Collie or Sheltie crossbreeds). Collies or Shetland Sheepdogs cannot have injections of ivermectin or its related compounds. The dose present in the once-a-month heartworm tablets is at a level which is quite safe for use in Collies and Shelties. Following initial heartworm treatment, Collies and Shelties go straight on to the once-a-month heartworm tablets.

In the arsenical intravenous treatment, it is estimated that over 90% of the adult heartworms are killed. Some dogs will require a repeat treatment, particularly where there are large numbers of female worms, which it appears are quite difficult to kill while they are under 12 months of age.

Treatment 2 Immiticide intramuscular injections. Dogs are given two injections, one day apart, into the deep lumbar muscles. This form of treatment has far fewer side effects, particularly on the liver, than the intravenous arsenicals and has a higher rate of clearance of the adult heartworm, i.e. lower rate of re-treatment needed.

Severely affected dogs are stabilised first with pre-treatment of low doses of aspirin as well as other drugs needed to stabilise the heart. These dogs will only be given on injection, and 4–6 weeks later will often tolerate the two consecutive injections. The initial injection may relieve the heartworm burden by more than 50%. The dog usually improves considerably in overall health and its heart and lung situation is more stabilised.

As with the intravenous arsenicals, the same initial care and confinement is needed for the first 10 days. The dog is returned to the veterinarian and checked out and allowed moderate exercise for 20 days.

Subsequent treatment is the same as for *treatment 1*.

Advantages to *treatment 1* — less side effects, fewer injections, better clearance rate of adult heartworms (rarely if ever have to have a second treatment to clear the heartworm infection).

It is essential that care is taken especially after arsenical injections of either kind.

Treatment 3 Homoeopathic drops of arsenic are given in various potencies over 10–12 weeks. The treatment is very mild and is particularly suited to the older and/or severely congested patient. This form of treatment gives very small amounts of arsenic that gradually kills the heartworm over the first 3–4 weeks. The dog should be kept very quiet for this period. This method can completely clear a dog of heartworms, but only about 20% of cases will clear up completely in one treatment. It is estimated that 60% of the heartworms will be removed. In elderly dogs, in particular, this method is preferable as it does not knock the liver or the body systems around as much as do the standard forms of treatment. Even if the heartworms are not all killed, enough are removed to greatly improve the general health of the dog, which often puts on weight, the coat improves and there is a new lease of life. Even if these dogs are treated this way once a year, it keeps the burden down. If they improve sufficiently, they may be candidates for Immiticide treatment. A copy of this treatment regime is in the appendix.

Heartworm prevention

Daily Heartworm Tablets. All the daily preventative tablets, liquid and powder, contain the same drug. They are all equally as effective at the correct dose rate. Preventatives have a good side effect; they control roundworms as well. The drug concerned is diethylcarbamazine citrate (DEC). The dose rate should be 10 mg/kg given daily.

The dose on most bottles has been at 6 mg/kg, but it is considered by many authorities to be insufficient to cover dogs adequately, and there have been reported cases of apparent breakdowns of the efficiency of DEC. We have been using the 10 mg/kg dose for many years and have not had a breakdown in efficiency.

Puppies. In the mosquito season start them early at 3–4 weeks of age using a powder, tablets or liquid form. If they are born during the winter months, start them at 6–8 weeks. To be absolutely sure, dogs should be kept on preventatives all the year round.

Adults. Adults and any dog over 5–6 months of age should be heartworm tested before starting heartworm tablets. If the dog is put onto daily preventative heartworm tablets and it has heartworm, it may show signs of toxicity — usually vomiting, occasionally jaundice, depression and lethargy. These signs may not show up for several months or even longer. If they do occur, stop the tablets immediately and retest the dog.

It is important to know and remember how daily preventative heartworm tablets work. The drug prevents development of infective larvae and gradually kills them while they are in the tissues under the skin. The effect lasts 24 hours. If the larvae have matured and started migrating through the body (at around three months after infection), it is not effective. It does not greatly matter if an occasional day is missed, but the dog must not miss weeks at a time.

Once-a-Month Heartworm Tablets. Ivermectin tablets (Heart Guard®) and its chemical relative milbeycin oxime (Endovet®) have been developed for use as a once-a-month preventative tablet and are proving very popular. These drugs work by eliminating the developing stages of heartworm that the dog may have acquired from mosquitoes over the previous month. The drugs are very safe and convenient. They are at low enough doses to be safe for use in Collies and Shelties.

Newer versions are capable of worming the dog for other intestinal parasites at the same time, saving money and reducing concurrent worm burdens. They generally cover hookworm and roundworm, some cover whipworm as well. Most are not currently effective against tapeworm.

These tablets are ideal for litters, saving the daily dosing with the tablets. If you are erratic at giving the daily tablet or you go away frequently, then this form of treatment may be the one that suits you. Stickers are supplied to attach to the calender as reminders. Try to establish a date that is easily remembered, e.g. the first of every month.

Vaccination

When you get your puppy and bring it home it has usually been vaccinated. This means that you receive with your puppy a vaccination certificate which states that the puppy has been vaccinated against, when it was done and when it is due for re-vaccination. If you do not get a vaccination certificate the puppy probably has not been vaccinated.

If the puppy has not been vaccinated, but is apparently healthy, that is to say that there are no discharges from the eyes, there is no diarrhoea and the puppy is bright and eating well — then I personally would let the puppy settle down for a few days before vaccinating. Vaccinations on top of a change of environment, people and diets can quite often set off gastric problems. Providing the puppy is healthy, vaccinations may be delayed for several days, possibly up to one week; by which time there is considerably less stress on the puppy.

Most puppies have been (or should be) vaccinated prior to your picking them up, and should have had several days to settle down afterwards. If not, be very careful with the diet for a few days, i.e. no fatty foods, no milk, bland food, cooked chicken, cooked rice, natural yoghurt. Low lactose milk is very good, and will usually not upset the puppies' stomachs.

Once your puppy has settled in nicely and is doing all the right things such as eating well, behaving beautifully and never dreaming of messing inside, you then start to think about paying visits. *Don't!* The puppy has had a temporary vaccination, which means that the effects of the vaccine are temporary.

PUPPY VACCINATIONS

A puppy's immune system is underdeveloped at 6–8 weeks of age. Most puppies have a certain amount of maternal antibodies acquired from their mother. This can interfere with the uptake in effectiveness of puppy vaccinations. Recent developments have produced vaccines that are more effective against maternal immunity. Since the advent of these style of vaccines, two vaccinations at 6–8 weeks and again at 12–14 weeks are sufficient to give excellent cover for distemper, hepatitis and parvovirus. Many veterinarians and breeders still prefer the older style vaccinations, these still require three vaccinations with the third dose at 16–18 weeks of age.

It is most important that puppies are in good health and are relatively free of parasites at the time of vaccination. If there are concurrent stresses such as a high worm burden, poor nutrition and gastric problems, these will lower the puppy's resistance to disease. Combine this situation with vaccination and there is often a poor response to the vaccine. Gastric problems can be triggered due to the lowered immune status of the puppy.

It is not wise to take a puppy outside your own backyard before it has had its second vaccinations at 12–14 weeks. Should you wish to take the puppy to someone else's place — do so at the risk of your puppy's health. If you have to take the puppy with you, make sure you do not put it down in any public places (e.g. parks). If the puppy has to go into a yard where there are other dogs, only do so if all the dogs are vaccinated and have had no illnesses in the last few months. Do not take your puppy for any great distance in the heat as this will cause a fairly high degree of stress. Most important of all, do not even consider taking the puppy to a dog show at this age.

Re-vaccination is usually done at 12–14 weeks of age. The immune response from the first vaccine needs to be boosted as the puppy's immune system is now more mature, and it covers those puppies who had a poor response to the first vaccination. The 12–14 week vaccination will give a very good cover and should, with the newer vaccines, give nearly a 100% cover against a strong disease challenge. The vaccine will take 5–7 days to reach a good level of cover, after which you can start taking your puppy out into the big wide world for socialisation.

Those using the older style vaccines may not achieve a full cover against parvovirus with the second vaccination and may then require a third vaccination at this time. This vaccine is most important for those individuals who have had very high levels of maternal antibody.

The 12 weeks vaccination will usually give fairly good cover against all except the strongest challenge. The vaccine will take 7–10 days to reach an optimum level, after which you can start taking your puppy out for socialisation but preferably make few trips outside until after the third vaccination. This vaccine will provide a good cover if you have the general health and environment of the puppy under good control. This means that the puppy is regularly wormed twice weekly till 18–20 weeks if it is humid or in wet weather as worm eggs love to hatch in these conditions . Ensure that the puppy's environment is clean, that old food and/or faeces are not left lying around, and the puppy is not unduly stressed by long trips.

The 18–20 week vaccination is most important for those individuals which have had very high levels of maternal immunity. This can interfere with the response generated by the body to the earlier vaccinations. As the maternal immunity levels are seldom checked and it is not practical to do so in the majority of cases, it is in my opinion, necessary to give a third set of vaccinations to be absolutely safe.

This vaccination comes at a time when the body is able to respond in an immunologically mature fashion i.e. the body is capable of producing a high and long lasting response to the vaccines. It is important also to vaccinate especially for parvovirus at this stage as the maternal antibodies for parvovirus can theoretically last up to 16 weeks, so the last vaccine ought to be administered past the 16 weeks stage. This applies in particular to animals that are going travelling around the countryside and to those breeds that are particularly sensitive to parvovirus such as Rottweilers, Dobermans and Greyhounds.

Once this third vaccination has had time to respond, it is unlikely that a puppy being kept under good conditions will come down with parvovirus. It is worth having the third vaccination in the interests of the safety of the puppy and your own peace of mind.

With the third vaccination out of the way, the worming interval can be extended to once every 6–8 weeks until 12 months. Also, by this age the puppy or young dog as it now is, can be allowed to go to training, mix with other dogs and go on longer trips. Gradually expose the puppy to the outside world. Do not suddenly start hauling it all over the countryside, but arrange small trips initially which gradually increase in length. By this stage, puppies are far less prone to stress, although I would still take care to avoid long trips, especially in the excessive heat.

ANNUAL VACCINATIONS

Dogs should be vaccinated annually and yes, this does mean once a year.

This is particularly important in younger dogs especially the vaccination at 12–15 months. By this stage, for the dogs which only had two vaccinations, the level of immunity will be fairly low. Those dogs which had three vaccinations, should be reasonably well covered right up to the 12–15 month period.

Annual vaccinations are important in keeping the level of immunity high within your own kennel and are necessary if you wish to board your dogs for holidays at kennels. If you do not vaccinate for several years, then the level of immunity drops below the minimum level needed to protect against such diseases. The longest I would leave an older dog is 18 months to two years; providing the dog had been regularly vaccinated up to that point. Anyone who has seen a dog die from distemper will appreciate the need to vaccinate regularly; it is not a nice thing to see.

If not re-vaccinated, the level of immunity gradually drops, which is why in some areas there are outbreaks of distemper every 3–4 years.

ADDITIONAL VACCINES

In some areas, certain other diseases may have a higher incidence, e.g. tetanus, leptospirosis. There are vaccines for these bacterial infections, but they are generally only given to high risk animals or in the face of an outbreak in the vicinity. Ask your veterinarian what their views are on the likelihood of catching either disease and they will advise you accordingly.

I generally do not like giving these additional vaccines with the first vaccination. By 12 weeks, the puppy's immune system is stronger and by 16–18 weeks, it can take fairly varied challenges. Prior to 12 weeks, puppies are rarely in a situation that requires cover for kennel cough.

Kennel cough vaccinations are now available, but I would not advise giving these to young puppies. The 'kennel cough' complex consists of at least two viruses and one bacteria, and young puppies have enough to try to respond to without these additional ones. Para-influenza appears to be the most contagious of the three and it is well worthwhile giving the vaccine to racing dogs, dogs that are about to be kennelled and possibly show dogs that are being shown heavily (i.e. that have a high degree of exposure). Again, as with most viruses, you need two doses of the vaccine to obtain a good cover, preferably 3–4 weeks apart.

Kennel cough in itself does not cause much physical depression, the dog is rarely, if ever, off its food for more that 24–48 hours, but the sound effects can be quite alarming! The virus basically affects the larynx and any exercise or sudden excitement sets off a very hoarse croaking. Think of yourself with the same problem. The other characteristic of this virus is that it is extremely contagious. The effects are seen within 5–7 days of exposure, and they last around 10 days. Rest, antibiotics and a cough suppressant or low dose of buffered aspirin are often all that is needed. A mucolytic agent may also be helpful. The less the dog runs around, the less the larynx is irritated, the faster the recovery. Racing dogs need at least three weeks complete rest before racing again.

A section on parvovirus and related viruses which cause gastrointestinal disease is to be found in chapter 18.

Points To Notice in the Growing Puppy

TEETH AND TEETHING IN DOGS
I = incisor, C = canines, PM = premolars, M = molars.
Dental formula:
  (a) Immature (deciduous) dentition
  I 3/3, C 1/1, PM 3/3 = 28
  (b) Permanent (adult) dentition
  I 3/3, C 1/1, PM 4/4, M 2/3 = 42

Group	Tooth	Eruption Time	*Eruption*
Incisors	Central	4 months	*(cutting) of*
	Medial	4–5 months	*permanent*
	Lateral	4–5 months	*teeth*
Canines		5–6 months	
* Premolars	First	4–5 months	
	Second	5–6 months	
	Third	5–6 months	
	Fourth	4–5 months	
Molars	First	5–6 months	
	Second	5–7 months	
(bottom only)	Third	6–7 months	

  * occasionally an odd premolar may not erupt until 6–8 months.

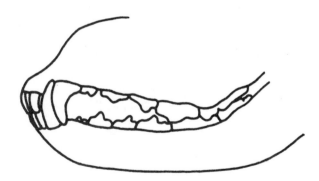

THE SKULL
The dog's skull is fixed, the lower jaw or mandible moves in relation to the skull. Points of reference are therefore taken from the skull. Try holding your jaw and talking at the same time — you will see how hard it is to do!

85

Head types   *Brachycephalic* — Short, wide-headed. This head type is often associated with a longer lower jaw, e.g. British Bulldog, Pekingese.

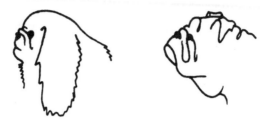

Mesaticephalic — head medium sized and proportioned, e.g. German Shepherd, Setters, Labradors, Beagles.

Dolichocephalic — long, narrow-headed breeds, e.g. Borzois, Collies, Greyhounds

FEATURES TO LOOK FOR IN A YOUNG PUPPY

Certain breeds have a longer lower jaw, giving a very prognathic appearance. These include the Boxer and the Bulldog. When choosing a puppy within one of these breeds, it is not really necessary to check bites as they are not really normal in the first place. In all breeds which require a correct scissor bite, the mouth should always be checked in those puppies which are being bought as show puppies.

In the vast majority of breeds, the adults should have a scissor bite. A puppy should at the time of purchase, have a scissor bite. If the lower teeth are slightly behind the upper incisors, this is often not sign-ificant in the eventual adult. If, however, the lower teeth are a long way behind the back of the upper incisors, giving the appearance of a 'shark', then the likelihood of this correcting is quite remote. It does not affect the majority of pet puppies, although care should be taken when the adult canines erupt to ensure the lower canines do not press into the roof of the mouth when closed.

In breeds with a shortened face and where a scissor bite is called for, it is important to select a show puppy carefully as these breeds are more likely to have the lower jaw overgrow the upper jaw. Examples of these breeds include the Rottweiler, Saint Bernard and the Cavalier King Charles Spaniel. The shorter headed individuals will usually have less 'bump' on the top of the nose; conversely, the bigger the bump at 7–8 weeks, the longer the nose (relative to the breed of course).

The placement of the immature canines is to me, the greatest eventual indicator of whether the bite will hold in the older or adult dog. The canines lock the bite. There is a short period when the adult canines are too short to hold the bite steady and this can be a period in which to watch the bite carefully.

In the puppy, when viewed from the side, the canines should interlock fairly snugly. Those mouths where the lower canine is appreciably further forward are more likely to have the lower jaw grow too much than those with the tighter fit. This is a common finding in breeds which regularly have mouth problems, e.g. Newfoundlands, Great Danes and Saint Bernards. A quick examination of the puppy before you buy it can save months of hard work and disappointment. Many of these puppies already have a very 'tight' bite by eight weeks of age.

Having said all this, there is one fairly notable exception to all the above generalisations. Cavalier King Charles Spaniels are about the only breed which I have seen where reverse scissor bites have corrected. This is not to say all such bites will so correct by puberty, but I have seen some remarkable bite reversals. I would select carefully with such a mouth, and preferably only those that were just a tight reverse scissor, avoiding those where the lower jaw juts out a long way forward from the upper jaw.

Teething   This starts at around four months of age and continues for another 2–3 months.

It is very important (particularly in the show puppy) to watch the mouth as the new teeth erupt. When the new or second teeth start to erupt, the immature teeth are sometimes retained, which can occasionally prevent the proper alignment of the mature teeth. This can result in wry bites with one tooth, or more, forward or backward of the correct position. This sort of incorrect positioning can often be corrected if noticed early enough and the offending retained immature teeth removed.

When the mature canines come down, the same thing as above may occur if the immature teeth are retained too long, resulting in a pinching of the position of the mature teeth. This may cause the adult canines either to come down too far forward of their correct position or to grow upwards inside the normal position and then push up into the roof of the mouth.

Occasionally the lower jaw may not quite catch up with the back of the upper teeth; this, if it is slight, can often be the result of incorrect diet, which can be improved. A good, well-balanced diet with a calcium additive that is well absorbed, usually works wonders. Again, this is often noted around 4–5 months, when the puppy is growing fast, and teething at the same time. If the lower canines are *behind* the upper canines when the mouth is closed, then the possibility of this mouth correcting is unlikely. *Growth of the lower jaw*

If, however, the lower jaw is starting to grow too far forward and looks as though the bite is about to be reversed, then occasionally this may be corrected by diet as well. This obviously applies only to those breeds that require a correct scissor bite.

A tight bite can often be a result of too much food, and these dogs will often benefit from a fairly strict reduction in the amount of food fed, providing they were overweight in the first place. A sudden reduction in the amount of food can slow down the growth rate of the lower jaw and it may be possible to hold the bite stable while the upper jaw grows a fraction.

A mouth which has the lower canines too far forward of the upper canines when the mouth is closed is often one that is going to grow forwards no matter what one does, so take heed when buying a puppy in the first place.

For breeds which have a longer lower jaw, e.g. the Boxer, Bulldog and Pekingese, the above comments do not obviously apply. In those breeds which call for a correct scissor bite and also have a short head, it is most important to check the placement of the canines on a puppy if it is being purchased for the show ring.

Occasionally at around 9–12 months of age, particularly in the larger breeds, these can be a late surge of growth of the lower jaw. This should be noted, particularly in those individuals which have a tight or close bite. It can be well worthwhile to regularly check the bite on these individuals.

Remember, weight and rate of development can affect the bite. If you do have a problem with teeth and/or the bite, the later you leave it, the harder and more unlikely it is to be corrected.

Dogs of the large heavy headed breeds may occasionally have their bites go level at around 3–4 years of age, e.g. Rottweiler, Newfoundland.

Missing teeth

This is is a genetic problem which cannot afford to be overlooked for too long as the amount of missing teeth in some breeds has to be seen to be believed! Dalmatians, Afghans, Borzois; to name a few, are among the more commonly affected breeds, but I am sure there are other breeds similarly affected.

Some of the worst mouths have only their incisors, canines and four to six other teeth in the entire back half of the mouth. This obviously leaves the affected individual with very few teeth with which to grind any hard food or crunch up bones.

Missing teeth should be considered a genetic problem, except where accidents have obviously occurred; and/or teeth have had to be removed for abscesses or gum infections, which are uncommon in young animals.

When breeding with an animal which has a lot of missing teeth, but hopefully many other redeeming features, try to use an animal with a 'full' mouth (or as close to as possible). The problem may appear to correct itself in one generation but it will still be around as a recessive problem for later generations. Do not forget the problem is always lurking in the background.

Ears and teething

Erect-eared dogs, e.g. German Shepherds, quite often will drop their ears when teething and occasionally they will not come up again. In drop-tip eared breeds, e.g. Collies and Shelties, the tips of their ears will usually rise while teething, and again, if they are not properly cared for, may stay in the incorrect position.

TESTICLES

Normal   Mon-orchid

A male puppy should, at the time of purchase, have two testicles in the scrotum. At worst one can be slightly in front of the scrotum, but it should be easily manipulable down into the scrotum.

The testicles develop up near the kidneys during gestation and then drop gradually through the inguinal canal and down into the scrotum. Testicles should preferably be in or near the scrotum by eight weeks of age.

Large fat male puppies quite often have one or both testicles further up towards the body. The fatter the puppy, the slower the sexual development. Excessive weight acts as an androgenic neutralising effect. If the puppy does have one testicle higher up that cannot be easily pulled down into the scrotum, trim the weight down and keep it that way until the testicle stays down in the scrotum.

It is not advisable to use male hormones on these puppies unless the weight is trimmed down first, otherwise a large amount of the effect will be negated. In the slightly older overweight male puppy that has normally descended testicles, these are usually very small and underdeveloped. If you trim the weight down, the testicles will start to gain in size towards normal for that breed.

Retained testicles can, at a later stage, cause trouble. Testicles that are trapped inside the body of the older age male dog (over eight years) can become abnormal. Tumours of retained testicles are not uncommon and, while not life threatening on the whole, do produce a feminisation syndrome. They become attractive to other male dogs, develop prominent teats and have bilateral hair loss. For this reason it is advisable to have the retained testicle removed at some stage before 6–8 years of age. If these dogs are sold as pets, it is usually done at castration. Retention of testicles is considered to be an inherited problem, and as such, affected individuals should not be bred from.

WEIGHT AND DEVELOPMENT

This aspect has already been covered to a large degree in the sections on diet and overnutrition earlier in this chapter, so the aim here is to give a reminder of the main points.

1. Weight in relation to rate of growth

This can become critical in the large, heavy boned individual, from medium-sized breeds upwards. The heavier the puppy is above the breed average for that age, the more likely that puppy is to suffer from soreness and/or cartilage defects. Increased rate of growth can affect bone development and the rate of mineral absorption.

2. Check the weight

Do this by lightly running your fingers over the ribs. There should just be a thin layer of fat, not centimetres thick! The ideal condition for the dog to be is trim — not too fat, not too thin — so that when it is moving, half of the dog's skin does not roll from side to side.

3. Check the legs and pasterns regularly

This is to ascertain that the puppy is coping with its diet and rate of growth; if in doubt, check with your vet. While you are there, have the dog weighed.

Do remember that while the puppy is teething there may be an increased demand for calcium in the diet. The pasterns and the ears in the erect and semi-erect breeds may reflect this need. Any additional calcium should be small amounts to effect, then reduce the dose or stop.

4. Tightness, firmness and soundness of ligamentation

These are very important in the younger dog, particularly in relation to the future soundness of the adult. Tightness of ligamentation is, to a large degree, a reflection of the dog's overall weight and diet during the growing stages. An adult dog can 'tighten up' as it matures and grows out of its 'puppy' fat, (rather as teenagers do). If the puppy is kept at a reasonable weight during the growing stages, then the ligamentation does not have the degree of looseness or laxity as an overweight animal would have.

On top of this there are of course **genetic influences** in this matter where particular lines are renowned for their soundness as opposed to excessive looseness. What, in effect this means, is that diet and weight can play a part as environmental influences, affecting genetic conditions such as hip dysplasia and osteochondritis.

This does not mean that excessive weight or inferior diets will necessarily cause these genetic conditions. If, however, the genetic predisposition is present, then the condition may be exacerbated by incorrect diets and excessive weight.

5. Excessive weight

On the younger dog, excessive weight can be very detrimental to the eventual breeding soundness of the adult. Too fat a youngster will cause slower gonadal development, i.e. the testicles and ovaries will be underdeveloped, causing possible decreased fertility in breeding life, especially with bitches.

The importance of not allowing a puppy to become too overweight in relation to overall soundness of the adult dog (movement, ligamentation and breeding soundness) cannot be overemphasised. Aim for optimal, not maximal, growth.

5

Puberty and Desexing

Puberty

Most dogs will reach puberty at two-thirds to three-quarters their adult weight. The smaller breeds are fast maturing and can reach puberty as early as six months. This early maturity can cause the occasional problem due to premature closure of the bone epiphysis, i.e. the growth plates. 'Legg Perthe's Disease' is an example and is caused by an insufficient blood supply getting through to the head of the femur, which in turn causes the head of the femur to semi 'dissolve'. This does not happen often and is considered to be partly genetic.

The larger breeds do not reach puberty until 8–12 months on average (varies greatly according to the breed). Some individuals who have been 'pushed' too fast due to overnutrition or incorrect additives, can get problems similar to those of the smaller breeds, causing hormonal upsets which in turn can prematurely close off the growth plates especially of the distal radius (bottom end of the forearm). This results in stunted front legs that may bow and bend.

The average medium-sized breed reaches puberty at around 7–9 months. However, bitches that have yet to reach three-quarters their adult weight may not cycle, i.e. come into season. Some of these dogs are hyperactive and, until you can put weight on them, they will not come into season. In the large to giant-sized breeds, bitches may not come into season if they are light in weight or very fit, i.e. carrying very little fat, until 15–24 months. Usually, owners should not worry, the inevitable will eventually happen and it is less trouble in the mean time. If you do get worried, try locking the bitch up for most of the day until you can put some weight on her.

So, for the medium to large breeds, puberty, along with its hormonal and psychological changes, occurs on average at 7–10 months.

Puberty marks the end of the rapid growth phase, where 75–90% of the dog's height and weight has been reached. Bitches tend to reach this stage 1–2 months before dogs. Male dogs will continue to grow after bitches have stopped. Final height, weight and maturity are now gradually established during the next 12 months.

PSYCHOLOGICAL CHANGES AT PUBERTY

At puberty, particularly in the males of the more dominating breeds, there is a change in attitude.

This is a fairly definite attitude change where the dog is saying 'I'm no longer a puppy, I'm a dog and I'm in charge — I think.' The trouble is that quite often they think they can boss you around as well as other male dogs they encounter. They try the 'dominance' scene, but do not let them get away with it. If you do, they will become aggressive to you as well as everyone else. Be firm, take the dog out and reinforce its obedience training. You may have to do this for several months before it really believes *your* side of the story! If you don't, the dog can end up a nuisance to all, and/or possibly dangerous.

While on this subject, there is a second major period when the dog reaches maturity where the same situation occurs, generally at 18–24 months of age, where the dog is now saying, 'I'm fully grown, and I *know* I'm in charge!' Again the dog is trying to establish its dominance, and he intends to dominate either you or other people. Get the dog out again and really pull it back into line with some firm obedience. If you 'win' and preferably win well and truly, on both occasions, the dog will rarely if ever try it on again (see also chapter 6 on Training your dog).

Bitches, unless they are very aggressive individuals, rarely if ever have these problems of domination. If you think that you may have trouble dominating a male dog, get a bitch instead. This also applies to the novice owner.

Desexing

Desexing of both sexes is normally done at 5–6 months of age or at any time after this age. More recently early desexing has been promoted, from as young as eight weeks onwards, particularly by the animal welfare groups. I feel that larger breeds can be safely desexed at 8–10 weeks, the smaller breeds from 10–12 weeks of age. Desexing of both sexes is most important if you do not wish to breed with your dog.

Today there are thousands of unwanted pets that are put down by councils every year, in every area. To prevent adding to this number, desex animals that you do not wish to breed from. The safest way to do this, and this applies particularly to the bitches, is to desex them *before* puberty, i.e. before they ever have a season.

Some people have the erroneous idea that a bitch is not 'complete' or will have emotional hang-ups if she is desexed before a season — this is nonsense. A dog does not have the same emotional hang-ups as a human. **Desexing has a calming effect on both sexes**; so the people who say the bitch should have a litter first because it will settle her down are right, but why breed more neurotic dogs? If you are going to breed with an animal do so because of its good qualities, not to try to calm down a neurotic bitch, who inevitably has neurotic puppies!

Desexing is very easy on young animals, especially if they have never had a season. The ovaries are small and the uterus is not very vascular, which generally means that it is far less of a risk to desex at this time than later, especially if the bitch is in season. The nice thing about a bitch is that once she is desexed, you don't have to worry about her coming into season again, or getting infections or mammary tumours in older age.

If you allow the bitch to have a season first, there are commonly a large number of 'accidents' that occur. Remember, a bitch is in season for three weeks, and the ideal time of mating is 10–14 days into a season. One of the problems is that you may miss the first few days or even the first week and the first idea that you have of it is a yard full of male dogs attached (occasionally literally) to your bitch; or she may go and find someone to 'love' all by herself. If you want your bitch to have a season, then make sure you have a very good lock-up pen, that is very dog-proof — both for in and out traffic. Keep checking your bitch, and at the first sign of a bloody discharge and/or vulval swelling, lock her up. When all signs of swelling of the vulva have gone, then you can let the bitch out.

AVERAGE AGE OF FIRST COMING IN SEASON
Small breeds — 6–8 months
Medium breeds — 7–10 months
Large breeds — 8–15 months
Giant breeds — 9–18 months
Also, remember — if your bitch has a litter of puppies:

- Invariably *you* will end up keeping another dog (or two), particularly if you have young children.
- Nearly all the people who said they would have one of the little darlings at 2–3 weeks of age, either disappear or 'cannot take the puppy right now'.
- Only keep a few puppies on the bitch or you may end up taking them to the local pound or vet to be put down.

Think before allowing your bitch to have puppies!

CHEMICAL MEANS OF STOPPING A SEASON
There are several ways of chemically stopping a bitch from coming into season, or accelerating the bitch through the season.

One of the most common forms is the 'pill'. This is given to the bitch from the first day of season and continues for eight days. Lock the bitch up for 5–6 days as mismatings can occur. The drawbacks of the pill are that it must be started on the first few days of the season as it will not be as effective later in the season. Also the length of time that a bitch will stay out of season is highly variable — it can be as short as three months and as long as 9–12 months. Also, if it is a bitch that you may wish to breed from at a later date, the possibility of developing cystic ovaries as a side effect is not uncommon. Long-term use on a non-breeding bitch has its problems, including the expense (particularly in the larger bitches), irregular seasons and infections in older age.

Another form of control of the bitch's season is by an injection of various different hormones. These will last on average 6–9 months, but most must be given when the bitch is not in season. Again, with a bitch that you may wish to breed at a later date, the injections have their drawbacks. Some bitches may stay out of season for as long as two years, and again hormonal imbalances can occur with cystic ovaries or inactive ovaries which can develop as undesirable side effects.

Personally, all bitches should eventually get desexed, including older bitches which are no longer being bred. The older bitch, whether or not she has ever had a litter, is prone to mammary tumours and pyometra (severe uterine infection), from the age of 5–6 years onwards. Desexing removes the hormones that cause these conditions. A desexed bitch is a very easy bitch to look after; there are no reproductive worries.

DESEXING MALE DOGS

This is also an important matter to consider. Your male dog may not come into season and produce puppies, but it is very good at finding bitches who are in season. Some males, especially the terrier breeds, can be rather over-sexed, i.e. they can become over amorous to humans and aggressive when frustrated. Terriers and terrier crosses are generally 'escape artists', and will go kilometres to find their lady love, have all sorts of fights in the process (what terrier ever backed off from a fight?), and come back battered and torn. Many dogs of other breeds also fit into the same pattern of wandering and fighting. The vets don't mind, they get plenty of work out of it, stitching up the remnants.

Aggressive dogs who are beyond the control of their owners, and particularly if they are aggressive to children, should be desexed. Erratic male dogs that are nice one minute and trying to bite you the next also benefit from desexing. Some of these animals may have a prostate problem that is making them aggressive, more commonly seen in the slightly older dog, so have your vet examine him for this.

The actual desexing removes the ovaries and the uterus in the female and the testicles in the male. The net effect is to remove the sex hormones. This in turn has a calming effect on the dog or bitch. The animal will still be just as good a watch or guard dog, but the aggressive edge will be removed i.e. the dog will still bark and be protective, but will be less likely to actually go and attack, unless provoked.

Effects of desexing

The question that worries a lot of people, is will the dog gain weight? The answer for the most part is yes. With the removal of the sex hormones, the metabolic rate is slower and generally there is an appetite increase. However, dogs that are very active before desexing tend to retain their figures, very indolent dogs usually already have a generous figure before and are likely to add to it afterwards.

It is important to remember after your dog has been desexed, that as the metabolic rate has been decreased, then the amount of food needed has also decreased.

Feeding desexed dogs

Cut down a desexed dog's food by about a quarter to a third if they start to *gain weight* after desexing and in particular reduce the dry dog food intake. Hyperactive dogs should not have their intake reduced unless the animal starts to gain weight noticeably. Remember, it is a lot easier to diet the dog than diet yourself. Some people complain that they feed their dog practically nothing at all — don't think how little you feed your dog; think how cheap it is to feed it.

6

Behaviour Development, Socialisation and Early Training

Puppies start to open their eyes by the time they are 10–14 days old, followed by the ears opening at around 16–20 days, and they will respond to sound from this time on. The puppies should be handled as much as possible from 2–3 weeks onwards. Stimulation and handling in the early weeks can help the puppy tolerate stress better in later life and make for a more emotionally stable dog that is less fearful of new people, situations and noises. The more the puppies are handled and the greater the variety of situations they experience, such as different noises and objects to play with, the greater their eventual temperament. This only takes 10–15 minutes daily, and will make for better learning ability and responsiveness in the adult dog. The puppy should not experience fear or trauma — all new challenges should be experienced in a **positive** manner. Leave the radio blaring when you are not there — so that the puppies are used to sudden and loud variations of noise. Leave around a sack full of old drink cans, a few old children's toys — the more the better. Do not leave small objects that may be swallowed, puppies are similar to babies in this respect, they will put anything in their mouths and try to eat it!

The attention the breeder and their family have given to the puppy before the puppy has gone to its new home is of great importance to the dog's eventual soundness of temperament and ability to be trained; particularly in regard to a working animal. A greater ability to be trained for whatever purpose the new owner has in mind for the puppy, will increase the chances of success and enjoyment that the owner, and the dog, achieve between them. Breeders who are aware of the value of this early socialisation will gain a reputation for good easily trained dogs with soundness of temperament for both the show and obedience rings.

Puppies are extremely impressionable between the ages of 5–16 weeks of age. If they have not socialised with humans at all by 16 weeks, then the puppies may never properly attach to humans and have severe temperament problems.

Critical Stages of Behaviour Development

FROM BIRTH TO TWENTY-ONE DAYS
The brain in the neonatal puppy is very immature and does not undergo much development until the ears open at 16–20 days. Warmth and stimulation are provided by the mother and litter mates. Survival is the most important aspect of this stage — warmth, food, massage by the mother, and sleep.

TWENTY-ONE DAYS TO SEVEN WEEKS
By 21 days, puppies can see, smell and hear quite well. Between three and seven weeks of age, there is rapid development of the brain and neural pathways. From now on, the puppy's brain receives strong stimulation from everything around it, and it begins to learn quickly. The time

between 21 and 28 days is a particularly rapid stage of development, where close contact with their mother is necessary. Puppies should not be separated from their mother for long periods of time. If you are starting to wean the puppies, take the bitch away about an hour before feeding and allow the bitch back after they have finished. By 28 days of age, puppies are much better adjusted to their environment and will cope with longer periods away from the bitch. With larger breeds, the development appears to be more rapid and by about day 24 onwards, the bitches themselves will spend longer away from the puppies. Particularly boisterous bitches may need to be separated from their puppies during the daytime from 3–4 weeks onwards to prevent them from jumping on the puppies, but always keep the bitch with the puppies at night until at least 4–5 weeks of age.

Puppies need continued association with their litter mates and mother up to seven weeks of age, to develop proper canine socialisation. The mother, even if she is in with the puppies only part of the time, teaches the puppies and gives discipline. Litter mates play, fight and develop a dominance order. Puppies that are removed too early from the company of their litter mates and mother may never develop normal canine associations and become over attached to humans.

The more puppies are handled by different people and children (old enough to understand the situation), the better their ability to cope with everyday events in a stable manner when they are older. Puppies learn that sudden loud noises do not hurt them, squeaky toys will not bite, humans can be crawled over and played with. This starts their lifelong attachment to humans. Individual attention and handling even twice a week for 10–15 minutes in this early stage will be sufficient to develop adequate socialisation. For the best result, you should handle the puppies at least twice a day, sit with them, pick them up and gently play with them (5–10 minutes is quite adequate).

Handling by humans

The formal teaching of puppies can start as early as 5–6 weeks, although in the average litter situation little is done in the way of individual teaching.

The very rapid assimilation of the events and challenges that are occurring during this period stimulates the process of learning. A lack of stimulation will hamper their ability to learn.

SEVEN TO TWELVE WEEKS

By seven weeks, the puppy's brain and nervous system have the capacity of an adult dog, but not the attention span nor the experience. The 7–12 week stage is the best time for the development of the human-dog relationship. This is the stage when puppies are going to their new homes and should be receiving an abundance of individual attention. Individualisation allows the puppy to learn its self-importance as an individual, rather than one of a mob, where a more dominant puppy may have taken precedence.

When the puppy arrives at its new home, there is a whole new environment to explore, different people and other dogs to have to interact with. Never allow a young puppy to encounter an older dog's lack of hospitality; it can take time for an older dog to accept the 'foreigner' into its yard. Older dogs and puppies should have controlled exposure to each other until there is obviously no animosity between them. Many older dogs will immediately get on very well with a young puppy, others may take a few days to grow accustomed to the idea.

Begin to take a new puppy out and about after the second vaccinations at 12–14 weeks of age, and then gradually widen its environment. If you have to take the puppy out, go only to a few homes where you know there have been no sick puppies and all their dogs are vaccinated.

Training at this stage is mostly in the form of games, but the pack instinct is at work, so that cooperation with, and dominance by, humans is learnt. The human takes over the role of 'mother', i.e. a parent-offspring relationship. Basic obedience such as 'sit' and 'heel', can be taught, but it is best to concentrate on lead and house training.

The acceptance of restraint is an important lesson, particularly with the larger breeds, and should also be learnt before 12 weeks of age.

Restraining a puppy involves holding it firmly either in your arms or on its side, where it cannot get away. This is a short lesson that needs to be taught, on several occasions only, until the puppy realises that you will not let it go until it stops struggling. Use this method when a puppy gets over excited and starts to get nippy or when holding a puppy to cut its nails. All that is required is that you hold it firmly until it calms down. The puppy may scream and shriek, wriggle like a worm or try to bite, but if held firmly (not in a death grip!) next to your body, with one arm over the body and the other around the neck, slightly stretching the head forwards, the puppy cannot hurt itself or you, and will, after 1–2 minutes calm down.

When it is calm, ease your grip, speak words of praise, and release the puppy. This only takes 2–3 lessons and it is learnt for life.

Holding a puppy on its side when it is under three months of age is an extremely valuable lesson in restraint. When your Great Dane or Saint Bernard weighs 60–80 kg in later years, it will remember the early lesson despite the fact its weight has increased. It is particularly useful to hold a puppy on its side a few times so that it can get used to being tipped over and having nails trimmed, ears cleaned etc.

If the puppy has not had sufficient handling and socialisation with humans by 12 weeks, the bond with humans may never be properly formed. The same is true for association with other dogs.

TWELVE TO SIXTEEN WEEKS

This is the final critical stage in a puppy's life as it marks the end of the basic learning process that will stay with it for life. If handling, stimulation, and socialisation with humans and dogs have not been adequate, the dog will never improve its ability to learn beyond this point. It is also the independence from the parents stage; the puppy will want to do far more on its own — investigating, seeing what is or is not edible in the garden, wandering the streets nearby if allowed out (hopefully never on its own and preferably on a lead) and so on. At this stage, puppies, particularly males, will try to see who is boss — never lose on that point!

Training for lead and obedience to basic commands should definitely have started by now — if not, start without delay as it is the ideal age for the transition from playing to disciplined training. The best results are obtained when the puppy is free from other distractions, such as other dogs or loud noises. Take the puppy by itself to a quiet area and work with it. The puppy will concentrate on what *you* want it to do, not what Fido the other dog is or is not doing. Once the puppy is well disciplined and self-confident, then tackle more complicated situations.

Training should be limited to 10–15 minutes (maximum), as the attention span is still not very long. Twice-daily training is more than adequate. Play activities after a session are good as the puppy sees this as a reward for being good.

I like to limit outside excursions to brief trips in a car, short walks in the park and visits to friends. Until the puppy is fully covered by its vaccinations, I do not advise taking a young puppy out into places where there are many dogs. Over 16–18 weeks of age, the puppy is reasonably safe to take out and about.

AFTER SIXTEEN WEEKS

This is a final stage, where earlier lessons are repeated and reinforced. I see this as expanding the dog's ability to accept different situations as 'normal'; this is socialisation with the general public if you would like to call it that. It is the stage to take the puppy out and around shopping centres, friend's places or for training. Encounter different situations, shapes, noises, traffic; do it gradually, not all in one day. This allows a puppy, in particular a well-handled puppy, to experience everyday situations to which it should react calmly. Dog shows and market days are very good venues for such excursions. Even if the dog does not encounter traffic or similar situations for several years, the early experience will remain when it is re-exposed at a later date, and the calm response will be remembered and repeated.

People who wish to continue with obedience will find all that early work put in by the breeder and then by themselves will be repaid by easy training and good results in the obedience ring.

Socialisation and training is never wasted, it results in a more manageable dog that is a delight to own and is much appreciated by other members of the public — especially by veterinarians. If this training could be done with all dogs there would be a far better relationship between dog owners and other members of the public than there is at present and fewer poor tempered, unreliable dogs to deal with.

SPECIAL CASES

After quarantine Dogs which have been through prolonged periods of quarantine may require special attention afterwards to re-socialise them. The younger the dog, the greater the effort required in socialising once they are released. Most kennels are reasonably good, but it is not possible in the average kennel organisation to allow time for anyone to sit and play with or handle the dog for more than 3–5 minutes twice a day. Younger dogs, and puppies in particular, are deprived of normal stimuli which they would be receiving if they were in a home environment.

Treatment for such dogs requires that they be re-socialised as though they were stunted in their growth. If a puppy goes into quarantine at an age when it has never been lead trained or exposed to traffic, when finally released, it will need to undergo a gradual expansion of its horizons.

This can take quite some time, 3–4 months at least, for the dog to settle into the new environment and be re-educated. If the young dog has new owners to contend with in addition to everything else, it may take 6–12 months to catch up to others of its age.

The older the dog is when placed in quarantine, the quicker the return to normal behaviour as it will have previous experiences to fall back on. Even so, I would allow 3–4 months of re-socialisation of a newly imported dog prior to public exposure in a show ring, where all eyes are waiting to find fault. Quarantine has now been shortened considerably so the problems of socialising are no longer as dramatic.

Phobias and Temperament Breakdowns

In the last few years there has been a move to try to understand the cause of temperament aberrations that suddenly develop in a previously normal dog. There are now dog psychologists and animal behaviourists to help deal with these problems and several excellent books have recently been published.

For a dog to develop sudden abnormal behaviour the causes can be many and varied. Some of these are as follows:

- A new animal or human introduced into the household.
- Lack of attention when previously the dog received much more.
- Sudden change of environment — e.g. moving house.
- Death of another animal or human to which the dog was deeply attached.

The list of possible variable factors could go on forever. The average behavioural problem can be related to a recent sudden change in the dog's environment. 'Environment' includes place (home and surrounding environs), people and other animals. Hormonal changes, described below, can be a contributing factor in the temperament/behaviour problems found in the young maturing male dog.

Books on behaviour and behaviour patterns, the importance of territory and the defence of it, dominance and so on, make fascinating reading. If you are keen to delve into any particular subject, additional reading will greatly help your overall understanding of your own dog's behaviour.

HORMONAL STAGES OF DEVELOPMENT

Periods of hormonal upsurges tend to coincide with psychological/ temperamental problems in dogs of previously normal behaviour — although 'normal' always varies considerably from the owners' point of view! The majority of hormonal upsurge problems, as I call them, occur in **male** dogs. The will (or drive) to dominate other dogs and humans generally causes the most problems for anxious owners.

The major stages of hormonal upsurges are at:

12–18 weeks — associated with growth/teething area

8–12 months — associated with puberty

18–24 months — associated with adult maturity

Stage 1: 12–18 weeks

Puppies have a small 'flush' of sexual hormones when they change their puppy coat, which is around 12–18 weeks. At this time, you may notice a small rash of 'pimples' on the belly and down near the groin area. This will usually go away with very little treatment; at most, wash with warm water and dry. As the puppies have a small burst of hormones, there may be an occasional psychological change — the puppy tries to assert itself or it may suddenly develop nervous tendencies or peculiar habits. Usually one can easily overcome this by being firm, taking no nonsense and using minor discipline to bring the puppy back into line.

Nervous habits are usually overcome by the owner putting more effort into the puppy's socialisation with people; by visiting places and trying at all times to give the puppy **positive experiences** that are not fear inducing. If the puppy is afraid, reassure it, wait and let it see that, whatever it is, it is not going to hurt it. Do not leave the place until the puppy is calm — even if you have to sit down with it for a quarter of an hour. At the same time, *do not force* the puppy into a situation it does not care for and do not allow the puppy to run away. Encourage it to go halfway forward and then stand, but no running away; the next time three-quarters of the way and so on.

Keep the puppy on a lead at all times, as having it running away with you chasing after it will undo all the good work achieved. Inexhaustible patience and kindness will gradually bring about the required change. Poorly socialised puppies may never get over some fears and will remain neurotic in certain circumstances.

Occasionally a temperamental fault can be a genetic problem within certain bloodlines of a breed and, while good early socialisation may get rid of the most obvious signs, the dog could develop nervous habits as it gets older. However, they can often be minimised with good ongoing socialisation.

Stage 2: 8–10 months

Around 8–10 months, male dogs, particularly the bigger breeds, wish to assert their authority, which extends to defence of their territory or humans. In their relationships with humans this may translate into such habits as ignoring you when you try to discipline them, becoming aggressive over food and towards other dogs/bitches, and displaying jealousy towards another human that is standing next to 'their' one and only human. As this is often the partner of the owner, this temperament change can be very worrying, particularly to those that have not owned a large or stubborn dog before. Often these dogs have been rather spoilt as puppies and have lacked the basic discipline that should have been given in the formative stages, i.e. before 16 weeks of age. A dog with too strong a temperament may cause even an experienced person trouble at this age.

This defiance of the rules must be corrected. It is an urgent matter which should be dealt with as soon as possible. Basically the dog is testing you, trying to reverse roles, saying 'I am grown up and I am in charge, I think.' If you allow this, the dog will lose its respect for you, will try to dominate you and ignore your commands. He is pushing his previous limit to establish himself in a stronger position. As with adolescent humans, it is mostly bluff, but must be dealt with firmly as dogs need to know how much is acceptable and where the line is drawn.

The way to re-establish control of the situation is to put more work into re-training your dog and reinforcing the early training. Give more lessons in 'sit', 'heel', 'stay' — where disobedience is punished *immediately* by a sharp check on the collar so that the dog knows you mean business. Half-hearted attempts at obedience are no good, now is the time to stand your ground and be firm. You will both benefit greatly from the experience. Once the dog starts saying 'Yes Sir!' again, start taking him out and about, reminding him of his training responses which may have lapsed since the early basic training was done. Difficult dogs will often benefit from a return to obedience school where discipline in and amongst other dogs is a fairly chastening experience.

This is the last difficult phase to cope with if you have a strong-minded dog. Once the dog is through it, life should never again be so difficult. At this time the male is attaining adult maturity, and his attitude is 'I am the boss and I know it!' *Stage 3: 18–24 months*

Aggressive male dogs will have fights with any dog they meet, and resent anything displeasing such as 'the cutting of nails' or removal of food dishes. Dogs that have previously settled down from *Stage 2* may, for no apparent reason, revert to dominating ways. You must be just as determined as the dog! If you can both weather the storm, the result will be well worth it. The same treatment is needed: obedience, pulling the dog into line — *insisting* on firm discipline. If you persist, he will now know that you really mean to win, and that he has to keep his place — which is below you in the order of dominance. In this way you should avoid another power struggle.

Few dogs that are well handled and disciplined as youngsters will ever even try to dominate humans at a later date, so the early training and handling before 16 weeks of age is vital if you are to have an easily trained and controlled adult dog.

Training Your Dog

I am I suppose, a house trainer. I like a dog that will behave just as well in normal household situations as on outdoor expeditions. However, my dogs are not the best at long 'sits' and 'downs', so I will attempt to explain only the basics, as that is all I have ever done or had time for.

As with behavioural problems, there are many excellent books that have been written about dog training, helpful to both the novice and the more dedicated obedience person.

Many people wish to find a book that will cure a specific bad habit their dog may have developed, however, every dog trainer has a slightly different approach to the same problem. The hard part is finding the right method for *your* dog — which is not necessarily the one suggested in a book.

There are several basic methods of training and I tend to follow the 'bribery and corruption' system with the initial basic training. In relation to humans, this is more commonly known as the 'reward' system. This will probably horrify the dedicated dog trainer, but as we are only approaching the basics and the initial training, it is successful as it makes the puppies approach the work with a certain enthusiasm which they often retain long after visible means of reward have vanished.

BASIC TRAINING

1. House training
(This subject has been approached in more detail in the House training section of chapter 3.)

The important points are as follows:
- Take the puppy outside as soon as it wakes up from a sleep.
- Take the puppy outside as soon as it has been fed.
- Give the puppy a little time to settle in — at least 1–2 weeks.
- Remember, some puppies are very quick to learn, some are very slow.

The more work you put into this training the quicker the result.

2. Lead training
Lead training can start as early as 5–6 weeks or as late as you care to go. Reactions vary from screaming the place down to placid acceptance (rare!). This is a good time for the bribery and corruption brigade, as a little bit of food in the hand while encouraging the puppy to follow you will start the puppy in the right direction. By the time puppies realise they have a lead on, they have begun to understand that they should follow you as you are attached. If the puppy pulls back, allow a bit of slack, wait until it calms down, and then resume operations. When it moves forwards, even if only a few metres, give a very small tidbit and lots of praise. I always use a soft lead and collar. Do not use a check chain on a very young puppy as it has enough to deal with being attached to something, without also having a harsh noose around its neck. After several short sessions of 5–10 minutes, the bribery aspect is less important than your generous praise.

Following you around is a natural habit, acquired by the young puppy trotting after its mother. As you have become their new parent and are holding the food, they are fairly keen to follow you. The earlier you start lead training, the easier and quicker the response. If you leave it until 12–16 weeks, there will be more resistance encountered from the puppy.

Half-grown puppies and adults (or any dogs training for obedience) will require a check chain to 'break them in' to the lead. Be prepared for some wild behaviour! The noise they make as they try to turn themselves inside out in an effort to wriggle out of the check chain can be sufficient for you to imagine that your neighbours will be phoning the animal protection society!

A check *must* be used correctly or it is both useless and potentially dangerous.

There are three rules to remember when using a check or choker chain.

1. A check chain must always have the long end going over the neck no matter which side you are working from. The short end (loose ring) is always on the lower side of the neck. This allows the check chain to release when it is relaxed. If not on correctly, i.e. the short end on the upper side of the neck, the chain stays in the 'locked' position when released.

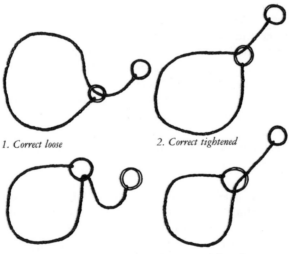

1. Correct loose   2. Correct tightened

3. Incorrect loose   4. Incorrect tightened

2. A check chain is used to 'check'. It is used to give a sudden quick pull and then is released immediately. The action of a fast hard yank pulls the dog back to you, and you regain its attention. If you pull continually on the check chain, it will act as a collar with no leverage, and the dog's airway will be restricted. If one hard yank does not gain a response, repeat it straightaway. Two or three hard pulls will gain the attention of the vast majority of dogs.

3. Never, never, never tie a dog up on a check chain. If a dog is tied up on a check chain, it can either choke to death if it gets tangled up or it

can hang itself jumping a fence. It is not a good idea to leave a check chain on a dog that is running free as if it gets caught up, it is possible the dog may injure or even kill itself. If you have to leave a check chain on, knot the long end around the other end, so as to have a firm collar effect.

Here are some final points on the subject of check chains:

- A thin one hurts more than a broader, heavier chain. Heavy breeds need a heavy chain; small, thin ones are likely to break, usually when the dog is lunging out at another dog.

- Overuse of a check chain can result in a dog that collapses to the ground as soon as it is even lightly checked, this will ruin it for obedience, so novice owners beware.

- Check chains are very effective when used properly and do not cause undue hardship to the dog. Puppies over 12 weeks graduate to a lightweight chain with no ill effects.

- When using a check chain on an untrained dog, you will obtain the best results as stated above, by a short sharp pull and an immediate release. This will have a greater effect if you are at a slight angle to the dog. Never pull a dog that is lying down on the ground as the dog has the advantage. Go back to the dog, stand slightly to one side, then a sharp pull will get his attention and make him come to you. Praise the dog when he comes to you.

- When you check the dog, give a command at the same time, so the dog will come to associate the command with what you want it to do. Use a firm no nonsense voice; Barbara Woodhouse, the famous TV exponent of animal training, had a voice which was very definite. 'Walkies' is what she wanted, and 'Walkies' is what she got. The gradual association with the command develops a response to the point that you do not need to check the dog unless its attention is wandering.

3. Heel   This can be well under way by 12 weeks and follows on naturally from lead training. When heeling, the dog's shoulder should be kept level with your knee or leg, so that it can see what commands you are making with your hands. Once the dog is leading well, the dog is brought to

heel by short sharp pulls on the check chain, while giving the command 'Heel' firmly at the same time. The dog will gradually associate the command with the position you want it to be in.

Give lots of praise and encouragement when the dog is working correctly, and you will help to create a keen, happy, obedient dog.

By this stage no bribery is given during a lesson, but you can sneak a little something in when you have successfully finished. Remember that a puppy's attention span is short. Lessons should be only 10–15 minutes duration until the dog is over 16–20 weeks of age. Try to do one thing well before moving on to the next.

4. Sit

Training the dog to sit can be done on or off a lead — preferably on a lead. With a puppy on a lead, give a short upward check of the check chain with your right hand, put your left hand on the dog's hindquarters and push down, saying 'Sit' while undertaking this manoeuvre. With the head raised and the hindquarters being pushed down, most dogs will automatically sit. You get the same result by raising your hand with a tidbit of food and gently pushing down the dog's rear end to the floor, giving the command to 'sit'. Several sessions are usually sufficient to instil this rule.

The sit lesson is a very useful one to teach with food as the puppy does not get any food until it is sitting. You will especially appreciate the value of this lesson if you have an 80 kg Saint Bernard! If it hasn't learnt to sit before receiving its food you could well find yourself knocked over and the food flung in all directions. These basic lessons, particularly if approached before 12–16 weeks of age, can make life much easier.

5. Stay

This command can save the dog's life when in a dangerous traffic situation. It is a **reprimand command**, and is done with the flat of the hand to the nose. The 'stay' command is generally first taught with the dog in a sitting position. It takes effort to get up from the sit position, and the dog is more relaxed. Make the dog sit, then move forwards after putting your hand flat against the nose commanding 'stay'. You can tap the nose gently if it breaks position, go a very short distance to start with, usually to just in front of the dog, and repeat the command. As the dog gets used to the idea, you can extend your distance to the dog and move in all directions around the dog, while still holding the lead. Once you are fairly sure that the dog will not break, drop the lead and try a little further away and so on.

Again, when you return to your dog and move around to the proper heel position and signal that the exercise is over, praise the dog.

6. Down The down command is most easily accomplished from the sit position. Push the forearms or elbows to the ground, saying 'Down'. This is a **submission** exercise. The dog is submitting to your authority, and some dogs have difficulty in learning this successfully. Once this hurdle is over, teaching the dog to 'stay' in the down position is relatively easy.

In wet weather, dainty dogs that do not like getting their feet, let alone their tummies, wet often refuse to do the down exercise.

Rules when ■ Teach one exercise well before going on to the next exercise.
training ■ All exercises are taught by **repetition, kindness and reward** with
your dog pats, play sessions and little snacks given after a successful session.

Training at This means training *with* you. It is rarely successfully if other people do
obedience it *for* you. Obedience schools are very good, and necessary, for:
school ■ Socialisation with other dogs and other people.
■ Making the dog a socially more acceptable animal.

Sending a dog away for training is useless unless you also go to learn as well. If training has to done elsewhere for you, you must learn the commands and practise often, especially during the following few months.

Serious training for obedience should be *an enjoyable sport*, for both the dog and the owner. There is nothing nicer than to see the dog enjoying itself at an obedience trial.

SHOW TRAINING

For show training, formal obedience training is not particularly desired. In obedience, the dog is trying to show you how well it can do something and is watching you all the time, waiting for the next command. In the show ring the dog is showing itself off to the judge and the people around the ring. Showmanship is an art. You, the handler are presenting your dog in the best possible way to exhibit its good points and hide (or minimise) the bad. A good dog that has 'presence' will catch the judge's eye time and again. Teaching your dog to stand, look alert, cheerful or dignified (depending on the breed) and so on, can take years, but it is as important as cleanliness and good grooming in overall show ring presentation.

1. Basic lead training (see above).

2. Teach the dog to stand and stay in the show position. Smaller breeds need to be taught to stand on a show table. Teaching a dog to stand in a show position is a matter of repetition and patience.

Stand the puppy in the approximate position or 'stance' that is applicable to the breed, hold the lead/collar up slightly in one hand (the right), and run your left hand along the side of the puppy saying 'stand, stand'. When you run you hand along, run it slightly under the belly, so if the puppy is sagging in the middle or is starting to sit down on the job, this encourages it to stand (or you raise it with your hand as you go). Even if it holds the position for just a few seconds, praise the puppy, pat it on the side and allow it to relax. If the puppy fails to respond, which is very common, give it a slight tap on the side both as mild discipline and a reminder of the matter in hand, and try again.

As the puppy learns to hold position, the length of time in the stand increases. Always give the puppy a congratulatory pat on the side or head at the end, to signal the 'end of the exercise'. The puppy learns to associate the pat not only as praise for being good, but as a sign to relax. Again a small titbit as bribery at the end of a session will keep the puppy keen to work next time.

Never train a puppy to show stand with a check chain when very young. Use a show collar that is soft and not too narrow for the breed, as the lead/collar is used as a bar or band for the dog to lean into as it is being held. If held on check, it can be very uncomfortable and the puppy will fidget or lean backwards to get away from the check chain.

A strong, heavy, older male dog or bitch that is obstreperous in the ring obviously needs to be shown on a check chain. However, if they have been taught that they are not going to be hurt when in a stand as a puppy, they will remember and not boat or bridge backwards. I allow a dog to slightly lean into a 'stand' so as to make its front look as good as possible.

Many people when they are training a puppy, will practise in front of a mirror if there is no one else to help them while training. This is very helpful as it allows you to see from the judge's viewpoint. Handlers are often amazed at the difference between how the dog looks from where they are standing (over or behind their dogs) to the view in the mirror. As they will then realise how the dog looks from a distance on the show side.

Know your dog's faults. If it has a steep front, get the dog to stand with its forelegs well under it, so as to create the impression of better angulation of the front. If the dog is very narrow in the chest, when picking the front half up to place it, spread your fingers slightly under the chest and push the elbows a little wider apart, so the dog lands on the ground looking correct. There are lots of little 'tricks of the trade', but they all take years to learn. Meanwhile, remember, the judges are dog breeders as well, and you can't fool them all (but you can have fun trying!).

Teach the puppy to allow its mouth to be examined by different people. Many exhibitors are, to my mind, too rough with puppies' mouths. If they are teething (4–6 months), the puppies have very sensitive gums and may become mouth-shy if handled without due consideration to this condition. Gently lift the lips up and look from side to side, as well as examining the bite — you do not have to apply a grip like death and/or force the mouth open; a quick glance, particularly with a baby puppy is quite sufficient for most judges.

3. Teach the puppy to do straight out and back, triangle, etc. This is really an extension of lead training. Again, breed peculiarities come into play as the method of exhibiting differs somewhat between breeds. The stand for examination is extended slightly for the ring situation, where the mouth and testicles in the males are also quickly examined whilst in the stand position.

'Out and back' is taking the dog away from the judge for 7–10 metres to see the hind legs in action from the rear, turning and coming straight back to the judge, showing how the front legs are during movement when viewed from the front.

Next the judge usually requests the exhibitor to move the dog out and around the ring in either a triangle or a lap of the ring. This gives the judge an opportunity to see how fluid the dog is in overall gaiting action, how all the parts flow together, particularly in side action. The reach (length of forequarter stride) and drive (the push or thrust developed by the hindquarter) are being assessed and the balance of the two is all important. Characteristic motion belonging to particular breeds is also taken into account.

A dog with long, loose hocks can be made to look better by slightly pulling back on the lead (with the dog pulling out in front marginally, this throws the dog back onto its hocks a little, having the effect of presenting a firmer picture). Returning towards the judge, a dog with loose elbows will look considerably better if slightly pulled up (so that it is not taking the full weight on the elbows).

These and other tricks in handling can be seen if you watch and try to figure out how it is done. The art of handling is to try to fool the judge without looking obvious, and so create the best possible picture of your exhibit. If you are too obvious, the judge will notice, and the fault which you wish to hide becomes very noticeable to an experienced person, particularly the judge and also a fair few fellow exhibitors.

Ring etiquette is an area that is seldom covered anywhere. There are certain accepted invisible 'rules' of conduct within a show ring, and offensive behaviour will lose you points with both the judge and other exhibitors.

Basically, the 'rules' are good manners between exhibitors, politeness to the judge, and most important of all, do not interfere with the other exhibits.

The last 'rule' is the most commonly broken one. A pushy exhibitor may overshadow or crowd your dog, thereby obscuring the view of the judge examining the class. This usually happens in the gaiting section of the class, when all exhibits being considered for places, are being moved together around the ring just prior to final placings. Crowding another exhibit upsets many dogs, particularly terriers, and often the blame belongs not to the dog who played up, but to the dog behind (and in reality the handler of that exhibit).

All exhibitors see the dog ring as a three ring circus, where you win some and you lose some: it can seem this way for both the judge and the exhibitor. Watch the handlers that consistently win and learn to show your dog to advantage, because a poor handler can (and does) ruin many a good dog's chances of winning.

At the end of a day at a dog show, always remember:

1. No judge is infallible.

2. The perfect dog has yet to be bred.

3. Your dog may not be the world beater that your slightly biased eyes see it as; and, finally, the best rule of all,

4. Another day, another dog show!

The fourth point means that you should not get rid of your dog because of one judge's opinion, particularly if it is a puppy that can change tremendously before rounding out as an adult. Very few judges (and breeders) are good at picking a puppy that will be a world beater throughout its show career, and many ugly gawky puppies grow into relative swans after the puppy horrors (the 6–12 month stage in many breeds). Every judge has their own ideal image of a particular breed, and that image varies considerably from judge to judge, but a good dog will do consistently well under nearly all judges.

Within the different breeds there is considerable specialisation of showing procedures, in particular stances and grooming. Get to know what is desired or acceptable in your breed. If you have a long coated breed, attend club grooming days, ask your breeder for advice and so on.

Novice owners, upon entering the previously unknown world of dog showing, will need to take time to learn the basics, and in the process are bound to make just about every mistake in the book. Take heart, the majority of people you are competing against have made precisely the same sort of horrendous bloopers. Make all your mistakes with your first dog and the second will greatly benefit from your increased knowledge. Good luck!

7

Care of the Pregnant Bitch

I f you have decided to mate your bitch, consider *why* you want to breed a litter. Do you wish to keep a puppy or do you intend primarily to mature the bitch? Have an objective in mind before you start; ideally you should aim to obtain a better dog or bitch.

Keep in mind that there will be other puppies in the litter besides the one you wish to keep and they should all be as sound, both physically and mentally, as you can produce. If you have a highly neurotic bitch, a litter may steady the bitch down, but what of the puppies? If the line is noted for dogs with temperament problems, don't breed any more of that particular line. This will only give you as the breeder, and the breed as a whole, a bad name.

Similarly, if the bitch has a bad physical or genetic problem, e.g. severe hip dysplasia, you will only do yourself and the breed a disservice to mate the bitch. *If you cannot guarantee that the puppies will be able to lead reasonably healthy lives of normal length, don't breed the bitch.*

The same applies to the dog that you choose to mate to your bitch. The dog should be sound in temperament and reasonably free of major genetic problems. Generally, a breeder is ten times more selective of a male as a stud, than they are of a bitch. Read chapter 16, Genetics and the Importance of Breed Soundness; if you do not want to delve into the subject in greater depth, at least read the section on Selection at the end of that chapter.

Age of First Breeding a Bitch

If you are going to mate a bitch, wait until she is at least 15 months of age. The actual age is not of vital importance unless the bitch is either too young or too old. Some breeds, especially the smaller toy and terrier breeds, mature very quickly and can have their first season at 6–7 months of age. *I do not suggest that any bitch be bred from under 12 months, preferably an absolute minimum of 15 months of age.* Larger breeds may not have their first season until 18–24 months of age and can still be immature.

If mating occurs on the first season while under 12 months (and I hope by accident only), the pregnancy that results can stunt the bitch's growth particularly in the larger breeds. It also means that the stress of pregnancy will drain the bitch far more than it would if she had finished maturing. Bitches of this age group commonly have difficulties in whelping as their pelvis may not have reached ideal size.

The age a bitch first comes into season is generally governed by weight. The sooner a bitch reaches three-quarters of her mature adult weight, the earlier the bitch may come into season. This is why the smaller, fast maturing breeds can have their first season so young. The larger breeds, or should I say the slower developing breeds, may not reach three-quarters of their mature weight until 18–24 months, especially if the bitches concerned are light in condition. Some of these bitches are hyperactive, and the only way to keep the weight on them may be to kennel them up for most of the day.

Health of the Bitch

The actual age that a bitch is first bred from is not so important as long as it is not too young. *The most important thing is that the bitch is healthy and in good condition.* By good condition I mean not too fat and not too thin. A bitch will not conceive well if she is too far either way from her ideal weight. If a bitch is too fat, especially for a first litter, she can often have fertility problems including low conception rates, whelping problems with slow parturition or inertia, and possibly sizing problems with puppies too large or too small.

On the whole, conception is better when the bitch is in good normal condition rather than overweight. Hyperactive bitches or those that are in very hard working condition often have poor fertility or irregular seasons.

I would not suggest that any bitch is left later than 4–5 years of age for a first litter. This also varies according to the breed. Some breeds e.g. Great Danes, are by this age fairly elderly. The oldest I would suggest breeding a maiden Great Dane bitch would be four years.

How Often To Breed

The average bitch will cycle every 6–8 months. Some breeds come into season very infrequently e.g. Basenjis, which only cycle once a year. Other bitches may come into season more frequently, some even as often as every 2–3 months.

SMALL BREEDS

Very small breeds, e.g. Chihuahuas, are heavily depleted of calcium and other minerals during pregnancy and lactation, even with a few puppies. This is due to the enormous strain placed on the reserves of the bitch from the ratio of the total weight of the puppies to the weight of the bitch, which is proportionally so high. It is not a good idea to breed these smaller bitches on consecutive seasons without greatly increasing the chances of milk fever and the possibility of pregnancy toxaemia.

LARGE BREEDS

With the larger breeds, the total weight of the puppies to the weight of the bitch is proportionally far less than it is for the small breeds. Because of this, bigger breeds can be safely bred on two consecutive seasons with little trouble providing the bitch is healthy and in good condition. If a bitch of a bigger breed has only a few puppies per litter, then a third litter could be bred, but this is the maximum in my view. After this the bitch should have 8–12 months rest.

Bitches that cycle very irregularly, e.g. every 12–15 months, obviously have plenty of time to recover and replenish minerals between litters, and could therefore be bred each season if need be.

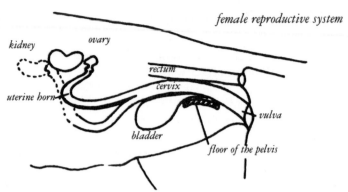

female reproductive system

Seasons

A season lasts for three weeks on average and there are three stages; **proestrus, oestrus** (true), and **dioestrus**. The first stage lasts for 7–10 days, the second for 4–7 days and the last stage for seven days.

Some bitches may stay in season as long as 4–6 weeks. This is uncommon, but may occur particularly with the bitch's first season. If this occurs, it is usually just after winter when there is a rapidly increasing day length which can bring young developing bitches into season a little early, making the season rather long. Bitches that have a season like this should not be given hormones to send them out of season. It is better to leave them alone to allow their hormones to readjust without interference. In older bitches that have prolonged seasons, this can be an indication of ovarian problems.

PROESTRUS

When a bitch comes into season, the vulva swells and there is a bloody discharge. This is called **proestrus** and usually lasts 7–10 days, but can last up to 12 days. Usually the bitch is swabbed on the third or fourth day. I prefer to wait until this time before swabbing the bitch, as by now the cervix is relaxed and there is a fairly true discharge from the uterus. If the swab reveals a growth there is usually plenty of time to treat this with antibiotics prior to mating.

Many veterinarians are dubious about the value of swabbing as it can be difficult to obtain a true indication of whether or not the bacteria present constitute a significant problem, i.e. will they affect fertility. It is difficult to decide, but in the interests of the genuine cases of uterine infections (around 10–20%), then it is a very worthwhile exercise. When bitches are going to outside stud dogs where you are paying a stud fee, the cost of the swab is minimal in light of other expenses yet it can give the owner of the bitch (and the stud dog owner) considerable peace of mind.

At this time I would suggest you make sure that the bitch is up to date on her vaccinations and worming. Some people prefer to vaccinate at the fifth or sixth week of pregnancy. Either method is quite acceptable. The main point is that the bitch's maternal antibodies should be high in order to give the puppies maximum protection possible during the first two months of life.

Male dogs are interested in the bitches at this time, but the bitches usually will not let them mount. Experienced stud dogs will not take any notice of the bitch until she is ovulating. Occasionally a bitch may stand for males for almost the entire season, but this is not common.

OESTRUS

This usually lasts 4–7 days. Counting from the start of the season, this can be anywhere from day four to day 16. On average, oestrus occurs between the tenth and fourteenth day from the start of the season. The blood discharge will usually change to a pale straw colour. This is the stage where the bitch will start to accept the male.

True oestrus lasts 3–4 days on average, and usually the best time to first mate a bitch is 48 hours into true oestrus. Oestrus can be detected by a 'smear' which will indicate when the bitch is ready. On a smear the cells on the slide are very thin, flattened out ('cornified'), and the nuclei have disappeared or are ghostly outlines.

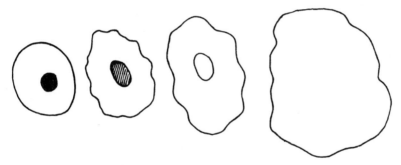

Usually this coincides with the bitch 'standing', i.e. swinging the tail to the side as soon as you touch the vulva and standing well when you press down on the back. The bitch will usually be fertile on the third or fourth day of the oestrus. The sperm will live at least 48 hours inside the reproductive tract (they can theoretically live for up to 5–6 days). Fertilisation generally occurs some 48–72 hours after ovulation, and takes place in the fallopian tubes. I generally prefer to mate a bitch 24–48 hours after first standing or when the smear indicates that she is ready and again 48 hours later, to try to catch the maximum ovulation period.

DIOESTRUS (METOESTRUS)

This can last 4–7 days and is the closing stage of the season. Keep the bitch locked up until the swelling of the vulva goes down and once all signs of discharge and swelling disappear, the bitch can be allowed to run with other dogs. Some bitches will accept other male dogs, particularly ones that they are used to running with for longer than normal, i.e. past ovulation and occasionally up to 7–10 days later. These same bitches may go to bite a strange male while still allowing a 'friend' to mate them.

ANOESTRUS

This is when the bitch is not in season. Some bitches have very long intervals between seasons, occasionally as long as two years. These bitches commonly have inactive ovaries. Particular breeds of dogs only cycle once a year, e.g. the Basenji and the Dingo. If you suspect an infertility problem in your bitch where she has very irregular cycles, read chapter 12, Common Breeding Problems of Bitches.

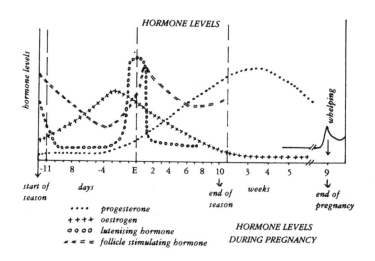

HORMONE LEVELS

start of season

days

end of season

weeks

end of pregnancy

• • • •   progesterone
+ + + +   oestrogen
○ ○ ○ ○   lutenising hormone
◄ ◄ ═ ═   follicle stimulating hormone

HORMONE LEVELS
DURING PREGNANCY

Mating the Bitch

When the bitch is ovulating, she will 'stand' for the dog. The majority of bitches will allow the dog to mount them and be mated with little or no objection. Experienced bitches will practically rape the male if he is inexperienced or slow at finding the right spot!

Once the stud dog has penetrated the vulva, he will work hard for a minute or two, and as the gland of the penis swells, the gland locks the penis inside the bitch so that the dogs are 'tied' while the dog ejaculates into the bitch. The length of tie basically depends on the dog. The average tie lasts 15–30 minutes but each dog has a fairly regular time that is particular to that dog. Occasionally a bitch may develop a muscle spasm that can keep the dog in for longer than normal, but this is rare. If this happens and the dogs have been tied for over an hour, an antispasmodic injection can be given to the bitch which will allow her to relax after 10–15 minutes.

It is often necessary to hold the dog and bitch together when they are tied. Some dogs are slower to swell in the glands and may 'slip' out if not properly tied. Occasionally when a dog has entered a bitch and has started to swell, particularly if the dog is well endowed in that area, a bitch may suddenly decide that this is not for her. She may wriggle, moan and groan, attempt to lie down or attack the dog. Too much of this sort of activity can cause considerable damage to the dog if he is not supported. Dogs in the street may stand up to this, but a valuable stud dog cannot afford to be bitten or otherwise damaged. If he is bitten, apart from the damage to the dog, he may become reluctant to mate other bitches, especially if he is fairly inexperienced.

Some bitches may attempt to bite the stud dog or refuse to stand. Provided that the bitch is definitely ovulating, the bitch may then have to be muzzled and held firmly to be mated. If the stud dog has trouble either entering the vulva or being able to get a 'tie' and the bitch objects strenuously, the bitch should be taken to your vet and examined internally in case there is an obstruction. Occasionally the bitch may have a persistent hymen and/or a frenulum of tissue dividing the vestibule. In several breeds, the bitches commonly have very small and tight vulvas, e.g. Cairn Terriers and Collies. There is more detail given about matings in chapter 11, Stud Dogs.

Two matings, 48 hours apart, are quite sufficient for the average bitch. When the bitch first stands for a dog, I tend to wait 24 hours and then mate the bitch. A repeat mating 48 hours later gives you, the breeder, a very good chance of covering the peak fertilisation period. If the bitch is mated over a longer period of time, it becomes difficult to determine when the puppies should arrive; limited matings give a more exact range of whelping dates.

If the bitch has an obstruction or is very small in the vulva, an artificial insemination (AI) can be carried out. Obstructions should be removed if possible but if the obstruction is small, it will tear by itself while the bitch is whelping. Unfortunately, most obstructions are not noticed until the time of mating and many owners do not want their bitch anaesthetised unless the obstruction is fairly major. Removing the obstruction can make the bitch rather sore for a normal mating in that season. This means that the bitch will usually have to have an AI that season.

Occasionally a bitch may be too dependent psychologically on humans to accept a male dog and is another candidate for an AI.

ARTIFICIAL INSEMINATION

I suggest this only be done by very experienced dog breeders or preferably by your veterinarian.

Artificial insemination is very useful for bitches that cannot be mated naturally or who will not allow dogs to mount them. With elderly dogs or dogs that have had accidents that preclude natural matings, AI may be the only method.

To collect the semen from the dog and transfer it into the bitch is not very difficult. All that is needed is a collection jar and a length of tubing. The equipment used should be sterile and above all, dry. Any water or blood will destroy the sperm. I personally use sterile syringe casings combined with part of a rubber glove. All of this can be thrown out after use or you can re-sterilise the syringe casing. As the syringe casings come in different sizes, there is a fair variation of sizing to fit the different sized dogs. Some people manage to collect the semen with a glass container.

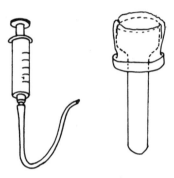

The main point to remember is that the semen must remain warm and away from direct light at all times. To get the dog to ejaculate, put the bitch in front of the dog and gently but firmly slide the skin up and down over the glands area. The dog generally gets the idea very quickly. Continue to hold the dog firmly on the glands once the dog has fully swollen and is ejaculating into the container. The ejaculate comes in several sections — first the prostatic fluid, then the semen followed by fluid from the various accessory glands. After about three minutes, there is generally sufficient material for an insemination. The quality of the sperm can be visually estimated; it should be a dense milky white, which then gets diluted by the accessory gland fluids. Keep the collection warm at all times. The seminal fraction is the most important.

To inseminate the bitch, I use a disposable dog urinary catheter which is soft and flexible enough to be introduced up the vagina without causing damage. The catheter is gently manipulated forwards as far as it can go (at least as far as the front of the pelvis). The urinary catheter is very useful as a syringe can be attached to the end.

The syringe and the catheter should be kept warm while the semen is being collected — normally held next to the body. The semen is then transferred from the collection jar into the syringe. I have one person holding the syringe (to keep it warm), while I insert the catheter into the bitch. The syringe is then attached to the catheter and the semen is slowly pushed into the bitch, stimulating the clitoris gently at the same time. This causes the uterus to contract as it would when the bitch is being mated normally by the dog and assists the semen to be drawn up into the uterus. When the semen is all inside the bitch, keep stimulating the clitoris for a further 1–2 minutes, then gently remove the catheter. Send the owners and the bitch out for a little run. Try to keep the bitch as calm and placid as possible during the whole process.

As with normal matings, repeat the insemination 48 hours later.

RECENT ADVANCES IN BREEDING CONTROL OF BITCHES

Blood tests to determine the progesterone levels in the bitch have been developed which give both the breeder and the veterinarian a greater degree of accuracy of timing the events as they occur within a season. ELISA tests will give a broad outline of the changes occurring, whereas a progesterone assay (using a radioactive labelling test) will give an extremely accurate reading. Progesterone assays are a must with bitches being inseminated with frozen semen and are very useful for bitches travelling interstate or with a history of poor fertility.

As a rough guide, the following progesterone levels equate to:

LH Surge (stimulus for ovulation) 1.5–2.0 mg/mL (4–5.6 nmol/L)
Ovulation   5.0–5.5 mg/mL   (15–18 nmol/L)
Fertile period   10–30 mg/mL   (30–90 nmol/L)

Time between events (average)
LH to ovulation 2 days   Ovulation to fertilisation 2–3 days.

POINTS TO REMEMBER WHEN MATING YOUR BITCH

1. Make sure your bitch is ready for mating before going to the dog. This can be done by a smear test by your vet to examine the state of the cells lining the vagina or more accurately nowadays by a blood test to check the progesterone level. If you have a experienced reliable stud dog in your backyard, one who is only interested when the bitch is ready, he can be very useful. When he decides the bitch is ready and she is backing up to your dog, wait 24 hours and then go the stud dog.
2. If you are travelling any great distance to the stud dog e.g. five or six hours by road or a short flight, I would definitely have the bitch blood tested to determine the progesterone level prior to travelling. The stress of travelling and changing surroundings can delay events by several days, particularly with nervous bitches.
3. Nervous and/or neurotic bitches often fail to conceive when left somewhere strange to be mated. This means that they are not good candidates to be sent away to stud dogs, particularly for the first litter.

ETIQUETTE AND THE STUD DOG OWNER

There are several points of etiquette that should be observed when using an outside stud dog. As a stud dog owner myself, it has amazed me that some bitch owners think that because the dog is at stud, ordinary courtesies can be ignored. The stud dog owner, contrary to popular opinion, owns the dog and may choose to refuse your bitch.

The polite method of inquiring about a stud dog is to inform the owners that you would like to use the dog, which bitch you are thinking of mating to him and some facts about her bloodlines and show history. A stud dog owner naturally prefers to have bitches of an above average calibre and of suitable bloodlines to go to their dog. Ask for copies of the dog's pedigree and relevant certificates.

Once it is agreed that the bitch can go to the dog, give the approximate time when the bitch is due into season. When the bitch does come into season, ring the stud dog owner and tell them of the good news, giving an approximate date of mating if you know when the bitch is normally mated. This allows the stud dog owner to plan around other bitches coming to the dog. Make sure your bitch is swabbed and if carrying an infection, is treated before going to the dog.

Care of the Bitch in Whelp
The most important points are good nutrition and exercise.

FIRST THREE WEEKS
During the first three weeks (trimester) of pregnancy, do not give extra food or vitamins as the bitch is not under any great demand at this stage. During these first delicate weeks, rapid developmental changes are taking place. This means that the developing foetus is particularly sensitive to external temperature and chemicals. Do not worm or treat with heavy doses of chemicals during this time. During excessively hot weather, care must be taken that the bitch is kept reasonably cool in the heat of the day, especially during the second and third weeks.

The bitch can be examined at 3–4 weeks after mating for pregnancy diagnosis if need be. The first signs of pregnancy are enlarged nipples, the still enlarged vulva and a slight swelling behind the ribs. The bitch should be re-checked at 5–6 weeks.

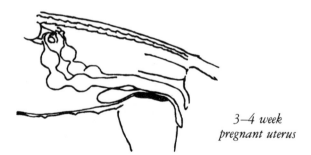

3–4 week
pregnant uterus

During pregnancy keep a check on any discharges. There is usually a clear discharge (slight) all the way through pregnancy but if there is a very heavy-coloured and/or smelly discharge at any stage, take the bitch to your vet for a check.

SECOND THREE WEEKS

During the second trimester of pregnancy, food can be slightly increased by one-quarter to one-third more than normal. If the bitch is already rather overweight, do not increase the food. It is particularly important that a maiden bitch does not become overweight with her first pregnancy as this occasionally results in very large puppies. Repeat breeders tend to 'size' the puppies much better.

If your bitch was overweight at the beginning of the pregnancy, *do not* put her on a diet during pregnancy. Keep the food level constant rather than create a strain on her system, as dieting a pregnant bitch can cause pregnancy toxaemia which can kill her.

Vitamins and calcium can be added to the diet *in moderation*.

Usually I ask for the bitches to come in at 5–6 weeks for a check-up. Vaccinate at this stage if not up to date. Worm the bitch at 5–6 weeks and repeat at seven weeks, but no later. Make sure that what you use to worm your bitch is suitable for use on pregnant animals.

It is a good time to check the health and weight of the bitch. Don't get the bitch too overweight as overweight bitches are often very slow whelpers. A good check on the weight is to run your fingers over the ribs of the bitch; they should have a light layer of fat present, not centimetres of it.

LAST THREE WEEKS

Feed the bitch twice daily up to twice her normal intake. The amount varies according to the bitch, her weight and the size of the litter she is carrying. As the bitch's uterus starts to occupy more and more space, the bitch can only eat smaller amounts at any one time. If a bitch is carrying a particularly large litter, it may be necessary to feed her three times a day.

I do not suggest worming the bitch in the last two weeks as it can upset the gut or put her off her food. Some compounds may be too strong and could possibly cause irritation to the uterus. Stick to bland, one-day type wormers during pregnancy.

Calcium should be doubled in the last two weeks of pregnancy, particularly in the smaller breeds as the calcium drain is proportionately higher. If using chelated calcium tablets, you may need up to one tablet per 10 kg with the small breeds. If you have a bitch that has a tendency to develop milk fever, then you may need to go as high as one tablet per 4 kg in the last week, and keep this up during the period of lactation. Larger breeds only need one tablet per 15–20 kg, and mainly in the last three weeks of pregnancy.

I usually re-check the bitch at eight weeks or the last 5–6 days prior to whelping. The bitch is usually starting to 'drop' the bulk of the puppies down and back towards the pelvis by this stage.

Pregnancy Toxaemia

Pregnancy toxaemia is a metabolic disorder which can occur in the pregnant bitch and is seen mainly in the last two weeks of pregnancy in the smaller breeds carrying large litters. The reason for the toxaemia is the drain of nutriments (primarily sugars) that the growing puppies require from the bitch. If the bitch is small and is carrying a large litter (for her breed), then the strain on the body's resources can be in excess of what the body can cope with. Because of this, the body then starts to break down its own reserves in an effort to maintain the pregnancy. Toxic side effects from excessive tissue breakdown make the bitches weak and nauseated, thereby decreasing a food intake that may have been inadequate to start with.

The symptoms of pregnancy toxaemia are depression, lethargy, weakness, lack of appetite and vomiting. Pregnancy toxaemia can also lead to the deaths of first the unborn puppies, followed quickly by that of the mother if it is not treated fairly rapidly. If these symptoms are noticed, the sooner the bitch is examined by your veterinarian the better.

Treatment consists of replacing lost sugars and the quickest method is the use of intravenous fluids containing dextrose. Milder cases or those that are detected by watchful owners in the early stages, may respond to oral doses of glucose, honey or Energel®.

Factors which predispose a bitch to pregnancy toxaemia are as follows:
1. Small breeds carrying a large litter, especially Chihuahuas, Miniature Pinschers and Pomeranians.
2. Weight: either thin bitches or overly fat bitches.
3. Diet: inadequate amounts of food and a diet that is low in digestible proteins and energy sources.
4. Stress: nervous and neurotic bitches are at a far higher risk than placid bitches as they are disturbed by sudden changes to the environment.

The first sign of trouble noticed in these bitches is a failure to eat. If you have a bitch with any of the above predisposing factors, you must be particularly observant. These bitches can not afford to be off their food for longer than 24 hours and if they appear to be depressed or withdrawn, immediately start on some form of sugar replacement. If there is not a good response within a few hours, go straight to your vet.

Preparation for Whelping

The Bitch

Last 3–4 days prior to whelping

The bitch will usually whelp at 60–63 days (smaller breeds 63–64 days) after mating. Three to four days prior to whelping, the bulk of the puppies 'drops' down from the rib cage and then gradually shifts back. In the last 48 hours the bulk is half way between the end of the ribs and the front of the pelvis.

The bitch is near to whelping when you can feel a puppy close to the pelvis, i.e. within 5 cm of the front of the pelvis. She will start to lose a clear or creamy, thick discharge from about 24–48 hours before whelping — this is the cervical plug and should not be discoloured (i.e. green).

The milk starts to come from the back teats about 5–6 days prior to whelping, and gradually more easily from the teats further forwards. When you gently squeeze the front teats and the milk comes out very easily, whelping is usually 12–24 hours away.

The bitch is often very loose in her motions in the last 24 hours due to hormonal changes taking place at this time.

Many people are frenetic temperature takers at this stage. It is normal for the temperature of the bitch to drop 12–24 hours prior to whelping, from a normal 38.0°–38.5°C to around 37.2°–37.5°C. Remember, this drop can be of quite a short duration and may be missed, as occasionally a bitch's temperature may drop up to 36–48 hours prior to whelping. Temperature taking can be a *reasonably* sound indication of approaching parturition, but should be taken in context with other symptoms mentioned above.

FOOD

The bitch usually goes off her food the night prior to whelping, but not all bitches will do this and some will eat at any stage. Pregnant bitches, particularly if they are carrying a large litter, run out of blood sugars very quickly and can run the risk of pregnancy toxaemia if they are not eating any food. Energel® and honey are highly concentrated food supplements which are very good for keeping the bitch's blood sugar and energy levels up.

If the bitch is off her food for more than 24 hours, is depressed or has a discoloured discharge at any time during pregnancy, particularly in the last week, take the bitch to your vet.

If there is anything seriously wrong, the sooner the bitch has veterinary attention the better. If the owner is worried, I would rather see a bitch though preferably not during the middle of the night, unless she is actually in labour, than wait several days and end up with an emergency that might cost the lives of the puppies and seriously affect the health of the bitch.

If your bitch regularly has trouble either holding a pregnancy or has heavy discoloured discharges, care must be taken to prevent this in subsequent pregnancies. Read chapter 12, Breeding Problems in Bitches.

THE WHELPING BOX

Get the whelping box ready at least 4–5 days prior to whelping. Ideally it should be long and wide enough for the bitch to stretch out on her side.

It is a good idea to have a small bar about 10 cm high and 10 cm out around the sides — this is a roll bar to prevent the bitch from squashing the puppies. This is particularly necessary for the larger breeds, as many of the bigger bitches are careless when sitting down and can squash puppies very easily in the first few days.

Newspaper is the best bedding to use while the bitch is whelping. It is readily available, easily ripped up by the bitch, and soaks up excess fluids well. When the bitch has finished whelping, remove all the wet papers and replace them with new clean ones. Put an old blanket or sheet down on top of this and change this daily. Puppies need to be able to grip with their feet. People differ in their preferences for bedding materials. See the section below about bedding, and remember what not to use in summer!

TEMPERATURE CONTROL FOR THE FIRST TEN DAYS

Puppies cannot control their body temperature for the first 5–6 days of life. This makes them extremely vulnerable to fluctuations in temperature, *particularly the cold*. Puppies that have to cope with extremes of temperature use up their energy reserves trying to keep either warm or cool, depending on the season. Puppies will fail to thrive and can quickly die due to adverse temperature conditions.

It is, therefore, very important to be ready before the bitch is due to whelp. Have the whelping room secure from draughts and be prepared for the worst, be it summer or winter. It is better to be over prepared than be racing around desperately at the last minute, or after whelping, in order to save the puppies' lives.

- The easy way to check puppies is to touch them, they should be warm not cold to the touch.
- Puppies that are warm will spread out over the box.
- Cold puppies will huddle in a pile and be very grizzly.
- Hot puppies will spread out; if they are too hot, they will be screaming.
- At the right temperature, puppies are quiet and warm to the touch.

The puppies must be kept cool in the heat of the day if the temperature *In summer*
is high. If the puppies are very hot, they will be spread out all over the
box and will be yelling and screaming. If you find them like this, cool
them down by wiping them over with a wet cloth — they usually
quieten down very quickly. Give them a few drops of water once they
have settled. If the puppies are thirsty, keep giving the water slowly.
Once rehydrated, they will nurse from the mother.

The best way to keep puppies cool is to have a fan in the room. Have
the fan blowing over the box to circulate the air in the room but do not
have the fan blowing air directly onto the puppies. If it is very hot, place
wet towels under the puppies, but only over half the box. If the puppies
get cold, they will move off the towels.

The problem is obviously reversed during the colder months. It is harder *In winter*
to keep the temperature of the puppies constant, especially at night. Do
not use fan heaters as they cause the air to dry out and the movement of
air creates a chill effect. Use a bar heater or radiator instead. It is a good
idea to have an electric blanket under the puppies, or a heated whelping
box (well covered by a thick layer of papers with either a blanket or a
bean bag on top). Never have either of these at top heat as you may 'cook'
the puppies, i.e. they may overheat from underneath. Usually put the
box or blanket on low, or on medium if it is very cold during the first
couple of nights.

The best idea for conserving heat in winter is to create a 'cave' effect.
You can do this by having a lid on your whelping box or by placing a
table over the top of the whelping box. Place a blanket over the table and
drape it around the sides, leaving an entrance at the front. In this fashion,
any heat is kept in and around the puppies but remember that hot air
rises.

Bitches feel more secure in a 'cave' as it is natural instinct in the wild
to whelp in a den or cave. This method also considerably reduces your
heating bill as the bitch's heat is kept down near the puppies together
with whatever additional heating that you supply.

As a cheap but very effective means of heating the 'cave', hang an electrician's light inside the top and about 10–15 cm down from the ceiling of the cave. A 40 or 60 watt (for larger areas) light is ample to provide a steady heat source. With this type of heating, where the heat is kept in by the cave, no other heat source is required in the room. As the light globe is within a wire cage, it is safe to be left on even when the bitch is unattended.

After 7–10 days, the heat source can be turned off during the day, depending on the weather. By 14–20 days, it may be possible to turn the heating off at night. Any external heat source must be very safe in both position and stability of construction. Heaters should never be left where they can be knocked over.

The temperature of the whelping room should always be assessed from the puppies point of view, i.e. from near the floor, not where your head is when you are standing up in the whelping area.

Bedding materials

■ **Newspaper** is good, readily available, easily disposed of and quick and easy to change. Newspaper is excellent for whelping a bitch as it soaks up the fluids. Once the puppies are dry after whelping, and all the wet whelping papers have been removed and replaced with clean, dry paper, I suggest that a sheet (in summer) or a blanket (in winter), is put on top of the newspaper. The puppies have a tendency to slip and slide on the newspaper. The top covering and any damp newspaper should be changed at least daily.

■ **Straw** is too hot to use in summer as it retains a lot of heat. If you are going to use straw, I would be inclined to wait until after the bitch has whelped and been cleaned up before using it as it tends to retain the moisture and stick to the puppies. Straw should be changed regularly as it can get damp and mouldy; it also harbours fleas. It may get into the puppies' eyes once they start to open and can be the cause of conjunctivitis. Straw is commonly used in the colder climates, as it retains heat.

■ **Vet bed/Dry bed** is a synthetic material that was originally developed for the prevention of bed sores in humans. Vet bed is easily washed and has the advantage that any urine or fluids soak straight through it. Because the vet bed is nice and fluffy, it has however two major drawbacks. One disadvantage is that newborn puppies nuzzle into the vet bed trying to find a nipple to suck (mistaking it for mother). This in turn leads to the second disadvantage where puppies can inhale the fluff, which can cause severe respiratory distress.

The safe way to use this material is either to cover the vet bed with a sheet, or wait until the puppies are at least 5–6 days of age before using it. By 5–6 days of age, puppies have learned what 'mother' smells like and generally will not bother hunting for her in the depths of the vet bed.

■ **Bean bags** are good for use in the whelping box, especially in winter. The air between the beans retains the heat extremely well from an electric blanket (on the lowest level only). Bean bags are very good for prevention of and use with 'swimmers' as the beans shift under foot as the puppies move. This makes the puppies exercise more and they cannot lie flat, as the surface is constantly changing. The depth of the bean bag need be only about 10 cm.

■ **Sawdust** is not good for use under the puppies while they are still in the whelping box as it can cause skin and eye problems. After the puppies are up and about however, it is very good as it absorbs moisture well and faeces stick to it, but it must be changed regularly. Damp patches should be removed daily.

8

Whelping the Bitch

No matter how many books are read on the subject, few owners actually believe that their bitch will cope very well with little or no assistance during whelping. Others can go to the opposite extreme of ignoring the bitch entirely and leaving her to whelp on her own. (With some novice owners, this is quite understandable but owners' and bitches' temperaments vary widely. However I believe that the person who decided to mate the bitch (or the careless person who allowed the bitch to 'get out') has a responsibility at least to be present and give moral support to the bitch.

Support of the Bitch

Maiden bitches are often extremely dependent and will not let you out of their sight in the last day before whelping. If you go out, or are asleep they may wait with crossed legs until you appear so that they can deposit a puppy at your feet (with a great sigh of relief). Not all bitches are like this and the more independent bitches may insist on hiding under the house, shed or bed, strenuously resisting any attempts to bring them out into the open where they imagine everyone will try to steal their puppies.

To avoid all the variations, make sure the bitch has been well exposed to the proposed whelping area by sleeping or kennelling her in that area for at least a week prior to the due date. If the bitch is desperate for your presence, sit in the box (large breeds, obviously) or beside the box, and gently give her little tummy rubs but not too much or she will prefer this to actually whelping. If the bitch is coping very well, (the 'no fuss and bother' type), leave her more or less alone and sit in a chair on the other side of the room, getting up only to check if a puppy is still in the sack, or is particularly sluggish. Try to keep strangers out — viewing audiences are not required nor desired by the bitch, it is, after all, a fairly private affair.

Large-headed breeds, e.g. Pekingese, Dandie Dinmonts, Bulldogs (of all kinds), Bull Terriers, Staffordshire Terriers and Chihuahuas, must be watched closely during whelping, as they are all breeds that have puppies with large head size but the bitches often have small pelvic diameters.

Your presence and support, while not necessarily interfering, can greatly reduce stress in the whelping bitch, and the number of puppies that survive can be increased by judicious assistance, preferably by an experienced person based on a sound knowledge of what is occurring, how to cope with it, and how to avoid panic.

Normal Presentation

Puppies, unlike human babies, can present head first or rear end first with no appreciable difficulties. The chance of a puppy being born either way is evenly divided.

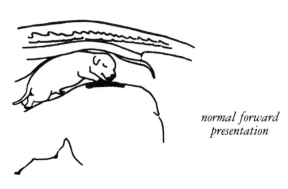

*normal forward
presentation*

Novices watching a bitch whelp for the first time are often horrified to see back legs appear, carrying this fear over from human 'whelpings', where breech births are uncommon and generally cause considerable problems. Breech births or rear end presentations are for the most part no more troublesome than forward presentations. The only time difficulties may occur is when the puppy in rear presentation has been wedged inside the bitch for a long period of time.

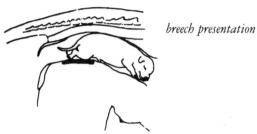

breech presentation

When the puppy is being expelled through the pelvis, the force of the contractions and the squeezing effect of being propelled through the pelvis, assists the lungs to be emptied of fluid. When a puppy is in breech presentation, the fluid is expelled but often re-inhaled to a certain extent as the head is still in the membranes. Thus a puppy wedged in the pelvis in rear presentation for longer than normal is more likely to have breathing difficulties once it is expelled than one in a forward presentation.

Afterbirths

Puppies, like humans, are surrounded by fluids and membranes during pregnancy which control the environment of the puppy. There is an inner and outer sack. The central part of the membranes (the placenta) is deeply embedded in the wall of the uterus in the form of a wide band. The puppy is attached to the placenta via the umbilical cord, through which it receives nutriment.

When the puppy is being expelled through the pelvis during birth, the pressure exerted breaks the membranes, leading to the term 'breaking water'. Occasionally a 'bag' may hang down from the vulva; this is just the outer bag that may not have broken and contains placental fluid. Leave this alone unless there is a puppy head or tail close by, as the fluid acts as a lubricant during contractions. If there is a puppy present, gently tear the bag open to allow the puppy to breathe.

Once the puppy has been born, the placenta (or 'afterbirth' as it follows the birth) may still be attached or the umbilical cord often breaks several centimetres from the puppy's stomach. The afterbirths may follow each puppy, but occasionally there can be several puppies born and then the afterbirths may follow in a little group. Do not panic if there is not an afterbirth with each puppy, just keep a rough count of the number of puppies to afterbirths and when the bitch has finished whelping, they should tally.

Normal Whelping

When the bitch actually goes into labour, there are three stages.

1. INITIATION OF PARTURITION

This is when the cervix is dilating and the first visible signs appear that the bitch is going into labour. The bitch is very restless, up and down, circling and ripping up paper. She is usually panting the whole time and constantly wanting to go outside and urinate, passing small amounts often. Some bitches have a very short (1–2 hours) first-stage labour, particularly the experienced bitches. First-stage labour can however, last as long as 12–24 hours in some cases, particularly with maiden bitches. Occasionally you find an odd bitch may appear to start, stop and then go into labour 10–12 hours later, but this is not common. This usually happens if there are too many people around and the bitch cannot get any privacy. Keep unnecessary people away while the bitch is whelping — the fewer present the better. Most bitches go off their food during the last 12–24 hours, but this is no foolproof indicator of approaching labour. No bitch should be off her food for more than 48 hours prior to whelping.

If this lack of appetite continues, take the bitch to your veterinarian for a check up to make sure all is well. Pregnant bitches cannot afford not to eat because of the danger of pregnancy toxaemia.

Delayed onset of parturition can also be due to the bitch being removed from her normal surroundings close to term. The less the bitch and her normal environment are disturbed in the last 5–6 days of pregnancy, the better. If the bitch is being whelped by someone else, away from her normal home, she should be installed and settled into her new environment at least a week (preferably two weeks) before she is due.

2. DELIVERY OF THE PUPPIES

This starts with the breaking of water, which means the foetal membranes have broken as the puppy is moving down close to the pelvis. As the puppy moves down through the pelvis, a bulge will develop under the rectum (anus) where the forward half of the outcoming puppy is pushing the vulva outwards.

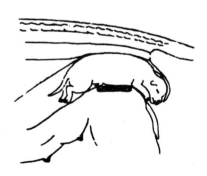

Once the puppy reaches the outer edge of the vulva, it is usually expelled fairly quickly. If the bag is unbroken at this stage, gently tear the membranes to allow the puppy to breathe.

A puppy is usually born within 20–30 minutes of the water breaking but it can take up to two hours. If a puppy has not appeared after 1–2 hours of the water breaking, ring your vet.

Most bitches will produce puppies without too much physical effort. Some bitches hardly seem to contract, yet the puppies appear to fly out as though jet propelled. Other bitches strain, groan and moan and make the most amazing sound effects for the birth of quite small puppies. Every bitch's pain threshold is different, like ours, but the smaller the breed the more discomfort shown would be a loose generalisation. Obviously very large puppies take more time and effort.

If a puppy is stuck half way out of the bitch, i.e. head or rear end presenting and not coming out any further after five minutes (10 minutes maximum), gently pull out and down, i.e. 45° out.

If head first, put your first two fingers — one on either side of the neck, just behind the head. Pull gently, and curl your fingers back into your hand as you pull.

If the rear end is presented first, pull above the hocks — never grab a puppy around the middle as you can rupture the puppy's liver. With a rear presentation where the head and shoulders are caught very firmly inside the bitch, gently put your little finger up the side and hook out one elbow. Repeat for the other side and then pull the puppy out and down. Once the shoulders are through, the puppy will pop-out very easily.

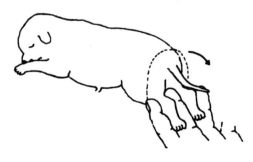

Pull with the bitch, i.e. as she pushes. If the bitch is very tired, she may not assist very much. The puppies tend to come in twos, one from each horn of the uterus so you will have two puppies being born fairly close together (10–30 minutes), then a break of ½–1 hour and then another two as the puppies gradually move down. If there is a large litter, the break between puppies tends to get longer towards the end as the bitch gets tired. Often if there is a large litter, the first 'half' will be born fairly quickly, then the bitch may have a break of 1–3 hours while the front half appear to shift down towards the pelvis. Once the 'break' is over, the bitch often gets back down to work and pops the second half out in reasonable time.

Some bitches will whelp very quickly whilst others are very slow. The average is one puppy per hour.

A fit bitch will usually whelp much faster than an overweight bitch. In the giant breeds, for example the St Bernard, the lack of muscle tone can create problems as the first half of the litter is usually delivered reasonably well, but then muscle fatigue sets in, reducing the chance of the puppies surviving up in the top (forward) end of the uterine horns.

3. EXPULSION OF THE FOETAL MEMBRANES

The afterbirths are passed either with or between puppies and the bitch is often very fast in cleaning the puppies and eating the afterbirths. This is quite a natural procedure and it is a good source of protein for the bitch, but it can cause her to vomit or have very loose motions after she has finished whelping. Generally, I allow the bitch to eat one or two afterbirths and then remove the rest as they arrive so that there is less cleaning up later on, but the bitch may still beat you to it!

When the bitch has finished, she will settle down, accept food and the panting will slow down. Some bitches do however have a rest mid-whelping, so be on your guard. A bitch that has finished whelping will have a reddish-brown discharge. If there is a green discharge, there are still more puppies or afterbirths. An empty bitch looks very 'hollow' in the flanks, unless she is very fat and has had only one or two puppies.

To be certain that the bitch has finished whelping and has passed all the afterbirths, take the bitch down to the vet several hours after you think she has appeared to be finished. If she whelped during the night (as 70–80% of bitches invariably do), wait until a respectable hour of the morning out of kindness to your vet, then take the bitch and the puppies for a check up and an injection to clean the bitch out.

If you think there is a problem and the bitch still has puppies left in her and it has been more than 3–4 hours maximum from the last puppy, ring your vet even, as much as I hate to say it, if it is in the middle of the night. Do try to consider the health of your vet before doing this. I like my clients with problem whelpers to notify me the day or night before they expect the bitch to whelp, so if there is trouble, everyone is (reasonably) organised around the situation.

With a bitch that is experienced and has whelped cleanly, passed all the afterbirths and settled down well, it may not be necessary to take the bitch to the vet. Ring your vet at a reasonable time, and explain how the bitch has whelped, how many puppies she has had and your vet will decide if there is a need to check the bitch.

Immediate Care of the Newborn Puppy

When puppies are born, occasionally the membranes may not have broken. Break these as soon as possible, wipe the puppy's face and nose and this will usually start a reflex breathing. If the puppy's chest sounds very moist and gurgly, the puppy may have to be shaken. To do this, support the head with one hand, the body with the other and swing the puppy out and down. Keep the puppy's head down while you give it a rub on the back and around the nose to clear any fluid.

If the puppy is weak as one can sometimes get towards the end of the whelping, it may be necessary to be fairly vigorous with your shaking and rubbing, but always support the head.

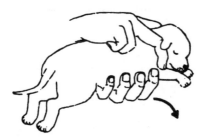

If the puppy is still sluggish despite the shaking, give it a couple of drops of brandy and water on its tongue or gums. Brandy is a heart stimulant so it can be very helpful with tired puppies. You can also add 1–2 drops of Calcium Sandoz (or a pinch of glucose powder) to the brandy and water, as it is a strong sugar solution as most tired puppies are also hypoglycaemic (lacking in sugar).

The recipe for this wonderful little mixture is:

1 drop of brandy

1–2 drops of Calcium Sandoz (or a pinch of glucose powder)

Mix with water to make up to 2 mL.

Have this mixture prepared before the bitch whelps so it is ready for use if needed.

Once the puppy is breathing reasonably easily, give it a rest. Gently rub the puppy on the chest and turn it over regularly until it picks up strength. After a rest of 5–10 minutes and if the chest is still very moist, give it another shake. Gentle taps on the chest will assist the clearing of the lungs. Lift the puppy to your ear and listen to either side of the chest to make sure it is clear.

The nose and feet of a puppy with clear lungs are nice and pink. If there is still a fair amount of fluid retained in the lungs, the puppy will have a 'bluish' appearance. Once the puppy is breathing regularly, give it a rest between bouts of rubbing and shakes, as too much may distress the puppy and it may die due to your over enthusiasm.

If the puppy has been expelled by the bitch, but is still attached by its umbilical cord, put your fingers on either side of the cord and go up as far as you can into the bitch, clamp your fingers and gently pull against the bitch. Never pull against the puppy. Usually the afterbirth will come out if you pull steadily. The cord may break as you pull, but the cord will usually stop bleeding if you hold it for 1–2 minutes.

When the cord breaks very close to the puppy, or the cord will not stop bleeding, clamp your fingers over the end and get some cotton or linen thread and tie around the base of the cord near the abdomen. Tie it firmly but *don't pull too hard* as the cotton can cut through the cord. Cut the knot off very close to the cord so the bitch cannot tug it off. The cotton will fall off with the cord when it dries out in 2–3 days.

If the cords are very long and/or the bitch does not eat the afterbirth or break the cord, cut off the afterbirth 8–10 cm away from the abdomen after 5–10 minutes with a blunt pair of scissors or tear it with your fingers. After a couple of hours when the cords are dry, cut them off about 5 cm from the abdomen, otherwise the cords can get tangled around the puppies' legs and toes and cut off the circulation.

Check the puppies for obvious defects such as cleft palates.

Healthy puppies are up and drinking from the bitch within two hours. Puppies may be rather clumsy to start with but once they have had a good drink, they are very quick to find the teat and will suckle vigorously. Puppies suckling will stimulate the natural release of pitocin, which in turn helps the bitch's uterus to contract, assisting the remaining puppies to be expelled. This same release of pitocin will occasionally cause the bitch to pant very heavily when the puppies are feeding, even after she has finished whelping and this may continue for some time. The uterus can still be over-sensitive to the pitocin release during the first 7–10 days and may cause concern for anxious owners about the restlessness of the bitch.

Assisting the Bitch

I find the best product to use is the chelated calcium tablets, e.g. Keylomin Calcium® tablets as they are rapidly absorbed and quite strong. For medium-sized breeds, I suggest one tablet per hour, one tablet per half hour when tired. For small breeds, give a quarter tablet and for large breeds two tablets.

Calcium given during whelping is particularly valuable in prevention of uterine inertia.

Calcium syrups can be helpful during whelping as the sugar in the calcium syrup will assist in keeping the bitch's energy levels up, however repeated high doses of the syrup can result in vomiting and very liquid diarrhoea due to excessive sugar intake.

Calcium is particularly important in those breeds or individuals that are highly strung or prone to milk fever. Some individuals become very stressed during whelping and can become aggressive towards their puppies as most commonly seen in Bull Terriers. High doses of calcium during and after whelping will reduce the incidence and severity of this problem. Highly strung or neurotic bitches will benefit most from the chelated calcium products. The average bitch will need little or no assistance during whelping, but in my opinion, someone should always be present to give the bitch moral support. Maiden bitches in particular are keen on having an owner present, and will rarely let you out of their sight in the last 1–2 days prior to whelping.

Medium-sized breeds generally whelp very easily and assistance is needed only if the bag fails to break, or where you need to shake a tired puppy at the tail end of whelping. Giant breeds are often very slow whelpers as they have a tendency to be slothful, especially in late pregnancy. Good exercise all the way through pregnancy can be very beneficial. Giant breeds may occasionally require a caesarean if they become too exhausted to push out the last few puppies when there is a large litter of 10–14 puppies. Small breeds and those possessing large heads, e.g. Bulldogs, Pekingese and Chihuahuas, can have difficulties due to small pelvic size (internal). Overweight bitches, especially when they are carrying a large load, can also be very slow whelpers.

Uterine Inertia

Uterine inertia means that the uterus stops working. The reasons for this can include lack of calcium, abnormal musculature of the uterus where it cannot contract properly, and too full a uterus, where the bitch cannot contract sufficiently to expel a puppy. There can also be uterine inertia due to exhaustion of the bitch. Lack of muscle tone generally, i.e. being overweight, and lack of exercise are responsible for many cases of uterine inertia.

Treatment

Try giving extra calcium at home initially but if there is no improvement within a few hours and the contractions are weak or non-existent, then the bitch must be taken to the vet. At the vet, the bitch is usually given intravenous (IV) calcium *slowly*. If calcium is given too fast IV can cause the heart to slow down excessively and develop irregular beats (this is why intravenous calcium *must* be given by a veterinarian). If the IV calcium does not get the bitch working, then a caesarean may be necessary.

Caesareans

Caesareans are occasionally necessary for the following reasons:

1. **Malpresentation of a puppy.** This may be transverse, head back or down, or the rear end presenting with the legs forward. Some malpresentations are able to be manipulated so that the puppy can be

pulled through the pelvis; unfortunately quite a lot of malpresented puppies are not able to be manipulated. If the bitch has been in labour for quite some time and the puppy is dead, then the body may be rather stiff and dry and therefore very hard to move. If the puppy has only been stuck for a short time, it is a lot easier to shift it. Another aspect of the problem concerns the remaining puppies jamming up behind the puppy that is incorrectly presented, making it very difficult to move or manipulate it into a better position.

2. **The puppy is too large.** Occasionally there is an outsize puppy within a litter which may be too large for that pelvis. This is more likely to occur in a small litter. Monstrosities (oversized, sometimes bloated, fluidy looking puppies, 'walrus puppies') can occur as well, but these are fairly rare.

3. **Too small a pelvis.** Several breeds commonly have this problem, notably Staffordshire Terriers, Dandie Dinmonts and Chihuahuas. You will note these breeds have one thing in common; they all have large heads in proportion to the body.

4. **Slowness.** Some breeds, e.g. St Bernards and Great Danes, are more likely to need a caesarean because of their large size and the large size of their litters. They often lose the second half of the litter because of the slowness at which they whelp. This is usually because the bitch is overweight and has poor muscle control. The possibility of this happening increases with the age and heaviness of the bitch.

5. **Uterine inertia.** The bitch's uterus will not contract properly.

6. **Damaged or malformed pelvis.** Fractured pelvises are a common injury in car accidents. They may heal very well with rest but there may be a reduced pelvic diameter as a result. If such bitches then try to have puppies, they nearly always require caesareans.

7. **Overdue bitches.** This is a tricky situation where the veterinarian (and the breeder) have to decide whether the bitch is ever going to whelp naturally and for how long it will be *safe* to leave the bitch before taking action. Occasionally this could be a difficult decision for both the owner and the veterinarian. When is too early and when is too late? Basically speaking there are four important points to consider; if the bitch is bright, eating well, the puppies are wriggling around happily inside and there are *no* discoloured discharges from the vulva; then it is safe to leave the bitch a little longer. But if you are doubtful of even one of these points, then take the bitch to the vet for a check-up.

Some breeds and individuals will go a little longer than average but it is very hard on the owner (and usually the vet as well) to wait until the bitch is finally ready. This can be particularly difficult with a maiden bitch where there is no previous history to rely on. The odd bitch may whelp 2–5 days late on a regular basis.

8. **Elective caesareans.** These are done when the previous history of the bitch is such that a caesarean is necessary on an elective basis, e.g. broken pelvis, too small a pelvis, inertia etc.

Aftercare of the Bitch and the Puppies

Veterinarians differ with regard to the use of anaesthetics and techniques. The larger breeds quite often are given an intravenous anaesthetic, whereas the medium to small breeds are often given a gaseous anaesthetic. Depending on the type of anaesthetic used, the recovery period for the bitch and the puppies will vary. Some anaesthetics have to be used with care as they can cause respiratory depression in the puppies, which are likely to be very sluggish and hard to revive after the operation.

Ideally, the anaesthetic used should *not* cross the placental barrier, and therefore would not affect the puppies.

The best results are generally from gaseous anaesthetics, where there is usually little or no respiratory depression in the puppies and the recovery for the bitch is very rapid. If the bitch is large, very boisterous, nervous or perhaps a borderline milk fever case, it may be advisable for the veterinarian to use an intravenous anaesthetic.

Most healthy puppies come out wriggling and breathing reasonably well. Some puppies however, particularly those of a bitch that has been in labour a long time, may be very sluggish when pulled out. Care is needed to see that all the fluids are expelled from the lungs of these puppies and respiratory stimulants, e.g. Dopram®, may be needed to initiate respiration if they are not breathing. Gentle shaking, rubbing of the chest and occasionally mouth to mouth respiration may be needed.

If the puppy is breathing, but is very weak, a few drops of water containing a very small amount of brandy and Sandoz (or glucose powder) is a good pick-up. As mentioned earlier this chapter, the brandy is a heart stimulant and the sugar in the Sandoz gives a source of energy. Many puppies that are sluggish not only after a caesarean, are hypoglycaemic, i.e. lacking in sugars. Puppies become hypoglycaemic through chilling and dehydration. Use one drop of brandy and one or two drops of Sandoz to make up 2 mL.

Once the puppy is gasping on a regular basis, give it a little break. Leave it lying on its side on a heating pad or hot water bottle and gently rub the chest to stimulate it. Turn the puppy over fairly often and after a few minutes rest — if the chest is still very fluidy, give it a couple of taps on either side of the chest and then another shake. Always remember to keep the head down while shaking and keep wiping the nose after each shake.

The puppies that are sluggish should then gradually start to regain 'tone'. From being limp, they will start to firm up, curl up in the hand and move around, as would a normal healthy puppy.

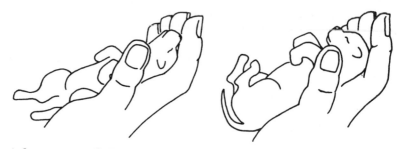

Aftercare of the Bitch Following a Caesarean

The majority of bitches recover quickly and with no complications from a caesarean. If gas has been used, the bitch is usually sitting up and taking notice of the world within 10 minutes. After an intravenous anaesthetic the bitch will take longer to recover, and it may be 1–2 hours before she is up on her feet. Regardless of what was used, the bitch should be watched carefully for the next few hours until she is really steady. While she is still under the effects of the anaesthetic she will be careless about where her feet go, and she may accidentally tread or lie on a puppy.

If the bitch was right on time, there should be minimal bleeding from the uterus. However, if the caesarean had to be performed before the bitch had gone into labour, there can occasionally be rather profuse bleeding into the uterus. The veterinarian will treat this with pitocin to shrink the uterus and use agents which will reduce the bleeding. Care must be taken to keep these bitches very quiet and to watch their colour. By this, I mean that the colour of the gums and the mucous membranes should remain pink not pale or white. If heavy bleeding continues from the vulva or if the mucous membranes are pale, ring your vet. Normally, the bleeding eases 10–15 minutes after the afterbirths have been removed during the caesarean.

Maiden bitches   Maiden bitches are a special case and require particular care. They do not have a chance to become maternal before they undergo the operation and wake up to a litter that arrived while they were asleep. Many maiden bitches have a tendency to look at the puppies and freak out. If they could faint, they would!

The best way for these bitches to accept the puppies is to get them, if possible, into their own surroundings. Alternatively, find them a quiet little corner without delay where they can have privacy and security. The average bitch will be somewhat bewildered for a short time, but will settle down very quickly if allowed complete peace and quiet. Stay with the bitch until she accepts the puppies and is steady on her feet. Make sure the puppies all get a drink within a few hours of birth.

Valium® injections may be required for the hysterical individuals who refuse to believe that the puppies are in any way related to them. The

Valium® relaxes the bitch and makes her more accepting of the puppies. It can be particularly useful in these cases if the bitch is given an injection of the drug before she is fully conscious.

Neurotic bitches may need to remain on decreasing doses for several days until they start to settle down and learn how to be mothers. Maternal bitches do not require doses of Valium®.

Once the bitch and the puppies have settled after the operation, the owner's first concerns should be the care of the wound, checking on discharges, and giving the puppies a small amount of yoghurt and possibly acidophilus tablets if the bitch is on antibiotics.

The wound

The majority of bitches are opened up down the mid-line for the caesarean. This means that if the bitch has a large milk production, then the wound may have a tendency to become damp. The bitch may also add to the problem by licking the wound. Try to keep the wound dry with antibiotic powders or a spray that tastes unpleasant. Do not put ointments on the suture line — keep it dry and gently clean with cotton wool twice daily. Stitches are usually taken out at 10 days post-operatively. If the suture line is not dry, the stitches are often left in a few days longer.

Discharges

Some bitches may not discharge for several days following a caesarean. Most bitches will discharge a reddish-brown mucous material that is rather thick. This discharge will continue off and on for the entire time that the puppies are feeding, as the bitch's uterus in this way is cleaned out and repaired, ready for the next pregnancy.

If a profuse heavy blood discharge continues, see your vet as soon as possible. Some bitches may need to be placed on vitamin K tablets (which helps the blood to clot) and given injections to reduce the bleeding. Excessive bleeding can occur after normal whelpings and the same treatment applies. These bitches should be kept very quiet and confined until the volume of discharge reduces.

Antibiotics

Most bitches are placed on antibiotics after the caesarean. The antibiotics can adversely affect the gut bacteria in the delicate intestines of the puppies. The puppies should be given natural yoghurt or lactobacillus acidophilus which help to maintain and return the gut bacteria to normal.

How Often and How Many Caesareans?

There are bitches that require caesareans every time they are mated. This can be because of anatomical abnormalities of the pelvis or the uterus. There are several breeds that have a high proportion of caesareans, e.g. Chihuahuas, Pekingese and Shih Tzus. The smaller breeds and those that have puppies with large heads and very heavy shoulders are more likely to have caesareans. Giant breeds that have poor musculature, e.g. Saint

Bernards, tend to be very sluggish whelpers and may require a caesarean to save the last few puppies. Bitches that have had fractures of the pelvis are also in this category.

If a bitch has had a caesarean, it depends on the cause as to whether it is likely that she will need to have a caesarean if she is bred from again. Consideration should be given to the value of the bitch's bloodlines; is it worth putting the bitch through all the trauma again? If the answer is yes, I like to give the bitch 12 months or a season free from breeding, before subjecting her to another caesarean.

The maximum number of caesareans desirable depends very much on the bitch. Consider how she copes with the operations, the amount of adhesions internally and the number of puppies that she has. The greater the number of caesareans, the more scar tissue and adhesions, and consequently a reduction in the number of puppies in the litter. On the whole, unless the bitch is an exceptionally good producer, three caesareans is a maximum for any bitch to endure. Even if the bitch is of very high quality, four caesareans should be her limit.

Care of the Bitch after Whelping

After all the excitement is over and the bitch has finished whelping and has settled down for a good rest, some people think they should disturb her rest in order to wash the bitch down. When a bitch has finished whelping, all I would do is to make sure that the bitch and the puppies are dry and warm and leave them to enjoy a good rest, especially in the middle of the night which is the time that most bitches finish whelping.

When the bitch has had several hours rest and is obviously finished, which is usually the next morning, then it is time to wash down or preferably sponge out any mess that is in the bitch's coat. Clean papers and bedding are essential and should be changed daily or more often if necessary.

Take the bitch to the vet for a check-up when she has finished. If all is well, it will not be necessary for you to contact the vet immediately, especially if it is in the middle of the night. Experienced breeders may be happy enough and knowledgeable enough not to need a 'clean out' injection of pitocin; but if the owner is inexperienced or if the bitch has a greenish discharge, then a visit to the vet's several hours after the bitch has apparently finished will give peace of mind and ensure that everything is out of the bitch, including any remaining afterbirths. If there is anything remaining and it is not removed, the dark discharge will continue and the bitch may be restless, depressed and off her food. She will be reluctant to lie down and feed the puppies for any length of time.

If in doubt, have the bitch checked!

Restlessness once a bitch has finished whelping can be due to several reasons. A common cause can be the pain of the uterus still contracting after whelping. When puppies drink from the bitch, there is a release of natural pitocin which allows the milk to let-down and also helps the uterus to contract, which is important during whelping and for the first few days following whelping. Once a bitch has had her puppies, the uterus gradually shrinks (involutes). Some bitches however, have spasms of the uterus which can be quite painful. Bitches which are overly sensitive to pitocin release and have uterine spasms will be very restless, pant a lot and be reluctant to lie down for very long.

These bitches may require an antispasmodic to allow the muscles of the uterus to relax. The best tablet I have found for this is Buscopan Compositum®, which is an antispasmodic and analgesic (pain killer). It is only necessary to use this for 4-5 days, by which time the uterus has settled down and is far less sensitive to pitocin.

Another common cause of restlessness can be the lack of calcium due to a strenuous whelping or insufficient calcium given during whelping. Bitches use up large amounts of calcium in muscle contraction, hence the value of giving calcium during whelping. If there is restlessness from this cause, it can usually be settled fairly quickly by giving several Keylomin Calcium® tablets.

FEEDING THE BITCH

The bitch should be fed 2–3 times her normal amount, depending on the litter size. In some cases the bitch will not eat well for the first week. If the bitch is not eating well, try to tempt her with milk custards or stews. It can be very helpful if you place the feed dish in the whelping box, where the bitch will often tuck into the food to stop the puppies eating it. Be careful however, as aggressive bitches may attempt to bite puppies that come near the food.

Avoid too much meat in the diet, particularly with the smaller breeds. Feed the bitch three times a day. With the very small breeds, if they are not eating enough or are losing too much body weight, give plenty of Energel®. If they won't eat readily it, stick it on the roof of the mouth (3–5 cm worth at a time). Most dogs really like it and will eat large amounts of it.

Calcium

The calcium given is proportionally higher for the smaller breeds as their output of calcium per unit of weight is greater. Also, the larger the litter the more calcium they will need.
Give either:
■ Keylomin Calcium® tablets — one tablet per 4-8 kg of the bitch's weight, depending on litter size. For bitches that are prone to milk fever, one tablet per 2–4 kg; or
■ Calcium Sandoz 10–15 mL twice daily; by 10 days increasing to 10–15 mL three times daily.

MILK FEVER (ECLAMPSIA)

Milk fever (Eclampsia) is due to a lack of calcium in the body to a degree which causes the animal to collapse. Calcium is not only used for the development of the bones, it is essential for the normal regulation of the contractions of muscle tissue. Too little calcium (hypocalcaemia) will cause muscle 'spasm' which is a trembling or twitching of the muscle, and a very rapid heart rate, resulting in the collapse of the bitch. The legs are extended, twitching, the breathing is extremely rapid and, if not treated, the bitch may die due to exhaustion of the heart muscles.

Small breeds and very **nervous** bitches are more likely to develop milk fever. The smaller the breed, the higher the litter number and the more nervous the bitch, the more likely you are too see this. If the bitch was bred the season before, she will be more likely to get milk fever, as she may not have had time to replenish her mineral supplies from the previous pregnancy. In proportion to their size, the smaller breeds produce more puppies per unit of weight than the larger breeds, so the demand on the resources of these small bitches is proportionally higher and must be taken into account. Breeds that are commonly affected include Chihuahuas, Cairn Terriers, Miniature Fox Terriers, Pomeranians and Cavalier King Charles Spaniels.

Bigger breeds very rarely develop milk fever as the proportional drain is not as high as with the little breeds. The only exception to this rule (on a consistent basis) is the Bull Terrier. The Bull Terrier appears to use large amounts of calcium during pregnancy and lactation. This terrier also has a tendency to live on its nerves to a large extent, which may account for the calcium loss. Bull Terriers may show early signs of milk fever or calcium deficiency by being particularly **aggressive** towards their puppies, which they may bite or kill. Breeders should be on the watch for this and start dosing the bitch with calcium at the first signs of aggression.

Stress is another very important factor in the incidence of milk fever. This particularly applies to the nervous, neurotic individuals. Bitches who are normally beloved house pets, are often locked up with their new litter, which they are not really sure they want, and are not allowed to be in among their familiar normal human family. Other bitches however, are very protective of their puppies and require a lot of privacy which they may not get with visitors 'viewing' the puppies at all times.

Insufficient calcium available during pregnancy and after whelping, especially when there is stress and large litter size, are contributing factors in bitches which develop the condition. Many of the smaller breeds in particular have inadequate diets or are picky eaters.

These little dogs become rather finicky during pregnancy and are often tempted with generous amounts of meat in the diet. This means that the availability of the calcium added to the diet is greatly reduced, resulting in a gradual loss of calcium during pregnancy. The bitch requires calcium in fairly large amounts to help the growth of the puppies and the supply of milk in addition to her own daily needs. Her needs increase with the size of the litter and her approaching parturition. In addition, there is the stress of whelping and the drain of calcium in the milk production for the puppies. By the time the puppies are two weeks of age, they have doubled or tripled their birth weight. This means that the drain of lactation increases dramatically as the demands of the puppies increase in proportion to their weight.

Milk fever usually occurs within three weeks of whelping. Bitches often refuse their food 1–2 meals before showing overt signs of the condition. The bitch is usually 'starry eyed', has a rapid respiration rate, shows a stiffness of gait, and occasionally may appear lame. The bitch will often go away from the puppies or refuse to feed them. She is usually running a high temperature and may have mild constipation. *Signs of milk fever*

If the early signs go unnoticed, the bitch then develops generalised muscle twitching and shaking. The animal is often unable to walk and will lie on her side, with legs extended and shaking, and a very rapid respiration rate. Loud noises and bright lights can set off convulsions, so it is important to handle her very gently and quietly.

When a bitch is found in a distressed state as described, she needs *immediate* attention by a veterinarian. This is not one of those things that can be delayed, it is a matter of life and death. She may already have been severely distressed for hours and any further delay may prove too much for her. *Treatment*

Treatment consists of giving the bitch intravenous calcium, which is given very slowly. Calcium, when it is given too fast, will slow the heart down. When a bitch has milk fever, the heart is beating very rapidly, so the vet monitors the heart rate as the calcium is given. The amount of calcium needed by a bitch varies. The drain on some bitches may be massive, and larger amounts may be needed for these animals.

The amount is regulated by the heart rate; once the rate settles down to normal or should there be beat irregularities appearing, the calcium must be stopped. As the animal's blood calcium levels improve, so the muscle spasms, twitching and respiration rate all become relatively normal. The recovery rate of affected bitches can be 'miraculous', where a bitch who looked to be dying several minutes before will stand up, look around and wonder what all the fuss is about!

It is occasionally necessary to give neurotic bitches Valium® to help keep them calm, even though the calcium has settled the majority of the symptoms. Some of these individuals may also need an injection of an ultra short-acting cortisone, which helps the body systems to return to normal and reduces the stress.

Aftercare is almost as important as the actual treatment. Even though the bitch has received calcium and has responded satisfactorily, the *Aftercare* body's reserves of calcium are still severely depleted. Recurrence of milk fever is common and can occur within 4–6 hours of initial treatment. To prevent this, the puppies must be taken off the bitch for at least the next 48 hours.

Large doses of calcium must be given every couple of hours for the next 24–36 hours, until a reasonable amount of calcium has been replaced. Give one to two Keylomin Calcium® tablet every four hours, depending on the dog's size. For small breeds, give one tablet and for larger breeds such as Bull Terriers, give two. After 24–36 hours, give one tablet per 2 kg (divide total daily dose into 2–3 doses) for 5–6 days and then cut down to one per 4 kg for the next 10 days. By the end of this time, the puppies should be almost fully weaned.

Bitches are often further stressed by the removal of the puppies and may require sedation with Valium®. I find that if the bitch can stay next to the puppies, but is not allowed to get in with them, she will not be so distressed.

After 48 hours, allow the bitch to feed the puppies during the night, and feed them yourself during the day. This takes most of the strain of lactation off the bitch, and reduces her chance of developing mastitis more than if she were to be taken straight off the puppies. If the puppies are over 2½ weeks old, start weaning them right away. Only allow the bitch in late at night after the puppies last feed, and take her out again first thing in the morning.

Some bitches, despite sedation, may continue to get distressed if they are not with their puppies. These bitches may have to be removed from the puppies and put as far away as possible for their own health. Bull Terrier bitches may need to be removed for the sake of saving their puppies' lives!

Prevention

Prevention in the first place is always better than the risk of milk fever. Milk fever is a 'production disease', and what can be produced, can be prevented 90-95% of the time.

Where there is a history of milk fever in a bitch, never mate her two seasons in a row. The bitch needs time to restore her body reserves of minerals before embarking on another depleting pregnancy. Keylomin Organic® should be given both throughout the pregnancy and lactation at one level scoop per 10 kg. This gives the bitch a trace element supply as well as calcium in a balanced ratio. In addition, Keylomin Calcium® tablets should be given from three weeks pregnancy at one per 10 kg of weight of the bitch, increasing to one per 5 kg by eight weeks. Keep small bitches on one per 2–5 kg daily during lactation, reducing after weaning to one per 10 kg for a further 3–4 weeks to make sure any losses are replaced into the body.

If the bitch is being mated for the first time and falls into the susceptible category as described above, treat in a similar manner. Avoid giving excessive amounts of meat in the diet during pregnancy and in the last two weeks in particular, try to keep the carbohydrates (cereals) and energy levels high. This is of great importance to the smaller breeds as it also helps to reduce the incidence of uterine inertia during whelping. Energel® and Calcium Sandoz are very useful in this area.

DISCHARGES AFTER WHELPING

The majority of bitches will have a dark reddish-brown discharge from the vulva after whelping that will persist for the duration of the bitch's lactation. The discharge will be heavy initially and then appear as sporadic blobs on the bedding. This is all perfectly normal and is nature's way of 'dry cleaning' the uterus, clearing out all the eroded and damaged tissue from the pregnancy and preparing the uterus for the next litter.

Most bitches will discharge for 6–8 weeks, some may discharge for up to three months; this tends to be related to the number of puppies and the length of time they are lactating. As long as the discharge is a dark red colour, not 'muddy', and has no smell, then it is perfectly normal.

If the bitch has a discoloured, profuse, or smelly discharge, she probably has an infection and should be taken to the vet.

In some cases, the bitch may have excessive bloody discharge, which can turn to a bright red and be passed in big clots. If this happens, there may be some areas of erosion of the uterine wall. See your vet immediately and the bitch will probably be placed on antibiotics as a precaution and vitamin K tablets as a coagulant. The bitch should be kept very quiet and preferably confined for at least 7–10 days.

Excessive bleeding after whelping can be dangerous. It is not common, but needs immediate attention. Some bitches become depleted of their reserves of vitamin K during pregnancy and therefore the blood may be unable to clot properly. Again, vitamin K tablets, and possibly injections are necessary for at least 10 days. If your bitch has a history of bleeding heavily after whelping, give vitamin K tablets during and after pregnancy as a precautionary measure.

Check your bitch regularly and monitor her discharges. Also check the teats daily for heat, swelling or discoloured milk, as these can be signs of mastitis.

MASTITIS

Mastitis is an inflammation of the mammary tissue which is usually localised to one teat, but can affect several. Rarely are all teats affected. Once a bitch has had mastitis, the chance of it recurring is fairly high.

Signs of mastitis are swollen, lumpy teats which exude a discoloured yellow-brown milk, often blood tinged. The bitch is usually restless, hot, drinking more than usual and reluctant to lie down with the puppies. The more serious cases are depressed, refuse to eat and run very high temperatures — these are signs of **toxicity** from the severity of the bacterial infection. Severe mastitis needs rapid and very prompt treatment by your veterinarian.

Causes of mastitis

1. Puppies scratching and damaging the teats — causing bruising and infections. The puppies' toe nails should be trimmed at least once a week to try and reduce this problem.

2. Insufficient puppies to drain the excess milk or too much milk causing an over production problem that can on occasions result in infection. This can occur when you are trying to dry the bitch up when weaning the puppies.

3. The bitch having infected milk prior to whelping and as a consequence the puppies not drinking sufficient amounts, creating congestion.

4. History of mastitis. Previous damage to the mammary tissue predisposes the tissue to repeated bouts of mastitis. This can even affect bitches with false pregnancies.

Types of mastitis

1. *Localised* There is discoloured milk coming from one of the teats and there are hardened areas within the tissue of that teat, which is hot and tender to the touch. Most of these milder types of mastitis can be treated orally with antibiotics and locally with warm compresses and regular draining of the teat, which must be done gently as the tissue is already fairly 'insulted'. Sometimes the mastitis has developed beyond this point or will not drain properly and then an abscess may form.

2. *Abscesses* These are swollen, hot and very painful areas within the mammary tissue which may have surrounding areas of discoloured skin. The bitch is usually running a high temperature, is off her food and is reluctant to be near the puppies. Abscesses should be lanced by your vet and can be done very easily with a small amount of local anaesthetic. Once the infected material has an exit point, the pressure is relieved and the bitch is a lot happier. The teat and the drainage hole should be gently massaged several times a day to get any remaining infected material out. If the abscess is not lanced and continues to swell, the skin over the abscess will eventually break down and a very large gaping hole may result. If you notice an abscess developing, the sooner it is lanced the better for the bitch.

3. *Gas gangrene or clostridial mastitis* Although it is an uncommon form of mastitis, when it does occur, it can kill the bitch within 48 hours. The symptoms of clostridial mastitis are: depression, loss of appetite, excessive drinking, hot swollen teat(s) with a small amount of bloody discharge, and a high temperature, often over 40°C. It usually only affects one or two teats.

To distinguish this type of mastitis from the other more commonly encountered forms, the symptoms develop with alarming rapidity, despite the seemingly small amount of mammary tissue involved and the bitch's depression is intense. Occasionally gas bubbles may be felt as a slight 'crackling' in the affected tissue, the skin is often white and cold and in longer standing cases (that is longer than 24 hours), there may be areas of blackened skin where the tissue has died.

Immediate treatment by a veterinarian is essential and as soon as possible if you wish to save the life of your bitch. The bitch will be hospitalised, given high doses of penicillin intravenously and put on a drip of IV fluids. Penicillin is often given locally into the affected area which should, if possible, have some form of drainage. If the problem is detected early enough and treated with proper hospitalisation, most cases recover with only the loss of the affected teat(s).

Mastitis results in damaged milk tissue and loss of productive milk tissue. This can cause hardened lumpy areas in the teats which when examined later on in life, can be mistaken as cancerous. The serious problem is however, that once a bitch has had mastitis, it is then very likely that she will develop mastitis again in the next and subsequent lactations. This factor should be taken into account before breeding the bitch again.

After all that doom and gloom, it is reassuring to know that most cases of mastitis are easily controlled and respond very well to treatment.

Blind Teats

Blind teats (inverted nipples) are not uncommon. Some breeds and lines are particularly prone to these. They can cause problems because the puppies try to suckle from them, but are unable to obtain milk easily. Then they move on to the normal teats. The affected teats will then overfill and can develop mastitis. If you know your bitch has several affected teats, particularly the larger back teats, pressure from behind will pop the nipple forward. Apply a hungry puppy and the teat will look like normal. If you can repeat this several times, the teat will be cured for life! As a rule, I do not worry about the very small front teats as the milk production from these is usually quite low.

9

Care of Puppies from Birth to Ten Days

The first 10 days is the most delicate time of a puppy's life. Puppies are unable to control their body temperature for the first 5–6 days so the temperature of the room must remain fairly constant.

Most puppies are born with their own fat supply, enough to last them for about four days. If puppies are placed under stress from adverse conditions such as lack of milk or infections, the fat supply will help them cope. Once these energy reserves have been depleted, the puppies will have great difficulty in picking up and improving from this position.

Normal Puppies

A healthy puppy will feel warm to the touch and, when picked up, will curl up in the hand, this is the normal healthy reflex. A sickly or cold puppy will remain flat and will not attempt to curl up. Healthy puppies will suckle vigorously and move around fairly actively to find a teat. Sluggish puppies have trouble finding a teat and will fall off the teat easily when pushed by litter mates. Once on a teat, a healthy puppy will suckle for 5–8 minutes (or longer) before dropping off and having a rest.

A healthy puppy gains weight steadily and feels 'solid' to lift. Weight gain is proportional to breed and birth weight, but a puppy should drink at least 10% of its body weight daily. Puppies should double their birth weight within 10–14 days.

Ideally, puppies should be loosely spread out in a box, happy to sleep on their sides and not needing to huddle on top of each other. They should not be making much noise apart from the usual little waffles and snuffles.

Daily Care of the Puppies

After the first few traumatic days have passed, life begins to settle down for both the bitch and the owner.

Weigh the puppies daily for the first 4–5 days. If they are gaining weight steadily then it is usually not necessary to continue weighing on a daily basis. Once a week weighing of an average sized puppy to gauge the worming dose will give you a relatively good idea as to their weight gain per week.

Puppies' nails should be cut once a week to make sure they do not scratch and damage the bitch's teats and possibly cause mastitis. Cut the little 'hook' of the end of the nails with a little pair of scissors.

Make sure the papers and/or blankets are changed at least once a day even if the bitch is cleaning up. Coverings get damp and if left, can cause bacterial skin infections.

Puppy Health

Healthy puppies are quiet, contented and gain weight steadily.

Daily weight checks for the first 4–5 days are especially important for the smaller puppies. Puppies cannot afford to lose weight at this age, and the sooner any failure to gain weight is noticed, the sooner it can be remedied. Puppies that fail to gain weight or lose weight, require supplementation. Once the weight has been lost at this early age, you may have a very hard struggle to return the weight to normal, and it may take as long as 1–2 weeks. The sooner you start to supplement, the quicker the response.

If a puppy is too weak to drink properly, it may be some time before you notice that it is not doing as well as it should. A good way to check if it is drinking enough is to feel behind the ribs. If it feels empty, the puppy is not sucking or swallowing enough milk.

A dehydrated puppy is fairly easy to recognise as it is very dry in the mouth and its skin is tight over the ribs. In normal healthy puppies, the skin slides easily over the ribs. If you pinch the skin up, a healthy puppy's skin slides straight back down; in a dehydrated puppy, the skin will remain elevated or take a while to slide back down to the normal position.

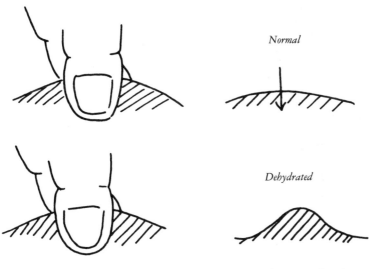

Normal

Dehydrated

If for some reason the puppies are not drinking from the bitch, get a watery solution of glucose and milk, or, preferably a watery low lactose milk (Di-Vetelact® or Biolac®) and feed them every ½–1 hour until they pick up enough strength to suckle from the bitch. If the puppies are dehydrated, make sure that what you feed them is very watery so that the condition is corrected. If you add glucose or honey, make sure it remains a weak solution.

Once the puppies improve, the mixture can be *gradually* brought up to full strength. Energel® is another very good product to help the puppies pick up as it is a very concentrated food supplement. You can put 5 mm of this on the roof of the puppy's mouth. Try to get the puppy to urinate before you feed it in order to make more room in its abdomen for food.

If the puppies have loose motions, give them natural yoghurt from the end of your finger on the roof of their mouths several times a day. Alternatively, give them acidophilus tablets, just a small amount crushed into some Energel®, again several times a day. If they have bad diarrhoea, give them a few drops of enteritis mixture several times a day, but only until the motions return to normal.

Constipation can be a serious problem if you have a gentle mother or you are feeding orphan puppies. Usually the puppies' stomachs are hard and tight, and they moan and groan continually. Normal and orphaned puppies should pass a motion after two feeds or approximately every four hours.

Puppies that are not gaining weight after 1–2 days at the latest should be taken to your vet. They may have an infection, you may have a management problem, or the bitch may be your 'management' problem.

SIGNS OF INFECTIONS IN PUPPIES

Puppies that are sickly are thin, ribby and very 'light' to handle. Sick puppies are colder to the touch than healthy puppies. Their motions usually smell unhealthy and are often loose and discoloured (greenish). The puppies will not stay on the teat for long, they suck poorly and fail to gain weight.

With newborn puppies you have very little time to correct problems. If they fail to gain weight within 24–48 hours of your noticing a problem and trying to correct it, go to your vet within 24 hours preferably, 48 hours at the latest.

If antibiotics have been prescribed, put the puppy on natural yoghurt as well. Give a fingertipful 3–4 times daily and/or a tiny bit of an acidophilus tablet crushed in Energel® or yoghurt. If the bitch has to have any antibiotic medication, again give the puppies natural yoghurt or acidophilus. As the newborn are very easily upset by antibiotics, this helps to return the gut bacteria to normal as it replaces the lactobacillus in the gastrointestinal tract. This is the bacteria needed for the digestion of milk. If you do not do this, the puppies may have diarrhoea and fail to gain weight. It is important to remember this especially after caesareans, when the bitches are usually put on a short course of antibiotics.

Puppies may fail to gain weight for several reasons:

1. An infection commonly called 'Fading Puppy Syndrome'. Usually this will affect a whole litter. The puppies are weak and weedy, they often have loose smelly motions, and soggy navel cords. Often the abdomens of the puppies are rather red and splotchy. Infected puppies are from the start, poor at sucking and will only drink in a very half hearted manner. Puppies that are born with an infection may die within a few hours of birth. Occasionally there are dead puppies within these litters, and these tend to look slightly 'mushy' (underdone), and have dark red abdomens.

If you think your litter has an infection, take the whole litter, the bitch and the dead puppies down to the vet. The vet will probably do a postmortem on the dead puppies and swab the bitch. The puppies are usually placed on antibiotics but be warned; it requires *very* good nursing to save the puppies. Constant care, little feeds often and good temperature control are essential.

Remember to feed the puppies natural yoghurt or acidophilus as their gut bacteria are already upset without the effect of the antibiotics on top. Use Energel® or a similar supplement to try and put weight on the puppies. Supplement feed as well, with Di-Vetelact® for instance, making sure the milk is *never* too concentrated.

If the bitch has an infection in the milk, which is uncommon, then the puppies are usually born quite robust and healthy but start to go downhill almost immediately. They fail to gain weight, become lethargic and may die within 3-4 days. This is a harder condition to recognise, as the puppies usually give no indication of any trouble until after 2-3 days of age, when the *lack* of weight gain is noticed.

The milk is usually discoloured, not a clean white colour. The colostrum is usually gone by 24 hours, so a persistent muddy yellow colour in the milk can alert you to the problem. Treatment is to swab the milk and put the bitch on antibiotics. The puppies are best hand fed or preferably put onto a foster mother. The puppies usually have to be put on antibiotics, preferably Chloromycetin Palmitate® as it is very good for settling down the gut bacteria as it is bacterio-static. Use only until the puppies start gaining weight which should be 3–4 days maximum.

Unfortunately the infection in the milk is very difficult to clear up totally and, with subsequent pregnancies the same problem tends to recur. If your bitch has this problem (English Cocker Spaniels seem to be more frequently affected), try antibiotics on that lactation, have a milk swab about a week before the bitch is due to whelp the next time and be prepared to have to *hand feed* the puppies. If the problem recurs a second time, I would seriously consider not breeding from that bitch again as it is not worth the hassle.

2. The bitch may be an unsatisfactory mother. Contrary to popular opinion not all bitches are maternal and will *not* stay in with the puppies. The puppies are usually born nice and healthy, but they scream for food all the time and slowly lose weight. This is more common in the litters of maiden bitches, particularly if they have had a traumatic whelping or a caesarean. If there has been too much interference with the puppies by the owner through constant picking up or too many visitors, the maternal bonding with the puppies will be reduced.

Nervous or neurotic bitches are very sensitive to too much interference and, in some cases, actually work themselves up until they get milk fever (eclampsia). These bitches have to be handled very carefully, especially if they have to be taken to the vet because of whelping difficulties. Valium® after whelping can help these bitches to settle down although occasionally I am inclined to think the owner needs to take it instead!

Maiden bitches that have had a caesarean can be tricky to handle. The poor bitch wakes up with a ready-made family and does not want any connection with the puppies. The sooner these bitches return to their own surroundings, the sooner they may start to feel maternal. Some of these bitches may need to go on to low doses of Valium® for several days. This reduces anxiety and the bitches usually become quite maternal after 2–4 days. In the meantime, the bitch has to be watched like a hawk and *made* to stay with the puppies. Some may even bite the puppies, so constant care is needed until she calms down.

In some cases the bitch may not have much milk at the time of whelping, although this problem usually rectifies itself within a few days. In the meantime, you will need to supplement the puppies. Always feed the empty ones first (they feel very empty behind the ribs). The bitch is usually producing 50–75% of what is necessary, so it is only needed to supplement the puppies every four hours. If you supplement too much, then the bitch has no stimulation to increase her own production.

Occasionally a bitch may refuse to settle down after whelping and be extremely restless, up and down, puffing and panting as though still in labour when she may have whelped one or two days before. This sort of bitch may be suffering from uterine cramp, particularly after a hard whelping. A bitch like this may need to be placed on an antispasmodic (e.g. Buscopan Compositum®) for several days until the uterus becomes less sensitive.

3. The conditions are too extreme. When the weather is cold and there is little or no heating, the puppies will be using all their body reserves to stay warm. The puppies will whinge and cry a lot, will slowly lose weight or be very slow to gain weight. Generally speaking, puppies that are cold will huddle together in a pile and complain, and puppies that are very hot will be spread out all over the box, panting and screaming.

For more on temperature control, see Causes of neonatal deaths later in this chapter.

Orphan Puppies and Supplementary Feeding

Supplementary feeding is necessary where there are big litters, poor mothers, bitches with very little milk or infected milk, orphans, weedy puppies or those that fail to gain weight sufficiently. Supplements should always be fed at body temperature, i.e. it should be warm on your wrist (approximately 36°–38°C).

Supplementation should start as soon as the need arises. The sooner it starts the better and the faster will be the result. Initial supplementation may need to be half hourly if the puppy is very weak, and the solution should be watery until the puppy rehydrates. As the puppy improves, so the feeds can be further apart and the strength of the feed gradually increased to full strength.

CHILLED PUPPIES
Chilled puppies should be warmed up slowly and gently stimulated by rubbing before attempting to feed, and then fed very slowly (small

amounts often) until they pick up. Feeding chilled puppies can be harmful as the vagus nerve, which controls the muscles of the oesophagus, is not fully developed in the newborn puppy. Chilling will slow down the swallowing and movement of food/fluids to the stomach, therefore the chance of the puppy regurgitating or choking is greatly increased.

Feeding Orphan Puppies

Start feeding every two hours for the first 1–2 days, gradually increasing the time between feeds to every three hours and four hours by 3–4 days. By 7–10 days, feeds should be every 4–6 hours, and at 10–14 days start feeding mushy solids. Basically, if the puppies are hungry, they will scream for food when they want it.

The teats used vary considerably, but babies' teats and bottles can be used. For the smaller breeds, there are various types of pet nursers available. One of the better type of teat shapes is illustrated below, where the teat is slightly flexible in and out of the top of the bottle, similar to the teats of the bitch.

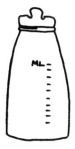

Hygiene is most important when hand feeding puppies. Make sure all bottles and teats are kept very clean. Milk that is made up and not used must be stored in the refrigerator.

A helpful hint: always urinate the puppy, as previously explained, before feeding it so that it will be able to take in more. To make the puppy urinate, gently rub a damp tissue around the appropriate outlet and the puppy will perform. Puppies should be made to defecate after every second feed. To make the puppy defecate, gently roll the puppy between your hands for half a minute and then, with a piece of wet cotton wool, gently rub around the anus while gently holding the puppy around the abdomen with your other hand. If the puppy is not defecating after three feeds you may need to give the puppy a small enema and some laxative orally.

The amount of milk supplement given in a single feed varies tremendously according to the size of breed and size of the puppy. Generally, a puppy is full when the stomach feels firm. To check, gently feel the stomach just behind the ribs, if it is still fairly empty try and give the puppy more. Some puppies will gobble into the food so greedily that they may start to choke. Check the flow on the teat as the holes may be too big; but if not, then accept the fact that some puppies are gluttons and keep them in check by giving them half the feed, feeding the others next and then giving the greedy one some more. Some puppies will overfeed in one feed and then not take much the next feed. This is all right as long as there is a drop in consumption in one feed only.

Puppies should take a regular amount that is steadily increased as they get bigger and as the feeds are less frequent.

Holding a Gently hold the puppy with one hand and the bottle forwards and *puppy to* slightly tilted upwards from the puppy's mouth with the other hand. *feed it* Never hold the bottle at too steep an angle to the puppy's neck.

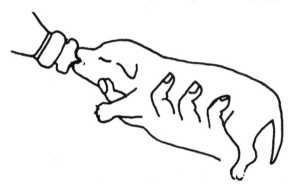

Tube Feeding. This is a method of feeding newborn puppies that are reluctant to suck from a bottle. It can be a fast way of feeding orphan puppies, but it does have definite problems. You need to be *very* experienced to tube feed successfully.

The vagus nerve, which helps control swallowing and movement along the oesophagus, does not develop fully until around 10-14 days. This means that when tube feeding, the whole amount may be delivered into the oesophagus instead of the stomach. Regurgitation or inhalation into the lungs sometimes happens, and could be expected with puppies that are chilled. *Tube feeding should be done slowly and gently.*

I would only suggest tube feeding for a puppy that is extremely flaccid and is unwilling to suckle. Give small amounts of fluid frequently until the puppy picks up, and then return it to the bitch or bottle. Fluids that are tube fed must be at body temperature. If too cold, they could cause stomach upsets or gripes.

When tube feeding, you should place a marker on the tube at the spot that is roughly equal to the distance from the nose to the end of the ribs. When inserting the tube, gently extend the head forwards — not up. Slide the tube in gently down the left hand side of the back of the puppy's throat. The oesophagus runs down the left side of the throat. If there is any resistance or coughing, remove the tube immediately and start again. Once into the stomach, insert a small amount of fluid at a time. If there is any resistance or signs of milk gurgling out the nose, stop and remove the tube immediately. **Do not overfeed!**

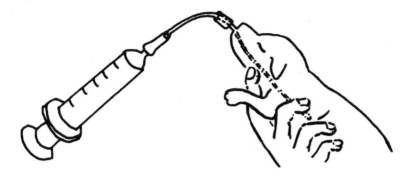

Personally, I feel that bottle feeding a sick or orphan puppy is the best and safest way. With bottle feeding, there is normal salivation and stimulation of sucking and swallowing. Puppies rarely take more than they need from the bottle unless they are really greedy.

Constipation

This can be a very real problem with orphan puppies and the puppies of bitches that are *too* gentle. There is insufficient stimulation of the intestines, so the faeces do not move along the intestines as quickly as normal. Large, lazy, fat puppies are also more prone to constipation as they do not move around as much as their thinner litter mates. Active puppies and those with good mothers who are just a shade rough with their puppies, very rarely if ever have any trouble with constipation. Once puppies are up and on their feet, constipation rarely occurs.

Older puppies (2–3 weeks of age) may develop constipation when being weaned and when they are experiencing diet changes. Make sure you make the food very sloppy and do not give meat alone. I mix everything together into a sloppy mixture and never have any trouble whatsoever. If you wish to be careful, add a small amount of cooking oil daily to the feed.

The signs of constipation are reluctance to drink, moaning and groaning, and a very hard and enlarged abdomen. Most constipated puppies will have bouts of straining.

Treatment is to give them warm soapy enemas and plenty of stimulation to the abdomen. Do this by picking them up between your hands and rolling them (rather like a rolling pin). Then gently rub the abdomen from the top right to bottom left, (the colon goes from the puppy's top right to left and then down the left side). Use wet cotton wool to stimulate the anus.

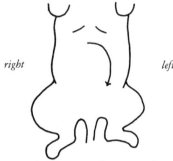

right   *left*

If all this does not work, you may have to give the puppy a lukewarm soapy enema.

Enemas must be given very gently and only with lukewarm soapy water. Do not use detergent as it irritates the gut. If the soapy water is too hot or too cold, the puppy will become distressed. Small amounts (2–3 mL) are squirted up the rectum with a syringe and then the puppy should be rolled and massaged. Stimulate the rectum after each flush out, and small amounts of faeces will start popping out. Treatment should only continue for 3–4 minutes and then the puppy should be rested. If you overdo it, you might kill the puppy. It is already under considerable discomfort with a blocked bowel, without the added stress of an enema.

It may be necessary to use a small soft rubber tube (5–7 cm long at maximum) to gently help sluice the soapy mixture further up the rectum; if inexperienced, leave it to your vet. After giving the puppy an enema, leave it alone for ½–1 hour before repeating any treatment. Usually after 3–4 treatments the puppy will have recovered. Concurrent small doses of oil or a mild laxative given orally can help shift the problem. Older puppies can have the same problem and sometimes are harder to fix when the diet is suddenly changed at weaning. If you cannot clear the blockage within 3–4 hours, see your vet.

To prevent a recurrence of constipation, give a small amount of oil and/or some other laxative in the diet on a regular daily basis. This is particularly important after a diet change of any sort, no matter how mild a change! Laxagel® is very good for preventing this sort of problem.

It is important that puppies that are supplement fed should be well stimulated after each feed. This will assist the movement of faeces along the intestinal tract.

SUPPLEMENTARY PRODUCTS FOR PUPPIES

There are various commercial supplements readily available which are quite good, but stay with those that are specially formulated for use in dogs and cats.

- Low lactose milk is well tolerated and does not irritate the gut — it can even be used with puppies that have loose motions; bitches love to drink it and you can wean puppies onto it (e.g. Di-Vetelact®, Biolac®).

- Specially formulated puppy and kitten milk are also well tolerated. Watch the recommended strengths as occasionally they can be too strong and may need further dilution (e.g. Animalac®).

- Energel® which is an American product is a highly concentrated energy supplement. It is very useful for the smaller, weak puppy. Energel® can keep older puppies going, even if they will eat nothing else. Squeeze out 1–2 cm on the roof of the mouth 3–4 times daily. It puts weight on sickly puppies and they really like it , often licking it direct from the tube. Energel® is also useful for older puppies if they are off their food for any reason, or refusing to eat.

- Natural yoghurt and acidophilus are useful for settling the gut bacteria. When there are loose motions, give the puppies yoghurt. We regularly use it on puppies during and following gastric problems. The acidophilus replaces the gut bacteria that are responsible for the digestion of milk.

- Laxatives (e.g. Laxagel®) and cooking oil are good for constipation, both during bouts and as a preventative.

1 cup of milk (Use long life or canned milk properly reconstituted. Do not use pasteurised milk as it can upset newborn puppies' gut bacteria.)
1 egg yolk
1 tablespoon cream
½ teaspoon honey or 1 teaspoon glucose
Can add 1–2 drops Pentavite to whole mix
Refrigerate and change every 2–3 days.

Temporary home formula for bitch's milk

Causes of Neonatal Deaths

SQUASHING

This occurs particularly with larger breeds which are generally very careless and sloppy when sitting and lying down. In some cases the owners may have to remove the puppies before the bitch gets up and put the puppies back in after the bitch lies down again. The breeds that are notable for this are St Bernards and Rottweilers, although it can occur in any breed, particularly if there is a large litter. As the puppies get a little older, they are better able to wriggle out of the way of the bitch. Once careless, a bitch tends to stay careless. Immediately after a caesarean, a bitch will not be very steady on her feet and might sit or tread on a puppy; watch for this for the first 12–14 hours.

If you hear a puppy screeching, dash in and pull it out from under the bitch. If the puppy is in shock, give it a gentle rub over the chest and put several drops of brandy and water on the gums. Keep the puppy warm until it appears to be improving. If you are worried, take the puppy down to your vet but keep it warm and don't forget the brandy (it's a heart stimulant, and you may need some as well). In order to prevent accidents like these, there should be bars around the inside edges of the whelping box which will give the puppies at least some protection.

If there are dead puppies and you are not sure of the cause of death, have a postmortem done. A postmortem reveals that squashed puppies have internal bleeding and heavy bruising especially around the chest. Also the bodies usually look very flat.

EXTREMES OF TEMPERATURE
As stated elsewhere, puppies are particularly affected by the extremes of temperature as they cannot control their temperature for the first 5–6 days.

Extremes of cold The temperature does not have to be very low for the puppies to start feeling the effects of the cold. Temperatures below room temperature (25°C), especially if there are any draughts in the room, can chill the puppies. Once the puppies are chilled, they start to use up their reserves of body fat and energy to stay warm. Obviously, the colder it is, the sooner the puppies start to deteriorate. Pneumonia and congestion of the lungs will set in very quickly. Trying to save puppies from this dangerous situation can be very difficult and will require extremely good nursing and environmental control.

When the temperature is too low for the puppies, they will huddle up in a pile and whinge and cry continually.

Puppies that are chilled should be *gradually* warmed up, however if you do this too quickly there may be tissue damage. Wrap the puppy up in a woollen blanket or jumper and put it on a hot water bottle. The hot water bottle should be wrapped up in a towel to prevent the puppy from becoming overheated. The puppy should be gently rubbed and regularly turned every few minutes and it can take 20–30 minutes or longer before it is thoroughly warmed. If you put the puppy and the hot water bottle in a little box and have a reading lamp angled so that heat is directed down into the box, this can help create a warm environment.

Once the puppy is showing more signs of life, with an increased respiration rate, warmer body and increased movement, then start to give it very small amounts of a weak glucose solution (a 'weak' solution is one that tastes faintly sweet to you). Give little feeds often until the puppy is stronger, and then start to increase the strength of the feeds gradually until they reach normal strength.

Antibiotics may be necessary after a bout of chilling as pneumonia is a very common result, but remember to give some yoghurt or acidophilus as well.

Puppies that are chilled quite often have intestinal paralysis as well so overfeeding a chilled puppy can cause a rupture of the stomach. Remember to warm the puppy up before feeding!

In controlling the environment to avoid chilling:

- Remember that hot air rises.
- Make sure that the room stays warm.
- Make sure that there are *no* draughts.
- Create a cave effect to keep the warm air down near the puppies (and reduce the heating bill). See chapter 17 for diagrams.
- Do not use a fan heater as the moving air will chill the puppies and will dry out the air too much.
- The room should be warm (about 28°–30°C) when you enter and the puppies should be warm to the touch. After the first 4–5 days, the temperature during the day can be lower (25°–27°C), but you should still keep the room warm at night. By 10–14 days, unless there is extreme cold, the heating can be turned off during the day but I like to keep a heater on low at night until the puppies are 3–4 weeks of age. These are approximate times and will vary greatly according to the geographical location and the amount of insulation in the whelping room or area. Remember, small areas are easier and cheaper to keep warm.

Prevention of chilling in the first place saves a great deal of trouble (and puppies). Postmortems of puppies that die from the cold reveal that they have very little fat reserves left on their bodies and often have little or no food in their stomachs. These signs, combined with the prevailing weather conditions clearly show the cause of death.

Extremes of heat

Obviously the reverse of the cold temperature situation applies in hotter weather. Newborn puppies will usually not require drastic cooling measures during the first 5–6 days unless it is very hot. Good circulation of the air in the whelping room is often all that is needed. Fans and air conditioners can be used with care and should be directed to send the air over the box, never directly into the box. With air conditioners, be careful not to reduce the room temperature too much. Air conditioners tend to dry out the air so leave a large bowl of water in the room to help keep the air humidified. If you do not have an air conditioner, a wet towel hanging in front of a fan acts as a home made 'cooler'.

As the puppies get older, on very hot days lay a wet towel down on the floor of the box, covering only half the available area. If the puppies are hot they will lie on the towel. Once they are cool enough they will move to a drier area. Remember that dogs do not sweat in the normal human fashion; they lose heat by panting and by sweating from their feet. Puppies that are hot will pant and flatten themselves out in an attempt to cool their bellies.

When puppies are too hot they will yell and scream and be too distressed to suckle properly. Treat over heated puppies by wiping them down with a wet cloth.

Do not put them in water or under a tap — too sudden a temperature change can cause brain damage. Wiping the puppy all over and then placing it on a wet towel will, in the majority of cases, be sufficient to help it to settle down. Keep wiping the puppies over every couple of minutes until they calm down; once the panting has stopped, stop wiping.

Leave the puppies on the wet towel and with a syringe, start giving them a small amount of water to drink. If they are very thirsty, keep going with the water but slowly! If they are very dehydrated, add a small amount of glucose to the water after the initial thirst has settled down. Puppies usually recover very quickly from overheating and have few setbacks once they are drinking normally.

Overheating can occur in winter especially when electric blankets and heated whelping boxes are left on the highest setting or where overhead heating lamps are too close to the box (they should be at least one metre above the box). The symptoms are similar to overheating in summer, but there may be more tissue damage as hot material will have been too close to the body.

Puppies that die from overheating have very bluish-purple tongues and are dehydrated. In hot weather conditions it is fairly easy to diagnose the cause of death.

INFECTIONS FROM THE BITCH

Puppies may be born with an infection which is usually bacterial (see above). Less commonly, in fact fairly rarely, there may be viral infections such as herpes or hepatitis.

Viral hepatitis Usually there will only be neonatal deaths from viral hepatitis in cases where the bitch has very little or no maternal immunity, i.e. she has not been vaccinated in the last 2–3 years. Viral hepatitis can cause sudden deaths of puppies overnight from no obvious cause. Postmortems show characteristic changes including an enlarged liver. Deaths can occur any time up to vaccination, but the sudden deaths usually occur in the first 2–3 weeks. Bitches that are up to date on their vaccinations should pass on sufficient maternal immunity to adequately cover the puppies for the first 6–8 weeks of life.

Viral herpes This is an infection carried by the bitch that can be passed on to the puppies at birth. The herpes virus infection causing death is usually seen 4–14 days after birth, and it does not necessarily affect all members of a litter. Affected puppies cry constantly, are weak, do not eat well and occasionally suffer from diarrhoea. As the condition progresses there is lung congestion and then death.

A postmortem reveals a characteristic picture of haemorrhage throughout the lungs, liver, intestines and kidneys. Because the virus replicates at a fairly low temperature, the problem is rarely seen once the puppies can properly regulate their own temperatures (over two weeks). Take sensible precautions to avoid hypothermia (chilling) in puppies at risk. Herpes virus occurs more commonly in crowded kennel set-ups where cross transmission is far more likely. Although uncommon, at present there is no vaccine for the canine herpes virus.

This is a generalised bacterial infection where the puppies are either sickly from birth or start to deteriorate soon after birth. Puppies will cry, feed poorly, lose weight and develop dark red blotches on the abdomen. There can be very small haemorrhages in the gums which will have a spotty appearance. Postmortems reveal widespread bacterial infection and multiple small haemorrhages. This condition is also called '**fading puppy syndrome**' (also discussed earlier in this chapter).

Neonatal
Septicemia

INFECTED MILK FROM THE BITCH
In this case, puppies are born healthy and start to fail and die within 2–3 days. On rare occasions, an incompatibility of the bitch's milk to the puppies can occur and the puppies may 'bloat' because of the production of gas and toxins. Treatment is to remove the puppies from the bitch and rear by foster mother or hand feed. The puppies need antibiotics but use these only until the puppies are gaining weight and then stop. Remember to give yoghurt and/or acidophilus as well.

ABNORMALITIES
Puppies with life-threatening abnormalities usually die within two days. An example of this would be an intestinal 'mistake' such as achalasia, where the gut is not continuous and there is no straight passage for food through the intestine. Some defects are very obvious at birth such as cleft palates, hare lips and limb defects, where affected puppies are invariably put down immediately.

Several breeds are more prone to cleft palates, notably the shorter headed toy breeds, e.g. Papillons and Chihuahuas, so check the roof of the mouths of newborn puppies, particularly if they are failing to thrive or are passing milk out through their noses. Not all puppies that have milk coming out of their noses have cleft palates however; they may just be drinking too much milk too fast!

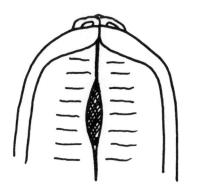

Cleft palate

Puppies with severe heart defects will often survive quite well for 2–3 weeks, but then start to fall behind the others. Pick the puppy up and put its chest next to your ear. A bad defect of the heart sounds like a washing machine instead of a clean beating sound. If you suspect a heart defect, take the puppy to your vet.

BIRTH INJURIES

These include internal injuries from whelping, resulting in damage to the liver, lungs or brain, and cases where puppies do not sufficiently clear the fluid from their lungs. This can occur after prolonged labour or where a puppy has been malpresented.

Puppies at the end of a litter and puppies that have been delayed in birth, are more likely to:

- have damage to their bodies in some way.
- retain more fluid in the lungs after birth.

Because the puppies are already under stress due to birth trauma, they do not progress well. In all of the above cases there is a gradual weight loss; weakening, then death. Trying to save some of these puppies can be heart breaking, as the response is often very poor.

Abnormalities and severe birth injuries are uncommon and usually only affect one or two puppies in a litter.

Common Puppy Problems

PUPPY 'NIGHTMARES'

Newborn puppies have muscle twitching episodes while they are sleeping. This is quite a normal event and indicates 'active sleep'. A puppy will spend 80–90% of its time during the first 10 days asleep and this muscle twitching is a way of ensuring that the muscle tone is retained. The twitching effect will gradually disappear after a few weeks. As the puppy gradually spends more and more time awake, getting increasingly mobile, so the need for this 'active sleep' decreases.

STAPH SKIN INFECTIONS

This condition appears as thickened, scabby patches of skin. Initially, there may only be one puppy affected, but the infection is spread by the bitch to the other puppies. Staph skin infection can usually be controlled by topical application of something to dry out the skin which tastes horrible enough to stop the bitch licking it. Avoid heavy ointments and creams. Gentian violet is very good, as are antibiotic powders. If there are large areas affected, antibiotics may have to be used. This type of infection is more commonly seen in humid conditions.

PUPPY STRANGLES

Puppy strangles is an infection that can affect one or two puppies in a litter, recognised by large 'mumps' under the jaw. These are abscesses of the lymph nodes and can appear fairly rapidly, almost overnight. The lumps are hot and painful and these abscesses need to be lanced by your vet as soon as possible, as the toxins from the infection and the pressure around the throat can make the puppies deteriorate fairly rapidly. If they are not lanced, the skin over the abscess may die, leaving a nasty hole. This condition is usually seen at around 10–28 days. Antibiotics are generally given afterwards.

INFECTED EYES

Occasionally at the time that the eyes are due to open (10–14 days), a puppy may develop what appears to be a grossly swollen eye. The puppy should be taken to your vet immediately to have the eye opened. The lids are washed and gently teased apart at the inner corner where the eye normally opens first and the purulent material released. The eye should be bathed with damp cotton wool and an antibiotic ointment used several times a day for 3–4 days.

If the irritation and discharge continues, the possibility of a problem with the lids such as entropion should be considered. Definite diagnosis often has to wait until the eyes are properly open.

DEAFNESS

Deafness in puppies is not usually apparent until 4–6 weeks of age as the ears do not open until around 16–18 days of age. Deaf puppies are always the last to respond to meal calls and if asleep will have to be shaken to wake up. Unfortunately, it is usually better if these puppies are put to sleep as many dogs who are deaf are killed within a few years by cars, quite often within their own backyard.

If they are kept alive, they must go to a home with adequate fences to keep them away from cars and they must be fairly placid individuals as some deaf dogs are very 'jittery' in temperament.

PIGMENTATION IN PUPPIES

Many people have misleading conceptions about the appearance of newborn puppies of a particular breed. To the dismay of their owners, most puppies are born with pink noses and pink pads. This is quite normal and the pigmentation of the offending areas will usually start to change within a week. Breeds that have pink skin on and around the nose take longer.

White
puppies
Some breeds which are not white as adults, are born white all over, notably the Dalmatian and the Australian Cattle Dog. Both breeds can have patches, but are otherwise born totally white. The puppies will start 'colouring up' at around 1–2 weeks and look like perfectly normal puppies of their breed by three weeks of age. Patches of solid colour are present at birth. Unfortunately, puppies have sometimes been put down at birth when owners (and occasionally the vet) were ignorant of the 'normal' birth colour of the puppies of these breeds.

Other breeds that are born predominantly white and change colour after birth are generally those that have heavy flecking through their coats, e.g. English Setters, English Springer Spaniels, English Cocker Spaniels.

In some breeds, white puppies are a major fault and these puppies are usually put down at birth, especially white Boxers which are particularly prone to skin cancers when older.

Breeds with white puppies that are prone to hereditary deafness include Dalmatians, Cattle Dogs and Bull Terriers, where the two genes are apparently closely linked. Old English Sheepdogs occasionally have a deaf puppy, this time associated with the blue eye gene.

Many breeds which should not have white on the adult dog, will often produce a puppy with small patches of white, generally only on the chest and the toes. Nearly 80–90% of the white area of these types of patches will disappear by three months of age. If there is white skin under the patch, then an area of white will remain — but it is usually small.

Puppies occasionally have dark pigment spots on their tongues, looking like a smutty ink spot. This is quite common and causes no problems whatsoever. These spots are occasionally looked for as an indicator of strong pigmentation in the adult dog but it is not certain whether this has any direct connection to the strength of genetic pigmentation.

Chow Chows and Chow crosses have excessive black pigmentation of the tongue, gums and skin. The Chows are born with bluish tongues and gums which darken to a blue-black, which can be very off putting to total novices. Blue-black tongues are also a trial for the vet when these animals are anaesthetised.

DEW CLAWS AND TAIL DOCKING

Some breeds have their tails and/or dew claws removed; this is generally done when the puppies are 3–6 days of age. The age that vets prefer to perform the operation varies slightly, but I prefer puppies to be a good size for their breed, in good condition and putting on weight.

Puppies that are in any way sickly, very small or weedy at the normal time of tail docking, should wait for a few days. It is far better to have a few days delay before putting the puppy through tail docking as an already poor puppy will only deteriorate. It is better to have a live puppy with a tail than a dead one without. If the puppy is a real battler, the tail can always be docked at a later date.

Tail docking should always be done by a veterinarian and the tails are stitched usually with a dissolving suture. Larger hind dew claws are also stitched. Small dew claws and front dew claws are usually cauterised by various means, often by using potassium permanganate crystals.

Tail lengths vary according to breeds, fashions, individual breeders and countries, so I leave it to individuals to tell me what length they prefer.

A word of warning however; the shorter the tail (especially the breeds docked right up to the base of the tail), the more likely that there may be problems in later life with prolapses of the rectum and perineal hernias. Fashions will, I hope, gradually remove the necessity of at least the excessively short tail docking.

Dew claws particularly on the hind legs can be a real problem in older dogs, especially with the hairy breeds. The nails can grow very long and actually grow around and into the back of the nail bed, creating abscesses and other problems. Dew claws often get caught and torn. Most breeds have the rear dew claws removed and some also have the front dew claws removed. This is a good idea in coated breeds, especially if they are clipped, as the dew claws can get cut while they are being trimmed.

KINKY TAILS

Some puppies are born with kinky tails but these defects are usually mild and will often grow out to a large extent so it is not as noticeable. Do not attempt to 'splint' the tail as it is very easy to cut off the circulation and lose the tail altogether. Leave most of these problems alone, unless the defect is very severe. Bad kinks should be shown to your vet who will advise you of possible treatment.

SWIMMERS

Occasionally you may see a 'swimmer'. This means that the puppy will look flat from the top of the back to the chest. It will move around in a fashion similar to a child first learning to swim. The rib cage will feel flattened out and the puppy is usually unable to stand, particularly with the hind legs, and has difficulty in moving around the box. Swimmers are usually seen at around 5–6 days onwards up to three weeks of age.

Causes

1. Puppies become overheated due either to excessive outside temperatures such as a hot summer day with inadequate cooling, or in winter from excessive heating, especially from underneath, with heated whelping boxes being left on the highest heat.

2. Occasionally a fat puppy will not move around the box adequately and tends to 'melt' into the swimmer state due to its weight and laziness.

Very young puppies are essentially very soft boned, as most of the bones are still cartilage at this stage. Excessive heat will cause the puppies to lie flat in an attempt to cool down, as the greatest cooling will occur on the stomach. Weight and too little movement will likewise cause the same situation through prolonged lying on the chest. The longer the puppies lie in this posture the flatter they become.

Treatment   Treatment of swimmers involves both correcting the causes of the problem and physiotherapy.

The causes are simply remedied. Arrange adequate cooling in summer and do not 'over-cook' puppies with excessive heat in winter. Make sure there is a mixture of surfaces so that it is difficult for the puppy to lie flat on its stomach. To do this, put scrunched up newspaper underneath the blanket or sheet. Placing a bean bag under the puppies is an effective way to help prevent the problem in the first place. This is particularly good in winter as the air between the beans retains the heat of the box very evenly. Bean bags can help to correct the problem of swimmers once you have the condition present, as the puppies cannot lie flat on the beans and have to exercise hard to move around. In summer, a bean bag may be too hot, so you may have to rely on rough surfaces.

Flat puppies or swimmers need to be exercised. Physiotherapy for affected puppies involves turning the puppy on its back, moving the legs together in a bicycling action, up and down, and massaging the legs and chest. If you can do this several times a day, most puppies, especially if caught early enough, will respond very quickly and will have returned to normal within 7–10 days. The more severely affected puppy may never entirely return to normal. These puppies have a triangular chest which is flattened over the base of the rib cage.

Anabolic steroids may be necessary to assist badly affected puppies and sometimes small splints may be needed for the pasterns (wrist). Splints should be left on for 2–3 days maximum, as that is usually quite sufficient at this age. If left too long, the affected tendons will stretch the wrong way. Occasionally the hind legs have to be taped together, rather like a set of horse hobbles, to keep them reasonably close together and stop the puppy doing the splits all the time.

See your vet and between the two of you, work out a schedule of physiotherapy. This needs to be done 3–4 times daily for at least five minutes at a time. Correct the environment and make fat puppies exercise. A good way to do this is to put the puppy in the farthest corner of the box away from its mother every time you go past, making the puppy exercise to get back. This also has the advantage of slightly reducing the puppy's food intake.

Nearly all puppies can be corrected provided that the problem is noticed early enough and they are given plenty of physiotherapy.

10

Care of Puppies from Ten Days until Leaving the Breeder

Worming

Worming of the puppies can commence from 7–10 days. I suggest starting when they are 10–14 days old and re-worming once a week until the puppies leave home. The drugs used can vary considerably but try to use one that acts on both roundworm and hookworm. If your bitch has been on heartworm preventative, and she is in any country that is affected, there will be little or no roundworm, as the heartworm preventative helps to control roundworm. Therefore, hookworm is usually the major worm problem in young puppies. Treat for tapeworm at 5–6 weeks if there is a concurrent flea problem.

It is important to remember that whatever you worm the puppies with, it will only remove the adult worms, *not* the immature worms that are undergoing migration through the gut which will be unaffected by the wormer. This means that if you worm them one week, you will remove the adults, but 1–2 weeks later you may have as many or more adults in the gut. If you worm them once a week, you tend to keep the burden to a minimum and at the same time reduce the possibility of gut problems such as diarrhoea or poor growth rates. The less you worm puppies, the more likely you are to have problems.

Once the puppies go to their new homes, the worming can be cut down to once every two weeks. This way, if the new owner neglects to worm the puppy for say 3–4 weeks, at least it is more likely to stand up to a worm infestation than a puppy that has not been wormed consistently.

Remember that worm eggs hatch in warm wet (humid) weather so that worm problems are at their worst in spring and autumn (also during a wet summer).

Problems that worms can cause include:

1. Failure to gain weight when puppies typically have a 'pot bellied' appearance.
2. Loose motions that are often tarry and foul smelling. Heavy burdens of hookworms cause severe anaemia which can kill puppies by three weeks of age.
3. Heavy worm infestation can occur particularly on contaminated grounds where there have been dogs for many years. This can set off gut infections like parvovirus and many others.

A motto for worming: it is better to be safe than sorry!

HEARTWORM

Heartworm is a problem that is worldwide. Many tropical and temperate zone countries are infested (see chapter 4).

During the mosquito season, the mosquitoes can start biting puppies as soon as they are born. Usually for the first three weeks, the puppies are kept indoors, but after this time they are allowed outside. If there are a lot of mosquitoes around while the puppies are still in the whelping box, spray the room every night or light a mosquito coil.

Heartworm prevention should be started early for the puppies' safety.

Daily tablets can be started from three weeks. For an average sized breed, ⅛ of 200 mg tablet each until 5–6 weeks of age then ¼ of a tablet each until 10–12 weeks, then ½ a tablet each until about five months and so on. The dose rate of the daily preventative tablet (DEC) is 10 mg per kg daily. Lower dosages may not adequately prevent heartworm developing.

In litter situations, I find that it is far more convenient to use the monthly preventative tablets. As they work by killing any developing heartworm larvae that may have been acquired over the last month, the first dose can be as early as four weeks of age. Generally, however, I start my puppies at 5–6 weeks of age and send the puppies home with a tablet to cover the next month's dose. The convenience of only having to dose your litter of puppies once a month rather than daily, appeals greatly.

Many dog owners (and breeders) used to wait until 5–6 months of age before starting heartworm prevention. *Don't!* If you do wait until this age, there will be a reasonable chance that the puppy has already been bitten and will have to undergo treatment.

Puppies that are born in winter can probably be started on the preventatives a little later, at 6–8 weeks of age, as they are less likely to come into contact with mosquitoes in the colder weather.

All new puppy owners should be told about the importance of placing their puppies on heartworm preventatives as soon as possible, and that prevention is far better than infection.

Recently developed is the ivermectin tablet (Heartguard®), which is the once a month tablet. Check with your veterinarian as to what age to start puppies with this type of tablet.

Socialisation and Behavioural Development

Chapter 6 deals with this subject in greater detail. Puppies start to open their eyes by the time they are 10–14 days old. If there is any unusual swelling under the lids there may be an infection, but this is uncommon. If this occurs, wash the eyelids with damp cotton wool and gently try to spread the lids. If you cannot release the infected material, take the puppy to your vet.

The ears start to open at about 18–20 days, and the puppies will respond to sound from this time on. I suggest that you start handling the puppies as much as possible from 2–3 weeks onwards.

Stimulation and handling in the early weeks can help the puppy tolerate stress better in later life and will make a more emotionally stable dog that is less fearful of new people, situations and noises. The more the puppies are handled, the more situations that they face, e.g. different noises and different objects to play with, the better their temperament on the whole. Leave the radio blaring when you are not there so that the puppies become used to sudden and loud noises.

Leave a sack full of old drink cans or a few old children's toys lying around — the greater the variety the better. Do not leave small objects that may be swallowed.

Puppies are extremely impressionable between the ages of five and 16 weeks. As the puppies get older, it becomes very important for them to have individual attention away from the other litter mates. This only takes 5–10 minutes every few days, and will make for better learning ability and responsiveness in the adult dog. Increasing stimulation and new challenges experienced in a positive manner (the puppy should not experience fear or trauma) will help develop the well balanced adult dog. Lack of socialisation in puppies can lead to poor development of the 'dog to human' bond and dogs may often have temperament problems in later life which make them unsuitable for many areas of work.

The attention the breeder and their family give to puppies before the puppies go to their new homes is of great importance to the animals' eventual soundness of temperament and ability to be trained; particularly in regard to a working animal. Increased ability to be trained in whatever direction the new owner wishes to take the puppy, will increase the chances of success and enjoyment that the owner, and the dog, will achieve. Breeders who are aware of the value of this early socialisation will gain a reputation for the soundness of temperament of their dogs and will have good, easily trained dogs in both the show and obedience rings. It just takes a little effort to achieve a good reputation for life.

Do not have aggressive, noisy bitches near the puppies from 4–5 weeks onwards, particularly when visitors arrive. The barking and jumping around not only scares the puppies, but the bitch starts to instil in the puppies a fear of strangers. Visitors like to see friendly puppies that run up to say hello and not run away because their mother has made them fearful! Think of it from the point of view of the bitch and the puppy, not to mention the visitor or customer angle.

Weaning

This should start by 2–3 weeks of age. With large litters, especially of the smaller breeds, milk fever (eclampsia) can be a big problem. The smaller the breed, the bigger proportionally the drain of calcium from the bitch. The smaller breeds put out a far higher 'proportion of puppy' per unit of weight than the larger breeds. For example, a Cavalier King Charles Spaniel weighing 5–6 kg may have 4–5 puppies weighing a total of 1 kg in contrast to a Great Dane weighing 55–65 kg having 8–12 puppies weighing a total of 6–7 kg. This means that the smaller breeds need a higher level of calcium added to the diet during pregnancy and especially after whelping than do the larger breeds.

Puppies of the smaller breeds are harder to wean on the whole. Take the bitch away from the puppies for 1–2 hours prior to feeding. Usually by the time they are between 3–4 weeks of age, the bitch should be removed during the day. If she is upset, put her next to the puppies so she can see them, but cannot get in with them.

At 4–5 weeks of age the bitch should be away from the puppies except to give them a quick drink to take the excess milk once or twice a day. By six weeks, let the bitch in for a few minutes twice a week. By the time the puppies are 7–8 weeks of age she should be completely dry.

My own philosophy on weaning puppies is that once their eyes are open, they are weanable, particularly with those bitches that are in a high risk group for developing milk fever. The larger the litter, the sooner you should start weaning so that the drain on the bitch will be reduced. A bitch should be fed 2–3 times the normal amount of food by the time the puppies are three weeks of age. However, in spite of the extra food, the bitch may still be losing weight because of the high output necessary to feed the growing puppies (little parasites might be an apt description).

If the bitch has a small litter of only 1–3 puppies, obviously you would start weaning a little later, say 3–4 weeks but no later, especially with the smaller breeds like Chihuahuas, Cavaliers and Miniature Fox Terriers.

Feeding
(See section on Feeding very young puppies in chapter 4).

Basically, puppies are fed on soft mushy food when just starting to feed. This usually consists of 75–90% soaked dry dog food and 10–25% very finely minced meat or canned puppy food. Use a good quality puppy dry food, one that soaks down readily. When using a puppy dry food, do not add vast quantities of milk, as most already contain a milk component. Add natural yoghurt rather than milk powder, as it does not irritate their intestines.

Many of the newer speciality dry foods are excellent, particularly with puppies, as they have higher digestibility, available protein and fat levels than those previously available. When selecting a puppy dry food, aim for at least 20–24% protein with around 10–14% fat levels. The greater the amount of meat based protein present, generally the higher digestibility. Giant breeds which are growing extremely rapidly have very high requirements for energy to sustain optimal growth and may require in excess of 26% protein levels in the diet during these early weeks.

Dry dog foods are far better 'starter' cereals than human baby food preparations as they are formulated specifically for canine rather than human requirements.

Milk products are beneficial to puppy diets on the whole as they add good quality protein and fats. However, many dogs will not tolerate pasteurised milk. To avoid irritating the intestines, use canned, powdered or long life milk; better still use goat's milk, natural yoghurt or junket. Slowly increase the level of milk in the diet as the intestines take several days to become accustomed to milk products if not previously used. Too rapid an increase in milk levels may cause diarrhoea.

PREPARATION OF MEALS

Soak the dry dog food first. Mix into the soaked kibble (biscuit) a small amount of low lactose milk (e.g. Di-Vetelact®) or natural yoghurt which is very good as it does not upset the gut. This mixture represents three quarters of the meal. The fourth part, consisting of finely minced meat, or a canned puppy food to make a sloppy porridge is fed three times daily. The entire day's feed can be made in one batch, providing it is refrigerated until needed, and then each meal can be diluted with hot water at meal times. The remaining mixture should be stored slightly dry. This saves time in meal preparation. Another advantage of preparing a day's feed at one time is that additives can be spread evenly over the feeds.

Try to avoid giving a separate meat feed to puppies when first starting to wean them as they tend to gorge on it and frequently become constipated as a result. Also, if they fill up on the meat, they become fussy and refuse to eat the soaked dry food. If the meat is well mixed with the soaked dry food, the puppies will eat virtually everything placed in front of them.

Feed the puppies three times daily until 7–8 weeks of age. If they are fed any more often the puppies will become very finicky and their owners will start complaining about poor eating habits. Also never leave soaked, sloppy food out in the hot months; the food will go off and is a common cause of gut upsets. By six weeks, the dry food should just be semi-soaked as puppies do like chewing on things other than humans. Always leave a shallow dish of water with the puppies.

By 7–8 weeks of age, the puppies will naturally start to cut down on the number of meals eaten per day. At this stage, I usually cut the meals down to twice a day and start to give unsoaked dry dog food in the medium to large breeds. Also at this age, most puppies are going to their new homes and, overnight as it were, may start to dislike soaked or sloppy food. Smaller breeds however may need semi-soaked food for longer as they often teethe later than bigger breeds.

ADDITIVES FOR PUPPY DIETS

(See diet sheet) These apply also to older puppies and adult dogs.

If puppies are fed properly and receive a balanced complete dry dog food ration with the addition of a small percentage of fatty meat or canned puppy food, table scraps or chicken (maximum 25% for larger breeds), they need very little by the way of additives.

Always remember, the greater the quantity of meat (which is high in phosphorus particularly kidney, liver and heart) then calcium should be added to the diet. This is because the higher the level of phosphorus in the diet, the more it will reduce the rate of calcium absorption.

Most good quality dry foods are already supplemented with sufficient calcium, so little or no supplementation is needed if feeding the correct proportions of dry food to meat.

If feeding in excess of one third meat, then small amounts of calcium supplementation may be required. Only use low doses of supplements if and as needed.

Very heavy boned puppies and/or breeds may occasionally need small amounts of calcium added to the diet if the feet and pasterns suddenly change. Use only low doses to effect and when you get the response, reduce the dose and if okay, stop. If there is no improvement within a week, the diet should be looked at. The problem may not be calcium related, rather any one or combination of the following: zinc, iron, B group vitamins, or trace element deficiencies. Often a small addition of zinc (Keylomin Performance® tablets are excellent) will result in a dramatic improvement.

Flat and splayed out toes can indicate an inadequate diet, such as a lack of available calcium or other minerals in the diet or occasionally a lack of vitamin D. Overcast weather and indoor housing can cause a vitamin D deficiency in the puppies. Vitamin D is able to be manufactured by the dog when it is exposed to sunlight and assists the body to absorb calcium. During overcast weather add a very small amount of cod liver oil or sardines to the diet (both of which contain vitamin D). If you add cod liver oil, twice a week would be the maximum, as too much can be as bad as too little.

When your puppies finally leave home, have a diet sheet ready to go with them. Preferably this should be reasonably detailed, yet not too long, otherwise the puppy's new owners will not read it. If it can be pinned up on the wall for reference, all the better.

An example of a diet sheet, for a medium sized dog, is given below.

This can be varied and/or modified for smaller breeds. It is actually a copy of the one I hand out with my own puppies. As a rule I do not put down the exact amounts of food fed, as the amount varies tremendously between individuals as to what is necessary to maintain a good weight. I tend to feed according to the needs of the dog in front of me; if it is too thin, I give more food; too fat, I give less food. A puppy with ideal weight has a light layer of fat over the ribs. Lightly run your fingers over the ribs to check this.

Remember to mix three quarters dry dog food to one quarter of what ever else you wish feed — this will grow just about any breed with the minimum of trouble. Smaller breeds can go down to two thirds dry to one third variable.

PUPPY DIET SHEET
Pin this up near where you prepare the puppy's meals.
8–16 weeks
Breakfast: A good quality, well digested puppy dry food e.g. Supercoat Puppy® or Meaty Bites Puppy Formula® mixed with a small amount of fatty meat. If necessary add a small amount of powdered milk, goat's milk or natural yoghurt.

Dinner: ¾ Dry puppy food to ¼ amount of fatty meat plus a small amount of powdered milk, goat's milk or natural yoghurt.

Between 12–16 weeks gradually decrease the amount of breakfast and increase the evening meal accordingly. By 16 weeks one meal per day should be sufficient.

Vary the diet now and then with a tin of sardines, leftovers, chicken, cheese or eggs.

Bones, particularly mutton flaps, or brisket bones, (raw chicken wings for smaller breeds) are very good for keeping the teeth clean and healthy and can be introduced at this age quite safely.

16 weeks and over

Dinner: ¾ Good quality puppy or junior dry food mixed with ¼ amount of fatty meat. Occasional mutton flaps or brisket bones are excellent.

Remember:

- Only give additives if really necessary. Use small amounts to effect. Check the diet if no response after one week.
- The heavily boned individuals require careful attention to diets and growth rates and may require some supplementation of trace elements.
- Too much calcium is as bad as too little. Go by the dog in front of you!

ONCE A MONTH HEARTWORM TABLETS

Once a month heartworm tablets such as Heartguard® and Endovet® work by eliminating the developing stages of heartworm that the dog may have acquired from mosquitoes over the previous month. The convenience, effectiveness and safety of the once a month tablet makes it superior to the daily tablets.

Newer versions are capable of worming the dog for other intestinal parasites at the same time, saving money and reducing concurrent worm burdens. They generally cover hook and roundworm, some cover whipworm as well.

DAILY HEARTWORM TABLETS

All the daily preventative tablets, liquid and powders, contain the same drug. The dose rate should be 10 mg/kg given daily.

It is important to remember how the preventative works. The drug prevents development of infective larvae (and gradually kills them) while they are in the tissues under the skin. The effect lasts 24 hours. If the larvae have matured and started migrating through the body (at around three months after infection), it is not effective.

The convenience of the once a month tablet is the telling factor. If you are erratic at giving the daily tablet or you go away frequently, then this form of treatment may be the one that suits you. Stickers are supplied to attach to the calendar as reminders. Try to establish a date that is easily remembered e.g. the first of every month.

Here are a few do nots in case you forget:

- Do not leave food lying around all day, especially dry dog food as this encourages the dog to pick at its food instead of eating proper meals.
- Do not give the puppy more meat because it prefers it. Too much meat can cause bone problems as meat is very high in phosphorus which lowers calcium absorption. If in doubt give less meat and more dry food.
- Do not give too much milk, give yoghurt, goat's milk or junket instead.
- Do not overfeed. The puppy should be nicely covered with a thin layer of fat over the ribs.
- Let common sense be your guide.

Give the puppy lots of love and attention, a firm hand when needed, a nice warm safe place to sleep, a few playthings (old slippers or hard rubber toys) to replace the games with litter mates and you will be rewarded with love and loyalty tenfold.

Healthy Environments for Young Puppies

This is often a neglected area of puppy raising. It is most important to raise puppies in a healthy, clean, dry and sheltered environment. Most puppy gastric infections e.g. parvovirus and coccidiosis often have as their origin, a problem in hygiene due to either contaminated ground or bad habits on behalf of the breeder.

Usually puppies are put into outside runs or garages once they can climb out of the whelping box. Obviously puppies go outside much later in winter; sometimes not until 5–6 weeks if the weather is severe. However the principal remains the same, that puppies need to be kept clean and dry as much as is possible. The puppies unfortunately tend to take the opposite point of view and seem to take perverse delight in becoming as dirty as possible, as quickly as possible.

The space they need depends on the size of breed. I personally like to see puppies in an area where they can be closed in at night and have an exercise area outside that is sheltered from the worst of the elements. Also, it would be a great advantage to have an identical second area, so that one area can be cleaned, disinfected and dried off while the other is being used.

The type of kennelling and materials that needs to be provided, again depends on the size and weight of the adult members of the breed. Puppy runs should preferably have concrete floors inside and outside. If the run inside has wooden floors, linoleum or tiles, this is usually all right if you put down newspaper or anything similar that is removable and does not have a slippery surface and can be easily cleaned and disinfected. The concrete on the outside runs should not be too smooth. There should be a slight roughness so that both puppies and adults do not slip and slide.

Dirt runs for young puppies are to be discouraged. Dirt or grass runs will gradually build up contaminating levels of worm eggs or coccidia over a period of time. By regularly liming or salting the runs, the accumulation can be minimised, but it still is a less than desirable situation. These runs also become almost unusable in wet weather (see also chapter 17 on Kennelling).

CLEANING

Cleaning up after the puppies should be done at least **twice** a day. This means the papers should be changed, everything cleaned and disinfected (once a day may be sufficient for this), and the puppies should be put back only when everything is *dry*. It is an idea to wait until after feeding to do the major clean ups, as puppies always urinate and have a bowel movement about 5–10 minutes after feeding.

If puppies are kept in damp, dirty conditions, their resistance to infection will be low and they will be more susceptible to skin, gastric and worm problems. Remember, never leave dishes of soaked food lying around in the hot weather; it attracts flies, goes off very fast, and will cause gastric upsets.

OUTSIDE RUNS

As previously mentioned, these should be made of concrete for young puppies. The runs should also be sheltered from driving rain, excessive heat or wind. Go out and check the puppies in such weather conditions and ensure there is somewhere for the puppies to shelter safely. Preferably there should be at least one solid wall to the run, some form of permanent shade or roofing that covers half to two thirds of the run and a slight slope on the concrete for easy drainage.

INDOOR RUNS

If puppies are completely raised indoors, there should be plenty of ventilation and preferably skylights or a full sized doorway to the shed, garage or outhouse. If there is inadequate ventilation, the air becomes very humid and stale — this will encourage the spread of airborne viruses such as kennel cough. Do not go to the other extreme and have strong draughts around the puppies, especially in cold weather.

In very cold weather puppies may need 24 hour a day heating for several weeks. Smaller breeds and those with thin coats obviously need a longer heating period.

In very hot weather the problem is reversed, and keeping the puppies cool can be a difficult job. Wet sacks or towels left down in one corner of the run will give puppies a simple way to keep cool. Another idea if you are going out for the day, is to freeze a shallow dish of water and leave it with the puppies. It will slowly melt and give the puppies something cool to drink.

Vaccinations

Different veterinarians have differing vaccination schedules. However, as the average breeder wishes to sell and disperse their puppies when they are 6–8 weeks old, the vaccinations usually take place during this period.

MATERNAL IMMUNITY AND ITS EFFECT ON VACCINE EFFICIENCY

It is important to understand maternal immunity and its relationship to the first vaccinations which puppies receive. Maternal immunity is the immunity from diseases that is derived from globulins which are passed to the puppies via the uterus and via the colostrum ('first milk').

Puppies that have little or no maternal immunity will usually respond well to the first vaccination as there is little interference from the maternally derived antibodies. However, the puppies that have high levels of maternally derived immunity are very well protected by this maternal immunity for at least the first 6–8 weeks, and quite often it will protect them until 10–12 weeks of age.

The problem is that usually you do not know the exact level of maternally derived immunity in any given puppy unless you have each puppy blood tested to find out, which can be very expensive. High levels of maternal immunity can interfere with the puppy developing a correct response to the vaccine, seemingly particularly so in the case of parvovirus. The average puppy from the average bitch will have sufficient immunity to cover it for the first 6–8 weeks, provided it is not subjected to high levels of challenge or stress.

With some of the newer vaccines, the uptake from the vaccine is faster, giving good responses within 5–7 days of vaccination. These vaccines cut across the maternal antibodies and 80% will respond well to the first vaccination. By the second vaccination at 12 weeks, there is nearly a 100% cover.

Occasionally, there appears to be a 'vaccine breakdown'. What this generally means is that puppies may develop signs of gastric problems within several days of vaccination or several weeks later. A vaccine is designed to create a response to a disease so that the immune system will recognise future exposure to that disease and protect the body. Vaccines are either killed or attenuated live vaccines, that will stimulate the immune system without causing disease. However, any vaccine requires a good healthy immune system in the recipient (i.e. the puppy) to gain the best response.

For those that react within several days, various aspects of puppy health and management should be examined. Any concurrent problems such as heavy worm burden or sudden dietary changes will affect the health and stability of their immune system and can adversely affect their response to the vaccine. If the puppy is not really healthy, the additional stress of being vaccinated can precipitate gastric problems which you least need. The puppy's immune system is undergoing change and stress in trying to respond to the vaccine, so it is unable to respond as well to concurrent infections from viral, bacterial or parasite induced causes. Should the puppy be further stressed by travel, change of home or diet, then gastric infections are almost certain to result. Very small toy puppies are particularly vulnerable to this type of post-vaccine stress reaction as it requires very little to force these puppies into a negative sugar balance (sugar drop) from which point, without active care and attention, it is easy to lose puppies.

The occasional appearance of gastric infections in puppies that were vaccinated 10–20 days previously can again be the result of a stressed immune system as well as an inadequate response to the vaccine.

Therefore it is very important to only vaccinate very healthy, trouble free puppies. The puppies should be well grown, a good weight for their breed and age and have no sign of illness. Any signs of sickness, worm infestation, poor appetite and particularly diarrhoea, should be noted and cleared up prior to vaccination.

Toy breeds should not be vaccinated before 7–8 weeks if they are in any way underweight and preferably, even then, given a reduced dose of vaccine. Make sure the puppies eat well over the following 48 hours in order to avoid sugar drop.

I prefer to vaccinate puppies a little older if at all possible i.e. at 7–8 weeks of age rather than exactly on the six week mark. The puppies are checked out for health, physical defects and weight. At this time, any major problems either physical or environmental (feeding, parasites or failure to thrive despite proper care), can be noted and corrected prior to vaccination. Although it may seem time-consuming for the breeders, I am sure they willingly pay attention to details, as their aim is to send puppies out in tip-top condition with no problems.

After the vaccinations are given, wait 4–5 days before you allow the puppies to go to their new homes. The puppy's body is trying to react to the vaccine, and if you transport it long distances, or change the environment, you will be adding to an already stressful situation. Remind the new owners that the vaccinations the puppy has just received are temporary. Vaccination given at this age will cover mild exposure to those diseases but not heavy or continued challenges. Tell the new owners not to take their puppy out to show it off and to especially avoid public place such as parks.

New puppy owners naturally tend to be fussy and over anxious, but when it is obvious that, through the breeder's efforts, the puppy is well and healthy, they will have a confident start and will not feel the need to consult their vet as often.

The puppies should basically stay within their own backyards as much as possible until they have received their second vaccinations at 12–14 weeks old. A third vaccination with parvovirus at 16–18 weeks is still advocated by many veterinarians so discuss this with your vet. Kennel cough can be given from 12 weeks onwards.

SUGAR DROP IN PUPPIES OF TOY BREEDS (HYPOGLYCAEMIA)

Some toy breeds of dogs are prone to 'sugar drop' (hypoglycaemia) when young. It is generally seen when they are under six months of age and most commonly in Chihuahua, Pomeranian and Maltese puppies. It can occur as early as 4–6 weeks of age. These breeds have somewhat small livers and with the higher metabolic rate of the toy breeds, small changes in eating habits or diet, stresses such as cold temperatures, infection of the gut or chest, will quickly place these puppies into a negative sugar balance.

Affected puppies often appear weak and disorientated, may be unable to stand and can fit. Severe cases may be found unconscious or dead. Often only one puppy in a litter is affected, usually the runt of the litter. Severely affected puppies need immediate treatment of glucose, preferably intravenously. Milder cases often only require oral doses of glucose solutions or Energel®.

Prevention of sugar drop is the main aim. Small, fine boned puppies of susceptible breeds should be fed high quality, highly digestible, energy diets. Feed frequently, 4–5 times a day if necessary. Avoid stress wherever possible. Be vigilant if puppies are off their food for any reason.

Most susceptible puppies will stabilise by 6–8 months of age as they have finished growing.

Checking the Puppies' Health

When you take your puppies to the vet at around 6–7 weeks of age for their vaccinations, the vet will check the puppies' health, weight, heart, testicles and mouths. This is the time when you may learn that the runt of the litter really does have problems.

HEART

Heart defects are not common, but neither are they rare. Heart defects are more likely to be seen when the bitch has carried the puppies through a very hot summer period, and especially during the first trimester of pregnancy. Should this happen, you may find that more than one member of a litter is affected. Defects of this type are not usually genetic. Generally heart defects will cause affected puppies to be smaller and slower to gain weight. Some heart defects will cause the puppy to have difficulty in swallowing solid food. Very bad heart defects can easily be palpated by placing your fingers on either side of the chest and feeling the erratic beats, or by lifting the puppy's chest to your ear. The heart beat may sound and feel like a leaky washing machine. If you are not sure, check another normal puppy and the difference will be immediately obvious.

Puppies with bad heart defects should be put down unless you or someone else is prepared to take on a problem dog which is likely to have a short lifespan. Minor defects, although undesirable, may not prevent a puppy from leading a fairly normal life. Make sure it keeps very fit and active, is kept trim, and continues to take heartworm pills at all times. A weak heart cannot cope with heartworms winding around the valves. It is vital that your vet should be told about the dog's heart condition *before* it is given an anaesthetic.

TESTICLES
Testicles are usually checked at vaccination time, especially with potential show dogs. Very fat males may not have their testicles down at 6–7 weeks. If this is so, slightly reduce the weight of the puppy and 1–2 weeks later ask the vet to re-check the puppy. By that time testicles have often come down. Some breeds do not 'drop' their testicles until later (10–12 weeks). Breeders generally like to be sure that both are down in the scrotum or very close to it, by eight weeks i.e. *before* they leave home.

TEETH
A vet will check a puppy's mouth to see if it has a correct scissor bite. If any puppy has a drastically over or undershot mouth, make sure an adequate diet is being fed. The vet should warn the breeder that the mouth may not correct. Where the bite is very 'tight', I warn the breeder that these may not hold as the jaw may overgrow the skull (see section on Teeth and bite in chapter 4).

KNEES
Breeds that have knee problems (luxating patellas) can have the looseness of their patellas checked. Slight looseness will generally tighten as the puppy matures. Excessive looseness indicates a possible problem in the future.

TATTOOING
This I recommend for all breeds with reasonable ear size (except breeds like Collies which have drop tips), as in today's world, dog theft is a very common occurrence. Normally tattooing is done at 7–9 weeks of age and is very quick, relatively painless and the puppy is back to normal immediately. Tattoos allow easy recognition of the origin of an animal and the tattoo can be used to identify an animal when being x-rayed for a hip dysplasia scheme. Most of the bigger breed clubs advocate tattooing, which should be done on a national basis in connection with any breed rescue schemes.

MICRO-CHIPPING
This can be done at any age and is a very good means of positive identification. Preferably, these micro-chipped dogs should have a small 'M' tattooed in their left ear at the time of micro-chipping to allow easy public recognition. Scanners are available at all pounds and at many veterinary clinics.

The initial vet check of puppies at 6–8 weeks is, as you can see, very important especially to your credibility as a reputable breeder of sound stock. I like to get the puppies back a week later to re-check any minor problems that were identified at the first visit. Although serious problems are rare, a large number of puppies have some little matter that needs to be corrected.

Leaving Home — Bags Packed

Finally the big day comes and some or all of your precious puppies are leaving home. Understandably some breeders will be thankful for less mess to clean up.

Have a good sound diet sheet ready, as well as some of the particular dry dog food that you use. It is also advisable to have a short note about the breed, its temperament and needs as far as exercise and socialisation are concerned. Breeders of puppies of coated breeds should give out notes on coat care and grooming, together with information about breed club grooming days. You should be particularly careful about the diet sheet that you give out for bigger breeds. It must be sound and trouble-proof, as what can go wrong, often does go wrong.

Information about when and what type of treatment was used to worm the puppy, as well as when it is next due for worming should be written down for the new owner. A vaccination certificate stating the date the puppy was vaccinated and when it is next due for vaccination must also be packed in the puppy's overnight bag.

When the new owners come to pick up their puppies, they are excited, their kids race around, your dogs are barking and there may be quite a scene. Because of all excitement, often very little of the advice that you give to the new puppy owner is retained. I suggest that the breeder should phone new puppy owners (especially novices) within two weeks and carefully check in detail what the puppy is eating, ask how often it is being fed and whether food is being left around. Try to solve problems as soon as possible, as it is a lot easier to fix problems early!

11

The Stud Dog

1. From the Bitch Owner's Point of View

CHOOSING A STUD DOG

Choosing a stud dog would seem to be very simple, yet it is in fact one of the hardest aspects of dog breeding. Newcomers often make mistakes such as seeing a popular show-winning dog and announcing 'I want one by him', or worse, they consider their own often inferior backyard male to be suitable. Some people give little thought to the bloodlines or conformation of the prospective parents and do not know what is needed in the breed at the time.

One should be ten times more selective with a male than a bitch as the male dog has the greater influence on the breed in the long run. Without wishing to offend those concerned with genetics, we all know that either parent is only responsible for 50% of the genes. However a male dog which is heavily used within a breed, will have a far greater influence via his numerous offspring than even the best bitch that is limited to 4–6 litters before becoming too old.

Breeding better dogs is what this game is all about, and the majority of breeders have a limited time to produce a definite improvement on their stock, let alone on the breed as a whole. By limited, I mean 10–15 years, by which time, if you have not produced good results, you will be more than ready to quit. Several wrong decisions on the way can delay that 'ultimate' litter, so think carefully before each litter. You should aim to breed a better dog or bitch than you already own. Remember that the perfect dog has yet to be born.

In choosing a stud dog, consideration should be given to the following:

(a) The genetic aspects such as the virtues or faults behind the lines and the good, the bad and the ugly. Additional information in this area is found in chapter 16, Genetics and the Importance of Breed Soundness— in fact you should read that first.

Knowledge of bloodline faults (and occasionally virtues) is not gained easily and you need to have been around for a few years, gaining experience by studying bloodlines and a wide range of representative offspring. You need not take all you hear as gospel; few people are objective about a stud dog, particularly their own or their major rival's. By the time you have been in the game for several years, if you are lucky you·might have met a few dedicated breeders, who may give you a more realistic view of a dog's genetic value.

The people I would be most inclined to believe are those who will praise even the opposition's dog and admit their own dog's faults. These breeders will often be rather critical of your precious bitch and will give constructive advice as to which structural faults need the most attention, and which bloodline should blend well with your bitch.

Read books and articles about your breed, preferably those with local knowledge as to the current status of the breed in your country.

Always enquire whether the dog you are interested in has the relevant certificates of soundness that are desirable in your breed e.g. covering hip dysplasia in the larger breeds, eye clearance for those with hereditary eye defects and so on.

(b) Look at what the dog is **producing** and assess:

- The suitability of the dog's **type** or **style** for your bitch and whether this will correct the major problem areas in your bitch.
- If the dog is too young to have mature progeny, assess the appearance of the dog, his virtues and faults, and consider whether he resembles the bloodline which you wish to use. If he is of the same type as the desired ancestors, hopefully he will then throw the same style. The more the dog resembles his genetic bloodline, the more likely he is to reproduce his type. If he is a one off, he is unlikely to reproduce his virtues to any great degree.
- Is he a 'prepotent' sire? This follows the point just raised. Few sires are considered to be prepotent. Prepotent means that the majority of the dog's offspring resemble the sire's body type, head and colouring. Prepotent can also refer to a fault that a sire may throw, e.g. bad mouths, poor pigment or bad fronts. This term is generally used in its positive aspect during discussions about stud dogs and their progeny.

A dog which is prepotent for good body type, will generally become a strong foundation dog in a pedigree. These dogs can often be inbred upon when further back in a pedigree.

Do not expect the stud dog to do all the genetic work. A litter is the sum of its genetic/phenotypic components and, at best, you can only hope for a half way improvement from the bitch to the dog (or vice-versa).

TYPES OF STUD DOGS

It is difficult to assess a stud dog's worth when you are dealing with those breeds that are numerically small, as consequently the choice for stud dog will be limited. In the smaller, faster maturing breeds, where maturity is reached as early as 8–9 months, a stud dog's worth is rapidly determined for that breeder at any rate. The converse is true of the larger breeds, where final maturity may not be reached for 2–3 years.

'Stud dog of the moment' syndrome

This usually means the top show dog of the last 6–12 months. Often this dog does not have sufficient progeny for anyone to make an accurate assessment of his future potential beyond opinion expressed that 'his puppies are very promising', or 'they are the best I have ever seen'.

I do not like to assess a stud dog until his oldest progeny is reaching 12–24 months and you can see how the mature offspring have shaped up. It is preferable to wait until there are enough of them before you attempt to make a reasonable assessment over several different bloodlines/types which have mated to the dog. The vast majority of breeders do not wish to wait this long and will often take the gamble that the progeny will be wonderful. As they will be amongst the first to use the dog, they are confident that the market for the puppies will be good and one cannot blame them. However consideration should be given as to the suitability of bloodlines, structural strengths and weaknesses as mentioned above. Otherwise the litter may eventually have been a waste of time, which, while producing nice pets, has left you the breeder, with little to go on with into the next generation.

'Expensive stud dog' syndrome

This syndrome is common worldwide, where it is believed that a large stud fee indicates, to the novice at least, that this dog must be worth more money than other stud dogs within that breed.

There is often justification for this high fee, particularly in the case of an imported dog. The owners have gone to considerable trouble and expense to import the dog, so a reasonable fee proportional to this is not unexpected. However, not all imports are well selected. The new owners are not necessarily at fault, as this may be due to original owners having claimed that the dog is a wonderful specimen of the breed. When the dog finally arrives, little may be seen of the original glowing description. Occasionally a stud dog may have been bought as a puppy, so it is a gamble whether he turns out well or not. Sometimes you are lucky, but Murphy's law loves to confound matters for the dog breeder.

The question still applies as to whether the dog is producing what you want, does he suit your bitch, both in conformation and bloodlines? Do you need the new bloodlines? If the answers are yes, then use the dog. It will be a lot cheaper than going overseas and buying your own and enduring all the hassles which are inevitable when importing a stud dog.

Free or 'cheap' stud dogs

The cheapest you can find is free but preferably not your own backyard dog unless he really is a good example of the breed and suits the bitch's bloodlines.

Some outside dogs are offered 'free' for a variety of reasons:

1. The owners may have quite a good young dog that they wish to 'rove' i.e. his fertility or his ability to produce worthwhile stock. This is in my view somewhat denigrating to the poor dog, but understandable when there may be a limited brood bitch pool available in certain breeds or within geographic locations.

2. The dog owner may want to have your bitch go to their dog if she is a good specimen of the breed or has compatible or valuable bloodlines which they consider will 'nick' well with their dog. They usually want the pick of the litter.

3. In lieu of a stud fee, the stud dog owner will take 1 or 2 puppies and sell them to recoup the stud fee.

4. They want a mating with their dog so they can have a puppy of their beloved Fido, even though it may be a scruffy flea-bitten individual.

Cheap stud dogs, with no apparent strings attached, often fall into one of the following areas:

1. He has never been shown but 'there are champions in his pedigree'. Just because a dog has a couple of good ancestors, does not mean that he is a good specimen of the breed. The dog must have something positive to offer your bitch before you can consider him as a possible mate.

2. He may not be very well bred or may have serious conformational faults.

3. Accidents may have restricted his show career, yet he may be a good example of the breed.

4. He does not have the desired certificates for soundness to comply with breed club recommendations within that country. This refers to hip certificates and eye clearances.

'HANDLING' THE STUD DOG OWNER

There is a fairly well established set of 'unwritten rules' covering the approach to a stud dog owner. Admittedly, for some the rule is 'if you have the money, here's the dog', but they are definitely in the minority. The concerned stud dog owner would like to be approached, preferably before the bitch even comes into season, not on the day she is due to be mated. It is the stud dog owner's prerogative to refuse any bitch on any grounds, so be polite and *ask*, do not demand, to use a stud dog. An interested stud dog owner will prefer to know what *your* bitch is like both constructionally and genetically. A copy of the pedigree is helpful.

Once your bitch comes into season, phone the stud dog owners immediately and inform them of what is going on, approximately when the bitch should be due to be mated and ask whether a swab certificate is required. The more helpful you are, the greater the effort the stud dog owners are likely to take with you and your bitch, particularly if she is a problem bitch (difficult to mate or with a bad history of infertility).

Speaking from experience as a stud dog owner, a polite pleasant approach by a bitch owner helps both sides to be patient and good humoured, considering all the time and effort required to mate a bitch. Matings often involve fiddling around for 2–3 nights after work, taking up half the weekend, socialising with the owners, making endless cups of tea and coffee, and receiving weekly calls until the puppies are born. This sort of thing can continue until the puppies are sold, sometimes beyond. I occasionally have nightmares about puppies my dog has sired, eventually dying of old age and the original breeder phoning up to complain about their death. I suppose they think their puppies should have lived forever if they bred them!

WHEN MATING A BITCH

Bitch owners should remember:

1. Never consider a dog as a stud prospect if there are major temperament or constructional faults. Dogs that are aggressive, shy or

are fear biters should be avoided at all costs. Serious show and genetic faults in a stud dog, such as bad mouths and eye defects, are not worth the trouble you may get. There are usually many good dogs available, so there is no need for you to bother with those which will probably bring problems that may take several generations to remove from your bloodlines.

2. Both parties should always find out the exact arrangements committing to a deal. If it makes you feel happier, put the arrangements in writing and let each party keep a copy.

3. Always ask *before* deciding to use a dog, about relevant certificates that are recommended in that breed, for example hip dysplasia and eye clearance.

Between the bitch and stud dog owner:

1. Always settle details of the fee, how it is to be paid, and when, at the time of the mating(s).

2. The stud dog owner should *never* hand over the stud or service certificate until the complete stud fee has been paid.

3. If the bitch misses, clarify the situation regarding the stud fee that has been paid. There may be a handling fee if the owners of the bitch do not wish to, or cannot, return the bitch for another mating. In these circumstances, arrangements between owners of stud dogs vary considerably.

2. The Stud Dog

WHEN TO FIRST USE A DOG AT STUD

Generally, a male dog should not be used for mating before nine months, although some are quite capable of mating with a bitch and being fertile from five months onwards. The smaller breeds are sexually mature at a much earlier age than are the larger breeds. Some of the larger breeds may not be sexually active until 15–18 months of age. Terriers, especially the smaller ones, are willing and able by 5–6 months. A dog should not be used under nine months on the grounds that he is usually not mentally mature enough to handle the experience well. Some individuals become instant sex fiends and will mate anything indiscriminately, including your leg. Other dogs may become aggressive to people or other dogs. Nine months is not a long time to wait considering that the animal has not finished growing until then. By this time you should be able to get a clearer idea of his virtues and faults.

It is good practice to allow a potential stud dog a mating before 18–24 months of age to educate him as to how it is done. In an animal that may get heavy usage at a later date, this can be a valuable introduction. The dog learns what it is all about and will be very keen the next time. If the first mating does not occur until later in a dog's life, the dog may be a very poor worker or not wish to mate at all.

With dogs that are not among the top animals in the breed, the stud work is very limited and it is not a worthwhile exercise to undertake, unless a particular person wishes to use the animal.

Ideally the first mating should be between 9–15 months of age and the bitch used should, by preference, be experienced. If the bitch is a maiden or a difficult bitch to mate, the dog may have a bad experience and could subsequently become a poor stud dog.

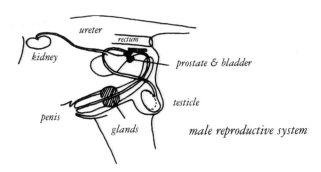

male reproductive system

Mating the Dog and Bitch

There is a definite art in mating dogs. If the bitch is ready and the dog is willing, it (usually) results in a quick and fruitful result. On the other hand, if both sets of owners and both dogs are relative novices, long hours can be spent trying to get the dogs to achieve a tie. I am sure novices often wonder how the canine race ever got started. There are advocates of different methods of mating dogs, novices in particular liking the idea of letting true romance take over. This method often has 5–6 neighbourhood males in hot pursuit and may well add some variety to the litter.

It is far safer to mate dogs in an enclosed area where complete control can be maintained. This is an absolute necessity in the case of visiting bitches. I prefer, particularly in the case of valuable stud animals, to have both dogs on leads at all times. If the bitch is friendly, allow a short play of 2–3 minutes before getting down to business. Long periods of playing can be detrimental to a young stud dog as he may develop a habit of auditioning as Romeo (for the entire length of the original play). Aggressive bitches have to forego the foreplay in the interests of the stud dog's safety. Over keen stud dogs with the 'bull at the gate' approach, also need to be restrained, particularly with nervous, shy or maiden bitches.

It is often best, particularly with an inexperienced dog, for one of the owners of the dog to hold the bitch. The novice dog, seeing one of his owners at the front end, usually works better than with a strange owner at the head of the bitch.

Handling the bitch

With novice bitch owners who are unused to assisting in matings, or are not used to firmly restraining their bitch, it is preferable that you (the owner) ensure that the bitch is not going to whip around at a critical moment and bite the dog. A valuable show and stud dog cannot afford to get attacked by an aggressive bitch.

Experienced stud dogs are usually indifferent as to who holds a bitch as long as she (the bitch that is) stands reasonably still. Aggressive bitches need a firm hand and whoever gets the job of holding her, should be strong enough to do the job.

Holding the bitch

The bitch should be held by the head in a firm grip, one hand on either side of her head, with a good grip on both the check chain and the skin around the neck. If the bitch is good natured, minimum restraint should be used. A light but firm grip of the check chain is often all that is needed, particularly with an amorous bitch who keeps playing even while the dog is trying to mount.

If however, the bitch is very objectionable, a muzzle made of soft material such as a stocking or soft bandage, should be applied for the safety of the dog and the handlers. Occasionally the bitch will want to sit or turn. If the handler of the dog holds the bitch's tail around to the side they are working from, and at the same time holds up the bitch under the middle of the abdomen, reasonable control of the bitch is obtained. For the long, low slung breeds, the handler can put the bitch over your legs whilst sitting down. Sometimes a paint can under the abdomen works very well, by keeping the bitch up off the ground and in a standing position.

Once the dog has mated the bitch, she may start to object strenuously as the glands of the penis swell to form the 'tie', especially if the bitch is very small in the vulva or the dog is well endowed. Hold the bitch very firmly until she accepts that she can do nothing about it.

Use of tranquillisers for difficult bitches

Aggressive or very nervous bitches may require tranquillisers before mating to save all concerned from wear and tear. Tranquillisers should only be resorted to if the bitch has definitely ovulated and is ready for mating. It may be necessary to have a blood test done to confirm this. Most bitches will object strenuously if presented for a mating when they are not ready, i.e. either too early or too late. Other bitches may be calm, even desperate to get mated, but when the dog has penetrated and the glands are starting to swell to form the tie, she suddenly wants to be anywhere other than attached to the dog.

Numerous antics are possible during a mating. She may try to turn inside out, she may throw herself on the ground, clawing her way up an owner's leg, even biting the owner. Unfortunately, you do not know until the first time the bitch is mated, what she may do. Bitches that have a past history of misbehaving should be tranquillised as a routine.

Valium® is the drug of choice, as it calms the bitch without making her keel over. She will still be able to stand and will be amenable to most of the proceedings. Acetyl promazine (ACP) is less effective as it tends to put the animal to sleep without having the mental calming effect of Valium®.

At the end of this harrowing little section, novices can be reassured that the average dog and bitch mate very easily, without resorting to restraints and tranquillisers.

It is advisable that dogs and bitches are not just left alone to mate in a yard, particularly if they are valuable breeding stock. Young stud dogs may get damaged by the bitch and some older dogs may start 'disciplining' a bitch that will not stand for them.

Assisting the dog

How to assist the dog during matings:

1. The dog and the bitch should be under supervision at all times and should only be tried for short periods, about 30 minutes at a time. If the dog is not interested, you will have long enough to find out. If he is interested, it is long enough for him to become tired if he is getting nowhere. After a break of 20–30 minutes, the dogs can be tried again. This keeps the dog alert and avoids exhaustion.

2. Try and use a small area, preferably one that is concreted and sheltered from the elements for matings so that the dog knows why he is there and will not waste time sniffing around the backyard. A garage, porch or small yard is ideal for this purpose. Once a routine is established, the stud dog will be very keen to mate when he is brought into that area, as he becomes conditioned to expect a bitch in season to be present.

3. Get the dog used to being handled during matings. Young stud dogs often prefer to do it all by themselves, but generally they do not manage to do very much. If the dog learns that he cannot mate the bitch without somebody holding on to her, he will eventually ignore the person holding the bitch and get on with the job at hand. Allow the dogs to play a little on leads before getting on with business. If the bitch is aggressive, muzzle her and forget the preliminaries.

With a maiden dog, encourage him to hop up on the bitch by telling him how good he is. Words of praise and enthusiasm for what he is doing will make the young dog work well. Never laugh at him, even if he tries to mate the front end (inexperienced dogs seem to be particularly interested in ears for some obscure reason). Once he gets the idea of which end to attack, he is generally up and running in a fairly short time.

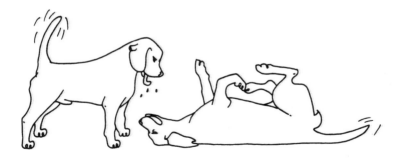

4. Holding the hindquarters of the bitch. If the hindquarters of the bitch are held up by an arm under the belly, just in front of her hindquarters, when the dog is attempting to mate her, then the bitch cannot sit down or move around at the crucial moment. This can greatly shorten the time for matings.

When the dog does jump up on the bitch's back, it often uses the arm as extra leverage to get closer to the bitch. Many younger dogs will try mating a bitch long distance as it were and end up poking around several centimetres from the target. If the dog is doing this, slightly push the bitch backwards as he starts to work. Once the dog hits the spot (the vulva), he will move forward and up, treading as he tries to gain the closest tie with the bitch. Once the dog has finished treading and attempts to get off the bitch to the side or turn, it is an idea to hold the two sets of hindquarters together until the glands of the penis fully dilate and ties or locks the two together.

Some dogs are slower to swell in the glands and may appear to slip out as soon as they turn; holding them together for several minutes will often ensure a proper tie. Even once they are tied, it is an idea to keep holding the hindquarters together until the tie finishes as one of the halves of the tie may want to lie down, leave, or bite the other half. Usually it is the bitch who changes her mind about being mated once the deed is done. Allow the dog to turn if he wants to, after the tie is definitely established. To assist, lift the dog's leg over and down.

Dogs do not have to turn, many prefer to stay parallel.

The length of time that a tie lasts varies between dogs. Most dogs have their own fairly standard time, i.e. the time it takes for the glands of the penis to relax but the average is 15–20 minutes. A particular dog may have a longer regular tie time of 30–35 minutes. Rarely, a bitch may have a muscular spasm of the vulva and lock the dog in. The normal time for the end of the tie will come and go, and ties have occasionally lasted 2–3 hours. This is not common, but the bitch may need an injection of an antispasmodic such as Buscopan® to relax her. Once she relaxes, the tie will end, much to the male dog's relief, not to mention the handlers.
5. Elevating the vulva of the bitch if she has a low vulva. Some bitches have a low slung vulva which may need to be elevated above the floor of her pelvis before the dog can mate her. Place a finger above and below the vulva, lift and slightly angle the lower edge outwards. The dog then has a clear go at the vulva. If not, the dog could bruise himself by continually hitting the pelvis as he attempts to enter.

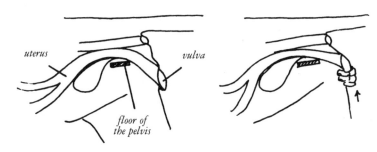

Bitches that have very small vulvas may not be able to achieve a tie. They can have slip matings, where the dog penetrates the bitch but knots outside. If the dogs are held together for 5–10 minutes (preferably 10 minutes), this is as good as the real thing. Some breeds rarely have ties as the majority of the bitches have very small vulvas e.g. Greyhounds.

When the vulva is too small to allow a natural mating, an artificial insemination may have to be done (see section on Mating the bitch in chapter 7).

If a bitch appears a normal size and the dog cannot mate her, it may be necessary to have an internal examination by a veterinarian to find out if there is a blockage.

6. Difference in height between the dog and bitch. When mating a dog and bitch of the same breed, there can often be a fair size difference. Males are larger than bitches on the whole, but all variations can and do occur.

(a) Small dog to a big bitch — face the bitch downhill. Some people have little potholes dotted around the backyard, so that tall bitches' back legs can be placed in them, but this is only really a last resort. Place the bitch facing down hill to give the dog a slight height advantage over the bitch.

Smaller breeds are easily mated on table tops if need be, preferably on top of a non-slip mat. Breeders of very small breeds like Chihuahuas, may in their effort to breed ever smaller offspring, use very small male dogs on comparatively giant bitches. A telephone book with a towel or mat on top is quite effective.

(b) Large dog to a small bitch — face the bitch uphill and/or slightly elevate the vulva. The pothole enthusiasts have trouble here as most stud dogs will not work with their feet in a hole.

7. When they don't mate, the dog may be right as the bitch may not be ready. Smears and blood tests to determine whether the bitch is ready are invaluable. Progesterone levels will give fairly accurate indications of what events have or have not occurred. Bitches that have travelled long distances, can be put off by the stress of travel or the new environment, and may not mate for a further 2–3 days after they have had time to settle down. I have known cases when a mating has had to be delayed by up to 7–10 days, as the bitch needed this amount of time to settle down in the unfamiliar surroundings. Occasionally a bitch may be having a strange season and fail to ovulate.

HOW OFTEN SHOULD A STUD DOG BE USED?

Younger dogs (12–24 months old), should have a maximum of one or two bitches per week; with two matings, possibly only one bitch per week.

Over 16–18 months of age, two or three bitches per week is a reasonable maximum. I would not give a dog under two years of age more than two bitches per week.

Older dogs are quite capable of studding every day during busy periods. Bitches tend to cycle in groups, so quite often, there is heavy work for a popular stud dog over the space of several weeks. In between groups of bitches, the dog should get a break every now and again.

Regular checks by the veterinarian are only necessary if the dog is constantly in use. If the dog develops a heavy prepucal discharge or has pain on mating or urination, then the dog should be checked out immediately by your veterinarian. Any swellings of the testicles, or sudden decline in fertility should likewise be swiftly attended to.

During a mating, the dog may get bruised or damaged, particularly if the bitch is very small in the vulva. He may also get traumatised by the bitch pulling away before the glands have properly reduced. Get the dog checked by your vet. Sexual rest and antibiotics may be all that is needed, but with a valuable stud dog it is better to be safe than sorry.

Occasionally the stud dog may have fertility problems or periodic prostatic inflammations. These individuals, especially if they are very valuable, need to be regularly checked. Dogs with prostatic problems should be checked by the veterinarian every 3–4 months. Never feed these dogs bones.

PROSTATE PROBLEMS
(For more detail see chapter 14, Breeding Older Dogs and Bitches). Signs of prostatic inflammation include aggression, constipation, urinating blood, straining when urinating and defecating, and reluctance to achieve a tie. Continued severe prostatic problems may necessitate castration in the long term.

ADDITIVES TO DIETS
A heavily in-use stud dog should have a high protein diet to sustain a good state of health and to cover the ravages of such an exciting lifestyle.

As a rule, do not feed a stud dog immediately prior to a mating. Wait until the dog has settled down after the service for a good half hour before giving him his meal. A dog with a full stomach will not work well and in the older deeper chested stud dogs, there exists the very real danger of stomach torsion. The excitement experienced by the dog from the mating can take ½–1 hour to subside, so delay feeding until the dog is calm.

Extra vitamins, especially vitamin E and the B group, are good for assisting the stud dog in maintaining a fit muscle condition and promoting sperm production.

VALUABLE STUD DOGS AND SPERM STORAGE
(See also chapter 14, Breeding older Dogs and Bitches). It is worthwhile to consider the storage of sperm from a valuable stud dog, not only for future use in case of accidents, but against decreasing fertility with advancing age. Sperm production does decrease with age, but the effect

is not marked in the *majority* of dogs until they are over ten years of age. Sperm quality does however, start to drop from around 7–8 years onwards.

Ideally, sperm collection and storage should be done at an age where the dog is still healthy and active, 4–6 years being an optimum. Collection is possible at under four years (and over 12 months) but it usually takes time to properly assess the dog's progeny and to estimate the dog's true value to the breed as a whole and your kennel in particular. Older dogs can still have sperm collected and stored, but an evaluation of the number of sperm and percentage of live sperm will give an idea as to whether it is going to be of sufficient quality to be a worthwhile exercise.

As transport has improved, so has the possibility of flying frozen semen around the world, instead of transporting the bitch. This new step may lead to a more efficient use of valuable stud dogs. To do this however, you do need capable people at either end, in sperm collection, dilution and correct storage, so as to maximise its viability when finally thawed out for use. Correct handling of the frozen semen during transport and in particular, the thawing process, can greatly enhance fertility levels.

If you are thinking of storing sperm from your dog, or using frozen semen on your bitch, ask around beforehand, to find out who is doing the most work in this field locally and what success they have had before going into any great expense. I am sure that as the techniques involved are constantly improving, there will be far greater use of frozen semen in the future.

STUD DOG INFERTILITY

Infertility is not as common in the male dog as it is in the female. Few fertile stud dogs ever develop serious infertility unless there is a history of injury or infection. True infertility is generally due to sperm abnormalities, being abnormal shape, too low a production (lack of production of any of the seminal fluids can create a lowered fertility) or complete infertility. Lack of production of hormones by the testicles can have a secondary type of infertility, namely lack of libido or desire to mate. Age can be a limiting factor on sperm production as can the frequency of use to a limited extent.

To obtain a clear picture of a stud dog's infertility, many factors need to be taken into account:

1. Age of the dog   (a) Too young when there is insufficient live sperm present, inexperience on the dogs part or lack of developed sex drive.

(b) Too old when again, insufficient live sperm is present, particularly if the older dog has not had a mating for six months or longer; lowered libido, prostatic infections, presence of testicular tumours etc.

(a) Litter numbers relative to the breed: if the breed average litter is eight, and the dog's past history is of litters of 2–3, then there is probably a problem of lowered fertility, often associated with higher than average percentage of abnormal sperm or a low sperm production.

2. Previous litters (if any) sired by the dog

(b) When was a litter last sired? Some dogs may have had heavy usage when younger and then lose fashion for several years. Even if the dog has a rest for several years, the fertility does not drop off markedly. An initial ejaculate may show large numbers of dead sperm, but a check after several ejaculates will give a more accurate picture of the dog's fertility.

(c) Number of litters sired. This is really relative to the number of bitches mated by the dog, which is further discussed in the following paragraph, so that a realistic assessment of the dog's fertility can be determined in the light of the bitches he has been put to.

(a) Previous litters of any of the bitches, what numbers, and when last conceived. An accurate picture of the bitch(es) put to a stud dog can often clear a maligned stud dog. Some problem bitches have a history of poor conception rates or muddled seasons, which can often damn a new stud dog as 'infertile', or 'a shooter of blanks'. Maiden bitches can present problems as they may or may not be fertile. If two or three difficult bitches who have been mated to the dog in succession miss, it will be enough to have the stud dog owner on Valium® or demanding weekly sperm counts.

3. History of the bitches put to the dog

(b) Age of the bitch, immediate history; has she travelled a long distance? How many litters has she had without a break? What is her genetic relationship to the dog?

(a) Testicles: size, weight, consistency.

4. Stud dog examination

(b) Examination of the penis and prepuce; can it extend fully, is there bruising or any sign of infection or abnormalities?

(c) Prostate: history of problems associated with the prostate; for example, is the dog unwilling to mate?

(d) History of matings and libido.

(a) Sperm: check for colour, motility, sperm shape and number of abnormal sperm as a percentage basis. The whiter the sperm fraction, the denser or higher the sperm count.

5. Collection of ejaculate and examination

(b) The other fractions of the ejaculate should also be examined. There are three fractions all together, for clearness, presence of blood or inflammatory cells.

Most veterinarians can assess the colour, number of sperm, motility, percentage of live to dead sperm, presence of 'streaming', and can examine the sperm morphology (structure). This would be an evaluation estimating whether the dog's sperm and ejaculate are normal or abnormal.

6. Sperm evaluation

If there are high numbers of dead sperm, do take into account how long it has been since the last mating. If there is a long time gap of several months, then the first collection is often misleading and several collections should be made over a period of 1–2 weeks, when a more accurate picture will appear.

Poor sperm counts can be as a result of many different causes; hypothryroid conditions, genetic abnormalities as well as a reduced sex hormone production. Routine checking of thyroid levels should be done on any dog with a low sperm count. If this level is low, thyroid replacement is necessary and should be commenced as soon as possible. Once the thyroid level is back in the normal range, wait 6--8 weeks before re-checking the sperm count.

If the sperm counts are still low, then sex hormone treatment may be required. The following applies to those with low sperm counts and normal thyroid levels. The hormones used to stimulate spermatogenesis are gonadotropins, which act indirectly to stimulate sperm production and as a side effect, also produce natural testosterone which stimulates the libido. Injections of testosterone are contra-indicated in fertility problems in the male. Giving injections of testosterone directly to a dog will not stimulate sperm production and in excess, can act as a contraceptive by lowering sperm production.

Large numbers of abnormally shaped sperm, e.g. kinked necks, double tails or heads, will cut down the fertility level of a stud dog. Levels of around 10% are considered reasonably normal, but over 40–50% is a real threat to having sufficient numbers to travel in the right direction to enable enough sperm to reach the fallopian tubes and achieve fertilisation.

If the ejaculate cannot be reasonably well evaluated, the next possible action would be referral to a specialist or a university clinic.

Once you have a comprehensive history for that dog, the veterinarian is in a far better position to make a qualitative diagnosis as to:

(a) Whether there is a problem.

(b) Where the trouble is to be found.

(c) Whether it can be treated.

FROZEN SEMEN EVALUATION

Dog semen needs to be evaluated prior to freezing. The concentration and value of the seminal fluid will give the final dilution rate of the semen and determine the number of straws to be obtained.

Medium sized breeds have ½–2 mL of seminal fraction with an average of 5–6 million sperm per mL. The ideal amount of semen needed for good fertility is 100 million live sperm. The volume which fits into the bitch (average size) is a maximum of 2 mL. Any more and the uterus will expel the excess. Frozen semen which is of low concentration and low post thaw motility is not a good candidate for use.

Ideally the concentration should be greater than 40 million/mL and the post thaw motility percentage. A test sample is always thawed for these values after freezing each batch of semen. Post thaw motility (PTM) should also be a minimum of 40%, the higher the better.

To work out the number of straws needed to be used, determine the concentration per mL and post thaw motility percentage. Ideally 100 million live sperm should be the target for adequate fertility, a minimum of 60 million live sperm. Small breeds need reasonably concentrated semen or the volume parameters become limiting.

Remember, nine out of ten fertility problems are associated with the bitch, rather than the dog.

12

Common Breeding Problems of Bitches

U nfortunately, not all infertility problems can be solved. This is a constantly expanding research field and our control over canine infertility improves as breakthroughs occur. Too little is known even now, about infertility in the bitch and specific hormone levels within different breeds. Because of this, I am reluctant to use hormone therapy on bitches unless they have a well proven history of poor fertility or specific hormonal problems during pregnancy. The more facts available to the veterinarian, the more likely a satisfactory result will be achieved.

The Importance of Good Records with Problem Bitches

It is most important to remember that every bitch is different and so is every case of infertility, poor fertility or reduced viability of puppies. If there is a good history with presenting bitches, the veterinarian can usually make a reasonable diagnosis as to where or what the problem is.

The main points to be able to tell your veterinarian about your bitch are as follows:

1. HER AGE AND GENERAL HEALTH CONDITION

The most important thing is that the bitch is healthy and in good condition at the time of mating. Good condition means not too fat and not too thin. If a bitch, especially for a first litter, is too fat, she can often have fertility problems including low conception rates, whelping problems with slow parturition or inertia and, possibly, problems of sizing, with puppies either too large or too small. In general, a bitch should be no more than 4–5 years of age for a first litter. However, this varies according to the breed as some breeds, like Great Danes, are by this time fairly elderly. The latest I would suggest breeding a maiden Great Dane bitch would be four years.

Older bitches have a greater risk of having developed hormonal imbalances and uterine infections. Any bitch over six years of age has a risk of failure to hold pregnancy for these reasons. Conception rates also will start to fall rapidly over the eight year mark and there is a significant decrease in puppy survival.

2. HOW OFTEN SHE COMES INTO SEASON AND THE LENGTH OF SEASON?

The season interval can be variable in the bitch, the average being 6–8 months between seasons. Some bitches cycle as frequently as every 2–3 months or have very irregular lengths of seasons, possibly due to cystic ovaries. Other bitches may have prolonged intervals between seasons yet still be quite normal, for example the Basenji, which is a once a year cycler.

Bitches that fail to come into season at all by 2–2½ years of age may need investigating further. The bitch's health should be assessed and the more obvious reasons for failure, such as poor weight or use of anabolic injections, should be eliminated. Thyroid levels in particular should be checked, as they are a very common cause of poor fertility and erratic season lengths. The possibility of chromosomal abnormalities should then be considered and karyotyping carried out. This is not often available by the average veterinarian, but if you are lucky, you might be able to have it done by a university veterinary laboratory .

Some bitches have silent seasons i.e. they do not bleed very much and because of this the season may pass unnoticed. If the owner does find the bitch in season, it may be assumed erroneously that she is very early in her season, when in actual fact she may be ready for mating. If you are unsure, have the bitch blood tested to determine the progesterone level at the same time she is swabbed. This way an accurate picture can be obtained of which stage in the season the bitch has reached.

If you cannot determine whether your bitch is coming into season and you own a male dog, kennel your 'non-cycling bitch' next to the dog. This way you may be able to catch the bitch when her behaviour (or his) shows that she is in season.

3. WHEN SHE IS NORMALLY MATED DURING A SEASON AND OVER WHAT PERIOD?

Quite a few cases of 'infertility' can be attributed to the owner going too early or too late to the stud dog. Bitches with poor litter size can occasionally fit into this picture. Too many owners believe that their bitch corresponds to the average bitch, and do not bother to have either a blood test or smear done to find out if she is ready before going to the dog.

Some bitches are very early or late ovulators and, if they go to the dog at the standard 10–14 days in season, may well miss the ovulation period. If your bitch has fairly standard seasons, but low fertility, have a series of blood tests taken every 3–4 days to check the rising progesterone levels and thus determine the ideal time for mating. You may find a dramatic improvement in her apparent 'infertility'.

A male dog in your own backyard can also be helpful. Some males are very accurate at pin-pointing the exact time of peak fertilisation, though unfortunately many male dogs become very hormonal, will howl, and go off their food for the entire three weeks of the bitch's season. However, if the male is sensible, he will only be interested during the 3–4 days that the bitch is fertile. If you have an accurate stud dog, he can be a very valuable indicator, saving much time and energy. When the dog says go, mate the bitch. If the bitch is very valuable and you wish to be sure, have a progesterone blood test done to ensure she has ovulated and is ready for mating.

Another important point to remember is that a bitch's peak fertilisation times may alter during her breeding life and they may occur earlier or later in the season. Some bitches can be mated at 3–4 days while others are not ready until 16–18 days into the season.

Matings should ideally take place 2–4 days after the onset of true oestrus.

Progesterone levels should be around 10–20 ng/mL (30–60 nmol) to obtain the best results (see also Mating the bitch and Timing of mating in chapter 7).

4. HAS SHE HAD PUPPIES PREVIOUSLY?

If so, when, how many, and at what time after mating i.e. how many days since mating?

The above point can be directly related to this one. If a bitch is mated too early or too late, litter sizes may be small. To work out if the mating time is at fault, count back the days from whelping to the day of mating. If the number is 58 days, you may need to mate the bitch 3–5 days earlier. Conversely if the bitch goes overtime, she may need to be mated later in the season. Use 63 days as the basis and adjust either way from that time, relative to the whelping date. If this is done, there may be a great improvement in litter size.

5. DOES SHE MATE EASILY OR DOES SHE REQUIRE ARTIFICIAL INSEMINATION ?

The bitch may have a physical problem or a defect which affects the mating. These problems are not common but when they do occur they can cause considerable trouble.

The most common problems encountered are:

(a) Too small a vulva. Either the vulva is physically too small for the dog to achieve full penetration, or a constriction may exist inside the vulva making the entrance to the vagina limited.

Occasionally problems of this sort can be fixed surgically and subsequently, normal matings can take place. If they cannot be fixed surgically, then an AI can be performed and at the time of whelping, the bitch will usually have no problems at all in passing the puppies. I always warn the owners that difficulties during whelping may occur, but they are infrequent.

(b) A constriction further inwards i.e. a persistent hymen, a constriction or frenulum (fibrous sheet of tissue) that can divide the vagina and restrict the passage of the dog's penis at the time of mating. These types of restrictions are occasionally difficult to recognise unless an internal examination is done and you are specifically looking for a problem of this kind. These bitches are often termed 'difficult to mate' as the best matings you will get are slip matings. This does not mean that all 'difficult to mate' bitches have physical problems. Again, the majority of constrictions like this are either self-correcting at the time of whelping or can readily be corrected surgically. If however the constriction or defect extends too far inwards from the vagina, then the chance of correcting this successfully diminishes rapidly.

It is uncommon to have defects, even minor ones like these. Some breeds do however have a slightly higher incidence of small vulvas and persistent hymens e.g. Collie Roughs (both) and Cairn Terriers which are very small in the vulva. Consider the possibility of minor abnormalities if your bitch has so-called fertility problems. Have your bitch examined during full season when there is more room for the internal examination and make sure that the bitch does not have a physical reason for not being able to be mated properly.

6. DOES SHE HAVE PURULENT DISCHARGES DURING OR AFTER SEASONS?

Infections of the uterus are not uncommon in the bitch. During a season the cervix is relaxed, permitting a greater flow both in and out of the uterus. The infections are generally mild and can be quite easily cleared up with a course of antibiotics. Many veterinarians consider these to be insignificant and are dubious as to the value of swabbing in the first place. However, discoloured discharges can be an indication of low grade metritis (inflammation of the uterus) and should be investigated. Bitches over four years of age, are more likely to have low grade inflammatory changes or infections than younger bitches.

Running more than two bitches together while in season can create problems not only because they are more likely to fight while in season, but also because they clean and lick one another, occasionally transferring infections. With valuable bitches, it is wise not to take them swimming, not to travel excessively, or allow them to mix with other bitches while in full season.

Unless the infection is severe or very resistant to antibiotics, a bitch is generally suitable for mating as long as she has been on the antibiotics for at least 3–4 days. It doesn't matter if the bitch is still on antibiotics while being mated as they do not interfere with the bitch's fertility, nor should they affect the stud dog in any way.

If the bitch has a very nasty, dark discharge that it is not clearing up after 3–4 days of antibiotics, I suggest that the bitch is re-swabbed and probably not bred from, in that season.

Before accepting bitches, most stud dog owners require certificates to state that they have been swabbed and treated if there was an infection.

Infections during pregnancy

During pregnancy, a bitch will normally have a small amount of discharge which is clear to cream. There should never be any brown or greenish discharge. If there is ever any discharge of this nature, your bitch should be checked over immediately by your veterinarian. Generally the vet will put your bitch on antibiotics or re-swab her. Some care must be taken when giving your bitch antibiotics during pregnancy as some antibiotics such as tetracycline, can cause permanent damage to the unborn puppies by affecting their adult teeth. Other drugs, if used in the first third of pregnancy can possibly, though rarely, cause birth defects.

If a bitch had an infection prior to mating, but was treated with antibiotics successfully, there is no need to repeat the antibiotic treatment unless there is a nasty discharge during pregnancy or the bitch has a previous history of problems. On the whole, if the bitch is going along well and is healthy, leave her alone and do not fill her with antibiotics unnecessarily. This is important especially in the last week of pregnancy, when if a bitch is on antibiotics (for no particularly good reason), and something goes wrong (e.g. the puppies' membranes start to break down), the antibiotics can mask the problem and allow the situation to get out of hand.

Where discharges persist, the chance of abortion or metritis increases. There may be hormonal reasons for the discharges e.g. failure to hold pregnancy. This is discussed later in the chapter.

7. DOES SHE HAVE FALSE PREGNANCIES?
This can occur without any obvious cysts on the ovaries. The reason for this can be persistent 'corpora lutea', where cells lining the cavities of the ruptured follicles produce high levels of progesterone, which cause the body to think it is pregnant. This is a common occurrence in the bitch. Occasionally, the follicles developed during a season do not all rupture, again causing a similar picture.

The false pregnancy usually lasts 5–6 weeks, with some thickening of the abdomen, swelling of the milk glands and behavioural changes similar to pregnant bitches. Rarely, a bitch may even go so far as to nest, go into labour and possibly pass a small amount of clear fluid. These bitches are often maidens on their first seasons, and most will go on to have normal seasons and normal fertilities. Signs will disappear without treatment and it can be harmful to future seasons to treat these with hormones unless there are very good reasons for interfering.

8. DOES SHE HAVE LIVE PUPPIES AND HOW LONG DO THEY SURVIVE?
If the bitch has live puppies but they fail to thrive, then the possibilities of uterine infection, infected or toxic milk, viral infections, and poor environmental control in temperature extremes must be considered. This area has already been covered in chapter 9, Care of Puppies in the First Ten Days.

Ovarian and Other Hormonal Imbalances
The reasons behind poor fertility or infertility are many and varied, both in their cause and effect. The common causes include: cystic ovaries, inactive ovaries, poor genetic fertility and chromosomal defects, infections before and during pregnancy, together with hormonal imbalances (secondary to cystic ovaries, inactive ovaries and/or overall problems with thyroid, adrenal or pituitary glands). Infertility can also occur as a result of interference to seasons (use of the 'pill', mismating

injections, anabolic injections). Less common causes of infertility can be seasonal variations, weight problems, concurrent health conditions — the list can seem endless.

CYSTIC OVARIES

A rather large number of bitches may suffer from cystic ovaries. Cysts on the ovaries can produce hormones which in turn upset the normal hormone levels and cycles. Ovarian cysts can produce excessive amounts of either oestrogen, progesterone, or no hormones at all.

Irregular season lengths can occur as the result of productive cysts on the ovaries. The seasons may be as close together as 2–3 months apart, or very infrequent e.g. every 12–18 months. There can also be seasons of abnormal length, sometimes lasting 5–6 weeks. The bitch may also be in season for one week, then out for a short time, and then back on again for several weeks.

Oestrogen producing cysts cause prolonged seasons with failure to ovulate.

Treatment involves the use of specific hormones such as chorionic gonadotropins which are injected into the bitch at the time of ovulation. This will help the cysts to rupture but if the bitch has a number of cysts it may take anywhere from 4–8 days. I usually suggest mating the bitch every two days for as long as she will stand. Usually the best results are 4–6 days after the injection. Take the date of conception from near to the end of that period. Quite often the bitch may not be fertile during this particular season, but the next time around she may not require hormone injections. Not all such cases are responsive to treatment and surgery may be required to drain the cyst.

Progesterone producing cysts can cause prolonged anoestrus (failure to cycle). This type of cyst can produce cystic endometrial hypoplasia and may be one of the predisposing causes of metritis. Persistent corpora lutea also produce progesterone.

Older bitches with pyometra (infection of the uterus), are often found to have large numbers of cysts on both ovaries when they are operated on to be desexed.

OVARIAN IMBALANCES

Occasionally, these occur where the bitch may have conceived but either aborts at around 5–6 weeks or has mummified puppies at term. Mummified puppies are dried out and look shrivelled. They appear as a greenish mess but do not smell or cause problems to adjacent puppies in the uterus. This is due to insufficient hormone levels to hold the pregnancy, possibly secondary to ovarian cysts. These problems tend to be recurring ones and injections of progesterone, usually at 3–6 weeks, are needed to hold the pregnancy safely.

Placental problems

Failure of initiation of parturition
This may occur when the bitch fails to go into labour at the right time, going over time by 4–5 days. When and if the bitch finally goes into labour the puppies' membranes have been breaking down, possibly for several days, and there may be dead puppies or very thin, weak puppies that fail to suck. Not all bitches that go over time have this problem. Quite a few bitches (and occasionally specific breeds) regularly go several days over and have no problems at all. In general this is considered to be an uncommon occurrence.

INACTIVE OVARIES

Causes of inactive or poorly developed ovaries can include chromosomal abnormalities, anabolic steroid and/or hormone injections, obesity, and reduced weight caused by either hyperactivity or too low a protein diet.

If the bitch is obese and has been so since she was young, the ovaries can be poorly developed. Many of these bitches will have poor fertilities on their first litter. Most animals so affected will gradually return to normal fertility if the weight is kept down near to the ideal, however, it may result in permanent infertility and/or low fertility. The same applies to the testicular development in male dogs. The excessive weight goes into rapid growth at the expense of gonadal (ovarian or testicular) maturity.

Hyperactive bitches, or those that are in very hard working condition, often have poor fertility and irregular seasons, rather like human marathon athletes. Obviously bitches that are grossly over or underweight should be placed on a suitable diet to return the weight to a normal level. The fertility of these bitches, if they do conceive, is generally low, with litters of only one or two puppies instead of the normal sized litters.

Inactive ovaries can occasionally be stimulated with hormones to promote follicular development and this is usually given during the first 3–4 days of the season. Some of the drugs used include follicle stimulating hormones or serum gonadotropins. This treatment may need to be followed up by an injection of chorionic gonadotropin at the time of ovulation, to ensure that the follicles rupture and hopefully normal pregnancy can occur.

Hormonal Interference with Seasons Causing Subsequent Infertility

MISMATING

This is the unfortunate mating between dogs that should not have got together, but somehow managed it. Even worse, often it is the horrid little shaggy creature from down the road that got in and did the foul deed. The mating can be aborted with the use of hormones, but the repercussions from drastically altering the bitch's hormones, can cause cystic or inactive ovaries.

IMMEDIATE MISMATING INJECTIONS

If the situation warrants the use of hormones to abort a bitch, then the bitch must be treated within 48 hours for the injection to be effective. The risk to the average bitch is not high, but the possibility of permanent damage is there.

It is important to know that the oestradiol hormone injection used tends to revert the season i.e. the season will last for another 10–14 days and the bitch is quite able to get mismated again. Also, the sudden alteration of the hormones causes changes in the uterine pH, which means that the bacterial population of the uterus is affected and this can set off infections. For this reason, most vets will give the owner of the bitch some antibiotics at the time of the mismating injection in case infections do develop.

The bitch is usually not fertile on that particular season, but she cannot afford to get mismated again and have a second injection — as the chance of the bitch developing pyometra (infection of the uterus), becomes very high.

USE OF PROSTAGLANDINS

The safest way to abort a bitch is by the use of prostaglandins (Lutylase®) injections. Lutylase® may be safely given to pregnant mismated bitches from day 32–34 of the pregnancy. This will abort the bitch in a natural fashion and not adversely affect future fertility. Injections are usually given morning and night for five days. Side effects include some vomiting and salivation. This drug is also used in cases of uterine infections as it evacuates the uterus.

Note: Sperm from a male dog only lives an average of 4–5 days in the bitch (technically they can live up to 10–11 days but fertility decreases rapidly after day four). If a bitch is mismated to a mongrel, the effects of the sperm only last for 4–5 days, not for years. Some people erroneously believe that a mongrel puppy is going to pop up in a litter several years later.

Infertility due to Systemic Hormonal Imbalances

Occasionally infertility of the bitch can be due to overall body hormonal disturbances and the infertility is secondary to the major hormonal imbalance. Thyroid and adrenal imbalances can cause secondary infertility varying from infrequent seasons to prolonged seasons. The end result of these types of disturbances is infertility or inability to hold a pregnancy. These types of infertility are accompanied by *other* symptoms such as lethargy, weight gain or loss, lack of coat changes or excessive loss of coat.

1. THYROID

Hypothyroidism, where insufficient thyroid hormone is produced, is the most common endocrine hormone problem in the dog. Behavioural abnormalities include lethargy, mental dullness and commonly obesity.

Abnormalities in the coat vary considerably but usually there is a thinning and loss of coat, and later on there may be thickening and scaliness of the skin. Heat regulation abnormalities occur where the animal cannot readily maintain the body heat and tends to become cooler and actively seeks the heat.

As the thyroid is one of the main regulator glands for the body, any upset in the production of thyroid hormone will have consequences in the reproductive capacity of the dog and bitch. For the bitch, reproductive abnormalities associated with hypothyroidism include: infertility, prolonged time length between cycles, failure to cycle, prolonged oestriol bleeding, and decreases in the intensity and duration of the oestriol cycles. For the male, abnormalities include lack of libido, testicular atrophy, and hypospermatogenesis (reduced sperm production).

If there are signs that are consistent with hypothyroidism and there is associated infertility, there are blood tests available to determine the thyroid levels. Once diagnosed, there are tablets that can reverse most of these effects. If however the condition is difficult to stabilise, then the chances of a bitch carrying to term are not good, nor of returning a male dog back to normal fertility.

2. ADRENAL

Infertility can occur due to adrenal hyperfunction known as Cushings Syndrome. Cushings Syndrome is where there is excessive production of cortisol from the adrenal cortex. Signs of adrenal problems include polydipsia, polyuria, abdominal distension, anoestrus, lethargy, muscular weakness and atrophy, bilaterally symmetrical hair loss, testicular atrophy, and polyphagia.

A persistent anoestrus (failure to cycle) occurs in over 75% of cases. An enlarged clitoris is present in a high proportion of cases, suggesting that some of the reproductive disorders associated with Cushings Syndrome may well be the result of abnormal secretions of androgens as well as glucocorticoids. Treating dogs with Cushings Syndrome is fairly difficult and delicate work. Unless the adrenals are well stabilised, the likelihood of a bitch having a normal season and then carrying to term, is negligible.

3. PITUITARY

The pituitary gland is another of the body's major regulators. Any upset of the pituitary gland will have a feedback effect on the ovaries and testicles.

Infections of the Uterus

The most common infections are E.coli and B.Haemolytic Streptococci, however, there are many types of bacteria. Some are far more resistant to antibiotics than the average, e.g. Pseudomonas which is extremely resistant to antibiotics. Luckily this is an uncommon infection of the uterus (more commonly seen in chronically infected ears).

Bitches are usually swabbed on day 3–4 of the season. It is best to wait several days from the beginning of the season to get a true picture of the bacterial status of the uterus, as a bitch may not start to discharge heavily until this time. Approximately 80% of bitches will turn up bacterial growths of some kind, which in most cases would probably have caused no problems. If however, you are mating a particularly valuable bitch, spending a lot of money on stud fees or travelling long distances for a stud service, having the bitch swabbed and treated if need be, reduces the risk of infection interfering with the conception of puppies. It also lowers the risk of the bitch not holding the puppies to term.

Bitches with Pseudomonas infections should not be bred from in that season as this bacteria is very resistant and very hard to remove. Pseudomonas infections are accompanied by a persistent dark brown-green discharge. A bitch may need several courses of antibiotics and several swabs before the problem clears up. I also suggest that she is swabbed to make sure she is clear before being bred from in the next season. Pseudomonas can be almost impossible to get rid of and bitches have had to be desexed because of it.

Severe or chronic infections of the uterus are quite common in the older bitch and are often as a result of ovarian cysts and chronic low grade infections. Metritis and pyometra are discussed in greater detail in chapter 14 .

Other Factors

INBREEDING

Inbreeding essentially increases the number of similar genes so that hopefully, the resulting progeny will more closely resemble the ancestor being inbred upon. Sometimes it can be a well proven combination of ancestors that provides a good result as seen in thoroughbred racehorse breeding. The good and the bad aspects of inbreeding are intertwined. While trying to increase the good points of the favoured ancestor, the bad points, which may have been hidden as recessive, will often come to light. If there is very close inbreeding, there may be increasing numbers of birth defects such as cleft palates and hare lips, abnormal limbs (malformed limbs, joints), abnormal intestines (sections missing), reduced viability, and less resistance to disease.

The real problems that may arise from very close inbreeding tend to occur later in life, as the developmental defects tend to be self limiting, i.e. they are put down at birth or die within a few days. These problems can include:

(a) Reduced viability with greater susceptibility to disease.

(b) Shorter life span.

(c) Temperament problems with a tendency to be very highly strung or neurotic.

(d) Reduced fertility of both male and female. This does not mean that they are necessarily sterile, but there are likely to be fewer puppies per litter in bitches and lower sperm counts and/or higher than normal numbers of abnormal sperm in the male.

To avoid the worst problems associated with inbreeding, avoid incestuous inbreeding i.e. mother to son, litter mates or father to daughter matings.

CHANGE OF HEMISPHERE

This can cause infertility, especially in older bitches that are sent from the northern to the southern hemisphere. Occasionally, it may take up to two years for the hormones to get used to the rearrangement of the seasons and the temperature changes. Younger bitches tend to acclimatise much more rapidly, usually within 6–9 months. It can take an adult dog or bitch up to two years for the coat to settle down properly after this drastic of change of environment.

SEVERE WEATHER/SEASONAL CHANGES

This problem is of a temporary nature. What may occur, especially around the turn of the seasons, is that heavy and prolonged rain and overcast weather, or lengthy hot, dry spells, may extend the season and delay the normal timing of a season. It may also make the bitch think that her next season has arrived, even if it has not. All these things can upset a normally very regular bitch and may, at the same time, affect the fertility. This type of problem is usually temporary and corrected by time and the weather. It is usual for many bitches to be affected at the same time. Maiden bitches on their first season, are often the most affected by this. They start and stop, and then finally get going into a normal season.

13

Importing Dogs

Before importing a dog or bitch, make sure you know why you are doing it. Obviously the main reason why most people import a dog is to introduce a new bloodline with an improvement in type and soundness.

Unfortunately many people buying an import, will have chosen the dog from photographs and pedigree alone. Some people imagine that the country of origin is the *only* place to go for the best type or bloodlines. However, in today's busy world many breeds have been re-established very successfully in other countries to the point that in those countries, better specimens may be seen than in their country of origin. This does not apply to all breeds, but it is worth comparing the local standard with that of the country of origin, and with the standard of the other major countries that exhibit the breed.

Once you determine which country produces the best stock and bloodlines, the fun really starts.

When buying an animal, especially long distance buying, you are, to a certain extent, at the mercy of the person selling you that dog. You are trusting in their honesty, reliability and integrity. You can be lucky and choose people who are reliable, truthful and honest in their dealings with you and in their selection of a good and sound animal. You can be equally unlucky and find yourself paying a dog dealer considerably more than you intended for an animal that may not be of top quality.

So the message from the dire warnings above, is do your homework well. Research carefully to determine what you and the breed in general (locally speaking) need. Do the local dogs lack type, bone, shape etc.? Consider which bloodlines are already present, which new lines overseas are doing well and most importantly, which bloodlines tie in with the local bloodlines.

Importing a Stud Dog

When considering importing a male dog, obviously thought should be given to the stud potential of the animal. This means that you should try to buy very *sound* and *productive* bloodlines. The other consideration is that most people wish to see the dog in open competition with the local dogs and obviously compare them. So the pressure is on the buyer to select not only a stud dog, but also an outstanding show dog which is easier said than done.

When buying an older dog (over 12 months), you have to ask why they are selling this animal. Is it the money, or does the dog not quite meet the higher local standards? Does the dog have a hip dysplasia certificate, clearance for eyes if the breed is affected by eye defects and working certificates if applicable at that age, indicating that the temperament is at least reasonable? If you know your breed, you should know what is required by your breed in order to make your dog an acceptable (and sought after) stud dog in your own country. You also need to know whether the dog has been shown, where and in what company, i.e. was it shown in the back of beyond or in top class company in the big shows and what results did it achieve? If the dog is over 2–3 years old, it is best to ask whether the dog has been used at stud, and if so what the fertility and puppies were like. If you are paying a lot of money, it may also be advisable to have a sperm count done on an older dog.

When you are buying a younger dog, under 12 months, there is a risk that the dog may not shape up as well as hoped or on the other hand, the breeder runs the risk of parting with the best thing he or she has ever bred. If the breeder decided to gamble on keeping the dog, it may be a nice dog but not good enough to beat the local competition. This is the risk inherent in any young animal; sometimes the transaction is to your advantage and at other times you may get a very unattractive dog.

If the dog you are buying is over six months old, preliminary hip x-rays can be done to give you some idea of the status of the dog's hips. This applies mostly to the larger breeds. Eye examinations can be done from 6–8 weeks onwards, so there is no excuse for not having them done.

If one is going to all this trouble and expense to import an animal, particularly a stud dog, then make sure that as many of the genetic faults that it is possible to test for, are checked.

When selecting bloodlines of a stud dog, do consider the bloodlines of other stud dogs that stand at stud either locally or in neighbouring states. *Do not* purchase a dog of precisely the same bloodlines. If you feel that you must have that particular bloodline, make sure the bitch line of the pedigree is not similar. Otherwise the situation will arise where there may be a few dogs of similar lines within a close vicinity, where one is producing well, while the others may be lucky to be used at all. Try to ensure that you bring in a dog with bloodlines that will blend well with the other top producing dog's daughters (and hopefully 'nick well' with them). This way your dog will have a ready-made line up of suitable bitches.

In selecting a stud dog, you have to be ten times as selective as with the bitch, because the reproductive capacity of a male is far greater than a bitch who has only a few litters in her lifetime. In the end, this means that the dog, especially if it is a top stud dog, after numerous matings, can have a profound effect on the whole breed throughout the entire country, not just locally.

Everyone dreams of getting one of those outstanding stud dogs, but they are very few and very far between.

Importing a Bitch

The pressure of importing a really top quality bitch is not nearly as fiercely competitive as it is for a dog. A bitch is essentially being brought in for *your kennel*, to boost or start new bloodlines. The bitch does not have to be an outstanding example of that breed, she can get away with looking rather ordinary. The most important condition is that she should be of very good bloodlines, and more importantly, from strong producing lines.

When buying an older bitch, the same conditions apply as for older dogs. The bitch should have all the necessary passes for hip dysplasia and eyes. If old enough, she should have working titles, if they apply to that breed, and again this tends to imply that her temperament is at least reasonable. Check on the bitch's breeding history including how often she comes into season, how long the seasons are, has she had a litter, when was she mated (i.e. what day of the season) and how many puppies she had per litter. If she is between 2½ and three years old, she should have had a litter and if not, why not? Often all this information can be rather hard to obtain, especially if the people you are buying from do not speak your language.

Young bitches under 18 months of age, obviously should not have been bred from. Similar conditions apply to bitches under 12 months as to younger male dogs.

IMPORTING A PREGNANT BITCH

Importing a pregnant bitch has advantages and disadvantages. Regulations and periods of quarantine vary from one country to another, so where a bitch is being imported from, determines whether it is feasible. For example, when importing a pregnant bitch from Germany to Australia, the bitch has to stay in quarantine for four months (120 days). The puppies have to stay for nine weeks and will be charged from six weeks of age at the adult rate. With large litters this can be expensive. If regulations change (as expected) and the time for either the bitch or the puppies reduces, costs decrease. If importing a bitch from England, the quarantine time has been reduced to 30 days, so most bitches can now arrive, do the time and be out to whelp at home which is a great help to owners and bitches alike.

If the bitch has to whelp in quarantine, make sure the facilities in quarantine are suitable. Inform the staff ahead of time that the bitch is pregnant and have a good vet available to make numerous trips for check ups if needed.

Some bitches can take up to 12–18 months to stabilise hormonally after a shift in hemisphere. This is more noticeable with older bitches.

Importing Frozen Semen

Dog semen can how be imported from most countries. However, to do so, you must obtain a copy of the regulations covering importation of semen from that country detailing under what conditions they will accept the semen (what diseases must be tested for before and after and what government clearances are needed). You must also apply for a permit to import the semen. The permit will usually last 3–6 months, so provided the semen is collected correctly and the relevant tests are carried out, the semen can be taken at any time. Find out the concentration of the semen and the post thaw motility before accepting the semen. Poor quality semen is of little value. See the section on Frozen semen evaluation at the end of chapter 11, The Stud Dog.

Importing semen can give access to valuable bloodlines that may be otherwise unavailable to you. However, many people are reluctant to allow semen out of the country (particularly the Germans in certain breeds) so find out the availability of the semen before applying for the permits.

When shipping the semen, ensure the container is full prior to leaving and that it has more than enough liquid nitrogen for twice the length of time needed. Occasionally some airlines may refuse to carry liquid nitrogen containers as they are listed as dangerous goods. Make sure the agent shipping the semen is aware of this and the semen has a direct flight into the country of destination.

The semen and its accompanying papers with the results of tests carried out and number of straws, are then checked by government officials before the semen is released. If the paperwork is not correct or complete, officials can refuse entry of the semen into the country.

Once released, the semen is stored in a semen bank. Keep one full set of papers and give a copy to the semen bank. Most cattle AI establishments will store semen at a cost of $10–12 per month per 50 straws. Semen will keep for in excess of 10–15 years with little loss of viability.

Importing Puppies

When contemplating importing a puppy, consider how long it will have to stay in quarantine and what the possible long term effects are on its temperament. I would not import a puppy under three months old as the trauma of the flight and new surroundings can precipitate gastric or other health problems. Generally a good age for importing a puppy is from 16 weeks old.

The puppies that handle the traumatic experience of quarantine the best are the very boisterous and out-going puppies. Timid, shy puppies may never recover from this period in which they are likely to have lack of handling and socialisation.

With recent reductions in quarantine times, importing puppies is not nearly as stressful as it was previously.

Government Regulations

The government regulations about importing dogs or semen from different countries have changed dramatically in the last few years and may continue to do so as vaccines and the accuracy of blood tests for the detection of diseases improve.

Currently dogs coming from rabies free countries (e.g. UK, Sweden, Norway) can be imported but have to stay 30 days in quarantine (this may be possible in private quarantine kennels at a later date).

Dogs coming from countries where rabies is under control (e.g. most European countries), may be imported if they have a current vaccine for rabies within 12 months but not in the last six months (i.e. vaccinated at least six months prior to importation), with a 120 days quarantine period.

Dogs coming from countries where there is poor rabies control e.g. India, must endure a nine month quarantine. When importing a dog from a rabies-free country to a country with rabies, usually there is no quarantine.

How to Import and/or Export a Dog

1. Go to the department concerned, usually the Department of Health or the Department of Agriculture. In the UK, it is the Department of Wildlife and Fisheries. Each government has its own name for the department concerned and its own set of rules and regulations!

2. Make sure that you comply with all the necessary pre-requisites such as blood tests and vaccinations.

3. Make sure that all the necessary papers are properly filled out and completed. Copies may be required ahead of time in the country of importation. When sent, the dog must be accompanied by the original documents as some countries may destroy an animal that does not arrive with the correct documentation detailing proof of blood test results and vaccinations.

4. Check and recheck the time that the dog is due to arrive. If the plane is delayed beyond the normal few hours, make sure there is some proof that the animal was not off-loaded anywhere. It is suggested that you make sure that the animal is placed on a direct flight if at all possible. There are occasional charter flights for livestock; these can be cheaper and the necessity of not off-loading in any country other than the final destination point is understood.

5. Try and have the dog sent early in the week so that it does not arrive on a weekend or holiday. Occasionally it can be difficult to have quarantine officials from the government station available on weekends.

6. If importing a dog, obtain as much information as possible before starting. Ensure that the people you are dealing with are honest and reliable (as far as possible) before even contemplating buying a dog. Even then you may be either lucky or unlucky.

14

Breeding Older Dogs and Bitches

The Bitch

WHEN TO STOP BREEDING YOUR BITCH

Some breeds and individual animals age sooner than others. As a generalisation, the larger the breed, the shorter the lifespan. With Great Danes for example, 9–10 years is about the maximum age but with Silky Terriers, 14–17 years is not uncommon. Dobermans are an exception, in that although they are not a giant breed, they are a relatively short-lived breed with an average of 9–10 years.

The breeds and some individuals that age faster, obviously need to stop producing at an earlier age or the pregnancy will cause a fair amount of stress to their systems, especially to the heart and kidneys. Added to this, the hormone levels required to maintain pregnancy, are not necessarily able to be produced in sufficient levels by the ovaries so failure to hold pregnancy or infections become more likely.

Most breeds have an average lifespan of 12–14 years and can, provided they are fit and healthy, keep breeding until eight years of age. It is suggested however, that you stop breeding your bitch at seven years of age. In a rare case, a bitch who looks and acts like a three year old, *may* be bred beyond her eighth year, providing there is no history of trouble during pregnancy. Greyhounds as a breed, are often bred up to ten years of age, but I would put nine years as an absolute limit even for a very fit breed or individual. The bigger breeds should stop being bred from by six years of age. The only exceptions would be very fit and healthy individuals with no history of infections or abortions associated with pregnancy.

Bitches should be desexed after they have finished being bred with. The reasons for this are due to the high risk of both uterine infections and mammary tumours. Either condition can kill a bitch, particularly an elderly bitch. Low grade uterine infections such as metritis can be very debilitating to older bitches and are often preliminary indicators of future pyometritis. Cystic ovaries can produce excessive amounts of hormones which again predispose bitches to infections.

1. PYOMETRA

This is a very serious condition and can cause a critical emergency. Pyometra is a severe bacterial inflammation of the uterus, which can develop rapidly into a very toxic condition. Toxaemia occurs through the absorption of toxins from increasing amounts of pus being produced by the bacterial infection.

It is usually seen in the older bitch, who is over 5–6 years of age and is within 2–4 weeks of having had a season. It can occur in younger bitches but is less common.

The **causes** of pyometra are varied. Older bitches often have poor hormonal control over their seasons and their cervixes no longer function properly. The cervixes are loose during, and do not close off tightly after, a season. This means that bacteria can more readily establish infections than in a fitter, healthier bitch.

The **symptoms** of pyometra are easy to recognise. The bitch will have had a season which has finished within the last 2–4 weeks, she will be off her food, drinking excessive amounts of water, vomiting and be very depressed. There may possibly be a discoloured discharge, depending on whether the cervix is opened or closed. Some bitches present to the veterinarian as having had a prolonged season with bleeding for up to 4–6 weeks. The blood picture (count) is also very characteristic. There is a very high white cell count in response to the severity of the infection and **immediate treatment is necessary.**

An **open** pyometra occurs where the purulent material from within the uterus is able to discharge through the cervix and so relieve both the pressure and the toxic build up. These bitches have a thick discoloured discharge, which is often rather foul smelling. *'Open' or 'closed' pyometra*

A **closed** pyometra is a very dangerous condition for the bitch as the cervix is closed, causing an increasing build up of purulent toxic material, which if not corrected fairly quickly, can cause death. These bitches have little or no discharge. Closed pyometras are often presented as medical emergencies

Antibiotics and drugs to relax the cervix and to promote better drainage are used immediately upon diagnosis. Surgery is often necessary on the 'closed' cases in order to save the life of the bitch, as the *toxic* effect from the bacterial build up within the uterus, can kill the bitch within 2–3 days.

'Open' cases can quite often be treated with drugs to assist in expelling the infected material from the uterus. However, despite this, the bitch may often have to be desexed within a short time if the condition does not clear up completely. Also, once pyometra has occurred, the likelihood of it recurring is very high. Younger bitches have a far greater chance of recovering and can be bred from in the subsequent season.

Newer drugs such as the prostaglandins offer some hope for non-surgical intervention, particularly in the younger bitches, but the above conditions in the older bitch still apply, and desexing is to be preferred once initial symptoms are under control. Milder drugs that may be used include Millophyline® and Buscopan®, both of which act as smooth muscle relaxants.

Mild cases of infection of the uterus are called metritis. Metritis can be in the form of a low grade and chronic infection of the uterus, causing infertility, irregular seasons, poor fertility or early abortions. Metritis can be the first sign of the uterus failing to cope (often as a result of irregular hormone levels coming from the ovaries) and may develop into pyometra at a later date. This condition needs antibiotics for the infection and drugs such as prostaglandins to assist with drainage. *Metritis*

Again, as with the cases of pyometra, if the bitch is old and you have finished breeding from her, desexing will cure the problem, as metritis can lead to pyometra on subsequent seasons.

2. MAMMARY TUMOURS

Bitches over six years of age that are not desexed, have a reasonably high chance of developing mammary tumours. Older bitches can develop mammary tumours whether they have been bred from or not. Many mammary tumours are 'malignant' and rapidly develop and spread.

Mammary tumours are most commonly noticed during or following a season when a natural enlargement of the mammary tissue occurs. At this time, the owners notice that instead of settling down again to normal size, the tissue is enlarged, hardened, hot and swollen. The first thing most owners think of is that the bitch must have mastitis or an abscess, where the affected tissue tends to be thickened but softer in the centre. With mammary tumours the tissue is hardened and irregular and there may be areas of discharge and ulceration. Despite the drainage, the size of the lump will not diminish.

Treatment   Treatment is usually surgical, particularly if the tumour is having a chronic debilitating effect. Usually, the veterinary surgeon will suggest that the bitch should be desexed at the same time in an effort to reduce the chance of new tumours developing. If the bitch is not desexed, then the problem will inevitably recur. Veterinarians generally x-ray the chest of the bitch when presented for surgery, to see if the tumours have metastasised (spread) to the chest and lungs.

When the bitch is very elderly and there are large numbers of tumours of varying sizes, or when they have spread to the lungs, the owner is usually told that surgery will not be of assistance. In those cases the only thing to do is to keep the bitch comfortable for as long as she is coping with the condition. When she shows signs of obvious discomfort, she will have to be put down.

On examination, if the lumps are not very numerous and they have not spread elsewhere, the bitch is desexed and the lumps removed. A sample is often sent away to determine whether the tumour is benign or malignant. If it is benign then breathe a sigh of relief. If the tumour is malignant and it has apparently been caught early enough, the bitch should have the chest x-rayed again 3-6 months later to make sure there have been no metastases in the lungs.

Not all lumps are cancers. This is particularly so in younger bitches following a bout of mastitis. I have known of owners panicking and having vast amounts of mammary tissue removed from the bitch only to find out on biopsy that the tissue is normal, either chronic reactive tissue (old abscess) or involuting mammary tissue that has developed a pocket or cyst of milk tissue. Mammary tumours are rarely seen in bitches under five years of age.

3. DECREASING FERTILITY

When the bitch is over six years of age, there will be a gradual decline in her fertility and there will be fewer puppies in each litter. The decrease is usually gradual with one or two fewer puppies in each successive pregnancy. The other aspect of the decreasing fertility is lower hormonal levels that are being produced by the ovaries. This can lead to failure to hold to term, or you may see the occasional mummified puppy. There is also a decreasing viability of puppies due to the older bitch whelping more slowly.

WHEN TO STOP

As stated above, bitches vary widely in their ability to continue breeding as they get older. Generally, most bitches have finished their breeding career before their health declines. Unfortunately however, many breeders do not have their older bitches desexed and consequently, end up with problems several years later. Very slowly, attitudes are changing and veterinarians are desexing some older bitches before problems develop. This way, the grand old ladies will enjoy their old age in health and comfort, even if they do get a shade tubbier. They have generally more than earned it. After they have had their final litter, bitches should be desexed before the following season.

The Dog

WHEN TO RETIRE YOUR STUD DOG

The decision to retire a dog at stud depends partly on the breed, the rate the dog is ageing and, most of all, the general state of health. The active stud life of a dog is much longer than the average breeding life of a bitch of the same breed.

The major problems associated with older dogs include:

1. PROSTATE PROBLEMS

The prostate gland is wrapped around the base of the bladder and produces fluids that go to make up part of the seminal fluids upon ejaculation. As a dog gets older, he is far more likely to get infections, abscesses, and tumours of the prostate.

The prostate gland sits just in front of the entrance to the pelvis and lies in a rather busy area with the rectum passing just over the top of it. The most common sign of prostatic trouble is constipation. When the prostate enlarges due to inflammation, there is pressure on the rectum, which narrows the passage of the faeces through the pelvis. Urine flow may be normal, but is sometimes reduced, with the occasional passage of blood at the end of urination.

Low grade and chronic prostate problems usually present with a straining, constipated dog who has often been fed bones in the last 2–3 days. Many dogs that have low grade prostatic problems will not have any symptoms at all until they are fed bones. Bones can cause mild constipation even in bitches, as the large pieces move more slowly through the gut and consequently, the intestine has more time to absorb water from the faeces, with the result that the dog has hard faeces.

On internal examination, the prostate is found to be enlarged and painful. Low grade prostatic inflammations tend to respond very well to an injection of female hormones (e.g. Delmadinone acetate — Tardak®), together with a course of antibiotics. The constipation is treated with liquid paraffin or other laxatives. Enemas are necessary to move the faeces in the worst cases.

The way to prevent constipation as a secondary problem to low grade prostatitis is never to give the dog bones; this alone may solve the problem. Chronic cases of prostatitis may also need doses of oil 2–3 times a week to help keep their bowel motions regular. Dogs (males and females) that have had pelvic fractures, should be similarly treated. Make sure there are no bones lying around in your backyard and explain to the neighbours who give your dogs scraps over the fence, how important it is that the bones should never be given.

Infections of the prostate

Infections of the prostate can be almost impossible to cure and dogs often require repeated treatments of antibiotics and hormone therapy. Dogs with chronic prostatitis with recurrent bouts of constipation and/or frequent passing of bloodstained urine, will require either periodic injections of hormones or castration. Castration has the effect of removing the hormones that are affecting the prostate. The hormones used in the injections are female so repeated injections will, over a period of time, lower fertility and libido. If the constipation is becoming hard to control and the breeding life of the dog has finished, castrate the dog. He will gradually settle down and be relatively trouble free afterwards.

Abscesses

These may be evident by signs of straining to defecate and urinate, and the presence of blood or pus in the urine. On rectal examination, the prostate will be extremely painful and the dog will object strenuously to its handling. Again, hormones and antibiotics are used. This treatment may settle down the abscess, but if it recurs, castration may be advisable and possibly the removal of the prostate gland. Surgical removal of the prostate is a very difficult operation and is not done unless absolutely necessary.

Tumours of the prostate

These can occur at any age but are rare under 5–6 years old. The typical symptoms are constipation, straining to urinate and blood in the urine. Treatment depends on the severity of the condition, but the prognosis is not good. Castration and hormones may help, but in many cases the dog may have to be put down eventually.

Stud dogs that have recurrent bouts of prostate problems need to be managed extremely carefully. Keep them well away from any bitch in season, as additional mating activity at this stage will result in the prostate becoming inflamed. Only present a bitch when she is ready and preferably for one mating only. Watch the dog carefully for a week afterwards for signs of an inflamed prostate in case the dog requires a course of antibiotics.

Managing a stud dog with prostate problems

2. TESTICULAR DEGENERATION
See also Stud dog infertility in chapter 11.

Infertility in a stud dog and degeneration of the testicles can occur as early as 2–3 years of age. Hormonal imbalances, particularly of the thyroid, can effectively render a dog infertile at a relatively young age. Chromosomal defects such as fragile X and XXY, can result in some dogs becoming infertile as early as 15–18 months of age. While genetic defects that affect fertility are generally uncommon, in some breeds there may be a higher incidence due to close inbreeding on a line.

As dogs get older, the hormone production from the testicles gradually deteriorates like the rest of the body. As a result, there is a reduced production of sperm and a lower level of associated fluids that form the ejaculate.

Decreasing the amount of hormones being produced by the testicular tissue, causes a reduction in libido (sex drive). Some people are very relieved to see a decrease in sex drive, but it may not be noticeable until the dog is getting fairly old. Again, this varies between individuals and between breeds. Many male dogs are still willing and able at 12 years of age. It is suggested that older dogs are used with caution as the dog's health and heart must be in satisfactory condition and the sperm count within acceptable limits (in other words, sufficient to warrant the mating in the first place).

I would have reservations in using dogs over 12 years of age unless the dog is in very good condition. Artificial Insemination (AI) is a better alternative so as not to overstrain the dog's heart with a natural mating.

If you have a very valuable stud dog, it is advisable to have his semen stored in case of sudden death, reduced fertility or accidents. The age of the dog when the semen is taken varies, but I strongly suggest that the semen is collected before he reaches eight years of age. After that time, the quality of the semen may not be as good, and therefore there may be a less successful result from the usage of his frozen semen. This does not rule out having semen collected and frozen after the dog is eight years old; it can vary with the individual dog. Unfortunately, the average dog owner waits until the dog is fairly decrepit before deciding that they must store some semen. By this time the dog's sperm quality has already deteriorated and after freezing and thawing, the viability of the sperm can be very poor.

3. TUMOURS OF THE TESTICLES

Dogs can develop tumours of the testicles, particularly if there is a retained testicle i.e. one that does not 'drop' down into the scrotum. Retained testicles can become cancerous and have a much higher incidence of tumours than normally descended testicles. Testicular tumours (even of retained testicles), are rarely seen under 5–6 years; most testicular tumours are seen from 8–9 years onwards.

Tumours of the testicles tend to be of a similar type where the testicle starts to produce excessive amounts of hormones (oestrogens), which creates a 'feminising effect'. The testicle will be enlarged, there may be some nipple enlargement, and the dog may become attractive to other male dogs. There is occasionally some increasing pigmentation on the belly and sides and, in more advanced cases, there may be bilateral hair loss on the flank area. The positive aspect of a testicular tumour is that it is nearly always confined to that testicle and it does not spread to other organs. The hormonal effects are reversible following the removal of the testicle.

Treatment   Treatment is castration. If the dog is very valuable, removing only the affected testicle is usually sufficient, but keep an eye on the other testicle for the next six months. Dogs that have obvious feminising effects are often given a course of injections of testosterone following the removal of the tumorous testicle.

WHEN TO STOP USING THE DOG AT STUD

The average stud dog is seldom used past 9–10 years of age. If the dog is still in demand and is very healthy, I would suggest that one (maximum two) bitch(es) a week is quite sufficient, and only one mating if there are two bitches. During the summer, the dog should only be studded in the cool of the evening and not at all during excessively hot weather. If the dog is over 12 years, use artificial insemination (AI), but check the sperm quality and concentration prior to use.

If the dog has concurrent medical problems, your veterinarian should check the dog prior to use and assess whether it is safe to allow the dog to have a natural mating. Dogs with heart conditions are obviously candidates for AI, provided that the heart can take even this amount of strain.

15

Geriatric Dogs

237

This is an increasingly important area of the pet owner's life. As veterinary care and knowledge improve, so dogs are living longer and enjoying a more active old age. As your friend ages and cannot get around as fast as it used to, you will find there are many ways in which you can help to make its life more comfortable.

Watch your dog's weight. Excessive weight can be detrimental to dogs with heart conditions, arthritis and pancreatic problems. Dogs that are obese will suffer greatly in the hotter weather, due to the increased strain on the heart.

Conditions Commonly Seen in the Older Dog:

The conditions described in this chapter are commonly seen and the underlying physiological changes effect the body. Once you can understand even the basics, then you can assist your elderly pet in a more competent manner at home. Elderly dogs need regular check-ups, at least every few months, to monitor their health. Dogs with serious heart, kidney and pancreatic conditions obviously need to be seen by your veterinarian at least every 6–8 weeks if they are on medication.

ARTHRITIS

Arthritis is caused by the wear and tear of the joints over the years and can often be the result of accidents and fractures in youth. Damage to any joint, whatever the cause, can result in the development of arthritis in older age. **Hip dysplasia** and/or **pelvic fractures** (particularly those that involve the hip joints), are generally the cause of the worst arthritis in older dogs.

Spondylitis is another very common problem in the older animal, particularly the larger and longer bodied breeds. Spondylitis is a result of spur formation between the vertebrae of the spine, which can gradually form bony bridges. When a bridge has been formed, the two vertebrae are linked and cannot move independently. The movement of the bony spurs against one another is very painful. The bridges can occasionally fracture because of an accident, for example slipping downstairs, which can almost totally incapacitate the dog.

Symptoms of arthritis

Symptoms include stiffness of movement, difficulty in getting up in the morning, slowness going up and downstairs, reduced ability of affected limbs to bear weight and consequent limping. The symptoms increase in severity in cold or damp weather.

Treatment

Treatment is aimed at reducing pain. Once arthritic changes are present, they cannot be reversed. With chronically arthritic individuals, pain relief is all important and drugs of some sort should be used to relieve discomfort and pain. Drugs act in various different ways to diminish the pain in the affected areas.

A large variety of drugs is available today to treat arthritis. Newer drugs such as Cartophen® (injectable or tablets) and Pentosan® can be used as adjuncts to other medications to give lengthy relief. Cortisone is still in use, but is generally used in the chronic, severely arthritic patient.

Some of the drugs available:

1. Cortisone is still the most effective drug in the treatment of spinal pain/injuries. For those on long term cortisone therapy, most advocate alternate day treatment so as not to interfere with the body's natural cortisone production. Cortisone should be used with care; there must be no concurrent infection as it slows the rate of healing and can allow infection to increase. Side effects include increased appetite (and weight gain), increased water consumption and occasional vomiting. If vomiting occurs, inform your vet and change the treatment. Cortisone should be used at a low dose to effect i.e. for the relief of symptoms, and only as often as necessary.

2. Aspirin can be very beneficial in the dog but *do not* use in cats as it can be lethal. Aspirin lowers the amount of fluid in the affected area, therefore reducing the stretching of the tissues and, as a consequence, the pain is reduced. Use small doses (¼ or ½ a tablet) to effect, twice a day for 2–3 days.

3. Cu Analgesic tablets are a non steroidal anti-inflammatory given once a day at night. It is very effective on most dogs and most tolerate it very well.

4. PBZ (Phenylbutazone) tablets, also a non steroidal anti-inflammatory drug, are given twice daily if severely affected, once a day if coping well.

5. Finadyne® tablets, an antiprostaglandin, acts as an anti-inflammatory. Finadyne® is used twice a week. However, some dogs will not tolerate the drug and there may be some vomiting.

(Do not use cortisone concurrently with Findayne® as severe gastric ulceration will result.)

6. Zyloprim® is a human medication used for gout. The drug works on the joint enzymes and reduces pain. This is particularly good for dogs with rheumatoid arthritis or osteochondritis.

Other alternative drugs that can be used concurrently with any of the above include Musseltone®, Selim E (selenium and vitamin E) and Ester C (calcium and vitamin C).

Selenium is a trace element and in very small doses, combined with vitamin E, can be used to reduce muscle and bone soreness and stiffness. These additives can be used for long periods of time with no apparent ill effects. They can succeed in keeping arthritis under reasonable control, so that the use of the heavier 'guns' (cortisone etc.), is restricted to the more severe bouts of inflammation. As science progresses, new and different ways of treating arthritis are constantly being developed, so that the drugs described above are only some of those available today.

Individual dogs react in various ways to different drugs and it may require a little juggling to find the best combination that suits your dog.

ASSISTING AT HOME

There are several ways of helping to ease the pain of the chronic arthritic sufferer to make daily living more comfortable:

1. Bedding — blankets, coats, electric blankets. All of these are useful with elderly animals, particularly the coats. Unfortunately some dogs, particularly the males, feel that a coat is beneath their dignity and will, under no circumstances, wear one. Good bedding is essential for the arthritis sufferer as it ensures that the dog is not sleeping on cold, hard concrete or tiles.

Trampoline beds, while being comfortable, allow the air to circulate underneath, which may be very cooling in summer, but can be irritating to stiff joints in winter. If you wrap an old blanket around the base to reduce the flow of air, the dog will be less affected by draughts.

2. Good shelter from the elements — Some older dogs refuse the comforts of home and hearth and will sleep where they are used to sleeping, outside under the stars and covered in frost. For their own good, put them inside at night in the laundry or in a shed with some form of bedding.

3. Weight — Many older dogs, like humans, have a slightly stretched waistline. A small amount of extra weight can be beneficial in case of illness, but obese dogs will really suffer if they have arthritis to any great degree. Weight should be kept reasonably controlled, particularly during winter. In summer, warmth minimises the effects of arthritis, so a slight addition in the weight can be tolerated (maximum 10%).

Many owners ask the question 'Is my dog in pain?' The answer to this question varies, as the individual response to pain is enormously diverse. Some dogs may have very little in the way of obvious arthritic changes, yet present a picture of being almost totally crippled; and the reverse can happen where there are massive bone changes, yet little obvious pain. Most veterinarians take each case on its own merits, according to how badly the animal is affected, how they respond to treatment and the supportive care given by the owners.

If, despite treatment, the dog is unable to get up and walk around by itself, then a decision must be made for the sake of the dog. Inability to stand and walk around indicates that the arthritis is at a point where drugs are insufficient to cope with the pain. It is kinder to put the dog out of its misery, because misery is inevitable if they are kept as virtual paraplegics. Unfortunately, many of these difficult decisions must be faced each winter, as the effects of arthritis are exacerbated by the cold. Be warned and be prepared to do a little extra for your dog if and when you have to make that final decision.

HEART CONDITIONS

With the creeping of the years, not only do the joints start to wear out, but the organs as well. The heart is no exception to the rule and would be the second most common condition that veterinarians treat in the older patient. Heart conditions are more common in some breeds e.g. Cavalier King Charles Spaniels, Pekingese and Chihuahuas, and the wear and tear on the valves of the heart may show up as early as 7–8 years of age. Other breeds may keep going past 14–16 years of age with hardly any heart problems at all e.g. the Australian Silky Terrier, which on the whole, have remarkably hardy hearts.

Heartworm infestation, either current or previous, can lead to signs of heart failure caused by the blockage of the valves or previous damage by the heartworm. When talking to your veterinarian, remember to tell him/her of any previous infestations of heartworm, so that the damage done to the valves can be assessed relative to the dog's age.

Symptoms

Signs of heart conditions are:
1. Coughing.
2. Reduced exercise tolerance.
3. Weight loss and/or the development of a 'pot belly' — ascites.

As your dog ages, you expect it to slow down, but occasionally the slowing down occurs rather earlier or more rapidly than expected. Often there is a slight cough first thing in the morning or after rest; the dog cannot walk as far and stands with the elbows out after even mild exercise, trying to get enough air into its lungs. Any chronic coughing, or sudden decrease in exercise tolerance in an older dog should be investigated by your veterinarian, as many useful drugs are available to help the heart cope with its developing insufficiencies.

There are several possibilities as to what is causing the heart to fail. The valves may no longer be closing correctly, the heart muscle may have enlarged and is not pumping at full force, or the heart is developing irregularities in the beat or rhythm. Because of any of these failings, blood is not effectively cleared from the lungs, causing a pooling of fluid in the tissues of the lungs. The lungs are particularly congested after a period of rest, when the heart has also been resting, so the congestion needs to be cleared when the dog starts to move around. The dog does this by coughing, a heavy clearing of the throat.

If the left side of the heart is involved, fluid in the abdominal cavity accumulates because the heart fails to clear the excess fluid from the body. Often these dogs look healthy, even slightly fat, when in actual fact they are losing weight over the ribs and the increasing girth around the abdomen is due to the retained fluid.

The heart is a marvellously complex organ and the body has many 'back-up' regulatory systems for it, but there is a limit to what they can do to compensate for the failing heart muscle or faulty valves. Many dogs suddenly appear to develop heart problems, when in actual fact the heart has been failing for a long period and it has reached a stage where the deficiencies can no longer be compensated for.

Treatment   1. Fluid tablets are given to reduce the volume of fluid the heart has to deal with. This is the most common medication given to patients with congestive heart failure. About one hour after being given the tablet, the dog will want to go outside to urinate. Tablets are usually given twice daily, so you should arrange to give the dog the tablets at times when it is convenient for you to let the dog out to urinate, and so avoid a mishap. Give the evening tablet at least two hours before retiring.

With a reduction of the volume of fluid the heart has to cope with, coughing should decrease or stop entirely. If the dog is on high levels of a diuretic over a long period of time, Slow K (potassium) tablets should be given once or twice a week. This will help to counteract the increased potassium loss which occurs with the use of most diuretics.

In heart cases which have a mild problem, a low dose of a diuretic is often the only medication needed to obtain a good control of the condition. However, once a dog has been placed on a diuretic, it usually needs to stay on some form of diuretic for the rest of its life. Never run out of medication, hoping that it won't matter. Always go along to your veterinarian several days before it has finished any heart tablets, as being denied medication can place a strain on the dog's heart.

2. Heart Drugs — Millophyline®, Digoxin®, Lanoxin®, Enalfor®.

These drugs regulate or strengthen the beat of the heart. Dogs with more severe heart problems, usually need to have these drugs in addition to a fluid tablet. The dog needs to be checked several times in the first few weeks after starting medication to make sure that the dose is effective and not too strong for that particular animal. Every dog is an individual and while the vast majority will regulate very quickly, some are more difficult or do not respond well to a particular drug. Even once a dog is stabilised on its heart medications, I suggest regular check-ups at 6–8 week intervals, at which time the owners usually renew their supplies of tablets.

3. Additives — Geribits®, vitamin E.

A well-balanced vitamin and mineral additive can often be beneficial to the older age heart patient. This can be a useful addition to the diet and can help to strengthen the heart. Geribits® are particularly good as they are specifically made for the elderly. A low dose of vitamin E can help strengthen the heart muscle but it must be introduced gradually. Avoid highly salted foods, as they increase the fluid intake.

4. Watch the weight. As a heart patient's system is already under considerable strain, effort should be made to keep the dog's weight to the optimum for that dog. Too much weight means considerable extra effort has to be made by the heart to pump blood around the body.

5. Exercise should be no more than the dog enjoys and playing around the backyard. Long walks, even at a very slow rate are inadvisable and especially dangerous in hot weather. If your dog has been a hyperactive individual and is a little slower now it is older, confine it in the heat of the day and find it somewhere cool to stay, inside the house or garage.

OVERWEIGHT

Many older dogs are grossly overweight from years of overfeeding by over-indulgent owners. Unfortunately many owners do not realise that the excessive weight may be causing health problems and/or aggravating existing serious conditions of the heart, pancreas, liver as well as arthritis. Tolerance of extremes of temperature and particularly of heat, is greatly reduced. Obese dogs are usually very unfit, so placing extra strain on the heart, as well as other health problems.

Elderly dogs do however, need to carry a *little* extra weight (maximum 10–20% over ideal weight), in case of illness. If old dogs become sick, they do not respond to treatment as promptly as younger animals, and take longer to pick up their health and eat normally again. Having a small amount of extra weight helps the dog to survive these hard times, but you should not allow the dog to become seriously overweight. As already explained, too much is *very* harmful.

It is your duty, as the owner of the dog, to do something about reducing its excessive weight. Dieting a dog is much easier than dieting yourself and your dog becomes cheaper to feed. The hardest part of dieting your over-indulged dog is to refuse it extra food when faced by those beseeching eyes. The problem lies with you and it is you who has to learn to be firm.

A good reducing diet aims to satisfy the dog while reducing his weight. It should be done gradually, particularly if the dog is *very* overweight. The best diet consists of cooked chicken and cooked pumpkin mixed together. The pumpkin bulks out the food and adds very little by way of calories. The chicken, with the fat removed after cooking, is mixed thoroughly with the mashed pumpkin. Generally, you mix 50% chicken mince with 50% pumpkin. In cases where the dog is particularly overweight, mix ⅔ pumpkin to ⅓ chicken.

- A small dog, e.g. Australian Terrier should be given one hamburger of cooked chicken.
- A medium sized dog, e.g. Cattle Dog should be given one handful (cup) of cooked chicken.

■ A large dog needs two handfuls and up, plus 2–3 times this amount (by volume) of the cooked pumpkin.

These amounts can vary considerably according to the present size and the eventual ideal weight of the dog. This diet will gradually reduce the dog's weight. Weigh the dog at least once a month. Give the dog a good vitamin supplement e.g. Geribits®, at least 2–3 times weekly. Alternatively, newer 'lite' dry foods have been developed as well as canned 'reducing' diets. These are balanced and will allow a steady rate of weight loss.

When the dog's weight has reached the desired level, stop the diet. Many people forget that the dog is on a diet, forget to weigh it, then return to the veterinarian complaining that the dog is too thin. When the dog is nearing the ideal weight, slightly increase its amount of food by adding a small amount of dry dog food (biscuit). Start to vary the diet if the weight is staying stable. Monitor the dog's weight and diet for several months, until you are sure the problem has been corrected. Ideally the dog should have a light layer of fat over the ribs, no more than 1 cm.

CONSTIPATION

A common problem in the older dog is constipation. Constipation is seen more often in elderly dogs as they lie around far more than when they were young and active. Reduced movement leads to a more inactive gastrointestinal system, causing faeces to stagnate and be drier than normal. One of the functions of the large intestine is to remove excess water from the faeces. Serious constipation in the elderly dog is caused for the most part by the feeding of bones. Add to this a sedentary lifestyle and the resulting faeces may resemble concrete.

Be very careful if feeding bones to older dogs, particularly those male dogs which have a history of prostate problems, or to any dog that has had a broken pelvis at any stage in its life. Both these conditions reduce the pelvic area, leaving less room for faeces to pass through.

Older dogs, with a history of constipation, should be given oil (e.g. liquid paraffin) at least once or twice a week to help prevent a serious blockage. Any excessive straining, failure to eat and vomiting that occurs with dogs that are prone to constipation, should be treated at once with 1–2 doses of oil. If there is no relief within 24 hours, it should be taken to your veterinarian (see section on Prostate problems in chapter 14). Older dogs with a history of repeated bouts of constipation should not be given bones unless oil (liquid paraffin) is given at the same time.

SKIN

Skin conditions in the older dog are a major cause for concern for many owners. Most of the skin irritations are of a chronic nature by this age and the veterinarian no doubt will have seen the dog for the same problem on many occasions. There are several major causes of skin problems: fleas, summer eczema, seborrhoea and hormonal problems. The methods of treatment used by veterinarians can vary widely, but essentially treatment aims at management, keeping the degree of irritation down to a comfortable level for the dog and the owners who both have to live with the scratching and biting.

The slightest irritation can set off these skin conditions, particularly flea eczema, as the older dog is by now so sensitised to fleas, that only one or two fleas biting the dog will be enough to start it scratching. With fleas, the aim is to control the dog's environmental exposure (i.e. reduce the pick-up), and to rinse regularly, to kill those fleas that it still gets.

Program®, the once a month flea control tablets are very good for reducing flea populations over the space of 2–3 months, thereby reducing the need for flea rinses considerably. Many dogs need cortisone tablets or injections to get through the summer season without developing bald patches above the tail area. The cortisone will decrease inflammation no matter what the initial irritation, but does not affect the agent causing the problem, so cortisone by itself is not enough. Care given to reduce the causative agents, is needed in addition to the cortisone.

Good shampoos, preferably mild, and not too high in detergents (tar based shampoos are excellent) should be used regularly (at least once a week) on those dogs which have greasy skins (seborrhoea). Cortisone, when used long term, should be given on alternate days in order to minimise suppression of the adrenal glands.

Quite a number of skin conditions seen in older dogs relate to hormonal imbalances, often involving the thyroid gland, causing a slight but gradual coat loss. Small amounts of thyroid hormone will correct this type of problem, but tests may be necessary to specifically locate which hormone is deficient (see information on fleas in chapter 18).

The secret of good skin care is management . What is required is a good diet (extra zinc, vitamin E and oil may help), regular skin treatment with good shampoos (Sebolyse®, Episoothe® etc.), and good control of skin parasites (flea and mites), both on the dog and in the environment in which it lives.

Kidneys and the Urinary Tract

Urinary tract problems can include prostate infections (see chapter 14, Breeding Older Dogs and Bitches), bladder infections (cystitis) and bladder stones, kidney infections, kidney degeneration leading to chronic kidney failure, and urinary incontinence. Kidney disorders can be secondary to other body system malfunctions. The causes and types of kidney diseases are too many and diverse to be dealt with in any great detail in this book, but it is important for you to be able to recognise the signs of kidney or urinary problems.

Symptoms   Symptoms of cystitis and bladder stones include frequent urination, regular passing of small quantities of urine, straining to urinate, and blood tinged urine. Common symptoms of kidney degeneration and inflammation include excessive drinking (polydipsia), excessive urination (polyuria), weight loss, vomiting in acute stages, and so on. There is a partial de-mineralisation of the bones with chronic renal failure. Prostatic infections in male dogs show symptoms of painful urination, often with the passing of a small amount of blood at the beginning or end of urination (see chapter 14 for further details).

Acute cystitis is a very painful condition. Blood-tinged urine is frequently observed and is mostly treated with antibiotics and urinary acidifiers to neutralise the urine. Dogs with cystitis often have histories of previous bouts of trouble and the condition may become a long term management problem. Long term treatment may include the use of antibiotics for extended periods (best given last thing at night, as the antibiotics will be concentrated in the urine) and continuing use of acidifiers like methionine, ammonium chloride, or vitamin C tablets. Cystitis will often flare up after periods of rain when the dog (particularly a bitch) is more reluctant to venture outside and so holds on to a large volume of urine. To avoid an attack of cystitis, you may have to forcibly take the dog outside, or leave it locked outside for 15 minutes, at least 3–4 times daily.

Bladder stones, while they may take a long time to form, can cause blockage of the outflow of urine (particularly in male dogs) which can lead to collapse, dehydration and, if the bladder ruptures, death if not treated. The average case of bladder stones is not as dramatic and the symptoms are straining after urination or frequent passing of small amounts of urine. Large bladder stones are generally removed surgically, while smaller stones may gradually be dissolved through correct medication. The method of treatment will depend on the composition of the stones.

The most common stones are struvite. These are best treated by adjusting the diet and giving medication for the acidification of the urine. This is helpful in dissolving struvite stones and reducing the chance of them recurring. Antibiotics are often needed for long periods. Newer forms of dry food can assist in the prevention of stone formation.

Dalmatians form stones, but these are always urate stones due to a lack of a particular enzyme being produced in this breed. Lower protein diets are of great benefit and these dogs often have to remain on Zyloprim® (Allopurinol).

Dachshunds mostly form cystine stones.

The most important point to remember is that the diet can play a major role in:

(a) The gradual reduction in the size of the stones.

(b) The prevention of stone re-formation.

RENAL FAILURE

Kidney degeneration, where loss of function of the renal tubules occurs, can, if the loss is severe or the inflammation is acute, lead rapidly to the dog becoming toxic. Kidneys are the body's strainers. They remove waste products that the body does not need and if the delicate balance is upset it can have a profound effect on the dog's health.

Acute renal failure has symptoms of severe depression, vomiting and dehydration despite the dog wanting to drink. Acute cases should immediately be hospitalised, where assessment of the severity of kidney damage can be checked by blood chemistry and fluid replacement therapy initiated as soon as possible. Long term prognosis of the dog is greatest where there is a quick return to normal.

Chronic renal failure is quite common in the elderly dog, often as the result of low grade tubular degeneration, in which the filtration of the blood is no longer very efficient. Consequently, there is an extra loss of protein, minerals and water from the kidneys. These dogs drink excessively (polydipsia) and urinate excessively (polyuria). There is an accompanying gradual weight loss and decreased activity. The urine is very 'watery' and the specific gravity is less than 1.012.

The treatment for both acute and chronic renal failure can vary widely depending on many biochemical factors that should be checked by blood tests, especially for blood urea (nitrogen) and creatine levels, dehydration, calcium and potassium levels.

Kidney failure or degeneration is a highly complex syndrome with far reaching effects on the body. However, once a dog has been stabilised after the initial diagnosis is made, the owner can help to a very large degree by feeding the dog correctly.

DIETS FOR TREATING DOGS WITH KIDNEY TROUBLE

The aim in feeding a dog with a history of some form of kidney degeneration and inflammation, is to reduce *stress and strain* on the kidneys. High protein levels in the diet force the kidneys to work harder, both in removing waste products and in making the urine more alkaline. Therefore, the dog's diet must be lower in protein. This is also true of humans to some extent.

A good low protein diet that can be made up, is as follows:

Ground beef (with fat) — 100 g
White rice — 2¼ cups cooked
Sugar — 1 tablespoon
Vegetable oil — 1 teaspoon
Calcium Carbonate — 500 mg (1 teaspoon) as a buffer

Add a vitamin and trace mineral supplement; extra B group vitamins in particular are helpful.

Total made up = 3000 kilojoules (720 calories).

The alternative to making up this set diet is to reduce the strong animal protein intake e.g. kidney, liver and heart. Keep red meats to a minimum; chicken, rabbit, veal are more suitable. Newer specific kidney dry dog foods are excellent, as are rice, spaghetti, small amounts of dairy products and occasionally an egg. The diet can be varied by the addition of vegetables — potatoes, pumpkin or cabbage.

Extra vitamins and minerals can be very beneficial to compensate for their loss through the kidneys. The B group vitamins in particular often need to be supplemented.

Dogs with chronic renal failure, particularly the elderly, need to eat on a regular basis, because of the loss of proteins through the damaged tubules. Anabolics may be needed periodically to assist these cases, as they increase appetite and improve metabolism.

URINARY INCONTINENCE

This is very common in the older desexed bitch. You will notice pools of urine near where the bitch has been sleeping or lying for some time. The loss is involuntary and very upsetting both to owner and the bitch who is often fastidious. Controlling this is very easy, as the replacement of small amounts of female hormone (Stilboestrol), generally given twice weekly, is sufficient to restore excellent control to the bladder. Another drug which is quite effective is pseudoephedrine (Sudafed®, Actifed® tablets) in low doses given twice weekly.

Urinary incontinence can be secondary to other urinary infections, so a good examination by your veterinarian and a good history of the problem is essential for correct diagnosis. Concurrent intake of cortisone can create urinary incontinence as cortisone increases the water intake. Cortisone should be used with great care in the older renal patient.

PANCREAS

The pancreas is the organ which produces enzymes to digest the food eaten by an animal (humans included). Its glands are situated near the stomach and deliver its enzymes into the intestines just below the outlet of the stomach. The pancreas is also the organ which produces insulin, and if chronic or severe damage occurs, diabetes can be a possible outcome.

Pancreatitis is a fairly common problem in the dog, not only in the elderly. This is predominantly seen in the chronically overweight dog who has been overfed for years. Pancreatitis generally occurs in bouts, where the common symptoms are vomiting and not eating. These bouts can indicate acute or more commonly, chronic low grade inflammation.

Acute Pancreatitis can be life threatening in severe cases if it is not treated immediately by your veterinarian. Diagnosis is often non-specific without a blood test to check the amylase level. The degree of elevation of amylase enzyme in the blood is the general indication as to the severity of the condition. Severely affected dogs are depressed, off their food, vomiting, and slightly dehydrated as they often refuse to drink. There is pain, particularly in the forward, right-hand side (the dog's right) of the abdomen. The dog is usually overweight but may have a recent history of weight loss. Dogs with acute pancreatitis are generally hospitalised and placed on antibiotics given once or twice weekly, and intravenous drips to replace lost fluids.

The main aim of treatment is to give the dog complete gastric rest, so as not to stimulate the pancreas and to give the digestive system a chance to settle down. After 1–2 days, a small amount of water may be given and if this is tolerated, the dog can be taken off the drip.

Very small amounts of water and food should be given for the next few days but absolutely no fatty foods. Aftercare generally requires a slow reduction in the dog's weight and a low fat diet. Digestion of fats places greater strain on the pancreas.

Low grade bouts of pancreatitis are often treated at home after the dog has been examined by the veterinarian. The treatment is basically the same; antibiotics, gut rest, with frequent small drinks of water during the following 2–3 days. Once the dog has improved, give small meals of low fat foods and if overweight, put the dog on a suitable diet to bring the weight gradually down to normal.

Pancreatic deficiency is a possible sequel to bouts of pancreatitis or to pancreatic atrophy (wasting). Failure of the pancreas to produce enough enzymes to enable the dog to completely digest the food, will lead to a gradual weight loss. Dogs which have a pancreatic deficiency are chronically thin and usually do not tolerate fatty foods very well. They have pasty, pale coloured faeces which are poorly formed like cow pats. Owners are often worried that neighbours might report them to welfare authorities for starving their dog.

This condition is diagnosed by a faeces test to see whether the dog has sufficient enzymes (generally testing for trypsin levels) present to carry out normal digestion. If there are insufficient enzymes in the faeces then the dog needs to be given some form of enzyme replacement, which is usually mixed with the food. There is a newer blood test called TLI which is also very accurate. Once this condition has been properly diagnosed, the dog is generally placed on gastric enzyme replacement medication for life. Diets consist mainly of carbohydrates (dry dog foods, rice, pasta etc.), and proteins. Specialised dry dog foods are now available that can assist in the management of this condition.

Pancreatitis and **pancreatic deficiency** are two different conditions which should not be confused. The second can be the result of chronic bouts of the first, but it should be remembered that most dogs with pancreatitis do not need to go onto a pancreatic supplement.

DIABETES MELLITUS

As we are on the subject of the pancreas, it would be advisable to explain diabetes. There are two forms of diabetes:

1. Mellitus which is a lack of insulin production. Insulin is produced by special cells within the pancreas.

2. Insipidus which is a lack of a particular hormone (ADH) which controls urination. Diabetes insipidus has similar symptoms in so far as it causes excessive drinking and urination, but it is otherwise totally different in its cause and treatment. This is seen mostly in Greyhounds in heavy work.

Diabetes Mellitus, contrary to general belief, can occur in many species apart from man. While it is not a very common problem in the average pet, there are several breeds which are more prone to diabetes, and these include the Dachshund, Beagle, Australian Terrier, Silky Terrier, and Cattle Dog to name a few, and yes, it can occur in the 'purebred' mongrel as well. The highest incidence however is found be in Dachshunds and Dachshund crosses.

Diabetes can be a result of damage from bouts of pancreatitis, but it mostly occurs on its own. The description of the affected individual is similar to pancreatitis, and the diabetic dog is usually chronically overweight (often called obese by the unkind).

Symptoms The symptoms are polydipsia (excessive drinking) and polyuria (excessive urination), often accompanied by recent sudden weight loss and decreased appetite. Cataracts in the eyes are fairly common in diabetics.

Diagnosis is by blood and urine tests which reveal high levels of dextrose (sugar). Insulin helps the body to metabolise sugars, so when there is insufficient insulin released, there will be excess sugar circulating in the blood. In an attempt to relieve the increasing levels of blood sugar, the body demands water leading to polydipsia and then on to polyuria.

Although the diagnosis of diabetes mellitus is reasonably simple, it often calls for a difficult decision regarding the dog's future. You will have to decide whether you are prepared to keep a dog which may need to stay on medication for the rest of its life, often receiving 1–2 injections daily. A diabetic dog will limit an owner's time, as the dog will require injections and feeds at set intervals. Small variations are allowable, but too much alteration in the daily schedule can be harmful. Elderly dogs with other concurrent problems should be assessed in the light of this additional burden. Not all dogs with diabetes will stabilise well.

Once the decision is made to proceed, the dog is hospitalised, the daily dose of insulin is calculated and the dog is fed 30–60 minutes after the injection. Blood tests are taken to ensure that blood glucose levels are coming under control. After they have been stabilised, careful control of the diet and weight of the dog is worked out by your veterinarian. Regular check-ups are needed, particularly in the first few months, to ensure that the dog's condition is stable and that you are carrying out instructions correctly. *Treatment*

Water consumption is probably the most crucial factor for the owner to keep an eye on at home. Increased water consumption indicates a rising blood sugar level and can be more accurate than a urine sample.

Blood tests are the most accurate method of checking glucose levels. Your veterinarian will do these at a standard time after the injection and the subsequent feed.

With good management and a good working relationship with your veterinarian, these dogs can live for many years and lead a relatively normal life.

Teeth

The teeth are not often examined, but dental trouble can be at the root of many an older dog's problems, particularly in the smaller toy breeds. The dog may eat badly, salivate, have atrociously bad breath and have a steady weight loss. Some dogs can become very snappy when you attempt to handle the mouth, as their teeth and gums are sore and ulcerated. If your dog has these symptoms, have a quick look at the teeth and you may get quite a shock. Plaque forms on the sides of the teeth, particularly the upper back teeth, which in turn irritates the gums and allows infections to set in. The infection causes the smell and eventually loosens the tooth in the socket. If you are not sure what is causing the smell or irritation of the gums, take the dog to your veterinarian.

If the teeth have an accumulation of plaque, they will need to be cleaned and the infection of the gums treated with antibiotics. Loose teeth should be pulled out, as the tooth root attachment rarely tightens following infection at the base. Iodine rinses or hydrogen peroxide mouth washes are very useful for treating severe inflammations of the gums (gingivitis), if used for several days following teeth cleaning.

In smaller breeds, the problem with the teeth is exacerbated by the feeding of soft mushy food. This is often a vicious circle: when the teeth are sore, dogs will only eat soft food, and when all the rotten teeth are removed, they have so few left that they have to stay on the soft food. Many of the smaller breeds need regular teeth cleaning.

Older dogs should have a thorough teeth examination at least twice a year. Any swellings or abscesses on the side of the face, especially below the eyes, can be the result of a rotten tooth which is abscessing out through the root and should be immediately seen by your veterinarian.

Eyes

Occasionally the older dog may have chronically irritated eyes which need to be treated every day. These types of problems are most commonly seen among the spaniel breeds and the short nosed, 'poppy-eyed' breeds e.g. Pekingese.

The most common condition in the older dog is the 'Dry eye' syndrome. This is where there has been years of low grade irritation and often, pigment deposition over the surface of the cornea. The tearing or moisturising system of the eye has become deficient and insufficient tears are produced to properly lubricate the eye. As a result, there is a very thick mucous sludge that is hard to remove from the surface of the eye. This in turn does not help any existing condition. Treatment consists of using 'liquid tears' several times a day to keep the eye moist. This gives the dog reasonable comfort, but the condition is not reversible, so treatment must continue for the rest of its life. Cortisone drops can occasionally be of benefit.

Another common problem with the older dog is Pannis, which is seen most often in the German Shepherd and the prominent eyed breeds e.g. Pugs and Pekingese. In this condition there is gradual pigment deposition across the surface of the cornea, usually starting at the edge, and there is a 'front line' of inflammation around the pigmented area. This is a slowly progressing condition which, again, is not reversible. The treatment here is the use of a strong cortisone drop e.g. Predneferin®, which is used when the eye is inflamed. Some dogs will need continuous therapy. This condition is rarely seen before 6–8 years of age. Gradually the affected dogs will go blind, but it usually takes at least 4–6 years for this to happen.

Ears

Many an older dog has a history of chronic low grade ear inflammation, where there has been a thickening of the canal or haematomas. This is seen particularly in the heavy coated, drop eared dogs, such as Cocker and English Spaniels. Once there is thickening of the inner ear canal, infections flare up easily, especially during periods of high humidity (i.e. following rain). Treatments vary greatly between veterinarians and in relation to the severity and cause of the condition, so a good all round maintenance programme is difficult to recommend. Owners of these dogs should be warned to watch the ears carefully after wet weather and possibly give the ears a good clean out if they are worried. If the condition flares up, the sooner it is treated the better (more on routine ear hygiene in chapter 18).

Cancers

As with humans, dogs can get cancers of every type and system. In the dog, some organs are more susceptible to cancer, e.g. cancer of the spleen, mammary tumours, mast cell tumours and lymphosarcoma (of the lymph nodes). It is very hard to generalise regarding the symptoms of cancer as they can vary considerably.

The most common symptoms are gradual weight loss, tiredness, decreased appetite and in some cases vomiting; note particularly the presence of swellings and lumps which have increased in size, particularly of the lymph nodes.

The treatment is as variable as the type and severity of the cancer. A definition of terms may be helpful:

1. **Benign** generally means slow growing, non-invasive and they do not metastasise (spread throughout the body systems). The tumours which are benign generally end with -*oma* e.g. Lypoma, a fatty tumour under the skin and occasionally between muscles, which is very common in the older dog, grows slowly and generally causes next to no problem to the dog's health.

2. **Malignant**. These are invasive, often rapidly growing and metastasise rapidly. Depending on the original tissue which has turned cancerous, the tumours resemble that tissue and often spread to the major filtration systems of the body i.e. lungs, liver, spleen, kidneys and lymph nodes. Once the effects are noticeable, the life span of the dog may be fairly limited. The cancers usually have -*sarcoma* or -*carcinoma* after their tissue description e.g. Haemangeosarcoma, a blood tissue malignant cancer, generally of the spleen.

Old non-desexed bitches are very prone to mammary gland tumours, which once they start spreading, will cause rapid deterioration. (See chapter 14, Breeding Older Dogs and Bitches). If your bitch is desexed after you have finished breeding with her, the chances of this occurring are reduced.

The important message about cancers or strange 'lumps and bumps' is the earlier they are attended to, the more likely that if it is serious, they can be treated and possibly cured. The attitude of 'I don't want to know', puts many owners through agonising months, when a simple trip to the veterinarian may relieve their anxieties.

When to Let Go — Dignity to Your Friend

The **quality of life** is the most important aspect of this often very difficult and soul searching decision. The decision should take into account whether your pet is still getting enjoyment out of life, its ability to get up and move about, whether it is eating and participating in general goings on, even if this is done at a very slow pace. Older dogs will spend a considerable amount of time sleeping and this is perfectly natural for elderly animals of any species, including humans.

Dogs with cancers or debilitating diseases, while they are still eating and reasonably happy, can keep going. Medication for many conditions will alleviate symptoms of failing body systems, but a stage may be reached where despite treatment, the dog is obviously not coping or is in pain. When they do not eat and start wasting away, or are unable to get up and down without assistance, then the welfare of the dog must be thought of.

It is not what you, the owner is going through, it is the dog that matters. Many people come to their veterinarian saying 'I cannot live without my dog, I want this and that done to save my dog'. Stop to consider the animal which is the one that is suffering. However upset you are, *you* are not the one in pain.

Decisions of this kind are very difficult to make with the dog in front of you, looking right up at you. If you cannot make up your mind, leave the dog with the vet, go home and think about it, without the emotional trauma of making the decision in the presence of your beloved pet. Decisions are then made without that emotional 'blackmail', allowing you to be more realistic in a calm frame of mind.

Your friend and companion of many years deserves a dignified end when the joy of living has gone. Do not ruin a good friendship. It is hard to make that final decision, but it is kind to give an old friend a painless goodbye.

16

Genetics & the Importance of Breed Soundness

Before you breed a litter, you should know why you are doing so and have goals in mind for what you wish to achieve. You should understand the basics of genetics to give you some idea of how different traits or characteristics are inherited. In contemplating a litter, you should consider the breed worth of the parents and their overall breed soundness. When breeding dogs, we are constantly trying to create better and hopefully sounder dogs.

Definition of Breed Soundness

Breed soundness is determined by assessing several areas:

1. Physical soundness. This relates to construction and health. Is the animal able to cope with the demands of ordinary life as well as stresses of heavy work in specialised areas if required? Health can relate to organ or system health e.g. reproductive soundness as well as problems such as heart function or joint soundness.

2. Mental soundness. This refers to the temperament, ability and aptitude of the animal to be of benefit in its chosen field. Different temperaments are required for the numerous fields of activity (or relative inactivity) that cover the wide range of dog types and diversity of use. The keenness to work that is admired in the working and utility breeds would be rather overpowering in many toy breeds.

3. Genetic soundness. This is reflected in many physically obvious attributes, as well as on cellular and hormonal levels, which may be less obvious. Recent developments have resulted in many more conditions being termed genetic in origin, however the means to readily remove these conditions from a breed are often not yet available.

4. Breed type. Before considering breeding, your dog or bitch should be typical of the breed i.e. look like the breed. It should be above average in order to improve the quality of stock within your kennel.

The overall picture covers many aspects within each area and may have different slants within various breeds. Compromises often have to be made when balancing out the relative importance of different problems both within that animal and the breed as a whole.

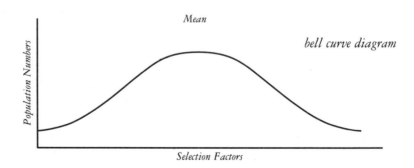

bell curve diagram

256

Populations can be described by a bell curve which can apply to any feature you wish to look at, be it height through a breed, litter size, hip dysplasia (HD) scores and so on. With this curve, the top of the curve is the mean of the population factor being assessed (e.g. height) with the extremes at either end of the scale (e.g. the shortest and tallest).

If your breed has no top height e.g. Great Danes, and the object is to breed tall dogs, you are obviously selecting animals from the top end of the scale, using the medium to large dogs and weeding out the 'runts'. On the other hand, with German Shepherds, there is a height limit and while we wish to breed strong, well boned dogs (who generally are on the large end of the scale), we have to fit (or attempt to fit) the vast majority of dogs under the limit, so the breeders will usually discard the tallest and the smallest, and generally work with the medium to large range of the population.

This same principle can be applied to any genetic problem within a breed. If the incidence of a problem is small across the whole breed, e.g. affecting 5–10%, it can be fairly easy for breeders or clubs to say not to breed with affected animals. If however, the problem has a variable expression and/or a complex means (polygenetic) of inheritance, this can affect virtually every member of the breed e.g. hip dysplasia, to some degree.

The most important point is to keep the problems a breed has within perspective. This means that if there is a minor problem that does not affect the animal's soundness, either as a working animal or its quality and length of life, it should be kept in proportion relative to other problems within the breed.

Genetic problems that result in a high incidence of blindness, crippling arthritis or vastly shortened life span (e.g. the storage diseases), where there is pain and suffering for both the dog and the owner (be it monetary or emotional stress), efforts should be made to decrease the incidence of these problems.

The major task facing any breed inherited disorder, is establishing the mode of inheritance. If you are lucky, it may affect a single gene, with a recessive/normal pattern, and if you are really lucky, there may be a blood test developed that can identify all three states of the gene i.e. affected, carrier and normal. This still allows a breed club to keep its genetic pool and breed the problem out within two to three generations. This happened in Springer Spaniels with the storage disease Fucocidosis. Would that all genetic problems were as easy to eradicate.

Most inherited problems have two or more genes affecting the inheritance pattern and not all genes behave nicely. Dominant genes can express one problem and hide another problem. The normal gene usually carries sufficient enzyme-making ability to hide the effects of the defective gene. The animal will appear normal but is in fact a 'carrier' of the abnormal gene. This can often be seen in sex-linked genetic problems e.g. Haemophilia A. As this gene is carried on the X chromosome, the problem can be carried or hidden by a bitch (XX) on to the next generation as she has two X chromosomes. If a male (XY) carries the affected X chromosome, the problem will be expressed as there is no other X chromosome to provide the correct enzyme to allow normal blood clotting to occur. There is at present no definitive test to determine carrier status in females for Haemophilia A.

Multiple gene problems are called polygenetic and are much harder to clear from the population as they are often a blend of effects of the genes and the environment acting together. The more genes that are involved, the greater is the chance that the environmental factors will affect the end result. Environmental factors include diet, rate of weight gain, level of activity and stress factors.

As stated above, the overall picture should be remembered. Trying to eliminate all dogs with hip dysplasia (HD) did not work (attempted in both German Shepherds and Labradors) and the end result was a greatly reduced genetic pool. Cases of HD were still occurring and breeds no longer resembled the standard. The main aim today of most hip schemes is a gradual reduction in the breed average while at the same time allowing breeders to preserve valuable bloodlines and decrease the incidence of really severe HD. The ability to inherit HD varies in different breeds. The higher the degree of inheritance, the more rapidly changes can occur within a breed when selecting for the characteristic. Also, a dog that has a good hip score, may not necessarily throw low scores in his progeny, while a full litter brother with a slightly higher score may have a far lower progeny average than his brother.

General Genetics

Every time you select a dog to breed to your bitch, you are practising the art (or science) of genetics. Genetics, in a basic form, is very simple to understand if you try. Unfortunately, a lot of people are terrified of genetics, deeming it to be too hard to understand unless they have a university degree in science. Because of this, few will make any attempt to understand the principles. I have tried to simplify, as much as possible, the basic principles and the effects of gene recombination i.e. what actually happens to the genetic material during reproduction and the subsequent effect that the environment has to play.

It is important at least to try to understand the basic principles of genetics and the laws of inheritance. Even in its simplest form, an understanding of genetic principles can assist you in the comprehension of what is happening and what might happen when you mate two dogs.

SOME BASIC DEFINITIONS:

Genes are the basic components of the genetic material that is passed on from generation to generation. A gene is composed of DNA and in effect the DNA is the blueprint of information to the cells. If the gene is defective or missing then the information controlled by that gene is also defective or missing. Genes can overlap in effect and only if the missing gene is controlling a life threatening process, will the lack of that gene be noticed.

Genes are connected to each other on long strands called chromosomes. Chromosomes are usually 'paired', with one chromosome of each pair deriving from each parent. Every species has a distinct number of chromosome pairs (diploid number), which never varies within that species e.g. dogs 39 pairs (78 individual chromosomes), wolves 39 pairs, cats 19 pairs, horses 32 pairs, humans 24 pairs. Similar species tend to have very close or identical numbers of chromosomes. The dog, wolf, dingo, coyote and the jackal have the same number of chromosomes. More remarkably, the sizes and types of chromosomes are identical in all these species. This is the fundamental reason why these breeds can interbreed.

The dog has a large number of chromosomes for a mammal and the larger the number of chromosomes, the greater the amount of possible re-combinations of the genetic material. This large number of chromosomes and the enormous variations that are possible has allowed the dog in all its numerous shapes, sizes and breeds, to spread and adapt to so many different climates and conditions throughout the world.

Mitosis is the process of cellular division and replication of the chromosomes. The chromosomes individually 'self copy'; and at cellular division, each daughter cell gets an identical set (and number) of chromosomes. This is the way that the body cells are produced during growth or replace worn out or damaged tissue.

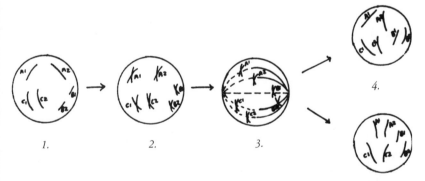

1. 2. 3. 4.

Meiosis is the process where the chromosomes come together as pairs (and undergo recombination) and then divide so that the each new cell has only half the 'pair' of the chromosomes. This is called the **haploid** number. This process halves the number of chromosomes so that upon fertilisation, the original number of chromosomes is restored. This process only takes place in the 'germ' cells, which are the ones associated with sexual reproduction, the ova and the sperm.

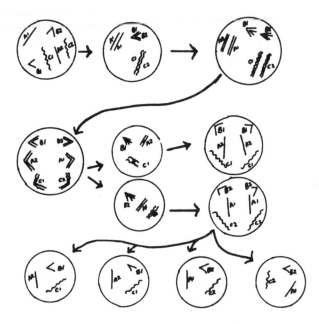

It is important to realise that this is the time that the chromosome linkage and recombinations are made that allow the incredible variation between individuals (even within litters) to occur. Recombination allows a random re-shuffling of the hereditary characteristics.

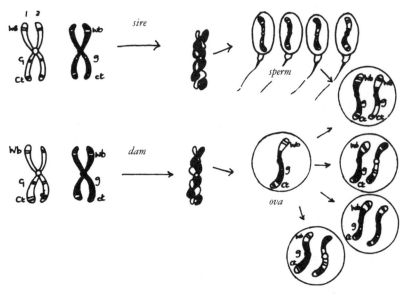

Linkage and Recombination — during meiosis

ALLELES

These are slightly different forms of the same gene. The different combination of alleles can cause variations such as in coat colour.

If the allele is the same on both chromosomes (i.e. the pair that carry that gene), then the animal is **homozygous** for that gene.

If the alleles are different on each chromosome, then the animal is said to be **heterozygous** for that gene.

An allele which, when present in a single dose, still manages to produce its full effect upon the animal is said to be a **dominant** allele.

An allele which has its effect blocked or masked by another allele is a **recessive** allele.

An example of these descriptions is given below.

A = dominant   AA = homozygous dominant (HOD)

a = recessive   Aa = heterozygous dominant (HE)

              aa = homozygous recessive (HOR)

HOD x HOD	HOR x HOR	HOD x HOR
AA x AA	aa x aa	AA x aa
AA,AA,AA,AA	aa,aa,aa,aa	Aa,Aa,Aa,Aa
All progeny	All progeny	All progeny
dominant	recessive	dominant (to look at)
(and will only		All carry the recessive
produce dominant)		i.e. all are heterozygous

HE x HE	HOD x HE	HOR x HE
Aa x Aa	AA x Aa	aa x Aa
AA,Aa,aA,aa	AA,Aa,AA,Aa	aA,aa,aA,aa
3 dominant:	All progeny	2 dominant:
1 recessive in	dominant in	2 recessive in
appearance	appearance	appearance
Genetically —	Genetically —	Genetically —
1 dominant	2 dominant	2 heterozygous
2 heterozygous	2 heterozygous	2 recessive
1 recessive		

Occasionally, when there are several alleles for a gene, it is possible to have an allele which is dominant to one allele, yet recessive to another, for example coat colour in many breeds.

Incomplete dominance of an allele can result in the apparent 'blending' of the effects of the dominant gene with the recessive gene.

Incomplete penetrance of an allele is where the dominant allele does not exert its full effect upon all the animals that carry it. This allows some which carry the dominant gene, not to show it in external appearance. The percentage of animals which show the character they carry in their genes is termed the *penetrance* of the gene.

MENDELIAN RATIOS

Mendel was the man who began the investigation of this often fascinating subject. Apart from his bad habit of growing masses of sweet peas in the monastery gardens, he worked out that the science of genetics follows fairly simple mathematical ratios. When working with a gene that has only two alleles, one dominant and one recessive, basic repeatable results will occur. This can be expanded to studying the effect of more than one gene each with two or more alleles, and again the results can be reasonably predicted.

Sex Determination: Males are XY, Females are XX

The Y chromosome carries all the differences that are between the sexes and it also means that the sex determination is very much made possible by the male. Females can only have an X chromosome to pass on as they are both Xs. The male however, has X sperm and Y sperm and which ever reaches the ova first, determines the sex of the offspring.

Sex linked. Some characteristics are sex linked as they are more common in one sex. Sex linked characteristics are mostly seen in the male as the character is usually carried on the X chromosome. This means with only a single X present in males, certain otherwise recessive characteristics can be expressed.

Sex determined. Only animals of that sex can exhibit the characteristic e.g. testicular abnormalities are only seen in the male.

Genotype. This term describes the genetic make-up (or blue-print) of an animal i.e. its genetic potential.

Phenotype. This means the actual physical make-up, or what we see physically. 'Phenotypically' much of an individual's genetic make-up is not visible, but the genetic potential will become more obvious through the offspring. The phenotypical appearance can be greatly affected by the environment.

Polygenetic. This is where more than two genes affect a characteristic or function. The important point to remember with 'polygenes' is that many genes are involved as a group, and that the effect of each one is small compared with the cumulative effect of the 'group'. The presence or absence of members of the group and the dominance or masking of the effect of one gene by another can each affect the overall expression of the group. This makes the understanding of genetics of these groups very difficult, particularly if large numbers of genes are involved.

There are many genes that inter-relate as far as function or metabolism are concerned. There are thought to be at least 4–5 genes involved in hip dysplasia for example, making this an extremely tedious problem to try and eradicate as a phenotypically normal animal is not necessarily genetically 'free' and may throw cases of HD.

Epistasis is the suppression of one dominant gene by another gene at a different locus. This is seen most obviously in colour breeding. In the Irish Setter for example, the red coat colour is the result of an epistatic gene in one position suppressing the normally dominant gene for black. The fact that there is a black gene is evident by the black nose, pads and occasional small patches of black hair.

Interaction Between the Genetic Make-up of an Individual and the Environment

The environment is considered by 'geneticists' as *anything* which has an effect on the development of the individual. In other words, the interaction of the genetic make-up and the environment is what shapes the individual.

The genetic material that is passed on at the time of fertilisation is the total sum of the parental genetic contribution. From that time onwards, the environment can and does affect the development of firstly the foetus as affected by the uterus, and secondly the puppy, as affected by the level of maternal care and the impact of the physical world.

The main environmental factors affecting the post-natal development are diet and temperature. How the individual is affected by these depends on its innate genetic constitution. Extremes of temperature, inadequate food and mineral deficiencies can cause stunted growth and increased susceptibility to disease. Given adequate food, the growth is then largely dependent on the genetic constitution of an individual.

Some characteristics are not affected at all by the environment e.g. basic colour and coat patterns.

Polygenetic characters such as hip dysplasia are more affected by environment than are the simple recessives as there are more factors that can be influenced by the environment e.g. diet, weight gain and exercise.

Difference Between Congenital and Inherited

Congenital means present at birth, i.e. 'something went wrong' at some stage of development during pregnancy. Congenital defects can be genetic or the result of accidents during development.

Congenital

Development of the foetus occurs rather like an assembly line that is highly complex and has many processes going on at the same time. Occasionally the right 'button' or correct sequence does not occur and an abnormality will result.

These abnormal 'happenings' can occur spontaneously (mutations), due to genetic make-up, or can be the result of external influences (these are not passed on to future generations).

External influences can be many and varied e.g. the effect of some drugs: Thalidomide which causes abnormal shortening of limbs.

Tetracycline, an antibiotic which if used during pregnancy can cause permanent damage to the enamel of the teeth.

External influences include any environmental factor e.g. periods of excessive heat. A heatwave lasting several days can cause all sorts of congenital abnormalities, particularly towards the end of the first trimester of pregnancy.

Excessive body temperature elevation due to a viral and/or a bacterial disease, particularly if it occurs during the crucial time towards the end of the first trimester of pregnancy, may cause the same assortment of abnormalities. The first trimester of pregnancy is the time when the most rapid developmental changes are taking place, especially during the second week and up till the end of the third week. Because of the rapidity of the development and the rate of cellular change and division, the cells are particularly 'sensitive' to outside changes, especially when these changes are dramatic. This is an important fact to remember particularly when having summer litters in hot climates. Veterinarians see more heart defects in puppies born in the late summer period than at any other time of the year.

Remember that the main point about a congenital defect, (providing that the fault is not life-threatening and the animal lives to reproductive age) is that it is *not* necessarily genetic i.e. passed on to future generations. Congenital defects that have occurred due to external influences are in no way genetic in origin.

There are congenital defects which have a genetic basis, such as cleft palates and hare lips in some particular breeds (e.g. Papillons), but not all breeds. If you suspect that the congenital defect(s) are inherited, ask your veterinarian or read several books on dog genetics.

Inherited This is the genetic material that is passed on to the next generation(s) unchanged by, although the 'expression of' may be altered by, the environment. Inherited generally refers to traits exhibited by the individual that breeders are interested in. Occasionally it may be a breed fault that they do not want exhibited e.g. incorrect coat colour or texture; but mostly breeders are interested in maintaining particular virtues and, at the same time, removing the undesirable faults.

As we have seen earlier, some characteristic methods of inheritance are relatively easily understood e.g. coat colour. When selecting matings for factors that have few alleles affecting them (e.g. coat colour), it is fairly easy to predict the resulting colours of the offspring. In some breeds with larger ranges of coat colour available, it may take a few matings to find out all the recessives the dog or bitch is carrying.

The more genes affecting a characteristic, the harder it is to eradicate or affect the characteristic. Where there are ways to measure the effect of the characteristic, then progress can be made in controlling the effect of the polygenes in the overall population e.g. x-raying of individuals and their progeny for hip dysplasia.

Determining whether a fault or defect is inherited: *Summary*
1. Does it affect more than one member of a litter? Obviously the larger the litter the more likely you are to get a significant result.
2. Has it recurred in a repeat mating, or in matings that are genetically similar?
3. Are there ancestors in common?
4. Test breeding can be carried out to see if the fault reappears.

Selection

Actual selection of animals for breeding is done by several methods with many differing aims in mind by the various breeders. The traits considered desirable in one country, may not be particularly sought after in another. Breed standards vary between countries, although there are moves to standardise these (i.e. the standards), to the country of origin. Breed preferences and aims do change over the years, some more quickly than others, especially in the 'younger' breeds. Nothing is static particularly where genes are concerned, nor should it be. Gradual changes within breeds and lines are desirable when aiming at improvements in soundness or working ability.

SELECTION FOR DESIRABLE TRAITS

Obviously, breeders will try to select the more desirable characteristics of the breed, but some of these characteristics may well have variable methods of inheritance. Some of these characteristics e.g. coat colour, have fairly well documented genes, so that you can plan with reasonable accuracy what colours you may expect to obtain within the litter before you even mate the bitch. As time goes on, and more characteristics are sorted out genetically, the breeder will be able to predict what a proposed mating will produce as far as type, colour or shape.

SELECTION AGAINST BAD TRAITS (FAULTS)

When trying to select for desirable characteristics, you are at the same time trying to reduce or eliminate the undesirable characteristics e.g. hip dysplasia, entropion (inturned eyelids), eye defects etc. Many genetic faults have well documented studies to sort out the method of inheritance of that fault.

Where the fault is a simple recessive, it is relatively easy to reduce the incidence of it in your lines, but unless there is a simple test to determine the carriers, the fault will be almost impossible to eradicate. New methods of enzyme assay are being developed daily and in the future this may be the way of determining the carriers of genetic faults e.g.

Fucocidosis (a lack of the enzyme which has a simple recessive inheritance) in English Springer Spaniels, which is now a relatively easy problem to eliminate from the breed within two generations if the breeders wish to blood test their stock. It would be great if all genetic problems could be as easily tested for and eliminated.

Breeders and clubs with the long term interests of the breed at heart are setting up schemes to test for the worst genetic faults (i.e. those that are detrimental to the health, comfort and mobility of the animals) and reduce the incidence of these faults. The more breeders participate in such schemes, the quicker the overall standard of the breed will improve.

SELECTION POTENTIAL

Selection potential is a term that appears every now and again, and refers to how 'heavily' an animal is selected for breeding compared to the rest of the population. This usually refers to the reduced number of individuals, particularly males, which end up being bred out of the total population available. With dogs, because they can have multiple offspring at one time (i.e. a litter) and can reproduce at a comparatively early age, a fairly high selection potential can apply.

When selecting a puppy in a litter, a breeder usually has 4–6 puppies to choose from rather than just a single offspring as in many species, for example, the horse. This means that rapid genetic 'improvements' are possible. With the smaller breeds, there is usually a small litter size as well (1–4 puppies), so the rate of genetic improvement is slower.

What this means in real terms to a breeder is that as far as stud dogs are concerned, there is a very high selection potential on the exceptional males. Average or mediocre dogs receive very few bitches compared to the very good dogs. Only about 10% of male dogs are used at stud, compared to about 40–50% of the bitches used for breeding. Breeders are willing to breed mediocre bitches to very good dogs, but very few people are willing to use mediocre dogs.

In the long run, a few males will end up having a fairly large effect on the breed, whereas a bitch has to be heavily bred from and be an exceptional producer to have the same effect, which by sheer numbers, places the bitches at a disadvantage. A well used stud dog can be out and producing 60–80 puppies during the same time as a bitch is producing one litter of 6–8 puppies.

Before you decide to breed your bitch or dog, make sure that she/he is a relatively sound animal in type, temperament and structure. If there are major genetic faults within your breed, at least try to discover them before breeding your bitch or allowing your dog to be used at stud.

As stated earlier, determine why you wish to breed a litter from that animal. Hopefully it is because you want to breed a better one for yourself, but the litter should also be as sound as you can make it for the sake of all the other owners of the puppies from that litter.

Different Types of Matings

There are several different types of mating systems that are used; quite often two or more systems are used simultaneously. The first two types of matings are often done without particular emphasis on pedigrees. The following systems are related to the pedigrees of the parents.

1. TYPE TO TYPE MATINGS

This is where the body and structure of both parents are similar in type. Generally one parent is the better animal (usually the dog), and you are attempting to correct minor faults while still retaining the same general body type. This system works very well, particularly if the parents are 'typical' of the litters from which they come i.e. the parents are not 'one offs' or flyers. Where information on the rest of the litter is not available, the parents should be typical of the 'bloodlines' (i.e. typical of the lines behind the parents).

2. CORRECTIVE FAULT MATINGS

This is where the 'types' of the parents are not necessarily similar, but one parent is particularly good in various areas and the other parent is weak in those areas. The resultant progeny will range in type between both parents, as will the fault you are trying to correct. This type of mating is generally done when trying to upgrade the quality of your stock. One generation of this type of mating will usually not be sufficient to remove the problem or it may merely hide it until the next generation.

3. INBREEDING AND 'LINE BREEDING'

Inbreeding and line breeding are often thought to be totally different. Inbreeding is generally considered by the older breeders to be close or incestuous breeding, whereas line breeding is thought to be where the common ancestors are slightly further removed. People differ in opinion as to where each one starts and stops. Basically it is all one and the same thing, only the degree varies.

Inbreeding, of either type is where an animal appears more than once on a pedigree. If this occurs after the fifth generation, the effect is held to be negligible. When inbreeding, the animal being inbred upon is generally held to be a very superior individual, having qualities which hopefully he/she transmits strongly. By inbreeding on this animal, or set of animals (e.g. a particular set of litter mates), you are trying to set or fix a type.

Genetically, you are trying to make the offspring homozygous for certain features, so that the offspring will:

(a) Exhibit the desired characteristic.

(b) Reproduce the characteristic.

Inbreeding of any degree results in the doubling up of an individual's genetic makeup. With increasingly close inbreeding, or heavy saturation of a particular individual, there are various consequences that may appear. As you double on the good points, you double your chances of producing the bad points, some of which may have been hidden until the individual was inbred upon.

As there are increasingly more points becoming homozygous, your 'type' will stabilise, but the potential for change is reduced.

As the chances for change are reduced, so are the factors that affect survival and reproduction. The effects of heavy inbreeding include:

(a) Reduced litter size in bitches; reduced percentage of viable (normal) sperm in males.

(b) Reduced survival rate; offspring are more susceptible to infections or changes of climate. The ability to adapt to these changes is reduced by too many factors becoming homozygous i.e. both parents have donated the same form of the gene, therefore the ability to change is reduced.

(c) Reduced lifespan for the same reasons as above.

(d) Increasing mental instability as the animals become more and more highly strung or neurotic.

To summarise, inbreeding is useful in helping to establish a type and should be done only on exceptional individuals. If grave faults appear on a regular basis, do not continue. For the average breeder, the best results of inbreeding occur using the third and fourth generations i.e. grandparents and great-grandparents.

4. OUTCROSSING

Outcrossing is where new bloodlines are introduced into a pedigree. Technically this means that no common individuals appear in the first 5–6 generations. Outcrossing enables new genes and gene combinations to occur where they are often much needed. If the parents themselves are heavily inbred but of different lines, the results can be very good.

The trouble with outcrosses, particularly with heavily inbred dogs, is that the genetic variation has been lost to such an extent that the first generation produced may be a total loss as far as the show ring is concerned. The value is often seen in the next generation, when they are crossed (not too closely) back into either parent's line.

5. LINE COMBINATIONS

Line combinations are where certain bloodlines 'nick' well together. The lines do not necessarily have to be inbred in themselves. They may either be sire lines, or less commonly, bitch lines. When this occurs, the lines 'blend' together favourably. This is a well known phenomenon in racehorses, Greyhounds and (as I know them) German Shepherds.

Good combinations are generally based upon exceptional sires or brood bitches with an effect that extends through their descendants. It is well worth keeping this in the back of your mind when outcrossing or inbreeding.

6. PREPOTENT DOGS AND BITCHES

These animals are generally those exceptional producers, whether male or female, whose effect continues beyond their own generation. Prepotent dogs or bitches always throw their own type, whatever dog or bitch that they are put to. Prepotent can occasionally refer to particular virtues or faults that a dog or a bloodline produces with characteristics showing up in the majority of the offspring.

Prepotency is held to be a very good sign in a stud dog. The most prepotent animals are, in my opinion, those that are from a very strong male and female family. If a stud dog comes from a good male line but the bitch line is weak (little of note has been produced), then the dog will probably not produce well, especially to average and below average bitches.

The best sires are those that come from a very strong female family as well as a good male line, particularly if both are fairly prepotent animals. This way the sire should produce reasonably good results, even to the poor and mediocre bitches.

The best brood bitches are those that come from prepotent bitches of strong family types. Occasionally sires may not produce an outstanding male, but the bitches from this sire may be of very good type and soundness and go on to produce offspring far above expectations. These sires are known as brood bitch sires and, while their male line may not persist, the effect of the sire is carried strongly through their daughters. The best brood bitches are by these sires and out of a good producing bitch family, i.e. the bloodline is being continually upgraded. As a tip, when choosing a bitch puppy out of such a litter, go for those that most closely resemble the mother's type. If the bitches line has not yet 'firmed' its type, go for the sire's type in the offspring.

Conclusion

Dedicated dog breeders must become 'relative' experts in many areas if they wish to produce sound healthy dogs. These areas include feeding and nutrition, housing and kennel management, basic genetics, disease control, breeding aspects (mating and whelping) as well as understanding the problems within their breed. All this in addition to attempting to breed the next world beater for the show ring.

Beautiful, healthy dogs who are sound in temperament and body, are the aim of all dedicated dog breeders. The end result is often a compromise of various factors, including economic ones. Where soundness relates to the dog's quality of life, we must make honest attempts to decrease the incidence of any problems.

The more we know of all the factors concerned, the quicker we can find solutions and reduce the numbers of unsound dogs being produced. It has benefits for all, particularly for the dogs.

Remember when breeding, aim for soundness, evenness and reliability as the age of guarantees is upon us.

Law suits abound.

17

Housing your Dog

This section is designed to give *ideas* to the prospective builder so as to avoid the more common mistakes associated with kennel construction. Some readers have far more experience and better ideas, but over the years of observing different kennel set-ups, I have seen what works and where simple mistakes have been made. With more thought and re-designing before you start, the kennel will be both easy to run and easy to clean.

Any dog, regardless of its size and age, should have adequate shelter from the elements and the extremes of temperature. Many house pets never need external shelters, but not all dogs are as fortunate.

The minimum essentials for humane care of a dog are shelter and an adequate water supply at all times. In milder climates, shelter may mean shade or protection from prevailing winds or rain. In very hot climates, having adequate shade and access to that shade, can mean the difference between life and death within the space of one hot day. If there is inadequate housing during cold weather, dogs with very thin coats and the very young or elderly individuals may be severely stressed and can die as a result.

House pets usually have the run of the laundry and garages even when the owner is away. This generally allows the majority of house dogs to obtain adequate shelter from the elements.

Portable or Temporary Runs

These are extremely useful if you own one or two dogs, particularly if you are absent for the majority of the day and wish to make sure your dogs are securely housed. A portable run (e.g. 2 metre high x 2 metres wide x 4 metres long) is ideal for most dogs, as there is sufficient area for them to move around as well as room for a kennel house. Paving can consist of paving bricks or slabs of concrete set on sand, with a non-slip surface, but if the run is not heavily used, leave the surface as grass. Shade cloth is easily placed over the top and the run can be placed in a sheltered area.

This is an excellent method of containing dogs which you do not wish to leave loose in the backyard, yet do not trust in the house. Many an owner has returned at the end of a day to what looks like the demolition of the inside of their house. These portable pens can save the owners considerable worry and money. I once had three mattresses ruined before I discovered who the culprit was!

Nowadays, if I have a puppy that refuses to be house trained and likes demolishing furniture in its spare time, I have only myself to blame for forgetting to lock the puppy outside before I go out for a short trip.

Building Permission and Siting of the Kennels

If you have more than one dog and wish to establish a permanent kennel, many factors must be considered. These include:

LOCAL COUNCIL REGULATIONS

These are highly variable, depending on the local shire concerned and the state regulations. What is acceptable to one council is often not allowed by the adjacent council. The more socially desirable the area, the tougher the dog laws are likely to be. The regulations mainly cover issues such as ownership, the number of dogs allowed to be kept and how the kennels (if allowed in the first place) are to be constructed. Rules often exist in up-market districts regarding the materials of construction, the distance from your house, the drainage, the distance from all neighbouring residences and fence lines, and so on.

Once you apply for a development application and learn all the conditions that must be met or passed by the council and its health and building inspectors, you will often wish that you had never started the whole business of making adequate kennel arrangements for your pets.

SIZE OF INDIVIDUAL KENNELS

Kennelled dogs should have an area large enough for them at least to stand, turn, move around a little and lie down. The space allowed per dog will obviously vary considerably with the size of the dog being kennelled. There should be some form of bedding and an area away from its bedding where the dog can defecate. Provision for a water container should always be made, preferably one that cannot be turned over. If the weather is inclement, the dogs should have a side wall to shelter them from the worst of the prevailing elements.

The height of individual kennels within a kennel block should be such that the dog can stand up on its back legs. For cleaning purposes, a height of 170 cm to 2 metres is workable for the average kennel cleaner, normally the female half of the kennel ownership. With too low a roof, the area will not get properly cleaned or aired. In large kennel establishments, where there is indoor accommodation with lock-up night kennels and outside runs, there must be adequate ventilation to prevent stagnation of the air or mouldy growths.

A concrete water trough is best as it is too heavy for most dogs to move and they are unable to turn it over. Automatic watering troughs can be a problem in that if the dog or puppy loves to play in the water, the kennel floor will always be wet and the dogs will be in danger of slipping and injuring themselves. The automatic systems do have an advantage of delivering water at all times, particularly when most needed in the hotter weather. In colder climates, the pipes should be adequately insulated from the cold. The demand for water intake is considerably lower in cooler climates than in the hot, arid or tropical areas.

SITING

Is the kennel to be placed at the top of a hill, in a sheltered valley or in a particularly exposed position where there are seasonal winds? When considering the site of the kennel, try to avoid exposure to the worst of the local winds. If you are new to the area, ask the older local inhabitants and gather all the information you can. It may save you thousands of dollars come winter.

If building on the side of a hill, back the kennels into the side that gives the greatest protection against the elements. The same applies if you have to build in an exposed area. Plant trees behind the kennels to provide additional protection.

The sun should move across the kennels rather than directly into them, so they should be set away from true east or west. The aspect should be carefully considered, as well as the planting of shade trees or vines. Choose deciduous plants to provide winter sunlight and summer protection.

Heating is very important in the colder climates, where thick walls could help insulate the kennels. There should be some form of insulation in the roof, no matter what the climatic conditions. Solar heating can be particularly useful to provide hot water systems for baths and washing. Too much heating is not advisable for the heavier coated breeds, as the thickness and length of coat can be affected. Thin coated breeds e.g. Italian Greyhounds, will revel in any extra ounce of heat that you can provide, so thought should be given to varying the specifications to suit the climate and breeds which are to be housed.

Kennelling Materials

CONSIDERATIONS
The adult size of the breed of dog and its temperament determine the strength and size of the kennel. This includes the amount of kennel area needed, the building materials, flooring, drainage and size of runs. What is needed for a Saint Bernard is a 'heavy duty' construction job, keeping in mind the strength of the walls necessary for keeping an 80 kg male in (or out as the case may be) when there is a bitch in season near by. Lighter framed materials are adequate for small, non-aggressive breeds. Terriers, despite their small size, are excellent fence climbers (Mount Everest is not beyond them) while the majority of the hound and gun dog group know how to tunnel under walls and fences.

Locks or catches that are used on gates should be bounce and lift proof as German Shepherds and others that have the brain power are quick to work out how to open the less complicated gate fasteners.

BRICKS/BUILDING MATERIALS
Concrete or masonry blocks are the ideal construction material as they are a hollow inside, providing natural insulation from extremes of temperature. The inside cavity can be filled if need be with foam to give a greater degree of insulation.

There are various widths of blocks that are available (10, 15 or 20 cm), so the wider blocks can be used with the larger breeds. Blocks have an advantage as they are fairly easy and quick to lay.

Occasionally there are disparaging remarks made regarding the use of blocks, claiming that they catch the coat in the longer coated breeds and absorb water and bacteria. To overcome these minor drawbacks, seal the surface with an exterior all weather paint that is easily cleaned and which, at the same time, will stop the catching of the coat.

Bricks , especially ordinary house types, are the next most commonly used building material, although there are several disadvantages in using them. You use more bricks than blocks and you need to be a more experienced bricklayer if you are going to do the job yourself. With longer kennel walls there is the need for an engaged pier along the back wall every 2–3 metres, which means extra work and extra bricks. Once erected, bricks present problems similar to block work.

Zincalum or colourbond sheeting can also be used, where council regulations permit, but unfortunately it is not considered desirable in built up areas. Ready-made garages of these materials can be bought quite cheaply. This material is not particularly good in climates with extremes of temperature, as they overheat quickly in summer and it is necessary to place them where they will derive maximum shelter from surrounding trees. Some ventilation is vital to prevent heat stress. In colder climates, kennels are expensive to heat during winter unless they are fully lined with thick insulation material. Insulation can also help in the hotter climates, but it does add to the overall construction costs.

FLOORING

Concrete flooring is most desirable as it is easy to clean and disinfect. The finish given is extremely important. If it is too smooth, such as with a steel float finish, then it can be very slippery, especially when wet. Frequently accidents occur where dogs may do the splits or fall over when they try to turn too fast. A smooth finish has the advantage of being easier to clean. A rough finish is too harsh on the pads and dogs become foot sore. Also it is difficult to clean and disinfect completely. The ideal finish is one given by a wood float finish, where there is a little bit of roughness in the surface to give grip to the pads, yet it is smooth enough to clean reasonably easily. If the finish is too rough, get a brick and rub it over the surface of the concrete about a day after it has been laid. This will knock the tops off the rough edges and points.

Before laying the concrete, the drainage within individual kennels and along the block should be carefully worked out. While you still have the concrete truck around, give a concrete bottom to your proposed drain away from the kennel. This will save constant re-digging.

Wooden floors are used quite extensively in some countries, particularly for temporary or movable kennels and for smaller breeds of dogs. Wooden surfaces are difficult to sterilise effectively and should not be used for puppies for that reason. When the wood is wet it can become slippery and greasy, so larger breeds can damage themselves when jumping around.

DRAINAGE

Adequate drainage in a kennel is absolutely vital for health and hygiene. Drainage considerations can be divided into two main areas:

1. Always take into account the natural lie of the land and the way in which the water drains. Gravity is a wonderful thing and it is free. Remember this if you live in a heavy rainfall area, so as to avoid the possibility of flooding after heavy rain.

2. Individual kennel drainage should allow water to drain out from the front of the kennel and then go into a common drain that does not flow into or across any other kennel.

One might ask 'why not out the back?' You should not have a hole in the back of the kennel as vermin may infest it; also the drain tends to be neglected if not in full view for daily attention. Drains should never flow through another kennel as cross contamination can occur, particularly when there are sick dogs or puppies with gastroenteritis.

Filters However much or little hair a dog has (unless it is a Mexican Hairless), there is always coat loss at some stage and hair will block the drain in a very short time. A removable filter is a necessity and, depending on the breed and the time of the year (i.e. when maximum coat drop occurs), it should be cleaned at least several times a week or even daily if need be.

Faeces disposal This is a problem of great importance to every kennel owner. The variations of this area of kennel management are many and consideration should be given to the following:

1. The amount of faeces to be dealt with varies depending on:

(a) Size of the breed owned. The size of the dropping can resemble a cow pat even with a medium sized breed. The volume that comes out always seems more than that which went in in the first place!

(b) Number of dogs involved. It is a simple mathematical calculation of the number of movements per day x volume x number of dogs = a lot of .... When it comes to a litter of puppies, I don't even try to count.

2. Method of disposal. This again can be subdivided into two parts; the solid matter and what I refer to as the left overs, the runny bits that refuse to be picked up. Some people prefer to hose the kennel out without removing the solids, but this usually results in the rapid filling of drains and disposal units.

The best way to attack this problem is by using a 'pooper-scooper'. First remove the bulk and then hose out what is left. Even if you own a large chemical disposal unit to try and reduce solids, the strain on the unit can be considerable within a short space of time and, in the long run, very expensive. Nothing competes with human labour and removal of solids prior to hosing with the kennel 'maid' reigning supreme. Solids are disposed of into thick garbage bags, sealed and taken to the tip, at least once a week.

3. Council Regulations. Local council regulations will often determine the size of the disposal unit that they require, governing methods or facilities for a sewerage system, filtration needed and drains. These must be fully investigated before building, to ensure that the position you decide on for the drainage/disposal unit will be approved upon final inspection.

Some councils have requirements over whether there should be open or closed drains. There should always be allowances for a hair filter before getting to the covered section of the drain so it can be easily and frequently removed for cleaning.

INSULATION

The amount of insulation needed is determined firstly by the type of kennels proposed, either open or enclosed, and secondly by the temperature variations in the local climate and the size of the kennel area. Consideration should be given to the following:

(a) Exposure to the elements. The kennels should be angled so as to give shelter from the worst of the prevailing winds and to avoid rain being blown into them. Strong winds can affect the efficiency of any insulation, as exposed areas will rapidly cool because of the chill factor produced by the movement of air. Very hot dry air, even if blowing hard, can dehydrate dogs very quickly.

(b) Temperature extremes and the breed to be housed. In colder climates, thickness of coat will determine the thickness of insulation required. Too much protection from the cold will reduce coat growth in the dense coated breeds whereas the function of the coat is to keep the dog warm. At the same time, heating will be needed for the very young and the very old for even the thickest coated breed. Very thin-coated breeds need all the warmth they can get.

In hotter climates, the thick coated breeds need to be kept cool or they will rarely develop the proper length of coat or undercoat. This is easily said, but rarely possible to achieve. The main aim in hot climates is to keep the dogs cool and comfortable during the day and prevent heat stress. The coat is often the last consideration.

(c) Size of the kennel complex. Large kennel blocks are obviously more difficult to keep warm as the volume of air is much greater than in small complexes. With open kennels, siting and alignment to give maximum protection against wind, rain and sun are of utmost concern.

The only insulation one tends to consider is the roof. Roof insulation will reduce the rate of heat gain or loss. With enclosed kennels blocks, roof insulation is sufficient for most climates. Roofs which are fully lined with fibreglass bats, while being more expensive, are the best insulation for extremes of temperature. The flow of air up under the roof can be used to help cool a kennel, so it is worthwhile giving consideration to the roof angle and configuration.

The thickness of the walls needs to be taken into account, particularly in colder climates. Masonry blocks are useful for both extremes of temperature and can be filled with foam for added insulation. Obviously the thicker the walls, the better the insulation achieved.

With good alignment to the sun, long block walls can be used as passive solar heat collectors and will retain heat for the late afternoon and evening. This can considerably reduce winter heating bills. In hotter climates, try to avoid placing the kennels next to a wall that retains the heat. Use that wall as part of a hall or walkway. Consideration should be given at the same time to exposure to the sun.

(d) Ventilation. This is considered in connection with the insulation/weather conditions and the type of kennel block. Obviously, ventilation of an enclosed kennel block is far more important than for an open kennel system. Ventilation should be sufficient to cope with the extremes of temperature. It is a good idea to have a louvre arrangement high on the walls so the amount of ventilation can be varied. As commented on above, roof configuration can greatly assist in this area.

A through passage of air is useful as a cooling system. Try to avoid causing areas where the air becomes stagnant. There should be some form of ventilation for corner or dead-end areas where necessary.

With open kennel blocks, the construction or use of a side wall can help to reduce cross winds.

LIGHTING

Good window location will give an ample amount of natural light to the kennels, particularly in hallways. Try to avoid dark, damp corners that have poor lighting. They tend to stay dark and damp as you do not 'see' them very often and they can become a source of bacterial or fungal growth.

Electric lights (preferably fluorescent lights) should be positioned in such a way that there is good internal lighting of the kennels at night, particularly in the whelping and kitchen areas. Position power points carefully and away from where dogs can get at them.

Skylights are a wonderful way of providing extra light, but not in districts that have regular hail storms, or in high wind areas where there are tall trees nearby. Skylights can also be used for extra ventilation during summer. Watch the positioning of the skylight as a large amount of heat could be transmitted through them, especially in mid summer. Skylights are generally used in the larger enclosed kennel complexes.

Have some form of external lighting (floodlights) for late night visits to the kennel block. The further away from the house the kennels, the more you need good lighting. It can save you from injuring yourself in the dark. Have two way switches, operable from both the kennel block and the house.

NOISE POLLUTION CONSIDERATIONS

In today's noise conscious environment, the need for indoor-outdoor kennels, where the dogs are locked inside at night, becomes particularly important. In the interests of keeping the peace with near neighbours, locking the dogs inside the kennels at night will greatly reduce the noise and strengthen good neighbourly relations.

It is worthwhile to have this type of set-up for the benefit of owners who are poor sleepers, even if there are no close neighbours. This also gives added security against theft of valuable dogs when you are away and protection during inclement weather.

Thick walls or well insulated kennels will appreciably reduce the amount of noise coming from the kennel block. When choosing the site, do not face an open kennel block or exercise area directly towards a neighbour's yard. Otherwise every time either the neighbours, or their dog, move outside the back door, the noise level from your kennel becomes unbearable. What the dogs cannot see, does not excite them. Erect fences which the dogs cannot see through.

Plans for Kennels

INDOOR AND OUTDOOR FACILITIES

As stated earlier, it can be very desirable to have indoor-outdoor facilities in your kennel set-up. This is in the interests of better temperature control, particularly in the colder months, and for noise reduction especially during the wee small hours of the morning. Have a doggie door large enough for the dog to go in and out of easily, preferably with a catch on either side so that the door can be locked from the inside or outside for easier cleaning of individual kennels.

The following are various plans for kennel blocks, given purely as examples of open and closed systems.

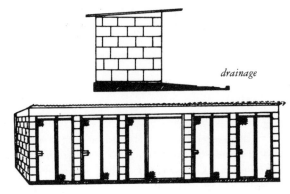

drainage

1. Open kennel block

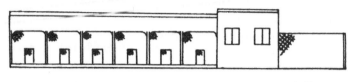

2. Closed kennel block

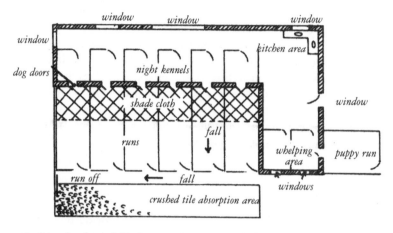

3. Circular kennel block

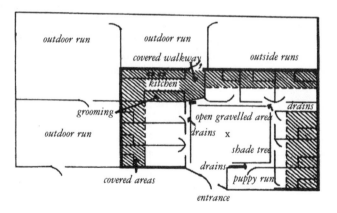

WHELPING ROOM

The whelping room should preferably be well insulated so that the temperature can be easily controlled if need be. Quite often however, the whelping area is either the laundry, a back bedroom, the garage or a corner of the kennel block. If you are building a kennel block, try to have a reasonably isolated area that can be partitioned off from the view of other dogs and from the noise of the rest of the kennels.

If you have enough money and the space, provide a separate room in which to whelp the bitch and raise the puppies. Ideally, have a kennel area for the bitch and the whelping box within the room. Access to an outside run or a puppy run is most useful as the puppies grow older. Separate hygiene facilities such as a sink and hot water, could be added.

WHELPING BOXES

The principle involved here is to provide an area for the bitch to have her puppies, where the puppies are safe and preferably there will be some means of temperature control. The size of the bitch will obviously be the determining factor on the size of the box. The length should be such that the bitch can lie flat out on her side and sleep comfortably. The width can be the same, although it is usually two thirds the length which is sufficient for the bitch to lie sideways.

Puppies cannot control their body temperature for the first 5–6 days and while they are born with sufficient fat to last them for around four days, the strain on the body's reserves through the effort of trying to keep warm is enormous and can often be beyond their capabilities. *Good temperature control for hot and cold extremes is essential in the first week.*

During the second two weeks, in hot weather, you will need some means for keeping the room cool in the daytime. In cold weather, heat will be needed throughout the night. By three weeks, the puppies are usually capable of controlling their body temperatures. However, thinner coated breeds will appreciate any extra heat in cold weather, so a good snug kennel house (or whelping box) can be very advantageous.

PLANS FOR WHELPING BOXES

Whelping boxes vary tremendously and one could carry out a fascinating study of all the variations and the reasons for them.

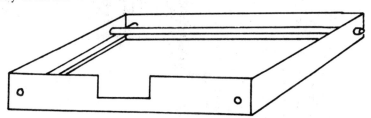

1. Frame only

This is basically four boards nailed together, with dowel rods placed 5–10 cm out and up from the corners and moved further out and up with the increasing size of the breed. The heavier the breed, the more necessary the rails become, as many bitches of the larger breeds are rather clumsy with their puppies. These act as 'pig rails' which the puppies can roll under when the bitch suddenly moves or sits down without checking to see who is underneath. These rails should be sufficiently high so that the puppies can easily go in and out of the 'safe' areas. Usually only three rails are used with the front section, where the bitch gets in and out of the box, having no rail.

The advantage of this type of whelping box is that it is easy to move, is useful as a temporary box, and can be placed over newspapers on top of a sheet of linoleum and set up anywhere you care to whelp the bitch. The drawback of this type of box is the lack of temperature control, but it can be quite adequate in hot weather.

2. Frame and floor whelping box

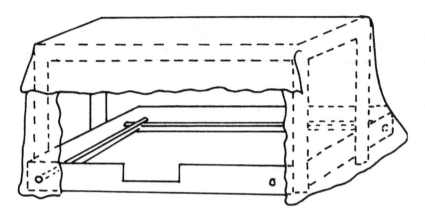

This type of box is heavier, but far more sturdy. The pig rails can be removable with a pin and hook arrangement, allowing more room for the puppies as they get older (it stops the bars being eaten as the puppies start to teethe). Provision can be made at the front of the box to have slotted rails added in, so the height of the front of the box can be raised as the puppies grow larger and try to climb out. The sides can be made of any height.

This box is a very commonly seen variant, but still does not offer good temperature control for the colder climates, where the heat needs to be retained down near the puppies.

3. Cave -type whelping box

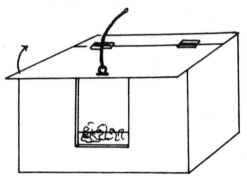

This type of whelping box is the ideal for temperature control, particularly in colder climates. The same basic box can be used as in number two, but a roofed or cave effect is created. If you wish to convert the previous box into this style, use an old table placed over the top of the box and drape a blanket over the sides and part of the front. This will stop any drafts and prevent any heat being lost. The bitch will feel more secure and, if need be, the sides can be raised as the temperature rises during the day. Remember, heat rises.

Another way to do this is to have a hinged lid placed over the top of a three sided whelping box. You can lift the lid to see how the puppies are and the bitch feels very secure. As the puppies get older, or when less warmth is required, the lid can be lifted and held in an elevated position by a chain. Slotted bars can still be used at the front of the box as can the pig rails around the sides.

The enclosed box has the great advantage of good heat control, whereby the heat is kept down near the puppies. Heating bills are considerably reduced and may even be eliminated in some areas. Often all that is needed is an electric blanket under the puppies set on low even in cold weather. The enclosed area also keeps the bitch very relaxed as it is the natural instinct of a bitch to go and hide in a cave or dark corner to have her puppies.

There are many more intricate ways and means for you to make the bitch feel secure and at the same time achieve good temperature control. The above examples may give you some ideas on the subject.

Outdoor Runs

The size of the outdoor run varies according to the size of the breed, as does the height and type of fencing material required. Chain or link wire is suitable for most breeds. A height of 2 metres is ample for all but the fence climbers (human and dog varieties). It is however, an idea to have the fencing embedded into the ground fairly firmly to deter the hole diggers and tunnellers. The most effective method is to have the bottom of the wire embedded into concrete, like a trough along the base of the fence. A thick steel hook driven deep into the ground every 2 metres will give added security.

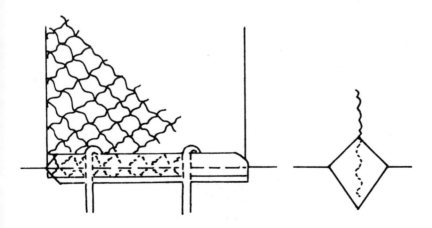

Rabbit proof netting is excellent (and cheaper) as a lighter gauge fencing material for breeds that do not climb fences, or those that are not destructive.

If the dog is a wire climber, metal fence panels such as colourbond or zincalum may be the material to choose as the dog cannot get a good grip on this type of surface. However, if the dog is a jumper (able to leap tall buildings) then a 'return' or overhanging section may need to be added. The other alternative to this is a thin wire placed about 20–30 cm out, and about 15–20 cm down, from the top of the fence which acts like a trip wire. The dog cannot see the wire very well and when it tries to jump, will hit the wire on the way up, losing balance and dropping back.

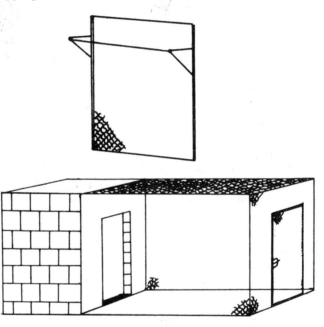

Failing all else, either build a small escape proof run, with mesh over the entire compound, or borrow somebody's electric fence and again place the wire near the top of the fence. The current only needs to be used for several weeks for the dog to gain the message that it is not supposed to leave the yard without permission.

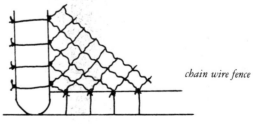

chain wire fence

It is a good idea to have a thin straining wire placed along the top, middle and bottom of the chain wire fence. The straining wire should be attached by wire ties at frequent intervals to the chain wire fence. At the end of each chain wire run i.e. at gate and corner junctions, bag ties should be used to attach the chain wire closely to the fence post.

Size of the Run

The size of the run should not be too large or the dogs will run continually. This can cause foot soreness, bloat in hotter climates and failure to retain weight. An ideal run should be 7–10 metres in length and anywhere up to the same in width. The running side is usually the side from where the house and people can be seen.

Runs coming directly off the kennel block on to a concrete run need be no more than 4–7 metres in length and 1–1½ metres in width.

The runs should have some form of shade and shelter and a water supply that is reasonably indestructible. Concrete water troughs are excellent as they are too heavy for most breeds to tip over. Old fashioned concrete pig troughs, which are reinforced with steel mesh, will withstand any dog, even an 80 kg St. Bernard. Water containers should be shallow in case of accidents (or suicidal individuals), although buckets which are wired on to the fences are very useful for the taller breeds as they can't go swimming in them.

Shade

Shade can be provided in two ways. In the runs connected to the kennel blocks, sheets of corrugated fibreglass (either the semi-transparent or green tinted versions), covering about half the running area, or all if you wish, will not only provide shade, but also some protection from inclement weather. Alternatively, shade cloth of varying densities, can be used in the same manner. Out in the open runs, shade trees (preferably deciduous), will create enough protection from the hot sun, particularly if there are several trees placed around the fences. Deciduous trees allow for increased light and warmth in the runs during winter time.

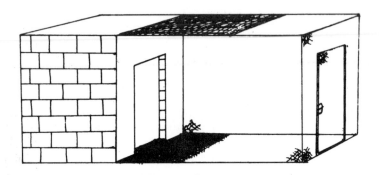

SURFACES

Within the kennels, concrete floors with a wooden float finish allow for ease of cleaning and thorough disinfection. Wooden surfaces will harbour bacteria, viruses and fungi, making it extremely difficult for you to be sure that adequate disinfection has taken place. Wooden bed boards or platforms are quite suitable for adult dogs, but if used for puppies they should be new or at least previously unused by any dog.

VENTILATION

Ventilation must ensure a through-flow of air. It is essential in hotter climates to provide adequate cooling for the dogs kept within closed kennel blocks. High louvres placed in strategic places can keep the air from stagnating as can oscillating fans on the ceilings and walls.

The opposite applies in colder climates where the reduction of air movement becomes the aim. However, in the interests of hygiene, some change of air is needed every day, so that the humidity does not rise too high. With higher humidity and an enclosed environment, diseases like kennel cough are far more likely to be transmitted.

In open kennels, the main consideration is the circulation of air near the roof (again in hotter weather). If there is a gap between the top of the block work and the roof, heat will be able to escape.

FOOD PREPARATION AREA

This section of the kennel should be away from individual kennels. It must be easy to clean, should contain an old sink preferably aluminium, with hot and cold water for cleaning dishes, and for the late night preparation of cups of coffee while whelping bitches. A small refrigerator/freezer for keeping the meat or perishable food is an absolute necessity in hotter climates. Dishes should be scrubbed out daily with both a detergent and a disinfectant and then rinsed thoroughly.

Meat which has been defrosted must be used within 2–3 days. Canned food which is opened should again be used within 1–2 days. Never give food that is not fresh as the gastric upsets that can result can be disastrous.

Dry dog food (biscuits) must be kept dry, as damp biscuits rapidly go mouldy, and could also cause some dramatic gastric trouble. Open bags of dog food are best stored in sealable containers, such as plastic or metal garbage bins. Too much exposure to the air over a relatively short period of time can cause the fat in the biscuits to oxidise and go rancid. All dry food bags should be stored off the ground.

INSECT AND RODENT CONTROL

Food must be locked up, particularly dry dog food. Plastic garbage bins with lock-on lids are good, but ideally metal garbage tins should be used as they are indestructible and less easily broken into by midnight marauders (rodent and canine types). Leptospirosis and Toxoplasmosis can be transmitted by mice and rats urinating on food sources.

When chemicals are used to control such vermin, the user must ensure that they are never left within reach of any dog (or cat), nor should they be placed where drainage of the baited area will go through kennels or exercise yards. Preferably try to use non-chemical means of control e.g. mouse traps or, best of all, good food management.

Hygiene

The products used for all purpose cleaning will vary widely in different countries. Basically, all that is needed is a good household detergent and a bleach (preferably chlorine based) for washing dishes and surfaces. For heavier disinfection a bleach will kill most bacteria, viruses and mould. Concentrated bleach solutions will remove just about any stain from the concrete. Any strong solution used on the floor, be it detergent or bleach based, must be rinsed off thoroughly before the dogs are allowed to run on it. Powdered bleach type products e.g. Halamid® or Halacept® are equally good for disinfection of surfaces.

With puppies, all surfaces must be thoroughly cleaned at least once a day with some form of disinfectant. The problem where puppies are concerned is that various materials are used to line the floors and consequently, the proper cleaning of the run is very difficult.

Newspaper is a useful material to use as a floor covering for puppies. The sheets which have been dirtied can be easily rolled up, either separately or all together. The newspaper will absorb fluids, but the faeces can create a problem as the puppies will walk all over them, making a thorough mess of the puppy pen, quite often making themselves, and you, very dirty.

Leave the cleaning until after a feed, as inevitably the puppies will have defecated and urinated within 20 minutes of feeding time. Particularly messy areas can be cleared easily by rolling up a few sheets as the advantage of newspaper is its ease of removal. Disinfecting can then be carried out and if you have two puppy runs, one can be cleaned and drying while the other is in use. This way the puppies are always on dry surfaces.

Sawdust is also used frequently with litters of puppies. It is very moisture absorbent and has the advantage of clinging to and coating the faeces, so that the puppies will stay clean and reasonably dry. The disadvantage is that it is difficult to change completely on a daily basis, so a load is often left down for 4–5 days before the run can be changed and disinfected. Damp areas and faeces are removed several times a day, but the moisture content will gradually rise. Sawdust can cause eye and skin infections, the first through particles getting in the eyes, the second because of damp conditions. Sawdust is, in my opinion, for use with older dogs where the need for daily cleaning is not as essential for their health and well-being as it is for young susceptible puppies.

Straw is widely used in the colder climates as it provides additional warmth. The straw has advantages and disadvantages similar to sawdust, although it is not as water absorbent. It has warmth advantage as puppies can burrow down into it but in hot climates it retains too much heat and can precipitate heat stress. It again has the disadvantage of not being easily changeable on a daily basis, but if used, the damp patches and faeces should be removed several times daily. A complete change of straw should be done at least every 5–7 days.

Bare surfaces such as concrete, wood, and earth are not desirable for very young puppies. Concrete can cause damage to the pads and it needs to be covered with some form of moisture absorber to soak up the urine and spilled water. Wooden surfaces need some form of covering for the younger puppy for the above reasons. Splinters can create problems along with moisture and the ever present drawback of wood: the surfaces cannot be properly disinfected. Earth floors and runs are to be totally discouraged for young puppies, as adequate puppy hygiene cannot be maintained against bacteria, viruses and parasites; disinfection of any kind is not possible.

FEEDING

Never leave food lying around, particularly soaked food. Older dogs can have some food left overnight if it is necessary, but in hotter climates the ever present problems of heat and flies will make this inadvisable.

Food sources should be standardised as much as possible. Preservatives added to fresh meat can often irritate young stomachs. Canned food has the advantage in that it is cooked and the batches do not vary. Dry dog food rarely changes in its formulation, but the dyes and preserving agents can be altered at the manufactures' whim (luckily this does not seem to happen very often).

Find a dry dog food (preferably a good quality complete dry dog food) which your breed of dog does well on and stick to it as long as you are getting good results. By this I mean that the weight gain is good, and is easily maintained.

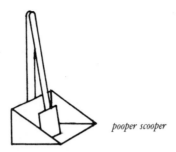

pooper scooper

CLEANING OF CONCRETE SURFACES

For the best results use a bristle broom or a hard plastic broom together with a hose, preferably under high pressure. Whatever is used should be capable of cleaning out the crevices and corner areas which try to defy ordinary cleaning. 'Pooper scoopers' are a necessary part of any modern kennel cleaner's equipment. These trusty little items allow the area to be cleaned up with a minimum of bending.

A cheap home-made equivalent is an egg-flip spatula and a dustpan which are very useful for either the shorter person or the smaller breeds.

Disinfection of all concrete surfaces and runs should be done at least once a week. Remember to rinse disinfectants off thoroughly before allowing the dogs back in the runs.

SUMMARY

Any kennel management scheme must be based on hygiene in feeding and cleaning methods, good environment control and adequate drainage. Routines for daily cleaning should be organised, as should regular worming and vaccination schedules, all of which will help maintain a good health level within the kennel and hopefully minimise disease.

18

Common Health Problems

Denise Dufferin '88

The advice given in this section is not intended to be used in place of a visit to your veterinarian, but to be used in conjunction with proper veterinary diagnosis. It will hopefully expand your understanding of your dog's condition. The theme is one of **good management**, to assist you in learning the reason for the problems and encourage you to practise **preventative** medicine in an attempt to minimise further episodes.

This section is not intended to provide advice for all aspects of animal health, but rather to give you an idea of:

(a) How some of the more common problems are caused.

(b) How to reduce the severity of the condition.

(c) How to prevent a recurrence, if possible.

Specific Areas of Health Care

1. Skin: fleas, mites, coat loss, grass allergies.
2. Ears: mites, hygiene, chronic infections, fly/sandbite irritations.
3. Gastritis and stress in young puppies and older dogs.
4. Invalid diets.
5. Pancreatitis and pancreatic insufficiency.
6. Foot and pad care.
7. Anal glands.
8. Viral and bacterial infections: a quick outline of the more severe, as well as common forms likely to affect the dog.

The basis of any health care programme, particularly if there are fairly large numbers of dogs involved, is overall cleanliness, routine worming, vaccinations, good diets and adequate shelter. All are necessary for a healthy lifestyle. There should be a reasonable standard of health, hygiene and housing so that dogs thrive with minimum problems. The areas concerning nutrition, housing and cleanliness have already been discussed. This chapter investigates specific areas of general health care.

Skin

With general skin care, the main rule to remember is do not over-wash.

You, the owner, can wash the dog whenever you like. However, many breeds do not need a weekly wash, particularly in the colder months, and generally washing is only necessary when the dog is dirty. Wash your dog more frequently if it:

(a) Has a skin problem or sensitivity due to mites, fleas, food or grass allergies, seborrhoea.

(b) Has a tendency to be messy and it loves to roll in all those rotten, smelly holes and among dead things.

(c) Is supposed to be white and you cannot stand looking at a grey-brown lump of hair.

Obviously all the dogs in category (a) have real skin problems and keep many vets in work. This section covers the methods of helping to manage these conditions. Completely eliminating these conditions is often an impossible task.

FLEAS

The flea prefers the warmer more humid climates and is therefore more of a problem in spring, summer and autumn. Tropical climates mean an all year battle against this resistant little monster.

Fleas are the cause of what is commonly known as 'summer eczema'. Summer eczema is a condition where the dog spends its entire time (as it appears to the owner) scratching and chewing its back, particularly around the base of the tail. Some dogs crawl under cars and tables of ideal height, to get a good overall scrape down the back. The result is hair loss, skin thickening and increasing deposition of black pigment on the denuded (bald) areas. Milder cases may have small patches of hair loss and scabbiness just above the tail.

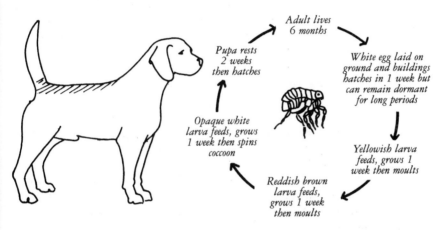

Adult lives 6 months

Pupa rests 2 weeks then hatches

White egg laid on ground and buildings hatches in 1 week but can remain dormant for long periods

Opaque white larva feeds, grows 1 week then spins coccoon

Yellowish larva feeds, grows 1 week then moults

Reddish brown larva feeds, grows 1 week then moults

The whole condition, and the severity with which it occurs, is related to the dog developing a 'sensitivity' to fleas. Over a period of years, this becomes a hypersensitive allergy to the saliva of the flea bite, in a way rather like humans becoming sensitive to bee stings (but not nearly as drastic).

Younger dogs may have little irritation of the skin and, if rinsed regularly to keep the flea population to a minimum, will have very little further trouble that season. Older dogs of certain breeds, some sensitive individuals and white skinned dogs can have enormous trouble keeping the reaction to fleas at a manageable level without resorting to cortisone. Older dogs have had time to develop flea hypersensitivity over the years. Particular breeds seem to have skin that is more sensitive than others to fleas, mange mites and grass allergies. These breeds include Golden Retrievers, Rottweilers, and Dandie Dinmonts. Before you become alarmed, understand that this does not mean every member of those breeds. However numerous members are more likely to have these types of skin sensitivities. Cross-bred dogs and breeds that have white coats or large areas of pink skin are particularly sensitive to fleas and grass allergies.

For the more sensitive dog, there is a constant battle between the owner, the dog's environment and bad habits and, that toughest of adversaries, the mighty flea!

The flea likes to live and breed in dusty, humid crevasses and of course on its preferred hosts, dogs, cats and rodents. Fleas will breed in the grass, in sandy areas, abandoned houses and in the dusty areas under the house.

Control Fleas must be attacked from all sides, or most of your efforts will be wasted. One of the major problems with flea control is that the flea population is constantly developing resistances to the chemicals that are used. Gammawash®, one of the organophosphates, used to be effective for 1–2 weeks, now it is lucky to last 24 hours! New products are constantly being developed, some of which are systemic i.e. the 'pour on' treatments developed from tick and lice products used on sheep and cattle. They are absorbed systemically and can last up to 2–4 weeks depending on the dose rate and how well they are applied. If they do not come into contact with the skin, they will not be effective for very long. Some animals do not tolerate these compounds and may become lethargic and vomit.

Whatever you use, wear gloves when rinsing the dog, as many of these compounds are absorbed through the skin and people can develop sensitivities to these chemicals to the point of becoming allergic. Symptoms of poisoning or sensitivity in humans include headaches, vomiting and skin rashes. If anything like this occurs, seek medical advice promptly. Always wear gloves and always wash exposed areas of skin afterwards.

Flea populations, with differing sensitivities can exist within a fairly small geographical location. Some breeders praise one compound, while others, in the same area may say that they cannot even control the fleas for one day with the same product. Generally speaking, use a compound that is strong enough to control your flea population and use it when you have a problem. The people that in my view, have the worst problems of flea resistance are those who over-rinse and stick to the same compound for years, increasing the strength and, at the same time, developing the fleas' resistance to that compound.

The environment in which the dog lives should also be treated as far as is feasible. If you just rinse the dog and forget about the kennel, sleeping areas, the cats and the area under the house, the dog will attract the fleas from all these areas, as soon as the rinse or whatever wears off.

Sand pits, under the house, kennels, floorboards and crevasses, should be treated as well in any determined effort to clean up the backyard. Surface sprays can be used in living areas, but leave the dog outside the kennel for several hours. Products like kerosene, were used years ago as a fairly effective spray around kennels and under houses. It coats the flea eggs and kills them and has the value of not being terribly toxic for the owners and pets alike. **Penny royal**, a herb, has been used successfully as a flea repellent in both its natural form and in flea collars and powders.

Others swear by daily doses of garlic in the diet which makes the dogs unattractive to fleas. I know of several kennels where this technique is followed with amazing success. This may not work for everyone but if you have exhausted all other means, it may be worth a try.

Another method is to lime your backyard regularly. Using builders' lime, do a patch of the yard at a time, allow to stand for a few days, then water into the ground thoroughly. This tends to 'burn' the flea and worm eggs and can be quite helpful for general yard control if done every 3–4 months. Do not allow the dogs to walk on the areas treated until the lime has been thoroughly watered into the ground as it can burn the pads of their feet.

In these days of heavy chemical use, often with toxic side effects, it is worth considering any alternative that may have a less drastic approach to this seemingly never ending, itchy problem.

New methods of flea control are constantly being developed. These include once a month flea control tablets Program® which, while not killing the fleas, will sterilise them. Over a period of 2–3 months the population levels will drop and only occasional minor topical control is required in addition to the tablets.

Another new product is Frontline®, a non toxic (to the dog and cat) product that affects the nervous systems of fleas and ticks and will give control for periods up to 12 weeks against fleas and three weeks against ticks. This is a topically applied product and it may have some effect against mite infestations as well.

Treatment for flea sensitivity

Flea antigen injections can be very beneficial, particularly with the younger dogs. These injections will help to desensitise dogs. Unfortunately the results vary, but it is well worth trying. The dogs receive intra-dermal injections, one week apart for 3–4 weeks. Once desensitised, the dog will often go through the summer without too much trouble. However, the effects are short lived and it may be necessary to repeat the injections the next spring or summer. There are apparently about nine different components to flea saliva and it appears that different dogs may be sensitive to different parts of the flea saliva. This could account for the variation of response to treatment with the flea antigen.

Cortisone is often used in the management of flea allergies. This is understandable, particularly with the older dogs, in order to make their lives more bearable. Cortisone injections and tablets are used to control the 'itchiness' and reaction to the fleas' saliva. Cortisone is therefore being used to control irritation caused by the fleas, but it *does not cure* the problem, it merely masks the effects on the body.

Long term usage of cortisone can have a depressive effect on the body's own natural cortisone production and the experts these days favour the use of shorter acting cortisone e.g. Prednisolone®, which if it has to be used over long periods, is given on alternate days. This way the body's own natural production of cortisone is not depressed.

Ideally, treatment for flea allergies is a combined effort by both the vet and the owner. The owner has the responsibility of rinsing or treating the dog and its environment, to keep the flea population under control. The vet has to try and decrease the dog's sensitivity by either the antigen injections or cortisone. With the younger dogs, I prefer not to use cortisone, except as a last resort when other methods fail to control the skin inflammation and biting. Tea tree oil rubbed into irritated areas can also be beneficial. With the newer flea control treatments available, the need for desensitising and cortisone treatments should decrease.

Mange Mites

Sarcoptic mange This is characterised by excessive itchiness, particularly of the lower half of the body, accompanied by varying degrees of coat loss and resistance to single dose treatments. Many of these dogs bring owners to desperation point, when several vets, treatments and cortisone, have all failed to cure the problem for any length of time. It is a problem which is on the increase as it is often misdiagnosed and treated as a skin allergy or grass sensitivity. Sarcoptic mange can often be recognised by the fact that more than one dog in the back yard has the same condition. It is a contact-spread mite which spreads between kennel mates and among dogs that have been moved around between kennels. It is also called 'fox' mange as many country dogs have presumably picked it up while hunting (on the other hand, it may be the dogs that are steadily infecting the foxes).

The typical appearance of a dog with sarcoptic mange is diffuse hair loss around the lower flanks, hocks, behind the elbows, under the chest, up the backs of the hind legs, down the tail in severe cases and, occasionally, on the backs of the ears. Upon closer examination, the skin can be seen to have numerous small pink spots which, unlike pimples, rarely have a 'head' to them.

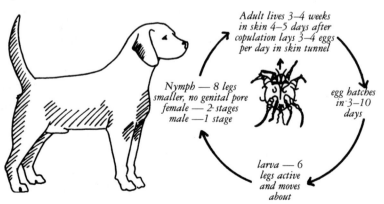

Adult lives 3–4 weeks in skin 4–5 days after copulation lays 3–4 eggs per day in skin tunnel

Nymph — 8 legs smaller, no genital pore female — 2 stages male —1 stage

egg hatches in 3–10 days

larva — 6 legs active and moves about

Diagnosis is by skin scrapings taken by your vet, but as the mite burrows under the skin, the absence of the mange mite on one scraping does not mean that the dog doesn't have sarcoptic mange. It can take 30–40 skin scrapings to finally turn one up. I have seen this done, but rarely go to such an extent myself. The mite burrows under the skin and lays eggs in the tunnels. Treatment is difficult and prolonged as the mites are only really 'killable' when on the surface. Repeated treatments are necessary to kill any remaining adults and treatment is not complete until all the eggs hatch and come wandering out to get their 'dose'.

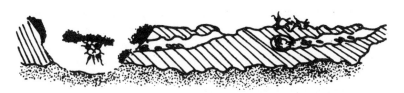

The burrowing nature of the mange mite explains the intense itchiness of the infestation. Imagine hundreds of them crawling around, just under the skin and you can understand why the poor affected dogs walk two paces, stop and scratch one spot, walk two more paces, stop and scratch somewhere else. As the mite is more active in warm humid weather, this condition is often mistakenly considered to be part of the summer eczema/flea problem. Unfortunately, many of the flea rinses are not effective against mange mite and those that are effective on the mite are not always very effective on the fleas. These problems are the trials and tribulations of the dog owner.

Treatment is of at least 4–6 weeks duration before the mite is eradicated. All dogs in your backyard should be treated simultaneously. The average treatment involves rinsing the dog all over once a week and rinsing just the affected areas in the middle of the week.

The affected areas can be found 'south' of what I call the high tide mark. This is generally a line above the elbow, straight back to the hip area; down to below the hocks on the hind legs, and below the elbows in the front (the low tide mark), and round to the same position on the other side. The backs of the ears should be treated as well.

Chemicals used include diazinon and amitraz with resistances to treatment being quite common.

The dog should be rinsed all over at least once a week, paying particular attention to affected areas. Wear gloves for any rinse, as many of the compounds are absorbed through the skin. Mid-week, a mite cream such as a benzyl benzoate lotion (Ascabol®), should be used very thinly and worked into the skin, particularly in the balder areas.

The use of ivermectin, which is an injectable wormer, can be very beneficial as you can achieve a measure of success from the internal treatment. This should not be used on Collies or Shelties as there are numerous recorded cases of lethal reactions. This treatment can be repeated at weekly or fortnightly intervals for 2–3 doses. Ivermectin can greatly facilitate concurrent topical treatment and should only be given under veterinary supervision.

The chemical used should be effective against fleas in addition to the mites. This way, reasonable control of both may be achieved. There has been resistance by the sarcoptic mange mite (in various geographical areas) to malathion and amitraz. Newer treatments such as Frontline® may prove beneficial in the treatment of mites.

Demodectic mange This is a mange/skin condition mostly seen in young dogs under one year of age. Demodectic mange causes diffuse to total hair loss in small patches and is most commonly seen around the eyes, sides of the head and muzzle, and occasionally under the chin. Areas of demodex can be found anywhere on the body, but the majority of cases are seen on the head. Older dogs may develop small patches on the head, neck or legs. The skin looks fairly normal under the patches, but there is occasionally a mild scurf, like a dandruff in humans.

The demodectic mange mite lives in the hair shafts, and if large numbers are present, the hair loosens and falls out. All dogs have a certain amount of mange mite as normal components of their skin flora, living there without causing any obvious hair loss. However, under conditions of stress the mite may start multiplying at a rate normally held in check by the body's immune system. Demodex is quite readily found in a skin scraping of an affected area.

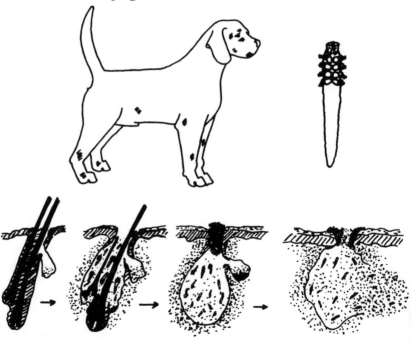

Bad cases may have pustules accompanied by thickening and 'bubbling' of the skin that may cover up to 80–90% of the dog's body surface. Severe cases of demodex are believed to occur in individuals that are deficient in their immune system i.e. the dog cannot develop even a mild immunity to the mange mite. Certain breeds have a 'sensitivity' to demodex: Dobermans, Boxers, Staffordshire Terriers, occasionally Bull Terriers and Rottweilers, and cross-breed offspring of these breeds. Severely affected animals have a definite immuno-deficiency problem. These animals, if they fail to respond to treatment, many end up having to be put down eventually. Badly affected animals, if they can reach one year of age, may develop some resistance to the mite but they should not be used for breeding.

Symptoms

If whole litters have serious demodex by 6–8 weeks and they are of the susceptible breeds, consideration should be given to having all the puppies put down, rather than pass problem dogs on to the general public.

Treatment is generally of 4–6 weeks duration. Mild cases with just a few patches on the head are fairly easily treated with amitraz. Make sure that what you use is effective against demodex. Patches are treated by applying the compound at the correct dilution (never neat from the bottle), and gently massaging it into the skin. Treat 2–3 times weekly until the scurf goes and the hair starts to re-grow.

Treatment

Cases that are moderately to heavily affected may need to be treated internally with Proban Cythioate®, which is a tablet usually used for internal flea control, and externally with rinses. Chemicals used include amitraz. Some vets advocate daily treatments, but there is a reasonable possibility of toxic side effects. I have found it just as effective when used every second or preferably, third day.

There is often heavy scaling as the chemicals dry out the skin. Good shampoos e.g. a tar based or aloe vera shampoo, can be beneficial when used before the rinse to help remove the scurf and oil in the skin.

COAT LOSS

There are many reasons for coat loss. The above conditions with external parasites usually cause coat thinning and are in well defined patterns of loss.

Hormonal changes, lack of, or occasionally excessive amounts of hormone production cause the next most common group of hair loss. These conditions will have well defined patterns of hair loss. Hormonal imbalances can include any gland which produces hormones (not just the sex orientated ones). Those which can commonly cause problems affecting the coat include the thyroid, testicles, ovaries and the adrenals. You need a veterinarian to diagnose and differentiate between these conditions as there are usually other symptoms apart from coat loss.

Treatments   Treatments differ according to the type and severity of the condition. Excessive pigmentation deposition (black pigment) can also be due to hormonal imbalances, particularly with ovarian irregularities in females and testicular tumours in the male dog. Testicular tumours cause a feminisation syndrome, with mammary development, hair loss on the flanks and increased pigmentation, particularly in the areas of hair loss.

There is another, less commonly seen skin problem which is characterised by excessive pigment deposition . **Acanthosis nigricans** is seen in several breeds including Dachshunds (most commonly), Chow-Chows, Keeshonds, and occasionally German Shepherds. There is no coat loss in the early stages, but a laying down of excessive amounts of black pigment in the skin, particularly in the groin and armpits. The skin is thickened and itchy, and gradually becomes very greasy. This is a condition which cannot be cured, but can be managed by the use of good cleansing shampoos when the skin is very greasy and by the correct use of cortisone. Topical application of a cortisone cream to affected areas can help control milder cases; oral doses of cortisone may be needed to help the more advanced cases.

'COAT CHANGE'

Some coat loss is perfectly normal, inevitable as day and night and there is little one can do to stop it. This is usually called 'coat change'.

The reasons for coat changes can be as follows:

(a) After seasons and litters.

(b) Periodic coat change on reaching adulthood.

(c) Seasonal coat change (after winter).

The amount of coat lost varies as to the cause, but undercoat is what is predominantly lost. Every two years or so, the top and undercoat are shed simultaneously in some breeds. Desexed dogs do not lose their coat nearly so dramatically and rarely lose their top coat.

ALLERGIES

Food and contact allergies can be very difficult to sort out and to pinpoint the exact cause.

Food   Food allergies can cause a generalised skin irritation with itching and
allergies   coat thinning. This condition may be accompanied by loose motions. Determining the food source which does not agree with the dog can be very difficult. In the majority of cases, the dogs are put on to a diet of cooked rice and chicken or fish. This is a very bland diet and the dog is kept on this for at least three weeks before adding anything else. The normal food sources are then added, one at a time, again for three weeks to see if there is any reaction in the skin. There are considerable numbers of dogs that cannot tolerate gluten in the diet, so a wheat free diet may be needed (see section on Diets in chapter 4). Once the offending food source is isolated, normal feeding patterns can often be re-established

around the removed food. There are low allergy prescription canned food and dry food diets available.

A point to remember about pet meat is that preservatives are often added, particularly in warmer weather, and many dogs will not tolerate these at all well, causing diarrhoea. Dry dog food manufacturers also use preservatives, many of which dogs will tolerate, but they can change these around every now and again . This may be the reason why dogs that may have been on one brand of dog food for a long period without any problems suddenly develop a reaction to a new batch of dry food.

Contact allergies

Contact allergies are easier to define as the dog will develop a reaction when it lies on the offending object. Many dogs are allergic to synthetic materials and when lying on a new rug, may develop a rash along the belly and flanks. Removal of the offending article will almost immediately reduce the severity of the reaction and it should disappear within a few days.

Grass allergies

Grass allergies on the other hand are often confined to the bottom of the feet, sides of the mouth and occasionally around the eyes. Wet, fast growing grass is the main irritant as it has a very fine layer of salt on it, which dries on the dog's skin, causing irritation. As a result the dog starts to chew at its feet and/or drag itself along the grass trying to scratch itself. This causes more areas to be irritated and so on. The rubbing of the face in the grass causes the edges of the lips and the rims of the eyes to react. Specific types of grass such as Buffalo, can be more irritating than others.

The way to control this type of allergy and irritation is to keep the dog off wet, fast growing grass. Sounds easy, doesn't it? Trying to keep a dog off wet grass in periods of heavy rainfall (most often spring time) can be nearly impossible. If the dog must venture out on to the grass, wipe its feet and face after it has been outside. Dogs that have white feet (pink skin pigmentation), are particularly prone to skin sensitivities. Keep lawns mown short and do not over water i.e. let it look like hoary, old, dried out grass and the dog will appreciate it, even if the lawn does not look aesthetically pleasing to the human eye.

Long term control of this problem for a badly affected dog may require the establishment of a small concrete yard for outside exercise during sensitive times of the year.

SEBORRHOEA

Seborrhoea is an oily, greasy skin condition which can, in some individuals, be almost impossible to clear up completely. It may have to be carefully managed for the lifetime of the dog.

Control is gained by regular washing, occasionally twice weekly until the worst of the condition is under control. The best shampoos are those that cut the grease e.g. peroxide shampoo, used until the skin dries out.

These shampoos have a disadvantage in the long run as they dry out the skin too much, so I tend to use them only every now and again if the skin is greasy and stick to a good tar or oatmeal based shampoo for normal washing. Shampoos such as Sebolyse® and Episoothe® are mild and do not irritate the skin. These dogs will often require weekly washing as a result of the skin condition, but it could be reduced to once every two weeks in colder weather.

Cortisone may be necessary to control the worst of the self destruction (ripping and chewing at the skin). Again, this should be used carefully, either topically, or longer term oral therapy should be used on the alternate day routine. Addition of zinc in the diet can be beneficial. Careful control of external parasites e.g. fleas, can reduce much of the irritation seen in these dogs e.g. use of Frontline®.

MOIST ECZEMA OR 'HOT SPOTS'

This is a common skin ailment that occurs with the thicker or double coated dogs and is mostly associated with coat loss, following wet weather or a bath by the owner.

When dogs lose their undercoats, particularly around the head and neck areas and around the hindquarters and then get wet on top of it; it can take a long time for the coat to dry out. The end result is rather like a hot steamy jungle, the top dries but underneath the humidity and heat make an ideal breeding ground for bacteria. If the dog bites and scratches the area, trauma to the skin occurs and leakage of serum results. This in turn scalds the skin (rather like a scraped knee), and combined with the moisture in the coat, the whole lot quickly turns into a wet smelly mess. The dog, attempting to ease the irritation, will keep chewing, so that it rapidly extends the original area involved. There is a certain amount of gravitational effect where the serum drips down the skin, scalding it as it goes, and thus 'growing' down the side of the face for example.

Treatment is aimed at drying out the affected area and in severe cases, may require the hair to be clipped very short to allow the inflamed skin to dry out. Wash the area with warm water, using moist cotton wool that is not dripping wet, so that you remove the serum and then dry the skin as much as possible. Add nothing to the water, get all the stickiness off, then dry and spray a drying agent or powder. Avoid creams as they keep the skin moist, in turn keeping the whole cycle going.

Wash the affected areas twice daily until the skin is dry and the scab is hard. As soon as the area is dry, leave it alone. Keep the affected area and surrounding skin as dry as possible.

If moist eczema is treated early, it can be brought under control within 24–48 hours. Use a spray that tastes terrible in order to deter the dog from chewing the affected area. Alternatively the micronised powders are very useful. Antibiotics are often necessary to treat the bacterial infection and cortisone may be needed to reduce self trauma.

Dogs that are prone to moist eczema tend to suffer repeated bouts, usually every spring when they are dropping their coat (particularly undercoat). Breeds that are most susceptible include the Labrador, Collie, German Shepherd, Golden Retriever and Saint Bernard. The areas most commonly affected are the thicker coated areas around the head, neck and the base of the tail.

Ears

The first sign of an ear infection is apparent when the dog is seen constantly shaking its head, or holding the head to one side. Upon examination the inside of the ear is seen to be red and inflamed and there is usually heavy waxy or slimy discharge. There is often an offensive odour. If there is no discharge but a sudden appearance of symptoms, then there is the likelihood of the presence of a foreign object such as a grass seed, particularly in spring.

Depending on the cause of the irritation and the severity of the condition, the treatments can vary tremendously. Different veterinarians have their own preferred methods of treatment for ear conditions.

Once your dog has had several bouts of ear infections (not including mite infestations), it can become very sensitive to humid weather. This is more apparent after a period of rain or high humidity, generally in spring and autumn when the dog's ear condition will flare up. Be alert for these periods and with a little care, the ears can be quickly treated and returned to normal.

Ear mites

Ear mites are mildly contagious, particularly in crowded (dog) living conditions. The picture here is one of irritation of the ears and the presence of a reddish granular wax which, when examined through an otoscope, will reveal lots of little moving objects. They obviously cause intense irritation and misery to the dog (it must be exquisitely itchy to have them trundling around inside one's ear canal). An easy way to see them is to put some wax out of the ear on a slide or a piece of glass, and mix a little oil with the wax. You will see the mites wriggling across the top of the oil.

Treatment There are various drops available for treatment of ear mites. The important point to remember is that whatever you treat them with, it will take some time to clear. If effective, the treatment will remove the adults and then their eggs will hatch, renewing the cycle. The best way to attack the problem is to treat the ears for 7–10 days, leave alone for one week, and then re-treat for 7–10 days. It is always a good idea to have your vet re-check the ears several weeks after you started treatment to make sure that the infestation has been cleared up completely.

Ear mite

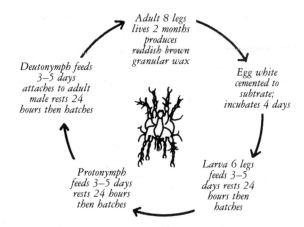

Adult 8 legs
lives 2 months
produces
reddish brown
granular wax

Deutonymph feeds
3–5 days
attaches to adult
male rests 24
hours then hatches

Egg white
cemented to
subtrate;
incubates 4 days

Protonymph
feeds 3–5 days
rests 24 hours
then hatches

Larva 6 legs
feeds 3–5
days rests 24
hours then
hatches

CANKER

This is by definition a bad smell. Chronic ear infections are usually accompanied by a very memorable smell, unpleasant to the owner and veterinarian alike. These infections have sometimes been present for several years. Once there is permanent damage to the bottom of the ear canal or the ear drum, radical surgery to open up the side of the ear may (eventually) be necessary. This may scare some people, but I am trying to show how important it is not to neglect an ear infection. The longer you ignore it, the longer it takes to repair. Once the condition becomes chronic, the ear takes very little irritation to flare up during suitable conditions of humidity.

The message is do not neglect ear infections, or you may pay the price for years afterwards.

EAR HAEMATOMAS

If there is an ear infection, particularly during hot weather, the chance of getting an ear haematoma is greatly increased. The blood vessels in the ears are fairly delicate especially in the heat, and vigorous head shaking can cause a rupture of a blood vessel, leading to a haematoma. The affected ear has the appearance of a stuffed sausage, with the fat ear drooping off to the side. Treatment is generally surgical.

When ear haematomas occur in the erect eared dog, it may be the end of the dog's show career as the scar tissue weighs the ear down and normal characteristic ear carriage may be lost. Once again, remember it is never wise to neglect an ear infection.

FLY BITES

Biting flies can cause considerable damage to the tips of erect eared breeds as well as the upper fold or creases of drop eared breeds. Fly bites are more commonly seen with the short to medium length coat types. A heavy crusting of dried blood is found on the upper 1–3 cm of the ear. If these are neglected by the owner, it can eventually cause severe

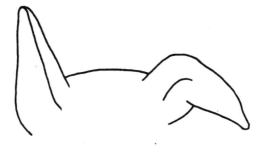

damage to the circulation to the tips of the ears, where the tips become thickened, curled and actual tissue may be lost. Badly affected ears may end up losing up to a third of their original length.

This type of ear irritation can generally be easily cleared up and managed. The whole treatment/management revolves around crusting off the dried blood before applying a fly repellent. The smell of the dried blood attracts the flies back to the ear. If the blood is removed before applying any treatment, the problem is halfway cured.

Preventing flies from attacking the ears is a regular maintenance chore. Some individuals are more prone to fly 'strike' than others, and will always be prime candidates for repeat attacks. I feel it is the dogs who are too lazy to flick their ears when the fly has landed, that are repeatedly affected. The type of fly repellent to use is an important consideration. I personally favour the use of a cream or ointment as the thicker the cover the better, particularly over area of damaged skin.

A good home made fly repellent can be made by mixing oil of citronella with warmed up Vaseline®; mix as much oil in as the Vaseline® will hold. When it cools, it will thicken. The resultant cream/ointment sticks well to the hair. Apply this every morning or evening, depending on when the worst attacks occur, to either side of the ear at the tip and spread a few centimetres below the tip. On the folds, cover bitten areas by a radius of 1–3 cm.

Remember to remove the dried blood before applying the fly repellent.

Routine ear hygiene
1. Check the ears at least once every two weeks; more often in the humid weather.
2. Clean out only as necessary. If you do this too often, you produce excess wax, or dry the ear out too much.
3. When there is an infection which can be recognised by smell, hanging of the head to one side, or pain when handled near the ears, see your veterinarian immediately and continue any treatment until the ears have returned to normal.
4. When cleaning the ears, wrap a piece of cotton wool around your little finger and use it like a big fat cotton bud. Your little finger can never reach down to the bottom of even larger dogs' ear canals. Dogs do not

mind big objects in their ears but they hate small ones like cotton buds. Massage the bottom of the ear canal from the outside to thoroughly loosen the wax/infection from the lower section and this will raise the infected material to the top.

5. Do not dry out the ear excessively. The ear canal is basically a waxy/oily environment and if it gets too dry, new problems are created.

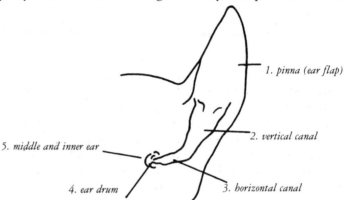

1. *pinna (ear flap)*

2. *vertical canal*

5. *middle and inner ear*

4. *ear drum*

3. *horizontal canal*

Gastric Problems and Stress

Gastric infections are seen mostly in the very young and elderly and are often stress-related. Stress results from sudden changes in environment.

Stress can include changes in weather, diet, or home e.g. going to a new home or a boarding kennel, The introduction of a new dog/person (usually associated with going to a new home), travel, vaccinations, heavy parasite burden/pickup (causing irritation to the lining of the gut), unhygienic and over-crowded living areas and any concurrent debilitating disease or condition can all affect a dog's stress level. Combinations of any of the above can cause or affect the severity of the disease or infection.

Stress has a more severe effect on the very young and the very old, where the immune system is either too immature to cope, or is failing because of age. It is very important to realise that stress can underlie many other clinical signs seen by the owner or veterinarian, *in particular* the gastric syndromes and viruses in younger puppies, under six months of age.

STRESS AND THE GASTROENTERITIS COMPLEX

This is an immense area to try to cover in one section, but they often have underlying factors in common, It is better therefore to list all the many and varied factors which can influence and predispose dogs and in particular puppies, to gastric infections, be they managerial, viral or bacterial in origin.

The following questions are commonly asked by your veterinarian about conditions which can affect the onset of gastric infections in your puppy or litter.

These individual points are discussed in detail further on.

Predisposing
factors to
gastritis

Questionnaire
1. Age of the puppy
2. Current health status
Questions which apply if the puppy is still with the breeder:
1. Vaccination status
  (a) Has the puppy been vaccinated?
  (b) If so, how long since it was vaccinated?
  (c) What is the vaccination status of the mother?
2. Worming
  (a) How often is the puppy wormed?
  (b) What chemical was used, when was it last done, was it effective?
  (c) Time of year?
  (d) Local problems?
3. Weight and diet
  (a) With what, and how often, is the puppy fed?
  (b) Has the diet been changed at all in the last week?
4. Kennelling
  (a) Hygiene
  (b) Are there concrete or dirt runs?
  (c) How often are the runs cleaned and disinfected?
  (d) Bedding — what materials are used and how often are they changed?
  (e) Crowding
  (f) Have there been sick puppies there before?
  (g) What shelter is provided?
Questions which will apply if the puppy is with the new owners:
  (a) How long have you had the puppy and what is its vaccination status?
  (b) Did it have to travel far to reach you?
  (c) Is the diet the same as when you purchased the puppy?
  (d) What is the vaccination status of the other dogs in the household, and have there been any sick puppies within the household in the last three months?

AGE

Relevant
facts
relating to
the above
questions

The age of the dog is often what governs the decision as to whether one is more likely to be treating a serious viral infection or a bacterial infection. With dogs under 12 months of age and particularly with those under six months, the viral infections are far more commonly encountered than at a later age. Once a dog is over 12 months of age, either it has been well exposed to the various gastric viruses or it has an adequate resistance to such infections via vaccinations. Gastritis in the older dog is usually as a result of management or stress problems.

The vaccination status of a puppy relative to its age can be critical in determining the likelihood of the puppy succumbing to infections. Under six weeks of age, most puppies are covered by maternal immunity to a reasonable extent. If the vaccination status of the mother is known, then a more accurate idea of the amount of maternal immunity received by the puppy can be estimated. If the mother was vaccinated within the last few months or during pregnancy, then the levels of maternal antibody that the puppies receive will be considerably higher, and can protect the puppy for anywhere up to 12–14 weeks of age.

The major problem is that one never knows exactly when the level of maternal antibody has fallen below what is needed to protect against viral challenge and, at the same time, low enough to not interfere with the body having an adequate response to the vaccine that has been given. Newer vaccines can stimulate better responses (see also section on Vaccinations in chapter 4).

If the puppy has been vaccinated in the last few days, its immune system is undergoing changes and stresses in trying to respond to the vaccine; so it is unable to respond as well to concurrent infections or stress from viral, bacterial or parasite induced causes. Should the puppy be further stressed by travel, change of home or diet, then gastric infections are almost certain to result.

WORMING

If the puppies have never been wormed, or wormed infrequently, then the presence of high worm burdens will cause considerable damage to the lining of the gut as well as debilitation from blood loss in the case of hookworm. These worm burdens have geographical areas of high risk, hookworm in particular preferring high humidity and moisture, so damp coastal belts are the usual areas where the problem is found. Find out from your local veterinarian or university veterinary school what worms are present in your local area, as it can affect your worming programme. (More information about worming schedules is found in chapter 4.) Damage to the lining of the gut can allow viruses and bacteria an easy entrance to the body, as does a lowered state of health from anaemia and poor weight gain, both of which can result from high worm infestation.

If the weight of the puppies is low, it may be the result of a bad diet or concurrent worm burden. A sudden change in diet can cause gastric upsets, be the change only in the batch of meat or brand of dog food. Different batches of meat, particularly pet meat, have added preservatives which can be very irritating to delicate little stomachs. If in doubt, cook all incoming meat, but preferably, stick to one source. Do not switch puppies with an upset gut on to canned food if they are not used to it.

KENNELLING

1. Hygiene

If soaked food is being left out, it will rapidly deteriorate in hot weather. The problem of flies carrying contaminated faecal material from elsewhere and infecting the leftover food is also extremely worrying. Soaked food for puppies should never be left down for longer than 30 minutes, particularly in hot weather or if there are flies around. Dry biscuits may be the exception to this rule.

2. Surfaces

Concrete is an ideal surface for puppies, as it has the advantages of being easy to clean and disinfect and dries out relatively quickly. Therefore, the chance of worm pick-up is greatly reduced. Dirt runs fail on all counts and are definitely undesirable for puppies.

3. Cleaning

How often are the runs cleaned? With what? Is the water supply clean? Is the drainage of the floors and runs satisfactory? Are the runs just hosed out, or cleaned only of faeces and not washed at all? These questions need to be addressed. Water bowls should be filled with clean water every day and scrubbed out preferably weekly. If the drainage is poor and puddles of water and urine lie about, puppies have the added problems of trying to stay dry and the danger of licking up contaminated material. Drainage from neighbouring runs or properties should also be considered and, where necessary, improvements should be made.

Good drainage and daily cleaning, with some form of a disinfectant, is a necessary part of running any kennel complex. Sweep out runs to remove excess water and allow the concrete to dry as soon as possible as a good 'house keeping' measure.

Bedding for puppies should be completely changed on a regular basis, preferably daily. Old blankets and sheets are good for use in the sleeping area. Newspaper, as already explained, makes a very easily changeable floor covering, which can be removed and replaced, several sheets at a time, or the whole lot if need be, several times a day. Straw and sawdust can present problems as they retain moisture, faeces and fleas, and are difficult to change on a daily basis. Straw is however very good for retaining heat in winter.

Ideally there should be two runs for a litter, one for use and one to be cleaned and dried straight away in readiness i.e. they should be alternated.

4. Crowding

The more overcrowded the conditions, the less likely the puppies are to stay clean and dry. If there is one puppy which is coming down with an infection, it will pass very rapidly between other puppies in the same run. Split puppies up into groups of two or three if there is any sign of a possible gastric infection. This will make it easier to contain the situation and help to identify who has the upset stomach if it is not obvious. The puppies will still have companionship, reducing the distress caused if they were placed separately.

Never put puppies into a run, particularly a dirt run, that has had sick puppies within the last three months, unless it is a concrete run that has had several heavy scrubbing/disinfection sessions. A dirt run cannot ever be considered as properly cleaned unless it has been empty for at least three months in hot dry weather with several layers of builders' lime watered into it. Even then it is doubtful whether it is suitable for use.

5. Shelter

Puppies that are exposed to cold winds and rain can develop gastric infections very easily. Sudden changes from warm to very cold, or prolonged wet weather, can again stress puppies. Make sure that if the weather is going to change, you prepare for it and do not leave the puppies outside that day. I know that this is not always possible to predict but you must use your common sense. If you have very good neighbours, you could ask them to put the puppies away if you cannot get home from work.

The other way to provide shelter is to have a puppy run that is sheltered from the worst of the winds and rain, is roofed over and has at least two sides enclosed. This may not be ideal, but may be the best that can be arranged.

New Owners

If you are a new owner and you have had the puppy for less than a week, the puppy may still be under considerable stress trying to adjust to a new household, new people, loss of its litter mates, change of environment and, quite often, the diet as well. This is the most stressful time of a young puppy's life and it is often trying to respond to a vaccination done the day before you collected it. No wonder so many puppies end up at veterinary hospitals within a week of leaving home.

When purchasing a puppy, try to determine when it was vaccinated. If the answer is within the last 3–4 days, delay picking the puppy up for several more days. If it has not been vaccinated (I personally feel that all breeders are morally obliged to vaccinate before selling a puppy), and you still wish to pick it up, do so, get it checked out that day and, if all is well, take it home, allow it to settle in for a week, then have it vaccinated, provided it is healthy.

The further the puppy has travelled and the more severe the weather conditions, the more stress it will have been subjected to.

Also the more quickly a diet is changed, the more stress is placed on the resources of the puppy. The gut bacteria are delicately balanced and a sudden change of food can be most upsetting. If the diet that was being fed to the puppy before you picked it up was very poor, give the puppy a very bland diet such as cooked chicken or fish, cooked rice and yoghurt or junket. Add in a small amount of semi-soaked dry dog food (or dry cat food for the small breeds) and feed the same food 2–3 times daily for several days before trying slowly to adapt the puppy to an appropriate diet.

If there are other young dogs within the household, make sure their vaccinations are up to date. The annual boosters for any older dogs should be up to date.

Do not allow a sick puppy to be in contact with another puppy under 16 weeks of age, particularly if it has not come from the same litter or is not fully vaccinated. This applies especially to Rottweilers, Dobermans and Greyhounds, as these breeds are often severely affected by gastric viruses and are very poor patients, making very little effort to live once they are sick. Do not handle other people's puppies, particularly if they are off colour, and restrain other people from handling your puppy.

The definitive diagnosis to determine which particular virus is causing the gastro-enteritis is often beyond the average veterinary hospital. An electron microscope (usually only available at universities) is needed and even then success is limited. New test kits are constantly being developed to eventually allow a more accurate diagnosis at the veterinary clinic level. *Diagnosis*

Because of the varied stresses discussed above, the presenting symptoms can vary dramatically, even for the same virus. Viral enteritis commonly has a secondary bacterial infection, which can also vary the presenting symptoms.

Treatment therefore has to be based on a symptomatic approach.

- Vomiting, is it related to eating or drinking, how soon after?
- Diarrhoea, is blood present, foul smell etc?
- Off its food or reduced appetite.
- Drinking excessively or not wanting to drink.

Symptoms which are usually seen:

These are the common signs presented by puppies which have a gastric infection. The severity can usually be gauged by the length of time the puppy has been sick and the presence or absence of the any or all of the above symptoms.

Puppies cannot afford to be off their food or drink for more than 24 hours. Their metabolic reserves are not equal to those of an adult dog. Within 24 hours of not eating and vomiting, the puppy can lose a large amount of its body reserves and fluids, which can result in severe depression and dehydration.

Apart from all the stress factors mentioned earlier in this section, the actual infective agents can be considered in two major groups, **viral** and **bacterial**. Two other groups, **parasites** and **protozoan infections**, can cause gastritis in their own right in addition to being precipitating factors to viral and bacterial infections. *Causes*

1. Viral There is a group of 5–6 viruses which can all cause enteritis, some more commonly seen than others and with variable severity of effect on the puppy. The following is a very short description of the differences between the two major offenders:

Parvovirus

- Symptoms include sudden onset, vomiting, not eating and diarrhoea (foul smelling at early stages may not show blood, later haemorrhagic), dehydration (moderate to severe), high fever, severe depression.
- Age group most commonly affected is 5–24 weeks.
- Incubation is short, between 2–7 days.
- Transmission is by faeces and contaminated materials.
- Duration of infection is 4–10 days (average).
- Severity is due to rapid spread, high infection rate and a mortality rate, often over 50% in young puppies.
- Diagnosis is possible from faeces in the first 5–10 days. (Kit Elisa Test)
- Vaccines available, live attenuated, killed.

Coronavirus

- Symptoms include sudden onset, vomiting, not eating, diarrhoea (very foul smelling yellow orange faeces which can be haemorrhagic in later stages), moderate dehydration, mild fever and mild to severe depression.
- Incubation is short, 2–7 days.
- Transmission is by faeces and contaminated materials.
- Duration of infection is 5–7 days (average).
- Severity is due to rapid spread, high infection rate and a low mortality rate with occasional deaths.
- Diagnosis is not precise as there is no definitive test currently available.
- No effective vaccine is currently commercially available.

These two viruses are the most commonly encountered causes of severe gastro-enteritis and because the symptoms are fairly similar, they are often lumped together as 'parvovirus'. The two viruses can affect a puppy simultaneously, or the puppy may be recovering from the one virus, only to succumb to the other in the lowered immune state following the initial infection.

Other viruses that can cause enteritis include rotavirus, retrovirus, adenovirus and distemper virus.

2. Bacterial E.Coli, Campylobacter, Salmonellosis etc.

Bacterial gastro-enteritis is generally related to contaminated food sources, overcrowded living conditions, poor hygiene and occasionally an asymptomatic carrier state in an older animal that acts as a continual source of infection. Bacterial scours are usually less severe apart from the odd case. These infections are also often seen as secondary complications to viral or protozoal infections.

3. Parasitic Round, hook and whipworm infestations are discussed more thoroughly in chapter 4 in the section on Worming, but need to be mentioned here in relation to gastritis.

Hookworm is very common in the more humid climates and heavy burdens can cause anaemia, periodic diarrhoea, dark 'tarry' faeces, weight loss and, occasionally, death. Puppies can die by 3–4 weeks of age from severe infestations of hookworm.

Diagnosis is by faecal examination and the presence of pale mucous membranes. With prompt treatment and supportive therapy, many puppies will recover, the less anaemic puppies obviously having a greater chance. Keep the puppies confined and treat them every five days for hookworm until there is a clear faeces test. After a positive test result, worm them every two weeks until 16 weeks of age. Remove them from contaminated grounds and place them on concrete runs to reduce the possibility of re-infection.

Roundworm is also a very common parasitic infection in the dog. Puppies have a 'pot-bellied' appearance and are slow to gain weight. Deaths rarely occur, but in some cases, the presence of large numbers can cause blockages of the gut leading to severe stress and eventually death, which can occur as early as 3–4 weeks of age. Signs of infection include vomiting up 'spaghetti' like worms, mucous diarrhoea, respiratory distress and stunted growth. Diagnosis is by faecal examination. The worming regime and removal from infected grounds mentioned above applies here as well.

Whipworm (seen after 3–4 months of age), affects the lower intestines and the motions are loose, often covered by a fresh bloody mucous. Tapeworm can cause occasional mild gastritis and an ill thrifty appearance with a dry coat.

4. *Protozoan infections* Coccidiosis is a common protozoan infection, most often seen where there is poor hygiene and overcrowding. The puppies are frequently in poor condition, have bouts of mucous diarrhoea with occasional streaks or spots of fresh blood present, and have poor weight gain despite routine worming. Carrier states are possible in older individuals who have had infections at a younger age. These older dogs become shedders of coccidial oocytes under conditions of stress (poor hygiene or concurrent worm infestations), and can re-infect new kennel areas where young puppies may pick up the infections.

Diagnosis is by faecal examination for the presence of oocytes which can be very difficult to find.

Treatment by various coccidiostats (most commonly the sulphonamides) is very effective together with relief from concurrent stresses that probably precipitated the outbreak in the first place. Chronic carriers may have repeated bouts of diarrhoea until a degree of immunity develops.

Giardiosis is another protozoan infection which is probably often overlooked as a cause of prolonged bouts of intermittent diarrhoea with mucous, or soft sloppy faeces. Affected individuals are chronically underweight while still maintaining a good appetite.

Diagnosis is by faecal examination for the presence of trophozoites but fresh faeces are needed and even then the protozoa is hard to detect. Infection is from contaminated water supplies such as ponds, dams and creeks and faeces ingestion.

Treatment of choice is the use of Metronidazole®. Giardiosis can be transmitted between species, including man, so affected animals can be considered a potential health risk. Isolation and treatment of affected animals and removal of the source of infection will minimise the spread of the infection.

The important fact to remember about parasitic and protozoan infestations is that they can predispose the gut to other clinical diseases.

TREATMENT OF GASTROENTERITIS.

Treatment varies according to the cause, the presenting symptoms, condition of the puppy or history of other litter members.

Treatment of parvovirus and coronavirus

Viral infections in particular require prompt attention, or you may lose puppies within 1–2 days.

Basically, any puppy that is vomiting, cannot keep water down, or is dehydrated and refuses to drink, should be taken to a veterinarian immediately. These puppies are usually hospitalised and put onto a drip. Intravenous fluids will reduce the dehydration, while at the same time giving the intestines a much needed rest. Antibiotics and supportive therapy are given until the gut can take fluids again. Added vitamins and sugars can all be given intravenously and it is most important that the puppy stays very clean, warm and dry. Affected puppies require a large amount of work when hospitalised, because of the continual vomiting and diarrhoea.

If your veterinarian is willing, daily visits to the hospitalised puppy can give it more incentive to live. If the owners of the sick puppies are very experienced, a puppy may occasionally be allowed to stay at home on the drip, with the owners bringing the puppy in morning and night to monitor the fluid intake and its progress. This way the additional stress of yet another strange place may be reduced. Seriously ill puppies which are passing blood are generally not allowed to be out-patients, as the amount of nursing care is generally beyond most owners' capabilities and the danger to other puppies still at home may be too great.

Aftercare and preventative care in the face of an outbreak of gastritis

If you suspect that your puppies are hovering on the brink of a gastric infection, immediately remove all fatty foods from the diet. Feed small amounts of bland food until the motions have settled. Give small amounts of watery electrolytes (a salt and sugar solution e.g. Heatade®), but do not allow puppies to drink large amounts of water (which they often promptly vomit back).

Avoid the use of pasteurised milk, many canned foods and high milk products. Use a predigested milk such as junket or yoghurt containing lacto-bacillus acidophilus which helps to re-establish the gut flora. Acidophilus tablets can be used on a regular basis whether the gut is upset or not. Corn flour or slippery elm powder are both very mild products which may help to settle irritated gut linings without further stress, and can be added to the bland diet. Cooked chicken and rice are about as bland as one can go.

If, despite your attempts to settle the irritated gut, the diarrhoea continues and/or there is any vomiting, see your veterinarian immediately.

The aim is to minimise stress of all kinds. This includes all of the following: *Prevention of gastric problems in puppies*

1. *Regularise feeding.* Do not vary the food sources or the meals, so that the food eaten by the puppies does not differ drastically either in quality, between feeds or the times of feeding. Never give stale food or leave soaked food around in hot conditions.

2. *Worming* should be done weekly from two weeks of age until leaving home. This way if the new owners neglect to worm the puppy for several weeks, it is more likely to survive a new worm burden or heavy stresses than one that has not been regularly wormed. After eight weeks of age, worm every two weeks until 16–18 weeks of age, then worm every 6–8 weeks to one year of age.

3. *Hygiene* is most important. Clean (and dry) runs and bedding, good food and freedom from flies, all make for healthier puppies that are less prone to gastric upsets. Cleanliness in all aspects of kennel management is essential, from washing bowls, bedding changes, and disinfectants to careful scrutiny of all the sources of food used, ensuring that the food is not contaminated and does not contain excessive preservatives. All these aspects should be considered and the list is almost endless.

4. *Establish a routine.* This means being organised with regular meals, worming, standard of care and protection from the elements. Do not vary the sources of food i.e. keep to the same brand of dog food, the same meat source and the same type of milk. If the puppies are not gaining weight or are loose in their motions because of something in the diet, try to work out what might have been changed that could have caused the gastric upset. Ensure that the vaccination cover of all the other animals in the kennel, particularly the mothers of any litters, are up to date, so the level of kennel immunity remains high.

5. *Travel and stress.* Travelling long distances, particularly in the heat, can stress any dog, regardless of its age. Long trips to dog shows, often with a change of water at the other end can result in the dog developing diarrhoea within 12–36 hours. It is a good idea to take your own water with you when you travel with your dogs or if this is not possible, take water sterilisation pills. Some districts are renowned for impurities in the water and for the gastritis that follows, if the dogs are unused to it.

Always take a supply of enteritis mixture and preferably some sulphonamide tablets if you are going on a long trip with the dogs and expect to be away for some time. This will at least cover emergency situations when you may find yourself in difficulties with no vet available for kilometres. During the hotter months, take some electrolytes (combination of salt and glucose in a powder or liquid form) in addition to your water, as the dogs can dehydrate over a long hot day.

Never travel long distances with puppies under six months of age. It is not worth the problems they will undergo from the sheer stress. Fly them there if you can, the time and stress involved is far less severe.

Summary   The vast majority of gastric infections can be avoided with a little extra care and attention, including the avoidance of additional stresses of all kinds, and rapid action in the presence of suspected gastritis.

GASTRIC OBSTRUCTIONS

Not all cases of vomiting are caused by infections or parasites. Foreign objects such as stones, rubber balls, large lumps of bone or plastic, can all cause obstruction of the inside of the intestine. In older dogs the obstruction may come from the outside in the form of a cancer compressing the lumen of the gut.

The symptoms are vomiting, usually without fever and with little or no faeces. The dog is often reasonably bright, wants to eat but vomits at a similar time after eating. The longer the obstruction has been present the more depressed the dog gradually becomes. These dogs need immediate veterinary attention and usually require surgery to remove the offending article. Some dogs are regular rubbish eaters and I have treated several dogs who have had 3–4 operations to remove weird and wonderful objects that they thought were edible.

Intussusceptions or telescoping of the gut can however be a possible sequel to a hypermotile gut as is seen in the more severe gastritises e.g. parvo and coronavirus.

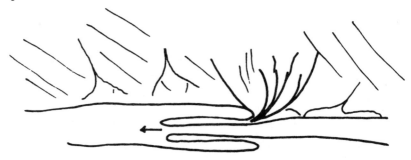

The presenting picture is the same as for obstruction and on palpation of the abdomen, a grossly thickened loop of intestine can be felt. These dogs require immediate surgery and the section of affected gut usually has to be removed as the blood supply has been interrupted for too long and the tissue is dead.

INVALID DIETS

These are good for feeding the chronically ill patient or one recovering from a gastric infection. The idea here is to aim for a bland diet, one that will not upset the gastrointestinal tract.

Dogs that are just getting over a gastric infection need a diet that is low fat that will not irritate the lining of the gut. Cooked chicken or fish with cooked rice mixed with a small amount of junket or yoghurt is about as bland as possible.

Acidophilus tablets or capsules are very helpful for any dog who has had a prolonged infection or course of antibiotics. These are particularly important in the younger puppy, as they replace the bacteria that help digest milk. Avoid giving fatty, greasy foods or pasteurised milk.

Those individuals that have had prolonged bouts of diarrhoea and are having trouble maintaining a formed stool, should have a small addition of either corn flour or slippery elm powder which can be very helpful to line the gut as they are non-irritant.

Give small feeds often, as an upset stomach can only cope with small amounts of food at any one time. If too much food is given, the dog may vomit. After several days, if the dog is eating well and the motions are normal, feeding can gradually return to normal.

PANCREATITIS

The definition of pancreatitis is inflammation of the pancreas (see also chapter 15, Geriatric Dogs). The pancreas is an organ which is divided into two sections across the greater curvature of the stomach and then down the first section of the duodenum. The pancreas produces enzymes which assist digestion. It also produces insulin (in specialised groups of cells) which regulates the sugar absorption of the body.

Susceptible individuals are mainly those that are chronically overweight or obese. They can have bouts when quite young, but pancreatitis is mostly seen in the middle-aged to older animal.

Symptoms

Per-acute pancreatitis is very uncommon, often fatal. Signs develop rapidly. The dog may be severely depressed, vomiting with acute anterior gut pain. In some cases the dog may be found dead and diagnosed on post mortem. The period between the onset of symptoms and death may be only 12–24 hours. Immediate treatment by a veterinarian is essential and even then, the prognosis is poor.

Acute to moderate pancreatitis is not uncommon and again, can be rapid in onset. Signs are vomiting, depression, not eating and soreness in the anterior abdomen.

Treatment

Treatment generally requires hospitalisation, placing the dog on an intravenous drip to give it total gut rest, which means that the dog must not be given food or water for about 48 hours in order not to strain the pancreas. Blood tests are generally carried out to determine the dog's state of health.

The severity of the condition is often determined by the level of amylase in the blood. Amylase levels can however (just to complicate matters further), be raised when the dog is under stress and are not necessarily significant. To give a loose interpretation of the level of amylase, up to 2000 is normal, between 2000–3000 can be as the result of stress. Over 2000 is considered to be elevated, but levels can go up over 10,000 in severe cases. A grossly elevated level of amylase will separate pancreatitis from other gastric problems.

Once the gut has had total rest for 2–3 days, small amounts of water are given often, until it is obvious the dog is tolerating it well. Small, low fat meals are then started. When the dog is drinking and eating, feed a bland, low fat diet.

Long term treatment. As many of these animals are grossly overweight, the long term goal is to reduce the weight to acceptable levels and avoid re-stressing the poor overworked pancreas. Particularly avoid excessive fats in the diet as they place a considerable demand on the pancreatic gland. A good diet is a mixture of cooked chicken and pumpkin, but commercially produced prescription canned food and dry diets are available as well.

As a final note, dogs may have recurring bouts of pancreatic inflammation until the weight returns to normal and some animals will have continued bouts, regardless of weight loss. Stick to low fat foods and keep the weight trim. Feed mainly dry dog food, chicken mince and avoid excess fat intake.

Chronic pancreatitis can occasionally develop into pancreatic insufficiency, where the addition of pancreatic enzymes to the dog's food becomes necessary. Because low levels of enzymes are being produced from the damaged tissue, insufficient food is digested, so the condition develops into chronic weight loss with loose putty coloured faeces.

PANCREATIC INSUFFICIENCY AND ATROPHY

This condition is very different to pancreatitis. In this condition, the pancreas is inactive, in contrast to the inflammation present in pancreatitis. The pancreas in this case is producing insufficient enzymes to digest the food properly so that its components can be absorbed. Pancreatic atrophy is a condition where the pancreas barely produces any enzymes at all.

Symptoms The symptoms of pancreatic insufficiency and atropy are the opposite of the typical pancreatitis dog, where the affected individual is overweight; these dogs are very thin, have a chronic failure to maintain or gain weight and have putty, greasy faeces with a cow pat consistency. Certain breeds are more commonly affected by this condition. These include: German Shepherds (pancreatic atrophy), Irish Setters and Cocker Spaniels.

Diagnosis is made from a small sample of faeces which is sent to the laboratory to undergo a faecal trypsin digestion test. Insufficient enzymes present mean that there are not enough to properly digest the food that the dog has eaten. The more recently developed TLI blood test is very useful in assisting diagnosis.

Treatment is by the addition of gastric enzyme combinations to the food. *Treatment* Some forms or brands appear to suit certain individuals better than others. If you find a particular combination is maintaining the weight of your dog nicely, continue with those tablets. The best effects from the enzymes are often obtained by the addition of the powder or crushed tablets to a slightly soaked meal 20–30 minutes before actually feeding the dog. Feed a lower fat diet, as the pancreas in its reduced state cannot handle appreciable amounts of fatty foods. Acidophilus tablets can be helpful in addition to the pancreatic enzymes.

Some of these dogs may have concurrent food allergies/intolerances to commercial dry dog foods and may benefit from a wheat or gluten free diet. Low allergy and low fat canned and dry foods have been developed and are now readily available (see chapter 4).

DIABETES MELLITIS
This can develop as a sequel to severe pancreatitis, but can occur independently as well. This subject is also discussed in chapter 15, Geriatric Dogs.

Some breeds which have a higher predisposition to diabetes include: all types of Dachshunds, Australian Terriers, Australian Cattle Dogs, Poodles, Beagles, Collies, Bearded Collies, King Charles Spaniels and Samoyeds.

Overweight older individuals are more likely to develop diabetes, particularly bitches.

- Polydipsia (excessive drinking) *Symptoms*
- Polyuria (excessive urination)
- Weight loss
- Vomiting and depression

The development of the above symptoms in a susceptible individual requires immediate veterinary attention.

Diagnosis is from blood glucose levels.

Treatment requires hospitalisation until the dog is stabilised. Thereafter *Treatment* injections of insulin are given, usually once (occasionally twice) daily.

Diet control after discharge from hospital is very important. Usually dogs are fed 30–60 minutes after the injection of insulin. Weight and diet must be strictly controlled in relation to the dog's ideal weight. Water consumption must be closely watched, as it is a good indication of how well the dog is stabilised. An increase in water consumption that continues for more than two days may necessitate a visit to your veterinarian for a retest of the blood glucose level.

Regular monitoring by your veterinarian is advisable, even when the dog is well stabilised. I would suggest 4–6 weeks is the maximum between blood tests.

Advice: A diabetic dog requires *constant* care and attention. Diabetic dogs are often blind, because of cataracts which can be a side effect of the diabetes. Caring for a diabetic dog can be a very rewarding experience and the dog may live for many years. However, it is a big undertaking, and you should think first whether, in relation to your lifestyle, this special care can be adequately maintained. If you are not able to do this, it would be kinder to have the dog put to sleep, as inadequate care of this condition will quickly lead to an unpleasant death.

Feet

TOENAILS

Toenails have a very simple construction, think of them as fingers where the nail has wrapped all the way around the end of the finger, and like your finger nails, the ends continue to grow if they are not worn down from exercise.

When cutting nails, cut off the hook on the end of the nail. Use the flat (straight edge) under the toe nail as the base line. Cut out at about a 45° angle. A second cut of the top 'half' backwards can level the end off and reduce sharpness. If you use this as a guideline, even black nails do not defy attention.

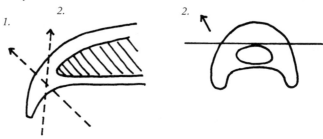

PAD CARE

Pads are often exposed to excessive wear and tear, cuts and abrasions. The foot does after all take the body where it wants to go, and with some dogs a considerable distance is covered daily. Some dogs have very hard pads and can put up with the most incredible terrain and distances. Others go for a few kilometres and are so foot sore that they can barely walk.

The signs of foot soreness are reluctance to stand and move, and when they do move, they walk gingerly with very short steps. The easy way to diagnose the problem is to walk the dog on soft grass first and then on a tarred road. The difference is dramatic as the dog's movement can go from nearly normal to that of an ancient geriatric in appearance. Examine the pads. Often there is a pink area in the centre of the pads (on those dogs that have black pads that is), or there is obvious loss of several layers of pad thickness in the centre of the pad.

Treatment for foot soreness is twofold. First remove the source of foot irritation (by rest or take off concrete runs), and secondly apply something to coat the pads to protect them while they heal. The simplest treatment is wonderfully cheap anhydrous wool fat, which is readily available from chemists everywhere. Apply this to the pads once or twice a day for 5–6 days and the problem will disappear. This will help feet that are very sensitive to wet conditions, as the wool fat acts rather like the waxing of the bottom of skis and gives added protection.

Dogs with chronically thin pads will benefit from the addition of Biocare®, a gelatin and biotin supplement usually used to improve hoof hardness in horses. Give ½ teaspoon daily in food.

FOOT INJURIES

Again, as the foot carries the dog around, it is often the first place to be injured by glass, caustic materials, lawnmowers (how dogs' feet manage to get under lawn mowers is beyond me), or by being caught in fences. The foot of the dog is very well supplied with blood vessels, which with any sort of cut or open wound will bleed profusely. As the dog does not have the intelligence to sit down and hold the offending member up in the air, but prefers to run around spreading blood far and wide, the most important thing to do is to apply a pressure bandage or tourniquet before taking the dog to the vet.

Many owners arrive with a blood stained car and the dog with a blood flow that is slowing down because of excessive loss. Tie a bandage or stocking above the injury (i.e. towards the body) fairly firmly before travelling, and loosen it for 10–15 seconds every five minutes. Once the tourniquet is in place, make for your vet as soon as possible.

Anal Glands

This is a seldom mentioned subject, but they do warrant a few words and the occasional emptying.

The anal glands are two sac like objects that are placed at the nine o'clock and three o'clock position on either side of the rectum. Their function is to place some 'personalised' scent on the faeces as they pass out, as a marker for other animals. It also acts as a 'skunk' gland, and in fright the dog will void the glands (usually all over the veterinarian's table), and by this deter various predators but not the hardy vet.

These glands have a small exit which can be easily blocked off, particularly when the dog has a concurrent worm (especially tapeworm) burden. Other causes of blockages include insufficient ventilation reaching the anus (heavily coated breeds) or any condition which causes irritation to the lower colon or rectal area.

Symptoms Signs of impaction include constant licking of the anal area, chewing of the sides of the tail and around the base of the tail (fat individuals can often not reach the exact spot, so will chew a few centimetres away), and scooting along the ground as if they have tapeworm. Some dogs will carry their tails hooked out due to the impaction.

These glands can become so impacted they can abscess, which as one can imagine, is a very painful condition. The area looks very swollen, inflamed and the abscess will often burst slightly below and to the side the anus.

Treatment Treatment of the impaction involves placing your first finger and thumb on either side of the rectum, slightly below and squeezing in, together, up and back. Now, I should warn you, you should have a big wad of cotton wool in the palm of your hand, as the foul smelling contents are very hard to remove (the lingering effects, that is), and they do come out at a fair velocity so stand out of the direct firing line.

If the glands have abscessed, the dog requires veterinary attention to have them drained and treated with antibiotics. If the glands have repeated bouts of inflammation, it may be necessary to have them removed. It is worthwhile checking the anal glands on a regular basis, particularly if the dog is constantly licking or chewing in that general area.

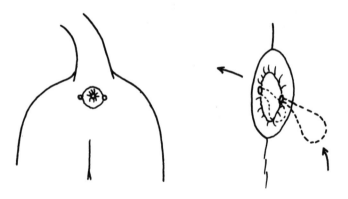

Common Severe Viral and Bacterial Infections

DISTEMPER

Distemper is a severe viral infection which attacks all mucous surfaces as well as lymphoid and nervous tissue. The symptoms of distemper are eye inflammation and discharge, pneumonia with a productive cough, gastro-enteritis and nervous signs such as twitching of muscles, temperament changes and depression. High fever is seen at days 4–6 and again at 14–18 days after initial exposure to the virus. Distemper has an incubation period of up to three weeks. By 3–4 weeks post infection, many dogs are either euthanased because of severe neurological symptoms, or the dog dies from cumulative systemic degeneration.

Treatment once neurological symptoms develop is often of no avail. Mortality is high (over 95%). Attenuated live vaccines are available and should be used in a correct vaccination schedule, both for individual immunity and for maintaining a high overall kennel level of immunity.

HEPATITIS

The adenovirus CAV-1 causes hepatitis and occasionally respiratory infections in dogs. The effects of viral hepatitis can be anything from subclinical to a severe and rapidly fatal infection. However, the majority of cases are often so mild as to be undetectable. The severe form is almost always seen in young puppies from 2–8 weeks of age, primarily where the immunity of the mother to the virus is very low. The disease is characterised by high fever, vomiting, diarrhoea, anorexia, abdominal pain and depression. Occasionally, puppies are found dead with little or no previous signs of illness. Puppies who recover may develop a 'blue eye', which while often only transient, may occasionally be permanent.

Vaccines are available and are usually derived from CAV-2, (which is antigenically similar to CAV-1) which confers good immunity to both CAV-1 and to CAV-2. CAV-2 is one of the causes of the kennel cough complex.

KENNEL COUGH

This is caused by a group of viruses and bacteria. The most common culprits are adenovirus CAV-2 (rarely CAV-1), para-influenza virus and Bordatella bronchiseptica (a mycoplasma) which is a commonly seen contaminant in kennel cough. Kennel cough is generally seen as an upper respiratory tract infection characterised by a hoarse cough, particularly noticeable after exercise of any kind. Incubation is from 3–10 days and the disease can spread very rapidly within a kennel, particularly in younger individuals.

The course of the infection takes about 7–10 days, with few dogs exhibiting any symptoms more severe (apart from the coughing, that is) than mild depression and occasionally inappetence for more than 24–48 hours. The coughing on the other hand, can last for any time up to three weeks.

Treatment is aimed at minimising coughing, so in addition to anything prescribed by your veterinarian, reduced exercise will help to lower the noise of the coughing and decrease further irritation in the upper trachea. Low doses of buffered aspirin are helpful to reduce throat irritation. Vaccinations are available for each of the viruses and bacteria involved, and are particularly useful for the older dog that may be going into a kennel for boarding, or for Greyhounds in work.

RABIES

Rabies is a virus which is capable of crossing species barriers and therefore can affect any warm blooded animal, including humans. It is a lethal neurological viral infection for which treatment is of no avail. Incubation is very variable, from as short as 15 days to as long as five months. Transmission is by the virus being inoculated via a bite from an infected individual. Symptoms presented are either the furious ('rabid') or the dumb form of rabies. Early signs include temperament changes, depression, viciousness, facial paralysis, drooling, inability to chew or swallow food. Any of these symptoms with a history of a bite wound, should, in countries where rabies is present, be treated with extreme caution, and immediate veterinary attention should be sought.

Vaccines are available in countries where rabies is present and should be used according to your veterinarian's advice and government health regulations (if any). Currently Australia, New Zealand, United Kingdom, Norway, Sweden and Japan are the only major countries that are rabies free.

HERPES

Herpes is a virus which can cause the deaths of newborn puppies. In older dogs signs are mild to subclinical. Bitches which are infected during pregnancy transmit the virus to the puppies at birth. Deaths usually occur from 5–16 days after birth. Symptoms are crying, rapid respiration, abdominal pain and anorexia. Affected puppies usually die within 24–48 hours. Treatment is supportive. No vaccine is currently available. Affected bitches can be bred from subsequently, with no further problems.

PARVOVIRUS AND CORONAVIRUS

These are discussed earlier in this chapter in the section on Gastric problems and stress.

Common Severe Bacterial Infections

LEPTOSPIROSIS

This is a bacterial infection which can affect many species, including man, and is a common infection seen worldwide. It is transmitted through contaminated water supplies and food sources as well as by direct contact with affected animals and their urine. It can also be transmitted via the uterus sexually or during pregnancy. Rats, mice, and cats are frequently the transmitters of leptospirosis by contaminating water and food supplies.

There are two more frequently seen serotypes which are Icterohaemorrhagica and Canicola. Icterohaemorrhagica infections are often very severe, with high fever, depression and anorexia, and show signs of damage to the liver, kidneys and the gastrointestinal tract.

Jaundice is seen in 70% of cases, and deaths can occur from widespread organ damage. Prognosis is often guarded. Treatment is supportive and the sooner initiated the better. High doses of antibiotics are necessary. Canicola is usually not as severe, and affects primarily the kidneys. About 15% of cases develop jaundice from severe liver damage. Affected individuals of both serotypes are likely to become carriers.

The potential risk to humans from contamination of water supplies and infected animals should be considered. Vaccines are available and should be given regularly in high risk areas.

TETANUS

Tetanus is not a commonly seen bacterial infection. It is caused by the toxin produced from a clostridial bacteria. Tetanus occurs in different species, mostly in the horse, but can also occur in humans and less frequently, the cat. Tetanus occurs following an penetration injury e.g. a grass seed, and is most commonly seen in spring or humid periods of the year, and in areas where there are horses.

Symptoms

Signs of tetanus in the dog include stiffness, spasm of the facial muscles and the third eyelids producing an anxious expression with a rigid erect carriage of the ears. Some individuals cannot eat because of the stiffness of the jaws. Hypersensitivity to external stimuli occurs. Symptoms can develop as early as 48 hours post infection, but may occasionally take up to eight days. Infection occurs via penetrating wounds or objects which carry the bacteria to an area where anaerobic multiplication can take place. The site of infection is often hard to find, but effort should be made to locate it and flush it out with high doses of penicillin.

Treatment

Treatment is to keep the dog in a darkened room, with minimal stimuli from light and noise. High doses of penicillin and anti-toxin are given, as are tranquillisers to reduce the severity of the muscle spasms. A prolonged course of antibiotics and tranquillisers is often required until the muscle spasms are reduced to near normal. Prognosis is guarded, as a reasonable percentage of infected dogs will die despite all efforts to save them. Vaccines are available and may be advisable in high risk areas. As a breed, German Shepherds appear to more susceptible to tetanus and may require vaccination if at risk. Tetanus can, on rare occasions, be transmitted to humans via bite wounds, so care should be taken with infected dogs.

BRUCELLOSIS

Brucellosis is an infectious disease which is characterised by abortions and infertility in bitches and infertility in male dogs. Brucellosis is transmitted via venereal contact and infected material. Brucellosis can be transmitted to humans and cases of owners contracting the disease from their infected dogs have been recorded. In bitches, abortions and early embryonic deaths can occur. Infected puppies that are alive at birth are usually weak and die within a few days. The uterine discharge of an infected bitch is highly contagious. In male dogs, infection can cause epidymitis and testicular atrophy. Treatment of brucellosis is often unrewarding, and success uncertain. Tests are available for brucellosis and, in countries where it is known to occur, all new breeding animals should be tested before being introduced to a kennel. No vaccine is available at present.

Brucellosis in dogs has been reported in many countries including USA. It has not been identified in Australia or New Zealand.

PROTOZOAN INFECTIONS

Coccidiosis and Giadiosis are protozoan infections and have been discussed earlier in this chapter in the section on Gastric problems and stress.

Toxoplasmosis is another protozoan infection, which again can cross many species. Transmission is via ingestion of contaminated material. Cats are the most commonly implicated transmitters of the disease. Cats' faeces, infected meat and occasionally flies and cockroaches can transport the oocytes. Toxoplasmosis in the dog can affect many different body systems. Diarrhoea, pneumonia, hepatitis, nervous symptoms, myosotis and ocular damage are amongst the many different presenting symptoms possible.

Treatment   Treatment is with sulphonamides, but correct diagnosis can be difficult due to the wide variation of symptoms. Deaths can occur in severe outbreaks. Vaccines are currently not available, but are being developed and tested. Toxoplasmosis can be transmitted to humans.

19

Emergency Conditions and How to Recognise Them

This section is to give you some idea of:
(a) What is an emergency.
(b) Emergency first aid.
(c) When it is necessary to go immediately to the nearest vet.

A basic definition of an emergency is any situation which could cause death or dire consequences if immediate action is not taken. In some cases, it may cause long-term or permanent disability to an organ or its normal function, for example the eye and sight. First aid may save the dog's life or prevent further deterioration before professional veterinary attention can be obtained, particularly in cases of trauma or poisoning.

Specific Areas
1. First aid.
2. Heat stress: how to recognise and prevent it.
3. Bloat: some of the causes and ways to prevent it.

FIRST AID
First aid kit
This is particularly useful on long trips, especially for the dog showing fraternity, with travel-induced stress e.g. diarrhoea or dehydration which can occur out in the wilds, a long way from any known veterinarian. The contents are on the whole, available from veterinarians or your local chemist. The value of having a first aid kit has to be experienced by the lack of one, when you are faced with an 'emergency' and you have nothing on hand.

Contents:
Bandage — 1 roll of Elastoplast, 1 roll of conforming gauze.
Dressings — gauze swabs, metho swabs (3–4), iodine swabs (3–4).
Cleansers — cotton wool, wound cleanser.
Instruments — scissors and tweezers, 3cc syringe and applicator.
Eyes — liquid tears, local eye drops.
Stomach — diarrhoea mixture, charcoal tabs, electrolyte sachet or liquid.
Creams — anhydrous wool fat (for sore feet), Stingose®, fly repellent.
Tablets — vitamin K, laxatives, Sulphonamide tabs (vet only), calcium.
Emetic — peroxide .
Antibiotic spray or powder.

I have highlighted the important items which should help you deal with accidents and stress type situations to the extent of giving you time to got to a vet, or get home to your own vet.

ACCIDENTS
Initial aims are to:
(a) Establish a patent airway i.e. make sure the dog can breathe easily.
(b) Cover or seal any deep wounds to the chest.
(c) Apply pressure bandages to heavily bleeding areas.
(d) Check for shock.

Shock is a defensive reaction from the body to cope with severe trauma. Signs of major shock are:

- Pale mucous membranes of the gums and eyes. Very pale to white indicates possible internal bleeding.
- Rapid shallow breathing.
- Lower body temperature particularly of the extremities (cold around feet, muzzle, ears).
- Haemorrhage from the nose, mouth, ears and/or anus can be indicative of major internal bleeding/damage.

APPLYING A MUZZLE

This is often necessary before moving an animal, even your own pet, as they are often in shock, and can automatically lash out if hurt or in a state of shock. Use a gauze bandage, stocking or length of thin rope, whichever is available at the time. Apply firmly but not excessively tight.

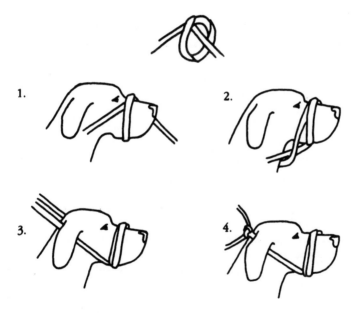

APPLYING A PRESSURE BANDAGE

Use a gauze bandage or swabs with a firm layer of elastoplast on top. Apply above (closer to the body) and on top of any heavily bleeding area. A figure of eight bandage tends to stay on better than applying the bandage in layers in one direction.

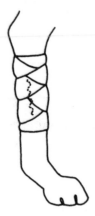

HIT BY CAR

What to do:

1. If the dog is conscious and in pain, muzzle the dog before you examine it. The animal is usually in shock and may not recognise its owners and bite out of fear and pain. Not all dogs require muzzling, but be careful when lifting an un-muzzled dog. Do not have the dog's mouth near your face.

2. Examine for signs of shock such as pale mucous membranes. The paler the gums, the quicker the animal needs to get to a veterinarian.

3. Apply a pressure bandage on any heavily bleeding site, if at all possible. This applies mainly to legs and feet injuries. Minor injuries and scrapes should be left alone.

4. Usually leave fractures alone, particularly if you are not far from the vet, and especially if the dog is in severe shock. If the animal is quite bright and alert, a quick and easy support splint can be made out of any available strong cardboard or thick layers of newspaper rolled up. Apply a bandage gently around the splint, with more above and below the fracture, rather than on the actual fracture site. On the whole this is better left alone, unless you know what you are doing and the animal is very placid. This would apply to very few people and even fewer animals!

5. Move the dog gently by lifting by the scruff or around the chest. Place the animal on a flat surface with the head extended. Keep the dog warm by covering it with a blanket, often covering the eyes as well. This keeps the dog calmer as it is not as exposed to external stimuli such as light or sound. Holding and rocking a badly injured dog, particularly one with broken limbs, is not a good idea.

6. Get the injured animal to a veterinarian as soon as possible to check that there is no serious damage.

If there is no way of getting to a vet for any appreciable length of time, keep the dog warm and somewhere quiet and dark. A small amount of brandy on the gums can help stimulate the heart, and leave some water in a bowl next to the animal. Ring your veterinarian if you can, and tell him or her the colour of the gums, the rate of respiration, whether the dog can stand on all four legs, and if it is bleeding heavily. If the dog is severely injured, the vet may be able to come out, but it is quicker for you to get there, than for the vet to find you. Remember that all the necessary equipment is on hand at the vet hospital.

N.B. Phone first if it is late at night or you have no transport, or you have a long way to travel to get to the vet. Time wasted may have been used saving your dog's life at the hospital.

STINGS AND BITES

Unfortunately, you often do not know *what* has bitten your pet and *when* it may have occurred.

Bee stings and **ant bites** are not generally life threatening and the reaction is usually limited to swelling around the area which has been bitten. When this occurs around the mouth and throat, it can be very alarming to the owner. Most bites of this nature do not cause respiratory difficulties unless the animal is particularly sensitive to the cause i.e. very allergic. Treatment with antihistamines will quickly relieve symptoms.

Dogs which have the habit of chasing bees can become so sensitised to bee stings, that they can develop a hyperacute, severe reaction which can indeed be life-threatening within 10–15 minutes of being bitten. The owners may need to (a) keep the dog locked in a pen (away from flowers) and (b) have some fast acting cortisone on hand for these emergencies (if your vet trusts you sufficiently to administer this). If the dog is seen to be in difficulties, give the cortisone immediately, and take it at once to your vet. By doing so you gain extra time to get your dog to the vet.

Snake and **spider bites** are far more difficult to deal with, particularly if you have no knowledge of the initial incident i.e. the time and/or the causative agent.

Signs are lethargy, trembling, vomiting and profuse salivation, progressing to inability to stand, rapid respiration, bluish mucous membranes (of the gums) and collapse.

There may be a hypersensitivity to noise and light in the form of minor fitting and/or muscle twitching. Signs vary according to the 'perpetrator', the time that has elapsed since the dog was bitten, and the type and amount of poison received.

Treatment

Take the animal to a veterinarian as soon as possible. Treatment differs according to the presenting signs, and the amount of knowledge as to the cause and time of the incident. Some snake bite effects can take 12 or more hours to manifest with owners often erroneously thinking that because there are no obvious signs within 1–2 hours, that the animal will not be affected at all, and/or that it may not have received any poison. Do not delay as precautionary treatment is preferable to being too late. The longer the delay from the initial incident, the lower the survival rate.

TICK POISONING

Tick poisoning is commonly seen in the warm humid periods of the year, especially along the eastern coastal belt of Australia. Ticks can kill affected dogs within 3–6 days of contact. Ticks like to crawl to the top of long grass and low shrubs, and will attach to the coats of animals as they brush past. About 80–90% of ticks are found around the head, neck and shoulder regions. Ticks look like small blue-grey coloured warts and can grow as large as your little fingernail, but (unlike warts) they have a thickening around the base where they are attached, called a 'crater'.

It takes several days for the effect of the tick to start showing and 3–4 days for the effects to wear off.

Symptoms　Signs are incoordination of the hindquarters, weakness of the hind legs, husky cough and loss of voice, loss of appetite and a rapid respiration rate.

Very early signs are easily missed, but if you are living in a tick area, you should be alert for any change in the dog's habits. Initially the dog may appear reluctant to walk very far, refuse a feed and be slightly off balance when turning. The further it walks, the worse it becomes. This progresses to a total paralysis with laboured breathing and bluish mucous membranes (gums). Death results from paralysis of the respiratory muscles and lung congestion.

Treatment　Treatment involves removal of all ticks; if no ticks are found, they may already have dropped off. There should still be a crater, which is an allergic reaction in the place where the tick was embedded. Removal of ticks is easily done by placing your thumb and first finger on either side of the tick, pinching down and almost taking a small piece of skin, and then give it a quick half twist. The tick will pop out. Ticks do not have a definite head; removal and/or killing the tick is the initial primary concern.

The effects of the tick are still wearing on over the next 48–72 hours, so that veterinary advice must be sought on all cases that are showing signs of paralysis and where there are respiratory difficulties, the dog should be seen by the vet as soon as possible.

The vet will administer tick serum from hyperimmune dogs. This is given intravenously, and quite often serum is injected locally around the skin under the crater where the tick was removed. The dog is hospitalised, and preferably kept very quiet and covered up to reduce external stimuli i.e. light and noise. Treatment for any respiratory and cardiac symptoms is initiated. Supportive therapy of high doses of vitamin C can be helpful. Sedation is often used to keep the dog calm.

Tick dogs are handled as little as possible to minimise respiratory distress.

Very mild cases with no obvious signs of paralysis should be put somewhere very quiet and dark for 24 hours. However, if it is the first tick they have ever encountered, it is wise to have the dog examined by your vet. Do *not* give food or water to the animal, as it is paralysed internally as well as externally. After 24 hours, give a small amount of water and if the animal drinks, and there is no vomiting or coughing, allow free access to food and water. If it is reluctant to drink, wait another 12–24 hours and repeat the process. *If the dog is not drinking after 48 hours or any signs of paralysis or breathing difficulties develop, consult your vet immediately.*

Dogs can (and do) receive a relative immunity to tick poison, but it develops slowly from short and repeated exposure to ticks. The immunity is short lasting (approximately three months) and variable, which means that by the end of winter, there is usually little or no immunity left.·

Prevention

Flea and tick collars can be very beneficial, provided they are changed once a month during the tick 'season'. The season varies according to the weather. Ticks prefer humidity and warmth, so the ideal times are spring and autumn. If, however you are having a particularly wet summer, they can stay out and about. Be on the lookout for ticks for 7–10 days after rain. In high risk areas, you can use Proban Cythioate® tablets twice weekly which will kill ticks as they attach. Unfortunately it is rather expensive, but it can be of great benefit.

Newer drugs and rinses are always being developed, for example Frontline®, a topically applied spray that will give three weeks cover, even if dogs are going in and out of water regularly.

Ticks prefer to live in thick, overgrown areas, and climb to the top of tall grass, small shrubs and bushes. If you live in a known tick area, keep the grass very short in the garden, and for at least 2–3 metres around it. High winds can blow ticks into a mown area, but the risk of picking up ticks can be reduced to almost nil in a well tended area.

Do not take your dog on walks through rough country, or allow it to roam through these areas.

Check your dog daily during the tick periods of the year, paying particular attention to the head, neck and shoulder areas. Beyond this area, the dog will usually bite out any small ticks which are trying to embed themselves into the skin. Despite this, the dog must be fully checked all over. Coated dogs are high risk animals in tick areas, as the ticks are extremely easy to miss in the thick hair.

Remember, it takes several days for the tick poison to take effect, and several days to wear off. Severe cases need hyperimmune tick serum to try to reduce the severity of the effects of the tick, but each case is different and unfortunately there are no guarantees of survival. Every case is treated according to its symptoms, and there should be as little external stimuli as possible at all times.

Poisons — Common Symptoms and Emergency Treatment

RAPID ACTING POISONS

The majority of poisonings which occur around the home tend to fall into the organophosphate group of poisons. Poisons of this sort include snail and slug killers, heavy plant poisons such as weed killers, fumigating poisons, strychnine, heavy applications of flea and other insect poisons. Poisoning can result from drinking water contaminated by run off from chemicals, e.g. following fumigation.

Usually the effects are seen within several hours of ingestion. The larger the amount consumed, the quicker the onset of symptoms and this can be in the space of 15–30 minutes. If you see your dog eating snail bait or a poison, take your dog immediately to your vet, or ring for advice which can vary according to the type of poison. Take the container or wrapper with you to the vet, in case there are specific instructions that may need to be followed in the case of ingestion.

Symptoms These present as the typical owners 'idea' of poisonings. The animal is hypersensitive to noise and light, the respiration rate is very rapid and shallow, the muscles are twitching all over and there is usually profuse salivation. The dog may be fitting or unconscious in the more serious cases. Symptoms can vary from very mild to extremely severe.

Treatment If the causative agent is known, the antidote or appropriate treatment is initiated. If not, the animal should be treated symptomatically i.e. by the presenting symptoms and the severity of the poisoning. Treatment usually includes Atropine to dry out the excess salivation, and anaesthetics or tranquillisers to allow the animal to sleep through the effects of the poison until it wears off. The animal is usually hospitalised until the effects have entirely gone from the body.

It is most important when going to the veterinarian, that these animals should be handled very gently, and above all quietly. Excess noise, light, handling or stimuli of any sort, will worsen the effect of most of these sorts of poisons.

SLOW ACTING POISONS

These include those that break down a body chain of reactions e.g. Warfarin rat poison. This causes a breakdown in the clotting of the blood, creating a 'haemophiliac' i.e. any small injury will start to bleed and will not stop. This poison can take from 3–7 days to take effect, according to the amount ingested. Newer potentiated versions of Warfarin are available in some countries which if ingested, can cause bleeding within 12–24 hours.

Severe anaemia, pale mucous membranes on gums and conjunctiva, tiredness, reduced exercise tolerance, rapid respiration and collapse. *Symptoms*

Blood transfusions for the very anaemic animals are a necessity, complete rest and confinement for 7–10 days, and large doses of vitamin K (particularly vitamin K1), which is the specific antidote to Warfarin. For animals who have only ingested this type of poison in the last 12–24 hours, treatment consists of giving vitamin K tablets for the next 10–20 days, rest and a regular eye kept on the colour of the gums. For the potentiated Warfarins, vitamin K1 tablets are needed. *Treatment*

Slow acting poisons can be very hard to identify until it is too late, as there is no fitting or other symptoms as with other poisons. If there are rat baits out, make sure they are out of reach of dogs and cats. If you are worried, precautionary dosing with vitamin K is harmless to the animal.

Fights, Wounds and Sores

Fight wounds and those that have been inflicted by accidents are all treated in the same basic fashion.

1. Clean the wound gently with damp cotton wool or a gauze swab.

2. Make sure there is no hair in the wound. Hair is often dragged under the skin in puncture wounds. If it is not removed, the wound will become infected and break open. All hair around the edges should be pulled out and then trimmed. Hair trailing into an open wound will delay healing and cause infection.

3. Large holes and deep wounds, where hair has been dragged too deep to retrieve, must be treated by a veterinarian. Small puncture holes and grazes are easily coped with by an experienced person. Any swelling which appears around a wound should be examined by your vet, as there may be a developing abscess.

4. Apply an antiseptic agent to the surface of the wound e.g. iodine or gentian violet and preferably try to keep the animal from licking it too much. Excessive licking can, contrary to popular opinion, cause more harm than good. Do not use Mercurochrome as it scalds the surface tissue, or Hibitane® as many dogs, cats and humans react adversely. Iodine or gentian violet are the safest.

5. Clean twice daily with slightly damp cotton wool. Keep wounds as dry as possible at all times.

MOIST ECZEMA

Moist eczema occurs in areas that the animal has chewed, often as the result of skin irritation from fleas, retained dead coat and excessive moisture retained in the coat following rain or a bath. The areas most commonly affected are around where the coat is thickest; the neck, cheeks, buttocks and the area above and to the sides of the tail. The animal has usually chewed continuously at the skin until the surface is broken and oozes serum, which in turn scalds the irritates skin. The aim is to dry these patches out, and apply something to keep the animal from further self damage.

Treatment Clean affected areas with damp cotton wool using nothing in the water, and try not to wet the surrounding area. Once clean, dry thoroughly and apply a drying agent such as a gentian violet spray. This usually tastes horrible and most have an insect repellent in them as well.

If these areas are large, they will need antibiotics and it may be necessary to shave off the hair. Smaller patches can be treated at home if you have enough experience, but larger areas do need veterinary supervision.

Points to remember when treating wounds:
- Dry out wet surfaces.
- Moisten dry surfaces such as calluses with creams.

Constipation

Constipation is a problem more commonly seen in older dogs and cats. Dogs, particularly older males, are prone to inflammations of the prostate. Very hairy breeds of dogs and cats can become constipated through ingestion of hair from licking and cleaning, especially when moulting. Bones given to older dogs and those that have had pelvic fractures, can cause constipation.

Symptoms Symptoms include straining to pass faeces, not eating, hanging over water and occasionally, vomiting.

Treatment Treatment is in the form of laxatives: liquid paraffin, Coloxyl® tablets and Laxagel®.

Give treatments several times a day until the animal is 'unblocked'. If the animal cannot pass any faeces after two days, it will need veterinary attention, see also chapter 15, Geriatrics.

Eyes

Any injury to the eye needs *immediate* veterinary attention, particularly in the case of scratches or tears to the surface of the eye. Penetrating wounds need to be stitched wherever possible, or the eye structure may collapse. The cornea has no direct blood supply, apart from diffusion, so when the cornea is damaged, it heals by having an increased water component, hence the blue-ish appearance. As the eye heals this gradually fades.

Dogs have a 'third eyelid' and it is situated along the medial (central) corner of the eye. When the eye is threatened, the third eyelid will automatically flick over the surface of the eye to protect it. Grass seeds and other foreign objects can be trapped behind this lid, and considerable damage to the surface of the cornea may result. Any obvious protrusion of the third eyelid, or noticeable closing of the eye should be investigated by your vet as soon as possible.

Ulcers or scratches on the surface of the eye often require careful handling after the initial treatment by your veterinarian. Ideally any damage to the cornea needs to have rest from direct sunlight until the sensitivity of the surface of the eye decreases. Sunlight can aggravate the surface of the cornea and dogs will scratch and rub the irritated eye causing further damage. Keep the dog out of direct sunlight for at least 4–5 days following this type of eye injury.

Grass seeds which get under the third eyelid can cause a fair amount of damage to the surface of the eye. Cloudiness or a blue-ish appearance to the eye indicates damage to the surface of the eye. The sooner this is treated the better, as delay may result in permanent damage or impaired vision. Any object that is scratching the eye and continues to do so, will cause the eye to be held closed as a protective instinct.

If this occurs, immediate treatment by your veterinarian is needed to ensure there is no foreign object under the third eyelid.

Dust inflammation. Many dogs will have a typical reaction to dust and high wind by having a heavy eye discharge. When examined by a veterinarian, the eye will show little by way of specific irritation, apart from a heavy discharge in the morning. If the cause is wind or dust irritation, then the simple treatment for relief of this condition is to rinse the eyes with a liquid tear preparation, particularly at night, to flush out any dust accumulated during the day. If the eye is inflamed, then an anti-inflammatory eye ointment may be needed after the flushing of the dust particles. In the morning, rinse any remaining ointment out with the liquid tears and do not add more ointment. If this is the only cause of the irritation, do not apply ointments in the morning to the eyes of a dog that will be outside all day, as the dust will attach itself to the sticky surface provided by the ointment.

Continuing irritation of the eye surface or any signs of ulceration requires immediate attention by your veterinarian.

Pannis is a chronic eye condition whereby the surface of the cornea is gradually covered by a heavy brown pigmentation. This condition, the cause of which is considered to be auto-immune based, results in the dog gradually going blind over a period of 3–6 years. It is seen most commonly in Pugs, Pekingese, American Cocker Spaniels, and German Shepherds. It is a condition which can be controlled but not cured, by the use of cortisone drops used correctly and under supervision.

Dry eye, see chapter 15, Geriatric Dogs.

Ears

Injuries to ears, especially where there is torn cartilage, must be stitched, as cartilage has a very poor blood supply and can take a long time to heal. Infections, once they get into the cartilage, are extremely difficult to cure and infected cartilage often has to be cut out. (See also chapter 18)

Milk Fever

(See chapter 8, Whelping the Bitch)

Blocked Bladder

Bladder stones can cause blockage of the outflow of urine (particularly in the male dog) which, in severe cases, can lead to collapse, dehydration and if the bladder ruptures, death if not treated. The average case of blockage from bladder stones is not as dramatic, with presenting signs of straining to urinate with frequent small amounts of bloodstained urine being passed.

Large bladder stones are removed surgically, while smaller stones may be able to be dissolved over longer periods using various means, depending on the composition of the stones.

Incidence   A higher incidence is seen during periods of high humidity and rain. Where there is a history of stone formation, recurrence can be common. The average stones are of struvite formation. Dachshunds are prone to form cystine stones. Dalmatians commonly form stones, but these are always urate stones and particular to that breed.

Treatment   The aim is to reduce protein in the diet and acidification of the urine, which is helpful in dissolving stones and reducing the chance of recurrence. Antibiotics are often needed for long periods (see the kidney section in chapter 15, Geriatric Dogs, for more detail and diets).

The most important point to remember is that the diet can play a major role in the gradual reduction in the size of the stones and the prevention of stone re-formation.

The aim of the diet is low protein and urinary acidification, depending on the type of stones found in the bladder.

Tetanus

Tetanus occurs following an injury, particularly a penetration injury e.g. grass seed, generally in the spring or humid periods of the year. Presenting signs include stiffness of gait, reluctance to chew hard food, an 'anxious' expression, with rigid upright ear carriage together with the third eyelid retracted laterally, and squinting in bright light.

Treatment   Treatment consists of hospitalisation with high doses of tetanus antitoxoid and penicillin. The site of the infection is thoroughly cleaned out and disinfected. Prolonged treatment of 10–14 days of penicillin and muscle relaxants are given if necessary. The dog should be kept in the dark to minimise reaction to light and reduce muscle spasm. Ledum drops are given as well. These are homoeopathic and excellent against tetanus (see also chapter 18).

Hypothermia

Hypothermia is a serious problem in cold countries. The effects are seen predominantly in the very young and old individuals. Cold can be the biggest cause of young puppy deaths, particularly if they get chilled during the first few days of life.

Signs of hypothermia are: reluctance to move, cold to the touch, lack of a shiver reflex, pale gums and a slow capillary refill (when the gums are pressed the colour takes quite some time to return whereas normally this is a very fast reflex), and cold extremities. *Symptoms*

Young puppies will whinge, refuse food and try to huddle together to gain some warmth. Cold puppies, particularly when they are less than one week of age, will not be able to swallow properly until they are warmed up as they can develop a partial paralysis of the vagus nerve. Food for these puppies must be limited to very small amounts until they fully return to normal body temperature.

Any cold or chilled dog should be gradually warmed up and given small amounts of brandy (acts as a heart stimulant) and glucose on the gums. Wrap the dog in wool, not synthetics, as wool retains the heat much better. Severe chilling can take some time to reverse. Gently turn the dog over every 10–15 minutes, massage the legs and stimulate the circulation. After effects usually include pneumonia, so an examination and treatment by your vet once the dog is fit to be moved is a necessity. *Treatment*

Heat Stress

Heat stress usually occurs on very hot or moderately hot days following several consecutive hot days. Heat gradually lowers the dog's body reserves of sugar and salts, so that the longer a hot period lasts, the sooner the heat stress can occur. In this situation, it only takes a little extra stress to set heat stress off.

Black dogs absorb more heat than lighter coloured dogs (as they do not reflect the light, but absorb it), so they are more prone to heat stress. Dogs that are exercising heavily in hot weather e.g. Greyhounds, are particularly at risk. It may also occur if a dog is in an area with restricted air circulation such as a closed car, crate, tent or dog trailer.

The dog's main ways of losing heat are:

1. Respiration through panting.

2. Sweating through pads. Dogs do not sweat in the same way as humans.

3. Heat loss through areas of minimal hair i.e. belly and anus.

Symptoms   The dog suffering heat stress is usually very sluggish and reluctant to move. Respiration is extremely rapid and the mucous membranes, i.e. the gums and conjunctiva, are blue-ish. The breathing is extremely laboured and there is usually very little salivation. The dog may vomit, stagger and collapse and if not treated at this stage, it will shortly die.

Treatment   The first priority is to cool the dog fairly rapidly. The most important area to cool is the head and neck, particularly the neck. The blood going to the brain must be cooled to prevent brain damage and to settle down the respiration rate. Turn a tap on full bore to wet the dog thoroughly and keep the water running over the dog, starting on the head and neck. If you have any ice, place some on the bridge of the nose (this is especially important on short nosed breeds) and on the sides of the neck.

Keep the water flowing over the dog until the respiration settles down. You can wet the dog's mouth, but don't expect the dog to swallow much water as it may be incapable of swallowing at this stage. Ensure that you do not give the dog too much water as this will choke it.

When the dog starts to breathe in a less laboured manner, turn off the tap and keep sponging the dog down with wet towels. Too rapid a temperature drop can cause brain damage.

As the respiration rate returns to normal, leave the dog sitting on a wet towel and give it a small amount of water to drink. Take the dog's temperature once the respiration rate is reduced and keep cooling the dog until the temperature is between 39.5° and 39°C.

- Do not wrap the dog up.
- Do not place the wet towel over the dog as it will not allow the heat to escape.
- Remember that heat rises.

As soon as the dog settles down take it to the nearest vet if it has not returned to normal quickly. The vet will usually administer a very short acting cortisone which returns the body systems to normal and helps the dog to recover from the stress. It is an idea to administer electrolytes, either intravenously if the dog is severely affected, or orally if it is less severe. The electrolytes replace the salts that the body has lost. Weak glucose solutions with electrolytes are a help. Nothing concentrated should be given as the idea is to rehydrate the dog by returning fluid to the body.

PREVENTION OF HEAT STRESS

Prevention of heat stress is of course better than cure.

1. Always ensure that your dogs have adequate shade and water. If the dog for some reason has to be left in a confined area ensure that:
   (a) Ventilation is more than adequate.
   (b) Shade is available.
   (c) Water is always available.

2. Puppies and old dogs are especially susceptible to heat stress. If your dog falls into either category, you should always leave a wet towel or wet newspaper over part of their living area.

If you freeze a large dish of water, it can be left out to gradually melt during the day. Leave a sprinkler going over the shed if it can be managed, or direct a fan over the animals to stir the air. If using a fan with puppies make sure it is directed over them and not on them.

3. In hotter weather it is a good idea to give your dog electrolyte salts to help prevent heat stress. There are two additives that are very helpful, especially after several hot days.

(a) Bicarbonate of soda is the main salt that is lost during heat and is therefore the most important to replace. Give large dogs ⅓ teaspoon daily. If it is very hot, double the amount. Put the bi-carb in the food as dogs do not like it in water.

(b) Electrolytes. There are various brands available. Give one level teaspoon for average to large breeds.

4. If travelling in hot weather, in addition to the salts or bi-carb, always travel with plenty of ice and water. If the dogs are at all distressed, place them on wet towels. The dogs will cool quickest through their feet, belly and anus. Hot air rises, so do not cover the dogs with wet towels.

Remember, in these circumstances, give plenty of shade, ventilation, water, and a small amount of electrolytes and glucose.

Remember that heat stress can occur on a relatively mild day, especially if it has been hot for the previous few days.

Bloat

Bloat is a dilation and/or torsion (twisting) of the stomach, which is usually accompanied by gas build up. Bloat can be accompanied by, and often caused by, a torsion of the spleen. It is a very rapidly developing and serious condition, which if not treated immediately, can result in a high mortality rate.

SIGNS OF BLOAT

The dog is usually found groaning with a swollen rigid abdomen which when tapped sounds hollow, like a drum. The dog is very distressed and the breathing very rapid and shallow. The mucous membranes are very pale to blue in colour, indicating a failing circulation system. Often, within 1–4 hours, it can cause death due to stress. What actually kills the dog is excessive pressure from the bloated stomach, pushing up against the diaphragm. This in turn causes pressure on the heart. The average dog, particularly an older animal, can only endure this kind of stress for a very short time before the circulation collapses and the animal dies.

If noticed in the very early stages, the dog may be seen hunched up, vomiting small amounts of frothy liquid, and often attempting to drink quantities of water which it promptly vomits back.

FACTORS AFFECTING BLOAT
Circumstances relating to bloat cases are many and varied, however there are common factors, which are listed below.

1. Age — Usually seen in older dogs (eight years and up), but it can occur at any age. It is unlikely to occur in a puppy. The older the animal, the poorer the muscle tone of the stomach and the muscles of the abdomen.

2. Conformation — Bloat is more common in deep chested breeds, especially in the excessively deep chested individuals. Affected breeds include German Shepherds, Irish Setters, Great Danes, Bassets, Borzois and the larger breeds.

3. Climate — Seen more frequently during the hotter months of the year, when more water is ingested. Bloat cases tend to increase after sudden temperature changes like a hot spell.

4. Exercise and excitement — Feeding immediately after excessive exercise and excitement or exercise just after feeding can also cause bloat. Dogs that are still very excited from running are more likely to drink large quantities of water immediately after their main meal. With dogs that are allowed to run after a meal, the risk that the stomach or the spleen will swing around and twist, and so cause bloat, is much higher.

It may be seen also in dogs that are **suddenly** having far more exercise than they have been used to. In consequence, these individuals will have a sudden increase in demand for food and salts. The increase in exercise may only occur because they have been put near other dogs and are running up and down the fence, when previously they have been house dogs.

5. The type of food, the salt content and the rate of ingestion — Bloat is most common after the feeding of a large meal, especially if the dog is the type to eat its food very quickly. Some dogs may bloat within 5–15 minutes of eating a large meal, particularly if they run and jump about. The problem of bloat occurring immediately after a meal appears to be volume and time related i.e. how much arrives in the stomach and how fast.

The type of food can be a contributing factor. Some people find that large amounts of dry food in the diet may be the causative agent, as the dog may drink a large quantity of water after a meal. The dry food swells considerably after ingestion and this can cause bloat. A dog that is fed a high proportion of dry dog food in a diet will usually have no trouble, especially if locked up before and after feeding, then kennelled with adequate, but limited amounts of water.

High levels of soya bean meal in the dry dog food seems to predispose dogs to bloat, as the bean meal ferments rather rapidly. It may also occur when large fatty meals of meat are given.

If the salt content of the food is too high, the dog will drink more water than normal. Never exceed 2% salt in the diet (this refers to straight salt or sodium chloride; electrolytes are a slightly different).

Many bloat cases tend to have a concurrent medical problem e.g. pancreatitis, where there is poor muscle tone of the stomach, and gastritis, where there is increased motility of the gastrointestinal tract. Because of this, there is increased water consumption. Other factors include generalised poor muscle tone in old age and debilitating diseases such as cancer.

6. Concurrent medical problems

GENERAL TREATMENT FOR BLOAT CASES

The majority of cases are opened up immediately. Alternatively, some dogs have a tube passed down to the stomach to relieve the gas, but most cases with torsion are unable to be relieved in this manner. If the tube cannot enter the stomach successfully, the dog has to be opened up and the problem surgically corrected. In many cases the stomach and/or the spleen are obviously twisted, in which case tubing is usually not attempted.

Because of the recurrent nature of bloat, many veterinarians elect routinely to remove the spleen, even though the organ may not have twisted. Quite often the spleen is heavily engorged from the build-up of pressure from the twisted stomach.

The twisted stomach is often heavily bruised and sections of its wall may have to be removed because of infarction (lack of blood supply). As the stomach torsions, the blood supply to the stomach twists also. When the spleen has undergone torsion, the ligament and blood supply from the stomach wall is twisted and damaged as well. Damaged areas can be obvious at the time, but occasionally the heavily bruised areas can develop additional blood clots, and in turn reduce the blood supply to areas of the stomach wall.

Some veterinarians elect to suture part of the stomach wall to the wall of the abdomen in an attempt to prevent further bloat attacks. If the spleen is removed, the chance of recurrence is also reduced. The stomach wall may be stitched down in cases where the animal has already previously bloated. Fluid and steroid therapy with high doses of antibiotics are the normal support therapy during and after the operation.

Despite the best of veterinary care, the success rate is not always high. The earlier treatment is initiated the better. Different veterinarians have varied regimes of treatment for bloat and the circumstances surrounding bloat cases can and do vary greatly.

AFTERCARE OF BLOAT CASES

This can be nearly as important as all the work the veterinarian has done to save your dog.

Feeding   For the next few weeks, give small meals often.

Older animals and those with continuing medical problems should go onto a fairly rigid routine for the rest of their lives. This includes giving 2–3 small feeds a day, reduced exercise before and after meals, and not leaving large buckets of water available. Additives to the diet should be given to try and reduce gas build up.

Additives to help prevent gas build up include:

1. Charcoal tablets, 1–3 tablets with every meal

2. Oil, cooking or liquid paraffin, to be added to each meal to help prevent rapid fermentation of food. About 1–2 tablespoons per meal

A good quality vitamin and mineral source will fill any deficiencies in the diet and hopefully improve the muscle tone e.g. Geribits®.

Other helpful hints may include removing soya-bean meal from the diet, i.e. check on the bags of dry dog food. If you wish, change to rice or spaghetti i.e. a natural food type diet. Those with permanently poor muscle tone could benefit from the addition of anabolics into their system, even if only given periodically.

PREVENTION OF BLOAT

1. If the weather is hot, feed the dog late at night after it has cooled down. This can be as late as 10–11pm. If necessary, give a reduced meal and do not leave large amounts of water around. It is most important to lock the dog up in a confined area.

2. If the dog is elderly or in poor physical and muscle condition, feed twice daily and soak the dry dog food. This way smaller amounts are eaten in any one meal.

3. If the dog has muscle wasting and has lost weight lately i.e. following illness, feed small meals often and limit the exercise after feeding. Build up the dog's muscle tone gradually i.e. over several weeks but don't suddenly increase the dog's exercise.

4. Avoid excessively salty food, usually 2% in the diet is ample. Cheezels, for example, are excessively high in salt content and should not be fed under any circumstances. Corned beef and food preserved in brine should not be fed. Ham and ham bones in particular should not be fed. Above all:

1. Do not allow the dog to exercise heavily before or after meals, particularly in hot weather.

2. If your dog eats too quickly, feed twice daily and leave limited amounts of water. With the taller breeds, it can be beneficial to raise the food bowl so that the dog has to stretch its neck up, and hopefully the rate of ingestion will be slowed.

Appendix

Homoeopathic heartworm treatment for dogs

(From treatment suggested by George MacLeod, MRCVS, DVSM, Associate of the Faculty of Homoeopathy, UK.)

Homoeopathic medicines are a system of giving a minimal dosage of a drug compound which, in this mild dilution, acts in a similar fashion to conventional drugs. Because the amounts used are so mild, there is never a problem of toxicity with these kind of medicines.

Administration action and storage of homoeopathic drugs

The medicines are best administered on an empty stomach. The area of absorption is the gums or tongue. They do not need to be swallowed, therefore they may be given to an unconscious patient. They may be given neat or with a little water. The dosage is not critical, rather it is the choice of medicine, the potency and the frequency that is important. The dose given to cats and small dogs is two to three drops, the dose for larger dogs four to five drops, while the dose for large animals, e.g. a cow, is ten drops.

The medicines are very sensitive and may be rendered useless if they are in contact with or stored with any strong smelling substances, e.g. linaments, rinses, camphor or perfumes. Store in a cool dark place away from all other medicines. If stored carefully, their effectiveness will last indefinitely. If given at the same time, some conventional drugs may render the homoeopathic medicines ineffective, in which case the former should be given either a while before or after administering the homoeopathic remedy. I usually wait half to an hour.

FOR HEARTWORM TREATMENT

Five medicines are employed and are listed in their order of use:
1 Arsenicum Album 6x
2 Arsenicum Album 30x
3 Heartworm Nosode 30x
4 Arsenicum Album 1M
5 Arsenicum Album 10M
The medicines are to be given as follows:
1 Arsenicum Album 6x — one dose twice a day for seven days.
2 Arsenicum Album 30x — one dose per day for 14 days.
3 Heartworm Nosode 30x — one dose on the day after the last dose of the Arsenicum Album 30x, i.e. on the 15th day. Then wait two or three days and start the next section.
4 Arsenicum Album 1M — one dose twice weekly for four weeks.
5 Arsenicum Album 10M — one dose once a week for four weeks.
Wait approximately one week and then blood test.

GENERAL COMMENTS

Homoeopathic treatment is generally reserved for dogs that are elderly and not capable of taking the standard treatment of arsenic or immiticide injections. Dogs that are depressed, not eating, usually very thin and requiring heart drugs and diuretics, are ideal candidates for homoeopathic treatment. The arsenic in such a low concentration acts as a tonic. Usually the animals are considerably brighter and eating within two days. The great advantage of this form of treatment is that it is extremely mild on the dog.

Dogs should be kept quiet for the first three weeks. The heartworms die after 10–14 days and there may be a slight cough around this time.

The dogs start to gain weight from after 7–10 days. By the end of the course their coats, weight and general appearance are greatly improved.

The dogs will not clear up completely in one go. The treatment appears to only clear some cases of heartworm (from American reports of this type of treatment the success rate is approximately 50%). Even though not all dogs are cured, the amount cleared improves the dog's health to the point that conventional treatment may be started several weeks later.

Elderly dogs come through improved and revitalised in situations where it may not be a good idea to institute conventional treatment. The homoeopathic treatment, while unconventional, offers a different avenue for the treatment of heartworm. This treatment should only be used on very depressed, fragile and/or elderly dogs that would normally not be expected to survive standard treatments.

Index